Introduction to Political Science and Policy Research

RICHARD L. COLE
University of Texas at Arlington

St. Martin's Press, New York

THIS BOOK IS DEDICATED TO MY PARENTS
Mary S. and Louis R. Cole

Editor: Beth A. Gillett
Manager, publishing services: Emily Berleth
Senior editor, publishing services: Doug Bell
Project management: York Production Services
Production supervisor: Dennis Para
Cover design: Lucy Krikorian
Cover art: Allied Artist's Studio/Nishi

Library of Congress Catalog Card Number: 94-74764

Manufactured in the United States of America.

0 9 8 7 6
f e d c b a

For information, write:
St. Martin's Press, Inc.
175 Fifth Avenue
New York, NY 10010

ISBN: 0-312-07192-2

Acknowledgments
Acknowledgments and copyrights are continued at the back of the book on pages 316–318, which constitute an extension of the copyright page.

Table 1.1: "Research Design Orientation" from Delbert C. Miller, *Handbook of Research Design and Social Measurement,* fifth edition, page 4. Copyright © 1991 by Sage Publications, Inc. Reprinted with the permission of the publisher.

Table 3.1: "Illustration of Operationalization of Variables" from Linda Brewster Stearns and Charlotte Wilkinson Coleman, "Industrial and Local Labor Market Structures and Black Employment in the Manufacturing Sector," *Social Science Quarterly* 71 (June 1990); 291. Copyright © 1991 by University of Texas Press. Reprinted with the permission of the publisher.

Box 3.1: "Correlational versus Experimental Research: The Link between Smoking and Lung Cancer" from Philip J. Hilts, " Cigarette Makers Debated the Risks They Denied, *"New York Times* (June 16, 1994). Copyright © 1994 by The New York Times Company. Reprinted with the permission of the *New York Times.*

Figure 3.1: "Illustration of Interrupted Times–Series Design: Monthly Automobile– Related Injuries in Illinois" from Steven M. Rock, "Impact of the Illinois Seat Belt Use Law in Accidents, Deaths, and Injuries, *"Evaluation Review* 16 (October 1992); 497. Copyright © 1992 by Sage Publications, Inc. Reprinted with the permission of the publisher.

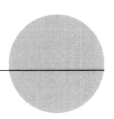

Contents

CHAPTER 3
Developing a Strategy: *Formulating Hypotheses,*
Operationalizing Concepts, Selecting a Research Design   **33**

CHAPTER 4
Gathering Information: *Observational Techniques and Survey Research*   **59**

CHAPTER 5
Gathering Information: *Making Use of Available Data*   **89**

CHAPTER 6

Measurement Strategies: *Data Processing, Data Entry, Index and Scaling Techniques*   **115**

CHAPTER 7
Data Presentation: *Charts, Graphs, Measures of Central Tendency and Dispersion*   141

CHAPTER 8
Searching for Relationships: *Contingency Tables and Tests of Statistical Significance*   175

CHAPTER 10
Sorting Out Relationships: *Analyzing Several Variables*   243

CHAPTER 11
Preparing the Report: *Writing and Rewriting*   277

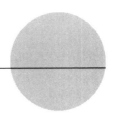

Illustrations and Tables

List of Illustrations

List of Tables

Preface

Distinguished political scientist, Charles O. Jones, once observed: "I must acknowledge what you all surely know. Writing about research methods always makes them sound more rational and systematic than they ever are in fact."[1] Anyone who ever has written about, or who has taught, methods of research recognizes the wisdom in Jones' comments.

But it is true, nevertheless, that even if there is no one "right way" to do research there surely are many "wrong ways." This book is intended to serve as a basic guide to the conduct of political and policy research; it offers suggestions and advice to assist the beginning researcher in the various stages of research and in avoiding some of the more common pitfalls of research.

As indicated in its title, this book is designed to introduce students to research methods appropriate for both political and policy issues. While the fundamental *techniques* of analysis are similar for both situations, the *focus* often differs. Students of politics, in the most general sense, are interested in discovering new information to help better understand the political world. Policy research is more narrowly focused. Policy analysts seek to identify those factors most related to the policies governments choose to pursue. Policy researchers, in addition, want to know whether programs are carried out as planned (sometimes called *process evaluation*), and they want to know the extent to which programs successfully accomplish stated goals (sometimes called *impact evaluation*).

Evaluation research, as Rossi and Freeman remind us, is both science *and* art. And, as Rossi and Freeman wisely note, there are "limits to which an art form can be taught."[2] I have found that one of the best ways to teach research methods, both political and policy, is by example. Accordingly, this text draws on numerous examples from both the political and policy literature, in roughly equal proportions, in illustrating the application of research techniques to political and policy issues.

A major feature of this text is that it attempts to carry the reader through all stages of the research process—topic selection, literature review, hypothesis formation, research design, data collection, data analysis, and report writing. Each of these, of course, is a very specialized topic, and each has its own areas of controversy and distinct body of literature. It is obvious that no single text can exhaustively explore the many complexities of each of these topics. Yet it is my belief that a useful purpose is served by a text that attempts to introduce to the novice researcher these issues in an integrated and illustrated fashion. What may be lost in depth of coverage is at least partially compensated by a greater appreciation of the entire research process, including a clearer understanding of the relationship of each phase to all others.

In selecting the topics to be covered and in deciding the emphasis to be given, I attempted to answer two questions: (1) which topics would the student find most useful in understanding and evaluating the contemporary political and policy literature?; (2) which methods and techniques would be found by beginning researchers to be most helpful in conceiving of and carrying out their own individual or group research projects? Thus, no attempt is made here to cover all possible research methods and techniques (extended discussions of time series analysis, and linear programming techniques, for example, are left for more advanced texts). But, I believe that the students completing this book will be able to intelligently and critically deal with the bulk of contemporary political science and policy research and will be in a position to carry out at least moderately challenging and sophisticated research projects of their own. I am confident that the energetic student may pursue, through the references and citations provided, any topic for which he or she desires more specialized information. Above all, I hope the text conveys the message that good political research is systematic, not haphazard, and that—in spite of major recent advances in computer technology, data availability, and packaged statistical programs—quality research is still heavily dependent on skilled and imaginative human judgment. It is this perspective which, it seems to me, often is missing in the more specialized and focused methods texts.

This text assumes no previous statistical knowledge and is indended primarily as an introductory guide to those having little or no training in empirical research. It is not a text overly concerned with mathematical derivations or statistical computation. Rather, in those sections where statistics are discussed, the stress is on the conditions under which such techniques should be applied and the proper interpretation of results. The exercises concluding each chapter are designed to further illustrate the points raised and to assist in student understanding and mastery of the concepts and techniques discussed. To illustrate various topics and techniques, I have relied in a few instances on data supplied by The Center for Political Studies of the Inter-University Consortium for Political and Social Research (Ann Arbor, Michigan) and especially its 1992 and 1994 National Election Studies.[3] Neither the Center nor the Consortium bear any responsibility for the analyses or interpretations presented here.

In preparing this text, I owe many debts of gratitude and many expressions of appreciation. Early in my own career, as a graduate student in the Department of Political Science at Purdue University, I was fortunate to have had a number of professors whose research and research techniques were so skillful as to, by their examples, carry me through much of my own scholarly career. Chief among these were Professors David A. Caputo, William R. Shaffer, and Myron Q. Hale. While preparing an earlier version of this book, I was fortunate to have had the excellent comments and criticisms of my colleagues and friends then at the George Washington University: Susan Carroll, John Dirkse, Eva Liebhold, Cynthia McClintock, and Stephen J. Wayne. Steve Wayne—now in the Department of Government at Georgetown University—has for many years, and also by example, inspired much of my own research. While on a research appointment at Yale University, I was fortunate to have been able to draw on the friendship and on the many research skills and talents of Michael Krashinsky, presently a member of the faculty of the Division of Management and Economics at the University of Toronto, Scarborough Campus. At the University of Texas at Arlington, I have benefited greatly from the research assistance (particularly in those areas dealing with use of the library) of Trudi DeGoede, Professional Librarian. Further, my faculty colleagues Rodney Hissong in the School of Urban and Public Affairs and Michael Moore in the Department of Political Science have read and provided invaluable comments on several chapters of this book. Barbara Moreland read and commented extensively on the book's final chapter, "Preparing the Report."

I would also like to thank those reviewers who offered helpful suggestions during the development of this text: Keith R. Billingsley, University of Georgia; James Campbell, Louisiana State University; John Frendreis, Loyola University-Chicago; Walter Hill, St. Mary's College of Maryland; Henry Hores, St. Mary's University-San Antonio; Myron Mast, Grand Valley State University; James Riddlesperger, Texas Christian University; Wallace Thies, Catholic University; and Fred A. Wright, University of California-San Diego. I have benefitted, too, from my association with Professor Delbert A. Taebel, a colleague for whom identifying researchable political topics has never been a problem. None of these, of course, bears any responsibility for any errors contained herein; but to all of these, and more, I express my sincerest thanks.

Richard L. Cole

NOTES

1. Charles O. Jones, "Doing Before Knowing: Concept Development in Political Research," *American Journal of Political Science,* 18 (February, 1974), 227.
2. Peter H. Rossi and Howard E. Freeman, *Evaluation: A Systematic Approach,* 5th edition (Newbury Park, CA: Sage Publication, 1993), 32.
3. Steven J. Rosenstone, Donald R. Kinder, Warren E. Miller, and the National Election Studies; *American National Election Study, 1994;* post-election survey [enhanced with 1992 and 1993 data]. [computer file.] Conducted by University of Michigan, Center for Political Studies. 2nd ICPSR, ed., Ann Arbor, Michigan: University of Michigan, Center for Political Studies, Inter-university Consortium for Political and Social Research.

    Throughout this text, the study is identified as: ICPSR, 1994 American National Election Study.

About the Author

RICHARD L. COLE (Ph.D., Purdue University) has been involved with the conduct and teaching of political science and policy research throughout his professional career. Currently, Dr. Cole is dean of the School of Urban and Public Affairs and professor of political science and urban affairs at the University of Texas, Arlington. Prior to that, he was a research scholar in the Institute of Social and Policy Studies at Yale University and associate professor of political science and public affairs at the George Washington University. Dr. Cole's research and teaching specialties include political science methodology, urban politics, and public policy.

Dr. Cole is a former president of the Southwest Political Science Association and former president of the North Texas chapter of the American Society for Public Administration. He has served as executive council member of the federalism and intergovernmental relations section of the American Political Science Association, and has served as an editorial board member for *Public Administration Review,* the *Journal of Urban Affairs, Amerian Politics Quarterly,* and other scholarly publications.

In addition to dozens of journal articles and policy evaluation studies, Cole's recent books include *The Politics of American Government* (St. Martin's Press, 1995) and *Texas Politics and Public Policy.*

CHAPTER 1

Conducting Political and Policy Research:

A Systematic Approach

It is no secret that students sometimes are put off by empirical research and by the prospect of having to endure textbooks and courses designed to provide instruction in research techniques. Research courses, some students believe, mainly involve statistical testing, data entry, numbers crunching, hypothesis testing, data analysis, computer instruction, and—in general—a tedious focus on scientific methods and techniques. Besides, research courses are thought to be devoid of the exciting political issues that attract many students to political science in the first place. Political science students are eager to debate contemporary political and policy issues and to discuss presidential elections, international terrorism, Supreme Court decisions, congressional politics, city council actions, and so forth. By contrast, research on these topics is viewed by many as dull and boring; courses in empirical research are viewed as regrettable and largely irrelevant diversions. Research, too frequently, is thought of as the "less glamorous craft" of political science.[1]

Actually, most students soon discover that conducting independent research can be one of the most rewarding of academic experiences. Finally, students are freed from the rigors of lectures, note taking, memorization, and class examinations and allowed to pursue their own intellectual interests. The product of the research represents their own work, reflective of their own talents, imagination, and creativity. Research is, in a word, fun. For maximum satisfaction, however, research should be carried out in a systematic and orderly fashion. Otherwise, the results can be meaningless and the effort frustrating, indeed.

THE FOCUS OF THIS BOOK

This book is a guide to the conduct of **systematic political and policy research,** in which the researcher carefully follows a well-planned series of steps for implementing research. However, to say that research should be carried out in an orderly way is not to suggest that good research is simply the rote mastery of procedures and techniques that, when applied appropriately, will always yield startling scientific breakthroughs. It is not even to suggest that seemingly haphazard research is bound to be unproductive: Occasionally, great scientific breakthroughs are made almost as if by accident (see Box 1.1).

Most important, to say that research should proceed in an orderly manner is not to deny the critical role of the *human imagination* as the true source of creative, innovative research. Observers of science, as well as famous scientists themselves, frequently comment on the important role of imagination in research. John Dewey, for example, stated, "Every great advance in science has issued from a new audacity of imagination."[2] Albert Einstein asserted the importance of imagination more directly: "Imagination is more important than knowledge."[3]

Scientific breakthroughs sometimes do happen almost by accident, and scientific research unquestionably involves the application of the human imagination to the solving of problems deemed important by both the scientific community and society at large. In solving (and even in identifying) such problems, talented imagina-

BOX 1.1 "Discovery by Misadventure"

Scientific historian Arthur Koestler recounts a number of examples of great scientific discoveries made almost by accident. One example is as follows:

We find, over and again, mishaps and minor laboratory disasters which turn out to be blessings in disguise, and spoilt experiments which perversely yield the solution— by brutally shifting the experimenter's attention from a "plus" to a "minus" aspect of the problem, as it were. One might call this pattern "discovery by misadventure." A classic case is that of . . . Abbe Hauy (1743–1822) a humble teacher at the college of Lemoine, whose leisure hours were devoted to collecting specimens of plants and minerals—until a small, embarrassing accident suddenly changed the direction of . . . his whole life:

One day, when examining some minerals at the house of a friend, he was clumsy enough to allow a beautiful cluster of prismatic crystals of calcareous spar to fall to the ground. One of the prisms broke in such a way as to show at the fracture faces which were no less smooth than those elsewhere but presented the appearance of a new crystal altogether different in form from the prism. Hauy picked up this fragment and examined the faces with their inclinations and angles. To his great surprise, he discovered that they are the same in rhomboidal spar as in Iceland spar.

He wished to be able to generalize: he broke his own little collection into pieces; crystals lent by his friends were broken; everywhere he found a structure which depended upon the same laws.

The result was Hauy's *Traite de Mineralogie* which made him a member of the French Academy and a pioneer of the science of crystallography.

SOURCE: Arthur Koestler, *The Act of Creation* (New York: Macmillan, 1964), 192–93. In this passage, Koestler quoted from J. M. Montmasson, *Invention and the Unconscious* (London: K. Paul, 1931), 137.

tions must not be harnessed; curiosity must not be bridled. To do so would stagnate scientific research, and that is *not* what systematic research is all about.

However to say that research *normally* proceeds in a systematic and orderly fashion is to imply that there exist techniques and guidelines that, if followed, serve to maximize the rewards and satisfactions of the research endeavor and to increase the *probability* that such research will have important payoffs. There is, in other words, a right way to conduct research, and there are agreed-upon procedures that can be learned. Learning these procedures is similar to learning to play a musical instrument. For the beginner, the process may at first seem awkward, cumbersome, and mechanical. For the established researcher, these procedures become second nature; they are followed with almost no conscious effort. Like the skilled musician, the skilled researcher seeks to meld technique with talent to produce a harmonious and well-blended outcome.

EMPIRICAL RESEARCH

This book is about the conduct of empirical political and policy research. **Empirical research** deals with actual (some would say, "observable") political phenomena. We want to *describe* the nature of the phenomena—that is, we want to accurately measure, label, categorize, and compare political events. Also, we want to understand how political events are *related*. We want to be able to use one variable (and sometimes several variables) to predict other variables. Ultimately, we want to know which events seem to be related in a *causal* way to other events. We want to assess cause and effect.

Empirical versus Normative Research

Empirical research sometimes is contrasted with normative political analysis. **Normative analysis** deals with political issues from a more *subjective* perspective; the goal of such analysis might be to develop principles and guidelines for political action. Normative questions typically begin with the word, "should." "Should the death penalty be abolished?" "Should Congress provide for universal health care coverage?" "Should the federal government reduce the number of rules and regulations it places on state and local governments?" "Should there be limits on the number of terms legislators are permitted to serve?" All of these questions are asking for conclusions about what should or should not be done or permitted. Questions such as these may be very important. They certainly are not to be ignored by political and policy students, and empirical research frequently can shed some light on these issues. (Violent crime rates for states having the death penalty can be compared with those not having the death penalty, for example.) However, empirical research alone will not provide conclusive answers to normative questions. Answers to these questions ultimately must be framed in the context of personal values and preferences.

Empirical research, on the other hand, usually begins with words such as "what," "who," "how," or "why." Consider some questions posed by recently published political and policy research:

"Why do some states have more interest [group] organizations than others?"[4]

"How do citizens who have long been governed by the same party in an authoritarian regime vote when there seems to be a chance that they could turn the incumbents out of office?"[5]

"How do voters use [information] to assess candidates?"[6]

"What are the reasons for the exclusion [of cost considerations] from the most important . . . decisions made by the Environmental Protection Agency?"[7]

"Who votes?"[8]

Questions such as these can be answered by reference to real political phenomena—to political *data.* This is not to suggest that any single study is likely to answer complex questions, such as the foregoing ones, finally and completely. Nonetheless, empirical research, properly done, will yield more satisfactory answers than those that currently exist. As Julian Simon put it, "empirical research [serves] as a bridge between scientific thought and reality."[9]

Empirical Research: Basic versus Applied

Empirical research may be classified as either basic or applied. **Basic research** (sometimes termed *academic, pure,* or *theoretical research*) is conducted primarily to satisfy the researcher's intellectual curiosity. Practical considerations (e.g., "How will results of my research be used?") are only of secondary importance; pure research advances basic scientific knowledge. The goal of such research is to produce new knowledge and to be able to predict outcomes, given certain conditions. Philip Shively calls this type of activity "recreational research." It is carried out, he says "for the twin pleasures of exercising [our] minds and increasing [our] understanding of things."[10]

On the other hand, **applied research** (sometimes termed *policy research, policy-related research,* or *action research*) deals with problems in need of immediate attention, such as drug use in public schools, crime in cities, waste-recycling options for urban residents, and so forth. Frequently, political scientists are asked (sometimes even commissioned) by public decision makers to conduct such policy-related research. Policy research "focuses on relationships between variables that reflect social problems and other variables that can be manipulated by public policy."[11] Here, the question often asked is, "Which policy should we pursue?" For example, what is the most effective and feasible way to reduce drug use in schools, reduce urban crime, or increase recycling activities? Empirical research can help answer these questions, and it frequently is conducted so as to present decision makers with cost and benefit comparisons among a number of possible options. Put another way, whereas basic research is conducted to satisfy the desire to *understand,* applied research is "expected to have a quick payoff."[12]

Some political scientists identify a third form of empirical research: **evaluation research.** Here the researcher is concerned with the application of scientific methods to the evaluation of agency programs or the outcomes of legislative policy. Evaluation researchers, it has been said, "use social research methodologies to judge

TABLE 1.1

Research Design Orientations

Defining Characteristic	Basic	Applied	Evaluation
Nature of the problem	Basic scientific investigation seeks new knowledge about social phenomena, hoping to establish general principles with which to explain them.	Applied scientific investigation seeks to understand a demanding social problem and to provide policymakers well-grounded guides to remedial action.	Evaluative research seeks to assess outcomes of the treatment applied to a social problem or the outcome of prevailing practices.
Goal of the research	To produce new knowledge including discovery of relationships and the capacity to predict outcomes under various conditions.	To secure the requisite knowledge that can be immediately useful to a policymaker who seeks to eliminate or alleviate a social problem.	To provide an accurate social accounting resulting from a treatment program applied to a social problem.
Guiding theory	Selection of theory to guide hypothesis testing and provide reinforcement for a theory under examination.	Selection of a theory, guidelines, or intuitive hunches to explore the dynamics of a social system.	Selection of a theory to fit the problem under assessment. Watch for ways to hook findings to a new theory or an established one.
Appropriate techniques	Theory formulation, hypothesis testing, sampling, data collection techniques (direct observation, interview, questionnaire, scale measurement), statistical treatment of data, validation or rejection of hypotheses.	Seek access to individual actions and inquire what actors are feeling and thinking at the time; elicit the attributions and evaluation made about self, other, or situational factors; regard crucial explanations as hypotheses to be tested.	Use all conventional techniques appropriate to the problem.

SOURCE: Delbert C. Miller, *Handbook of Research Design and Social Measurement,* 5th ed. (Newbury Park, CA: Sage Publications, 1991), 4.

and improve the ways in which human services policies and programs are conducted, from the earliest stages of defining and designing programs through their development and implementation."[13]

Delbert C. Miller has nicely captured the essential differences among basic, applied, and evaluation research in terms of their defining goals and techniques.[14] Those differences are shown in Table 1.1. However, as Miller also points out, all researchers—regardless of approach—must master the fundamental principles of basic research. These fundamental principles are emphasized in this text.[15] These principles guide the conduct of systematic political and policy research.

THE SYSTEMATIC POLITICAL RESEARCHER

Do not confuse a distinction between systematic and unsystematic research with a distinction between *honest* and *dishonest* work. It is assumed at the outset that all students recognize the difference between honest and dishonest research and that work that is plagiarized, faked, misrepresented, or otherwise purposely distorted cannot be tolerated.[16]

Unsystematic research can be conducted by the most diligent and conscientious of students. Many elements of unsystematic research, in fact, may be quite legitimate and may appear very scientific. The unsystematic researcher may even be unaware of the flaws in his or her methodology.

Perhaps an appreciation of the topics to be covered in this book can best be gained by first considering some examples of *unsystematic* research. While unsystematic research can take many forms, there are a few typical cases. Everyone is familiar with the "scrambler," the student who (usually the weekend before the paper is due) makes one hurried trip to the library, checks out a few books, makes photocopies of what appear to be some important journal articles on a particular topic, carries all these materials back to his or her room, spreads the materials in front of the television set, fixes a sandwich or two, and then scrambles through all these materials while watching an afternoon football game. The scrambler hopes that sometime during the third or fourth quarter of the game, a fully developed research product will emerge. What typically emerges is an unimaginative paper, poorly researched, poorly cited, and smeared with mustard. Both the student and the professor will be disappointed with the effort.

Also typical of unsystematic research is the method used by the "masher." This student at least collects some data on a particular topic, mashes the data through his or her personal computer (PC) using a statistical package program, correlates every variable with every other one, then frantically scans the results looking for significant correlations (the masher usually assumes that unless astonishingly high correlations are found, all is lost). Having found some strong correlations, the student then prepares, ex post facto, some hypotheses that can be supported by these findings and shapes the report accordingly.

The "shuffler" is also frequently encountered among student researchers. This student will find all the major works on a particular topic and, in cut–and–paste fashion, will shuffle, more or less randomly, the findings of previous research into a single paper. The result may have no uniform theme or may make no original contribution, but the student believes that the instructor will at least be impressed with citations from the major scholars and apparent familiarity with the terminology in a particular field.

In each of these examples, the students, in fact, are adopting *portions* of the systematic approach to research. It is certainly important to spend some time at the library, to become familiar with the major works and terminology in a field, to develop hypotheses, to find empirical evidence pertaining to the hypotheses, and, perhaps, to use a computer to perform some analysis. In isolation, however, none of these measures represents systematic research. It is not enough to selectively apply segments of the research process to your effort—these phases must be integrated in an orderly and systematic fashion. Otherwise, the process is likely to be tedious, the experience frustrating, and the results unrewarding.

Compare the scrambler, the masher, and the shuffler with the systematic researcher. This student first carefully develops several possible research topics, evaluates each, selects the one with the greatest potential for yielding interesting results, thoroughly reviews the literature in the selected area, clearly and precisely develops hypotheses that can be examined and tested within the time frame and with the resources available, selects an appropriate research design, collects the appropriate data for testing the hypotheses, applies the appropriate analytic techniques, and prepares a report relating the findings to some body of theory or to an important policy issue. Not only will such research be well received but also, even more important, the results will be personally rewarding and satisfying. The researcher is assured that his or her efforts add, even if only incrementally, to what is known about a particular issue. The results represent real contributions to knowledge. In addition, this sort of research is enjoyable and rewarding.

THE ELEMENT OF TIME

The systematic approach to research is the approach promoted in this text. The following chapters are organized according to the major stages in the research process. The student will find in those chapters many specific and—it is hoped—helpful research suggestions.

Additionally, a crucial overall consideration in conducting research is time. Perhaps no other single element is so crucial to research success as this one. Alternatives can often be found for the other research ingredients, but time is the one for which there is no substitute. Social science research is particularly time-consuming, and social scientists must be especially aware of the time available and must plan accordingly. Perhaps Aaron Wildavsky said it best when he reminded political researchers, "Your time is your most valuable asset. Do not fritter it away: Use it."[17]

Of course, the amount of time required for each stage of the research process will vary widely. A research project that requires you to collect your own data will obviously mean that you have to spend more time in the data-collection stage than a project that relies on data already available. A research design calling for in-depth interviews of a hundred or so elected officials will take more time than one requiring brief surveys of classmates and friends.

Still, a very rough guide to the amount of time that should be allotted to each stage may be suggested. Table 1.2 assumes a time frame of 15 weeks, about the amount of time most students will have in one semester. Obviously, those students who have differing time constraints will have to adjust these intervals accordingly.

The time suggested for the initial stages (topic selection, literature review, and hypothesis formation—6 weeks) may seem excessive. Indeed, with practice, much less time may be required for these activities. On the other hand, the initial stages are the most important phases of the research process. Beginning researchers, in particular, will have to invest a great deal of time in becoming familiar with library

TABLE 1.2
Suggested Time Allotments and Chapter Keys for Each Stage of the
Research Process

Stages in the Research Process	Suggested Time Allotment*	Chapter Keys
Topic selection	3 weeks	2
Literature review	2 weeks	2
Hypothesis formation	1 week	3
Research design selection	1 week	3
Data collection	3 weeks	4–5
Data processing	1 week	6
Data analysis	2 weeks	7–10
Report preparation	2 weeks	11
Total	15 weeks	

*Assuming that the project is to be completed within one semester.

utilization, with social science indexes and abstracts, with appropriate data sources, and with the other published materials required for the completion of these phases. Considerable time is required, also, for simply thinking through the feasibility and desirability of pursuing a particular project. In addition to every other consideration, students should always ask of themselves, "Am I *really* interested in this project?" Typically, beginning researchers will consider and discard several ideas before finally settling on the one that is to be pursued. Thus, about one third of the total time available may productively be devoted to the early stages of the research process. However, after this time, the student should be ready to proceed without delay to the remaining tasks.

SUMMARY

This book is a guide to the conduct of empirical political and policy research. Two themes are underscored: (1) Political research is an enjoyable and pleasurable opportunity, not a dull and tedious chore; (2) for maximum satisfaction, research must be carried out in a systematic, orderly process. The techniques of research can be taught; many suggestions are introduced in the following chapters. Nonetheless, the greatest teacher is personal experience. If this book serves as the introductory guide to political research for many students, it is hoped that this is just the first of what will be many rewarding and productive research experiences.

KEY TERMS

systematic political research
empirical research
normative analysis

basic research
applied research
evaluation research

EXERCISES

1. Empirical research versus normative analysis
   a. Discuss the differences between empirical political research and normative political analysis.
   b. What features distinguish each of these, and in what contexts is each appropriate for the political analyst?
   c. How can empirical political research contribute to a better understanding of important social problems?
2. Basic versus applied research
   a. Discuss the differences between basic and applied research.
   b. Under what circumstances might each of these approaches to research be appropriate?
   c. What is meant by the term *policy research,* and how is it distinguished from *basic,* or *pure, research?*
   d. Discuss the term *evaluation research* and the situations in which it might appropriately be conducted.
   e. From the political science and policy-related journals in your library, select at least one article that represents primarily basic research and one that is primarily applied. Describe the differences between each of these kinds of research, focusing especially on the techniques of research used in each, as illustrated in these articles.
3. Systematic versus unsystematic research
   a. Discuss the differences between systematic and unsystematic research, as those terms are used in this chapter.
   b. What are the advantages of systematic research, as opposed to unsystematic research?
   c. How does dishonest research differ from unsystematic research, and what are some consequences of each?
4. Time and political research
   a. Discuss some of the reasons why political science and policy research are especially time-consuming.
   b. Do you think that some strategies of research are more time-consuming than others? Why or why not?
5. Stages of research
   a. Select three empirical studies from recent political science and policy-related journals in your library, and report the approximate time the authors appear to have allocated to each stage of the research process, as discussed in this chapter.
   b. Could the time allocated by these authors to the various stages of research have been shortened without significantly sacrificing the quality of the research? How might this reduction have been accomplished?

NOTES

1. The phrase, "less glamorous craft" is used by Julian L. Simon, *Basic Research Methods in Social Science: The Art of Empirical Investigation,* 1st ed. (New York: Random House, 1969), 5.
2. John Dewey, *The Quest for Certainty* (New York: Minton, Balch, 1929).
3. Albert Einstein, *On Science.*
4. David Lowery and Virginia Gray, "The Population Ecology of Gucci Gulch, or the Natural Regulation of Interest Group Numbers in the American States," *American Journal of Political Science,* 39 (February, 1995), p. 1.
5. Jorge I. Dominquez and James A. McCaan, "Shaping Mexico's Electoral Arena! The Construction of Partisan Cleavages in the 1988 and 1991 National Elections, *American Political Science Review* 89 (March, 1995), 34.
6. Wendy M. Rahn, John H. Aldrich, and Eugene Borgida, "Individual and Contextual Variations in Political Candidate Appraisal," *American Political Science Review* 88 (March, 1994), 193.
7. Paul R. Portney and Winston Harrington, "Economic and Health-based Environmental Standards," Policy Studies Journal, 23 (Spring, 1995), 96.
8. Jan E. Leighley and Jonathan Nagler, "Socioeconomic Class Bias in Turnout, 1964–1988: The Voters Remain the Same," *American Political Science Review* 86 (September, 1992), 725.
9. Simon, Basic Research Methods in Social Sciences, 6.
10. W. Phillips Shively, *The Craft of Political Research,* 2nd ed. (Englewood Cliffs, NJ: Prentice-Hall, 1980), 7.
11. David L. Weimer and Aidan R. Vining, *Policy Analysis: Concepts and Practice* (Englewood Cliffs, NJ: Prentice-Hall, 1989), 4.
12. Simon, *Basic Research Methods in Social Sciences,* 6.
13. Carol H. Weiss, *Evaluation Research* (Englewood Cliffs, NJ: Prentice-Hall, 1972), 9.
14. Delbert C. Miller, *Handbook of Research Design and Social Measurement,* 5th ed. (Newbury Park, CA: Sage Publications, 1991), 67–102.
15. For a further introduction to some of the research issues unique to applied and evaluation research, see Carl V. Patton and David S. Sawicki, *Basic Methods of Policy Analysis and Planning,* 2nd ed. (Englewood Cliffs, NJ: Prentice-Hall, 1993).
16. Dishonesty in research is not a problem unique to students or to first-time researchers. Pressures to produce results are great at every level of research, and the history of science is filled with examples of researchers—even at the highest levels—taking inappropriate shortcuts in the research process. One of the most notorious incidents of this nature in American science occurred in the late 1980s and early 1990s when first a coresearcher and then later the Office of Scientific Integrity at the National Institutes of Health accused a team of biomedical researchers, including one member who was both a Nobel laureate and a president of a major research university, of publishing a remarkable finding that included faked data. (Their finding suggested that the human body might be coaxed into producing a variety of antibodies by inserting a gene for a foreign protein.) For background, see the *New York Times,* June 4, 1991, and May 4, 1991.
17. See Aaron Wildavsky, *Craftways: On the Organization of Scholarly Work* (New Brunswick, NJ: Transaction Publishers, 1989), 45.

CHAPTER 2

Getting Started:
Selecting the Topic and Reviewing the Literature

Starting the research process—that is, selecting a topic for study—is the *most important* stage of the research process. The topic selected for study sets the tone for the entire research effort and establishes the framework within which the other major stages of the research process—such as developing hypotheses, collecting information, analyzing results, and writing the report—will be carried out. It should be well understood that none of these other stages can substitute for poor research ideas. Research techniques—no matter how sophisticated—cannot turn a bad idea into a good research topic. As Julian Simon has put it, "a good idea is the keystone of an empirical study. . . . data collection and measurement are worthless unless the subject is important."[1]

In addition to being the most important stage of the research process, topic selection is frequently the *most difficult* one. Unfortunately, experienced researchers do not spend a lot of time describing how they come up with their research ideas. When they do describe the origins of their ideas, they often say their ideas are generated by competing theories of some political phenomenon. Alternatively, they sometimes say that their ideas spring from the conflict existing between some theory of political behavior and their own experiences with the real world of politics.

An example of a research topic generated by competing theories of a political phenomenon is provided by Taylor and Rourke in their recent study of the relationship between historical analogies (that is, lessons from the past) and the making of foreign policy. At the outset of their study, they noted,

> There exists, therefore, two propositions that compete for our understanding of the role historical analogies play in the congressional foreign policy process. On the one hand, there is the argument that analogies shape policy choices. On the other hand, analogies are viewed as secondary to our understanding of the process and are employed merely as rhetoric to justify choices made on the basis of ideology and party. . . . The task of this research . . . is to evaluate . . . the validity of [these] competing propositions. . . . [2]

An example of a research topic generated by a lack of congruence between some theory of politics and a scholar's own political experiences is provided by Roger Davidson in his study of Congress. The idea for this research topic, said Davidson,

> came to me several years ago in the midst of a panel discussion at a professional meeting. Several earnest and capable scholars were presenting papers analyzing the reform-era Congress of the 1970s. . . . All this was well and good, I thought, but the descriptions soon exceeded the bounds of reality. . . . Surely, I thought, an institution such as they described would be so lacking in coherence and cohesion that it could not long survive. This was by no means the Congress I knew at close range.[3]

A good strategy, then, is to seek topics in areas where there exist competing theories or in areas where existing theory is inconsistent with reality. Unfortunately, the Catch-22 for beginning students is that often they must select a research topic before they can possibly have time to become familiar with the literature or with the theoretical controversies in the field. More common is the situation described by Benjamin Most:

> Students—at least those with whom I have worked over the years—find it extraordinarily difficult to focus in on research questions. Failing all else—and confronted by the approaching end of the semester which raises the specter of (yet another) incomplete—they typically visit my office to discuss "what they should do." All too commonly they have no idea how to begin; if they do have an idea, it is not always a terribly useful one. Getting started appears to be very difficult for them.[4]

Most's experiences with his students are not unusual; his description is typical of students everywhere. In selecting research topics, students face special problems. Not only are they typically more limited by time and resources than are senior researchers, but also they almost certainly are not as familiar with the issues and controversies in the field. Advanced scholars frequently have ongoing research projects and interests; for them, the conclusion of one project often leads directly to the start of another. For beginning students, however, coming up with an idea for a research topic is frequently the hardest part.

DEVELOPING A LIST OF POTENTIAL TOPICS

Simply put, ideas for a research topic either must come from an outside source (such as when an instructor assigns lists of topics from which students are to make choices, or when a public agency requests an evaluation study) or from the student. When topics are assigned or requested by someone else, of course, the initial decisions have already been made or at least substantially limited in scope. Very frequently, though, students have to select topics themselves. Topics may be selected because they relate to the general literature in the field or because they deal with some relevant policy issues. In either case, the task is to take a large subject area—such as "the American presidency" or "teen-age substance abuse"—and *narrow* it down first to a *list* of potential topics, and finally to *one* manageable, meaningful research topic.

Actually, by the very process of selecting which courses to take, you already have begun the task of topic narrowing. You decided to take the course on the American presidency, urban politics, or health policy because you already have an interest in the subject matter. You may already know that you are interested in presidential campaigning, or in city council elections, or in health care. Course selection is a beginning. From here, you proceed with the process of developing a list of potential topics.

Reviewing Textbook Chapter Titles and Subtitles

One valuable, and easy, strategy at this early stage of topic selection is simply to examine the chapter titles and subtitles of the text(s) assigned for the course. This strategy will give a quick overview of the broad areas of concern in the subject area. A recently published text in urban politics lists the following chapter headings:[5]

1. Cities, Suburbs, and Power
2. The Urban Situation
3. Decision Making in Local Communities: Who Has the Power?
4. Formal Structure and Leadership Style
5. Machine Politics
6. Reform Politics
7. Citizen Participation and Decentralization
8. Urban Bureaucracy and Service Delivery
9. Suburban Politics and Metropolitan America
10. The Politics of Metropolitan Government
11. Metropolitan Governance: The Politics of Intergovernmental Cooperation

These chapter titles make clear some of the major concerns in the field of urban politics. Based on these titles, the student can begin to formulate questions and ideas about citizen participation in urban politics, urban bureaucracies, suburban politics, and the like. Looking at chapter *subtitles* refines these issues even more. This particular text, for instance, includes the following subtitles in the chapter on suburban politics: "A Diversity of Suburbs," "The Graying of Suburbia," "Minority Suburbanization," "The Political Attitudes of Suburbia," "Housing and Land Use," "Suburban Autonomy and Metropolitan Fragmentation." Even if this is the student's first course in urban politics, some of the important issues and controversies surrounding suburbanization are readily apparent.

Examining Journals and Periodicals

Also useful in identifying topics is an examination, even if cursory, of leading journals and periodicals. Specialized journals are available in virtually every field of political interest, and a simple review of the titles of articles appearing in the most recent issues of these journals will give the student a good idea of contemporary research interests in that field.[6] Listed in Appendix A are approximately seventy-five leading journals in political science and public policy. A review of the titles and descriptions of these provides a good idea of the focus and content of each journal.

Presidential Studies Quarterly	*Criminology*
Predicting Presidential Decision Making	Religion and Crime Revisited: The Impact of
The Appointment of a Supreme Court Justice:	Religion, Secular Controls, and Social
A Political Process from Beginning to End	Ecology on Adult Crime
The Impact of Presidential Selection	The Impact of Enhanced Prison Terms for
Methods on Executive-Legislative Conflict	Felonies Committed with Guns
Dumping the Vice President: An Historical	Delinquent Peers, Beliefs, and Delinquent
Overview and Analysis	Behavior
Are Senior Citizens Too Old for the Vice	Gender and Southern Punishment After the
Presidency? A Look at the Record	Civil War
White House Organizations as a Problem of	Parental Attitudes and Deliquency
Governance: The Eisenhower System	Deterrence or Brutalization? An Impact
Public Funding of Presidential Campaigns	Assessment of Oklahoma's Return to
and Elections: Is there a Viable Future?	Capital Punishment

FIGURE 2.1

Article Titles Appearing in Issues of *Presidential Studies Quarterly* (a journal specializing in studies of the American presidency) and *Criminology* (a journal specializing in the study of crime and criminal behavior)

NOTE: These examples were taken from 1994 and 1995 issues of *Presidential Studies Quarterly* and *Criminology*.

Looking at a few issues of *Presidential Studies Quarterly* and *Criminology*, as examples, the student will find the article titles shown in Figure 2.1. Even for beginning students taking courses on the presidency, or in criminal justice, these article titles are suggestive of appropriate research topics.

Overviewing the Appropriate Subfield

Another valuable exercise at the earliest stages of the research process is to review the state of knowledge and research in a particular subfield of interest. While many research reviews are available for the political science literature,[7] the most useful publication is *Political Science: The State of the Discipline II,* published by the American Political Science Association.[8] This publication includes chapters on the major subject areas in political science (Legislatures, Executives, comparative politics, voting behavior, etc.), prepared by leading scholars in each field. Each chapter presents an overview of the field, an assessment of the contemporary state of knowledge in each area, a discussion of the major theoretical questions and controversies, suggestions for research issues that need to be addressed in the future, and a lengthy and useful bibliography. A review of any of these chapters will yield numerous research questions and ideas, as well as suggestions for sources of information and data.

Using Encyclopedias

Students also should be familiar with the various **encyclopedias** and **dictionaries** focusing on political issues and controversies. Indeed, political science surpasses most other disciplines in the sheer number of such publications; a quick review of these two types of resources can be very helpful during the topic-selection phase of research.

The *Blackwell Encyclopedia of Political Thought* (David Miller, ed., 1986), the *Blackwell Encyclopedia of Political Institutions* (Vernon Bogdanor, ed., 1987), and the *Blackwell Encyclopedia of Political Science* (Vernon Bogdanor, ed., 1992) (all published in New York by Blackwell) are companion volumes dealing with political theories, theorists, thoughts, ideas, and institutions. Entries are arranged alphabetically, with a subject index provided. More specialized encyclopedias are found in the various subfields of political science. The *Encyclopedia of American Foreign Policy: Studies of the Principal Movements and Ideas* (Alexander De Conde, ed., New York: Scribner's 1978, 3 vols.) contains various articles on topics ranging "from broad concepts such as isolationism and national self-determination to specific topics, such as the Monroe Doctrine and the Marshall Plan."

The *Encyclopedia of American History: Studies of the Principal Movements and Ideas* (Jack P. Greene, ed., New York: Macmillan, 1984, 3 vols.) contains articles on political events, documents, issues, themes, institutions, processes, and developments. Topics range from ideas such as liberalism and Republicanism to specific topics such as the U.S. cabinet and suffrage.

The two-volume set, *Political Parties & Elections in the United States: An Encyclopedia* (L. Sandy Maisel, ed., New York: Garland Publishing, 1991), contains articles relevant to American political parties and elections, including "names and dates, basic data on the history and current operations of political parties, [and] rudimentary information on the individuals who have played and continue to play key roles in the functioning of political parties and the electoral process."

Excellent guidance to the three branches of American government may be found in *The Encyclopedia of American Government* (Washington, DC: Congressional Quarterly), along with its companion three-volume set: *Congress A to Z* (1993), *The Presidency A to Z* (1992), and *The Supreme Court A to Z* (1993).

The *Encyclopedia of the American Presidency* (Leonard W. Levy and Louis Fisher, eds., New York: Simon and Schuster, 1993), provides an excellent overview of the American presidency. The four-volume set includes long individual articles followed by bibliographies.

The *Encyclopedia of Third Parties in the United States,* (Earl R. Kruschke, Santa Barbara, CA: ABC-Clio, 1991), presents a "laundry list of examples of third parties that have existed throughout American history, ranging from some of the most important . . . to some of the most frivolous."

The *Encyclopedia of the United Nations and International Agreements* (Edmund Jan Osmanczyk, Philadelphia: Taylor and Francis, 1990) defines international terms, conferences, agreements, conventions, treaties, and declarations with cross-references.

The *World Encyclopedia of Peace* (Ervin Laszlo and Jong Youl Yoo, eds., New York: Pergamon Press, 1986, 4 vols.) contains articles on peace "from a very broad spectrum of perspectives; from the idealist to the realist; from the global to the subnational; from the cultural to the economic; from the religious to the feminist; from the historical to the contemporary." Included are essays dealing with concepts, terms, events, wars, movements, associations, and personalities.

The *World Encyclopedia of Political Systems and Parties* (George E. Delury, ed., New York: Facts on File, 1986, 2 vols.) consists of entries dealing with systems of government, institutions, and electoral systems, including suffrage, registration, and balloting procedures on a nation-by-nation basis.

Using Dictionaries

Least helpful, probably, are political science dictionaries. Nonetheless, these dictionaries may be useful for defining key terms and concepts, or for clarifying the role and significance of certain ideas, events, and people in the world of politics. Probably the best, and most current, of these *general* political science dictionaries is Jack C. Plano and Milton Greenberg's *The American Political Dictionary* (San Diego, CA: Harcourt Brace Jovanovich, 1993). Also useful, but somewhat dated, are William Safire's *Political Dictionary* (New York: Random House, 1978) and Jack C. Plano's *The Dictionary of Political Analysis* (Santa Barbara, CA: ABC-Clio, 1982).

Additionally, *specialized dictionaries* are available for most of the subfields of political science. It is impossible to list all of these, but in the fields of political science and policy studies, students will find especially helpful the dictionaries listed:

Political Theory: *A Dictionary of Political Thought* (Roger Scruton, New York: Hill & Wang, 1985).

American Government: *The HarperCollins Dictionary of American Government and Politics* (Jay M. Shafritz, New York: HarperCollins, 1992).

Public Administration: *The Facts on File Dictionary of Public Administration* (Jay M. Shafritz, New York: Facts on File, 1985).

International Relations: *Dictionary of American Diplomatic History* (John E. Findling, Westport, CT: Greenwood Press, 1980); and *International Relations Dictionary* (Jack C. Plano and Roy Olton, Santa Barbara, CA: ABC-Clio, 1988).

Public Policy: *The Public Policy Dictionary* (Earl R. Kruschke, Santa Barbara, CA: ABC-Clio, 1987).

State and Local: *The State and Local Government Political Dictionary* (Jeffrey M. Elliot, Santa Barbara, CA: ABC-Clio, 1988).

Foreign Affairs: *Dictionary of American Foreign Affairs* (Stephen A. Flanders and Carl N. Flanders, eds., New York: Macmillan, 1993).

In addition to the aforementioned, students should be familiar with the country-by-country dictionaries published in the ABC-Clio political science series, including dictionaries for Africa (by Claude S. Phillips, 1984), Asia (prepared by Lawrence Ziring, 1985), Europe (by Ernest E. Rossi and Barbara P. McCrea, 1985), Latin America (by Ernest E. Rossi and Jack C. Plano, 1987), the Middle East (by Lawrence Ziring, 1984), and Soviet and Eastern Europe (by Barbara P. McCrea, 1984).

Consulting with Instructors

All of the foregoing activities should yield a large number of potential topics for research. At this point, it is time to consult with your instructor and to proceed further with the process of narrowing the list. Your instructor will have additional ideas concerning topic feasibility, data sources, resource materials, and help with your answering the most important question at this point: "Which of these research efforts can I really complete with the resources and time available to me?" As you formulate answers to this question, a variety of additional criteria may be applied in narrowing your list of *potential topics* to the *single topic* to be pursued.

NARROWING THE LIST TO A SINGLE TOPIC

Student Interest

In narrowing a list of potential topics down to a single topic to be researched, a number of criteria may be applied. The most important of these is *personal interest*. When reviewing the list of topics, you should ask yourself, "What project would be of most interest to *me*?" In the case of a semester's project, several weeks will be devoted to the research effort. In the case of a master's thesis or a doctoral dissertation, several months (perhaps even years) will be required. It is mandatory that you select a topic that will be appealing for at least this period of time. Nothing can be so onerous as a dull research project, and nothing so detracts from the ultimate quality of the final product as lack of researcher enthusiasm. If, after your initial explorations, you find that the topic does not appeal to you, get another topic.

Discipline Significance/Policy Relevance

It is not enough that the topic be of interest to you; it needs also to be of interest to the broader community of scholars, or it should be related to some significant policy issue. A major purpose of research is to add to existing knowledge. Even brief semester projects should be placed in the context of existing theory or should be related to questions of obvious policy relevance. Studying the relationship between voters' choice for president and brands of coffee preferred would, undoubtedly, fail the test of significance to the discipline.

More substantial topics, such as a case study of waste-recycling activities in a particular city, become even more relevant when placed in the broader context of factors associated with success or failure of waste recycling in a representative sample of cities. Along a similar vein, a study of attitudes toward waste recycling, expressed by local decision makers, becomes more important when related to the process of policy making in those cities: "Do cities in which officials express more positive attitudes toward waste recycling have more favorable policies toward recycling activities?"

Graduate students and senior undergraduates will generally be familiar with the significant policy and theoretical issues in a particular area, so the application of this criterion will be almost automatic. For those unfamiliar with a discipline's major issues, a quick examination of political and policy indexes and abstracts (discussed here subsequently) will indicate other work that is being conducted in the chosen area. If, in checking such references, you find no other work related to the topic you are considering, the topic is probably of no interest to the broader discipline or is too difficult to be pursued. In either case, you should consider another topic.

Manageability

Usually, it is not too difficult to come up with interesting and even significant ideas. Often, the most difficult problem is selecting a topic that can actually be completed within the time allotted and with the resources available. Social science research can be very time-consuming and very expensive. Even a survey of a small sample (say, 100 individuals) requires considerable time to draft the survey instrument, select the sample, interview each respondent, enter the data into your computer, analyze the data, and write the report. An individual student will be better off selecting a project where the data already have been collected. (Chapter 5 discusses some of these important sources of available data.) Projects involving the collection of data are more appropriate for an entire class, or for a team of students, where different tasks may be assigned to different students.

You also have to be *realistic* in selecting a topic. Although it would be interesting and perhaps significant to conduct an interview study of state legislators in your state, politicians are very busy people, and it is doubtful that you could gain enough time with enough legislators to make the study worthwhile. On the other hand, an interview study of legislative aides, or of a small sample of legislators—when the legislature is out of session—might be possible.

All of these cautionary comments are intended simply to advise you that in selecting a topic, you must, at the outset, apply a good deal of foresight and common sense. Know your own time and resource limitations, and select a topic that is realistic and manageable.

Ethical Considerations

Political scientists, like all other people involved in research dealing with human subjects, are becoming increasingly sensitized to the moral and ethical issues arising in such research. As Mark S. Frankel has stated, "If political science is going to continue to matter, political scientists must face up to the civic and ethical implications of their work."[9]

In adapting the scientific method to behavioral research, social scientists cannot choose to show little concern for the subject matter.[10] Although the chemist need have little regard for the welfare of the elements in the test tube, the behavioral scientist must be totally concerned with the welfare of his or her human subjects. Human experimentation must be *voluntary,* and those participating in the study must be fully apprised of whatever risks may be involved. Maximum care must be taken to ensure that human subjects are not embarrassed, insulted, or otherwise psychologically or physically harmed by the research. Joan E. Sieber aptly expressed the ethical goals of the political researcher:

> The ethical researcher creates a mutually respectful, win–win relationship with the research population; this is a relationship in which subjects are pleased to participate candidly, and the community at large regards the conclusions as constructive. Public policy implications of the research are presented in such a way that public sensibilities are unlikely to be offended and backlash is unlikely to occur.[11]

Political and policy researchers must take special care to protect the privacy of subjects, especially when conducting surveys and when interviewing people in politically sensitive positions. In return for participating in a study, subjects frequently are guaranteed **confidentiality,** which means that particular responses will not be publicly identified with particular respondents (you will not, in other words, reveal who said what). Sometimes, subjects need to be guaranteed **anonymity,** which means that the study will be conducted so that even the researcher is not able to associate particular responses with particular respondents. Researchers must understand the difference between confidentiality and anonymity, and they must not promise one, when they actually mean the other. Illustrative of the concern with ethics in research, the American Political Science Association has issued a publication entitled *A Guide to Professional Ethics in Political Science.* Among the issues covered in the publication is a set of principles governing research on human subjects, regarding which the Association advises,

> The methodology of political science includes procedures which involve human subjects: surveys and interviews, observation of public behavior, experiments, physiological testing, and examination of documents. Possible risk to human subjects is something that political scientists should take into account. Under certain conditions, political scientists are also legally required to assess the risks to human subjects.[12]

When evaluating a research topic dealing with human subjects, ethical criteria must be considered carefully. Human subjects must be treated with *dignity.* If there is the slightest doubt that respectful treatment will not be employed, the topic should be abandoned.

TOPIC FAMILIARITY: MAKING USE OF THE LIBRARY

Following these steps, the student should have settled on at least a general research area and should be reasonably certain of the feasibility, desirability, and ethical efficacy of proceeding. It is tempting at this point to leap to the more exciting data-collection and analysis phases of the research process. First, however, attention must be paid to other matters, which are also important. One of these is *topic familiarity:* You must become thoroughly familiar with the available literature in the area.

A review of the available literature further assists you in narrowing the topic and in placing the research within a proper theoretical or policy context. Through a review of the literature, you become familiar with the approaches and techniques used by others, with the sources of available data, and with the important questions posed by scholars in the field. In short, the literature-review process tells us what has been previously attempted in the area, what approaches have been successful, and what issues remain unanswered.

It is at this stage that the researcher turns to the library. Although the library resources and personnel are essential aids in the conduct of research, use of the library can be a very frustrating experience. Hundreds of thousands of academic books and articles are published each year in the United States alone, so it is impossible even for experts to keep up to date with every piece of published research in their fields. For the library experience to be productive, this phase of the research process must be carried out deliberately and expeditiously. A number of guides may assist in the optimum utilization of the library's resources. These guides quickly alert the researcher to the materials that are most directly and immediately related to the topic of interest, so it is essential that the researcher become thoroughly familiar with these tools.

On-Line Catalogs

Beginning researchers generally are familiar with the traditional card catalog, where a library's book holdings are listed by author, title, and subject. However, upon entering most university libraries today, students will not see the familiar card catalog cabinets, instead, they will find a bank of computer terminals used for gaining access to an **on-line library catalog system.**[13] The on-line catalog is an indispensable aid to research. The computer is an ideal teacher. It is endlessly patient, always available, and amenable to much more imaginative use than the card catalog was.

By using only its most basic features, students will find the on-line catalog system to serve many of the same functions as the card catalog—only better. The on-line catalog gives the same kind of information as was provided in the card catalog, but the information available through the on-line system may be arranged differently, and there may be more information available. Typically, an on-line system can be searched by author, title, and subject, and also by call number and keyword—a significant word that may be found in the abstract, title, or text of any number of works. Many on-line systems are equipped with a printer so that the student may save time by printing records quickly and accurately directly from the terminal. Also, many systems make it possible for students to download records directly to computer disk, providing even more speed, accuracy, and convenience. On-line systems typically are *fully integrated*—meaning that users will find not only whether the library owns an item, but also other useful information regarding the availability of the item, such as whether that item is checked out, is being repaired, is on reserve, or is housed in a branch library or a specialized collection. All this information existed in the days of the card catalog, but it could not all be retrieved readily in one place.

In addition, on-line catalogs offer many features that were inconceivable in the days of a single, fixed-location card catalog. Today, investigators can also gain access to the catalog from their homes, offices, workplaces, or anyplace where they have access to a microcomputer and a modem. Additionally, researchers are not limited to searching only their own university's holdings. Many catalogs from North American, European, and other universities throughout the world are accessible to users on-line through the Internet system.[14]

A good exercise for beginning students is to visit the university library at the earliest possible moment and to become familiar with their library's particular on-line system. When locating a book through the system, you will find presented on the screen much useful information about the book, including the U.S. Library of Congress subject headings to which this particular book is indexed. The Library of Congress subject heading is very useful in conducting library research. In fact, most university libraries arrange books on shelves using the Library of Congress's classification scheme. This means that once you have identified a call-number sequence of interest, you may want to browse in the shelves for all books in that sequence. It is helpful to know that university libraries are consistent with one another in their use of subject headings and classification scheme. Table 2.1 presents the Library of Congress tables for political science.[15]

The library catalog (on cards or on-line) is a good place to begin the process of topic familiarization. These systems are particularly useful for finding books that have been on the shelves for at least a few months. Unfortunately, a time delay of weeks, or even months, may occur between a book's publication and its acquisition and cataloging by the library. Fortunately, other sources of information about library materials are also available. These additional sources include various reference indexes and abstracts.

General Indexes and Abstracts

An **index** is a publication, released regularly (e.g., monthly, quarterly, or semiannually, and nearly always with an annual cumulative volume) that tells you about the published research in the field for the time covered by each issue. Frequently, but not always, that research will be exclusively in the *journal* literature.

The indexes available for political and policy research may be arranged in a number of ways. Some indexes concentrate on a *single topic* (e.g., public policy), some on a *single publication* (e.g., the *New York Times*), and some on a *type of publication* (e.g., government documents). Indexes also may be classified by *format* of publication: Some are published in paper format, some are on compact disc, and some are available in other electronic formats. Students should be aware that the electronic version of an index seldom duplicates the entire span of that index and that to conduct historical research, the researcher must consult older volumes available only in print.

Some indexing services also offer **abstracts** (brief summaries) of works cited.

TABLE 2.1

Library of Congress Classification Scheme: Political Science

J	1– 981	General legislative and executive papers
	(1– 9)	Official gazettes
		The Library of Congress now classes this material in Class K
	10– 87	United States documents
		For congressional hearings, reports, etc., *see* KF
	80– 85	Presidents' messages and other executive documents
	86– 87	State documents
	100– 981	Other documents
		For documents issued by local governments, *see* JS
JA	1– 98	Collections and general works
JC	11– 628	Political theory. Theory of the state
	311– 323	Nationalism
	325– 341	Nature, entity, concept of the state
	345– 347	Symbolism, emblems of the state: Arms, flag, seal, etc.
	348– 497	Forms of the state
		Including imperialism, the world state, monarchy, aristocracy, democracy, fascism, dictatorships
	501– 628	Purpose, functions, and relations of the state
	571– 628	The state and individual. Individual rights. Liberty
		Constitutional history and administration
JF	8–2112	General works. Comparative works
	201– 723	Organs and functions of government
		Including executive branch, cabinet and ministerial government, legislative bodies
	751– 786	Federal and state relations
	800–1191	Political rights and guaranties
		Including citizenship, suffrage, electoral systems, representation, the ballot
	1321–2112	Government. Administration
	2011–2112	Political parties
		Special countries
JK	1–9993	United States
	2403–9501	State government
	9661–9993	Confederate States of America
JL	1–3899	British America. Latin America
JN	1–9689	Europe
JQ	1–6651	Asia. Africa. Australia. Oceania

Table 2.1 *(continued)*

JS	3 – 8399	Local government
	141 – 231	Municipal government
	241 – 285	Local government other than municipal
	301 – 1583	United States
JV	1 – 5810	Colonies and colonization. Emigration and immigration
JX	1 – 5810	International law. International relations
	63 – 1195	Collections. Documents. Cases
	101 – 115	Diplomatic relations (Universal collections)
	120 – 191	Treaties (Universal collections)
	1305 – 1598	International relations. Foreign relations
		Here are classed international questions treated as sources of or contributions to the theory of international law. For histories of events, diplomatic histories, etc., *see* D-F
	1625 – 1896	Diplomacy. The diplomatic service
	1901 – 1995	International arbitration. World peace. International organization Including peace movements, League of Nations, United Nations, arbitration treaties, international courts
	2001 – 5810	International law (Treaties and monographs)

Abstracts may be *evaluative* (describing the quality of the article or work) or *descriptive* (describing the subject of the work, the measures and techniques of analysis used, the population studied, and the results). The abstracted information may help you to determine whether the work is relevant to your research topic.

The crucial characteristic of all indexes is that they tell you what exists and where it exists. Further, indexes list all sources, regardless of whether they are maintained in your library. Having located a source that seems appropriate to your research, you next must determine whether your library has it. If the source you want is not maintained by your library, you may want to use your library's interlibrary loan service to secure a loaned copy of the publication. Many university libraries now subscribe to electronic services that both index the literature *and* offer document retrieval. That is, they not only tell you what exists, but they can also arrange to get a copy for you. You make loan arrangements yourself by following the instructions provided on-line.

Political science is a field for which many indexing services are available and, indeed, the array of published indexes is so extensive that beginning students may at first be overwhelmed. Typically, researchers become most familiar with those focusing on their own ideas of specialty. It is impractical to discuss here all available indexes, but some of the most general and frequently used of those available are listed next.[16]

Social Sciences Index.   The *Social Sciences Index* (New York: H. W. Wilson) is an extremely important reference source to recent articles appearing in social science journals. Published quarterly (with cumulative annual editions) since 1913, the *Social Science Index* (along with its predecessor the *Humanities and Social Science Index*) provides an alphabetized listing of authors and subjects for more than 350 periodicals in the fields of anthropology, area studies, economics, environmental sciences, political science, psychology, public administration, sociology, and related subjects. The *Social Science Index* is available on-line, and many libraries choose to make it available in conjunction with some of the other indexes discussed here subsequently.

Under the topic, *voting,* listed in the March, 1995 volume of the *Social Science Index* are found the following articles relating to the United States:

Comparing gubernatorial and senatorial elections. P. Squire and C. Fastnow. bibl Polit Res Q v47 p705-20 S '94

Let the good times roll: the economic expectations of U.S. voters. H.B. Haller and H. Norpoth. bibl Am J Polit Sci v38 p625-50 Ag '94

Rationalization and derivation process in survey studies of political candidate evaluation. W. M. Rahn and others. bibl Am J Polit Sci v38 p582-600 Ag '94

Religious voting blocs in the 1992 election: the year of the evangelical? L.A. Kellstedt and others. bibl Sociol Relig v55 p307-26 Fall '94

State legislative elections: what we know and don't know. M.E. Jewell. bibl Am Polit Q v22 p483-509 O '94

PAIS International in Print (PAIS).   PAIS (formerly the *Public Affairs Information Service Bulletin*) (New York: Public Affairs Information Service), which has been published since 1915, provides an index of publications on subjects that bear on contemporary public issues and the evaluation of public policy, with emphasis on factual and statistical information. PAIS includes in its index approximately 1,600 professional periodicals as well as books, government documents, and reports of public and private organizations. Because it is an international publication, you will find publications in other languages represented. PAIS issues monthly updates, quarterly cumulative updates, and annual cumulative volumes. In a February, 1994, volume, more than 50 titles were listed for the topic, "voting," including entries from *National Journal, Congressional Quarterly Weekly Report, Presidential Studies Quarterly, Weekly Compilation of Presidential Documents,* and *Electoral Studies.* PAIS is also available as an on-line database.

Social Science Citation Index.   The *Social Science Citation Index* (Philadelphia: Institute for Scientific Information) is a very powerful index, covering the gamut of topics in the social sciences and drawing on the bibliographies of the items indexed. Originally conceived as a machine-readable file, this index has been available in both print and electronic versions since it was first created. (In its on-line version, this index is known as *Social SciSearch.*) Through this publication, you can search for current work based on an index to previous work in an area of interest to you (in the "Citation Index"), you can search for writers in the present year whose names you know (the "Source Index"), you can search for significant words in titles (the "Permuterm Index"), or you can search by the institution at which someone works (the "Corporate Index"). All parts of the citation index give reference to the source index where complete citations are found.

ABC POL-SCI: A Bibliography of Contents: Political Science and Government.
This index (Santa Barbara, CA: ABC-Clio), available in print and on compact disc, provides table of contents information for approximately 300 journals dealing with political science, public affairs, sociology, economics, and law. Because of its arrangement, it is ideally suited to browsing the recent literature when searching for a particular topic. Because the publication has been around for more than 20 years and because it provides annual and 5-year culminations, it also is a powerful retrospective index.

Reader's Guide to Periodical Literature.   The *Reader's Guide* (New York: H. W. Wilson), published annually since 1900, indexes by subject and author approximately 200 general-interest periodicals. Less professional in orientation than indexes previously discussed, the *Reader's Guide* includes in its coverage a wide variety of periodicals, ranging from the *Wilson Quarterly, Foreign Affairs,* and *Bulletin of the Atomic Scientists,* to *Time, Newsweek, Psychology Today,* and *Rolling Stone.* Listed under the topic, "voting," in recent volumes are the following entries.

The couch potato vote [computerized voting] J. Alter. :1 *Newsweek* 125 34 F27 '95.

The people have spoken [charts] :1 *Scholastic Update* (teachers' edition) 127 4–5 Ja 13 '95.

Why women don't vote for women (and why they should) S. Henry :1 *Working Woman* v19 p48–51t Je '94.

Motor voter: Goin' mobile. A. Gowen. *Rolling Stone* p18 Jl 8-22 '93.

Bill will enable 15 mil. more blacks to vote [Motor-voter registration]. *Jet* v84 p11 My 31 '93.

It can be seen that the *Reader's Guide* is much more general and less scholarly in orientation than the other indexes discussed. However, a lag of some years usually exists between an area of current popular interest and the publication of scholarly research on that issue. For very contemporary issues (such as the "motor voter" bill—taking effect in 1995—requiring states to provide citizens the opportunity to register to vote at the same time they apply for or renew a driver's license), the *Reader's Guide* can sometimes be the most useful index available.

The Universal Reference System: Political Science, Government, and Public Policy Series (URS).   The URS (Princeton, NJ: Princeton Research) was first published as a 10-volume set in 1967, as *Annual Supplements* until 1979, and as *Political Science Abstracts* (New York: IFI/Plenum Press) since 1979. The URS is a computer-generated annotated bibliography of books, articles, papers, and documents based on a classification scheme developed by Alfred de Grazia. In explaining the uniqueness of this system, de Grazia writes,

> Its value derives in part from the depth of its indexing. Whereas most keyword indexes in bibliographies rely solely on titles (perhaps augmented with additional keyword(s)), the URS input is not only annotated but is also tagged with an average of twenty "Standard" and "Unique" descriptors per item. Moreover, from two to four of these descriptors are identified as "Critical" descriptors and are given special treatment in indexing.[17]

International Political Science Abstracts.   This volume of abstracts (Paris: Association Internationale de Science Politique), published bimonthly since 1950, provides over 5,000 indexes and abstracts of articles appearing in more than 900 political science journals, listed by major headings: methods and theory, political thinkers and ideas, government and administrative institutions, political processes, international relations, and national and area studies. Abstracts are presented in English for articles written in English; otherwise, the abstracts are in French.

Sage Public Administration Abstracts.   Specializing in the public administration field, the *Sage Public Administration Abstracts* (Newbury Park, CA: Sage Periodicals Press) provides abstracts for books, government publications, speeches, and more than 200 scholarly journals of organizational behavior, budgeting, financing, personnel, and comparative administration. It is indexed by author and by subject.

United States Political Science Documents.   This computer-based information service (Pittsburgh: University Center for International Studies, University of Pittsburgh) started in 1967 as a cooperative effort among the University Center for International Studies, the University of Pittsburgh, and the American Political Science Association. This service is noted for the quality control it exerts in its approach, surveying political scientists as to the journals they use, and then indexing in depth the journals they have selected. It is interdisciplinary, with the primary emphasis being on political science. Each year, two cumulative volumes are published. Volume 1 consists of the indexes with reference to citations: author/contributor, rotated subject descriptors, subject, geographic area, proper name, and journal. Volume 2 contains the citations with abstracts. Articles from approximately 130 journals are abstracted by this information service.

Dissertation Abstracts International.   *Dissertation Abstracts International* (DAI) (Ann Arbor, MI: University Microfilms International) is a monthly compilation of abstracts of doctoral dissertations submitted to University Microfilms International by more than 500 colleges and universities in North America and throughout the world. Because dissertations are not always published in any other form, and because they represent the cutting edge of research in any field, DAI is a very valuable indexing source. DAI is published in three sections: Humanities and Social Sciences, Sciences and Engineering, and Worldwide. An abstract of about 100 to 150 words accompanies each listing. Most dissertations listed in DAI are available on microfilm from University Microfilms. DAI is also available on compact disc.

Indexes to Government Documents

Much material of interest to political and policy researchers comes, of course, from state, local, and federal government offices, departments, and agencies. If your library is a depository site for federal and/or state government publications, if it has a strong United Nations collection, and if it has made an effort to collect relevant local government publications, then you have a very valuable research resource. Your library may have compiled its own indexing system for *state and local government* documents. Some of the more useful indexes for the vast amount of material published by the *federal government* are listed next.

Index to Publications of the United States Congress.   This compilation (Washington, DC; Congressional Information Service) gives access to everything issued by the U.S. Congress except the *Congressional Record*. Included are all published hearings, documents, reports, and committee prints since 1970. It is a monthly publication with annual and multiple-year cumulative issues. Since 1984, this index has also provided separate access to the legislative histories. It is available on compact disc.

Public Papers of the Presidents of the United States.   This information source (Washington, DC: Government Printing Office [GPO]), Federal Register Division, National Archives and Records, General Services Administration [GSA], published since 1957, has become the standard official source of public messages, speeches, addresses, letters, pronouncements, transcripts of press conferences, and other statements by U.S. presidents. Beginning with the presidency of Herbert Hoover, material is presented in chronological order. A name and subject index is included.

Government Reports Announcements and Index (GRA).   The GRA (Springfield, VA: U.S. Department of Commerce, National Technical Information Service) is the index to the National Technical Information Service reports. It is issued semimonthly with indexing by author, subject, contract number, and accession number. This index is available in several formats from on-line database vendors, including some intended for self-serve searching. While the literature indexed by GRA is largely of a technical nature, it also includes many subjects of interest to political and policy researchers.

Monthly Catalog of United States Government Publications.   This publication (Washington, DC: Government Printing Office [GPO]) indexes all documents released through the GPO. It gives access by author, title, and subject, and it gives a reference to the Superintendent of Documents number.

Index to Current Urban Documents.   Students of local government will find useful the *Index to Current Urban Documents* (Westport, CT: Greenwood Press). This index, containing abstracts, provides information about the operation of the major cities and counties in the United States. Included in the index are planning documents, budgets, demographic accounts of areas, environmental impact statements, annual reports, and zoning documents. This index is available in on-line format.

Newspapers

Newspapers are important sources for both current and historical information. They can be excellent sources for current statistics; for maps showing recent political, social, or economic change; for the names of important political figures; and current policy issues and legislative affairs. Among the important newspapers currently indexed are the *New York Times*, the *Washington Post*, the *Wall Street Journal*, the *Times* (London), the *Christian Science Monitor*, the *Chicago Tribune*, the *Denver Post*, the *Detroit News*, the *Los Angeles Times*, the *Saint Louis Post-Dispatch*, and the *San Francisco Chronicle*.

A number of indexing services provide coverage of *groups* of newspapers. For example, the *National Newspaper Index* (Menlo Park, CA: Information Access Corporation) provides coverage of three elite American papers: the *Christian Science Monitor*, the *New York Times*, and the *Wall Street Journal*. Topics covered by the index are identified by subject, name, or country. Similarly, *The Newsbank* (New Canaan, CT: Newsbank) provides an index of approximately 200 papers from American cities, listing articles under three major categories: (1) political development, (2) government structure, and (3) law and order. *The Newsbank* is available on compact disc.

On-Line Newspaper Sources

The Newsbank is typical of many newspaper services now available in electronic format. As another example, full text retrieval of all articles appearing in the *New York Times* since June 1, 1980 is available through a service called *The New York Times On Line* (New York: New York Times Information Service). Material can be retrieved by free-text searching, or by using index terms. Results may be viewed on screen, or printed offline, and articles may be retrieved within 24 to 48 hours after publication of the printed version of the paper. Another service, *Datatimes* (Oklahoma City: Datatimes Corporation) is an electronic index that now provides indexing service for more than 200 domestic newspapers for recent years. It also offers coverage of international news. Dow Jones, CompuServe, Nexis, and The Source are other well-known electronic subscription systems that offer access to news publications, and some even to wire services.

Additionally, a number of libraries are mounting these databases directly into their on-line catalog systems for even more convenient access. Electronic indexes typically do not go as far back in time as print indexes, but they do offer a number of advantages. They allow students to ask more complex questions than the print indexes because they permit the combining of concepts and the use of keywords, and they make it possible to search several years at one time. They may provide more information per citation than the print version does, and in some instances, on-line systems may even provide the entire text of the article, not just an abstract.

Database Systems

Many university libraries now subscribe to **on-line database systems** (computer-based body of data, organized in a manner that allows for multiple indexes and other means for gaining access to information. These database systems provide access to multiple databases simultaneously. Such systems include *CARL* (Colorado Alliance of Research Libraries), *FirstSearch* and *EPIC* (Dublin, OH: Online Computer Library Center [OCLC]), and *Newsnet* (Bryn Mawr, PA: Newsnet). Such systems act as gateways to many existing databases and greatly facilitate comprehensive and convenient reference searching.

SUMMARY

The foregoing discussion should provide many ideas for proceeding with the sometimes difficult task of topic selection, as well as with the crucial task of evaluating the probability of successful completion of the project. Additionally, the following suggestions should be helpful.

1. *Select a Topic of Limited Range.* Students sometimes select a very broad topic and immediately find themselves overloaded with information. For example, a student interested in a broad topic such as "Differences between Democrats and Republicans" will find literally hundreds of books and articles on various aspects of this topic, published in the past few years alone. Overly broad topics such as this one clearly cannot be managed in one or even two semesters of work. Better would be a narrower topic, like, "issue differences between Democrats and Republicans," or perhaps even better yet, "Contemporary domestic difference between Democratic and Republican college students." Selecting a narrow topic is not only more manageable, but is also likely to result in more interesting and certainly more definitive results.[18]

2. *Replication Is Okay.* Replicating the works of others is a legitimate and worthwhile exercise in scientific research. In any field, it is important to discover whether results reported by one investigator are confirmed by repeated investigations. Repeated confirmation, of course, gives greater credibility to the findings. Note, however, that the term *replication,* as commonly used in scientific research, is not limited to simply duplicating the works of others. You might want to examine similar political relationships, as reported by one study, using a different group of respondents, or conducting the study at a different point in time, or using a different research design, or using different indicators. If, in replicating some other work, you find similar results, then you have contributed additional confirmation to whatever theory or proposition is being tested. If differences are found, on the other hand, you can suggest ways in which the theory may need to be altered. In either case, you have made an important contribution.

3. *Abandoning a Project Is Okay, Too.* A very common mistake is to hold on to a topic after it become obvious that the data cannot be collected, interviews will not be possible, materials are not available, or the research topic simply does not interest you as you had thought it would. In such cases, do not hesitate to look for another topic. As distinguished scientist E. Bright Wilson has reminded us, "The scientist who gives up too easily is unlikely to reap any great harvest, but on the

other hand, it is also possible to be too tenacious. It is a wise [researcher] who knows when to abandon a research or a field of research."[19] Of course, early evaluation of a topic makes it possible to uncover problems while there is still time to switch topics; do not wait until 2 weeks before the project is due to begin the topic evaluation stage. It is much better to switch topics rather than to turn in a poor paper with a lot of excuses for a lackluster performance.

4. *Then, Just Do It.* A final word of advice comes from researcher Robert Kanigel, who has advised,

> And then just *do it.* Don't spend all year in the library getting ready to do it. Don't wait until you've gotten all the boring little preparatory experiments out of the way. Don't worry about scientific controls, at least for now. Just go with your hunch, your scientific intuition, and isolate that simple, elegant, pointed experiment that will tell you in a flash whether you're on the right track.[20]

Kanigel's advice is well-taken. It is virtually impossible to resolve every potential problem, to check every possible source, and to consider every possible option. There comes a point in any research project, at any level, when it is time to get out of the library, put all the books and articles down, and stop worrying about potential research pitfalls. You have committed as much time to the problem-familiarity phase as you can; you are as familiar with the topic as anyone could expect. As far as your research project is concerned, it is time now just to *do it.*

KEY TERMS

encyclopedias
dictionaries
confidentiality
anonymity

on-line library catalog system
index
abstracts
on-line database system

EXERCISES

1. Developing a list of topics
   a. Referring to textbooks, political science and policy journals, and your own interest areas, develop three possible research topics.
   b. Look up each of these topics in one of the major political science encyclopedias, report some of the major problem areas, and list some of the important reference works for each topic.
2. Narrowing the list to a single topic
   a. For each of the research topics developed in the preceding step, apply the criteria for evaluation suggested in this chapter (student interest, discipline significance, manageability, etc.).
   b. Which of these topics appear most feasible and most manageable? Why is this so?

3. Topic familiarity
   a. Select one of the research topics developed in the foregoing steps, and—relying on the various social science indexes and abstracts discussed in this chapter—thoroughly review the literature in this area. Ask your librarian for assistance with the on-line library catalog system that may be available at your library.
   b. Based on the review you just completed, list the ten books or articles that appear to be most relevant to your particular area of interest.
   c. Prepare a paragraph summary of each of the ten books and articles, listing hypotheses tested, sources of data, and findings.

NOTES

1. Julian L. Simon, *Basic Research Methods in Social Science: The Art of Empirical Investigation,* 1st ed. (New York: Random House, 1969), 5.
2. Andrew J. Taylor and John T. Rourke, "Historical Analogies in the Congressional Foreign Policy Process," *The Journal of Politics,* 5 (May, 1995), 460–469.
3. Roger H. Davidson, *The Postreform Congress* (New York: St. Martin's Press, 1992), vii.
4. Benjamin A. Most, "Getting Started on Political Research," *PS: Political Science & Politics* (December, 1990), 592.
5. Bernard H. Ross, Myron A. Levine, and Murray S. Stedman, *Urban Politics: Power in Metropolitan America,* 4th ed. (Itasca, IL: F. E. Peacock Publishers, 1991).
6. A thorough directory of journals of interest to political researchers, including a listing of journals by subject, is provided in *Political and Social Science Journals: A Handbook for Writers and Reviewers* (Santa Barbara, CA: ABC-Clio, 1983).
7. For example, see Rod Hague, Martin Harrop, and Shaun Breslin, *Political Science: A Comparative Introduction* (New York: St. Martin's Press, 1992).
8. Ada W. Finifter, ed., *Political Science: The State of the Discipline* II (Washington, DC: American Political Science Association, 1993).
9. Mark S. Frankel, "Ethics and Responsibility in Political Science Research," *International Social Science Journal* 30 (1978), 173–180.
10. This, of course, is not to imply that the laboratory scientists do not have to worry about the consequences of their research or the use to which that research might be put; it is only that behavioral scientists, in addition to this concern, have to be especially concerned with the welfare of their human subjects.
11. Joan E. Sieber, *Planning Ethical Responsible Research: A Guide for Students and Internal Review Boards* (Newbury Park, CA: Sage Publications, 1992), 3.
12. American Political Science Association, *A Guide to Professional Ethics in Political Science,* 2nd ed. (Washington, DC: Author, 1991).
13. An *on-line catalog* may be defined as, "A catalog of bibliographic records in machine-readable form, maintained in a computer system and permitting interactive access through terminals which are in direct and continuing communication with the computer for the duration of the transaction. Access is typically gained through predetermined procedures, utilizing search keys such as author, title, subject, International Standard Book Number [ISBN], or a combination of these." Heartsill Young, ed., *The ALA Glossary of Library and Information Science* (Chicago: American Library Association, 1983), 156–157.

14. The Internet system integrates many individual campus, state, regional, and national networks into one single logical network, all sharing a common addressing scheme.
15. Taken from the *Library of Congress Classification Outline,* Office for Subject Cataloging Policy, Collection Services, 6th ed. (Washington, DC: Library of Congress, 1990), 19, 20.
16. For more detailed listings of indexes, reference sources, bibliographies, and the like, see Frederick L. Holler, *Information Sources of Political Science,* 4th ed. (Santa Barbara, CA: ABC-Clio, 1986); Dermot Englefield and Gavin Drewry, eds., *Information Sources in Politics and Political Science: A Survey Worldwide* (London: Butterworths, 1984); or Henry York, *Political Science: A Guide to References and Information Sources* (Englewood, CO: Libraries Unlimited, 1990). For a listing of on-line database systems, see James H. Shelton, ed., *CD-ROM Finder,* 5th ed. (Medford, NJ: Learned Information, 1993); and Kathleen Young Maraccio, ed., *Gale Directory of Databases,* two volumes (Detroit: Gale Research, 1993).
17. Alfred de Grazia, "Continuity and Innovation in Reference Retrieval in the Social Sciences: Illustrations from the Universal Reference System," *American Behavioral Scientist* 10 (1967), 1.
18. A similar point is made by Herbert F. Weisberg and Bruce D. Bowen, *An Introduction to Survey Research and Data Analysis* (San Francisco: W. H. Freeman and Company, 1977), 223.
19. E. Bright Wilson, Jr., *An Introduction to Scientific Research* (New York: Dover Publications, 1990), 3.
20. Robert Kanigel, "The Mentor Chain," *F&M Today,* 10, no. 5 (1981), 1–8.

3

Developing a Strategy:
Formulating Hypotheses, Operationalizing Concepts, Selecting a Research Design

Once the literature-review stage is complete, you will be familiar enough with existing theory and research in your area of particular interest to continue with the research process. Your next task will be to develop, from this body of knowledge, hypotheses. **Hypotheses** are testable statements relating two or more concepts or variables. In contrast, theories usually are too broad and imprecise to be directly testable. Hypotheses are explicit statements of expected relationships. According to Simon and Burstein, "A hypothesis . . . is a single statement that attempts to explain or predict a single phenomenon, whereas a theory is an entire system of thought that refers to many phenomena."[1]

Hypothesis formation serves two critical functions for the research process. First, hypotheses provide a means of evaluating a theory. Any theory of a political phenomenon will generate numerous hypotheses. As a result of testing one or more of these hypotheses, researchers are able to offer some evidence relating to the utility of the theory itself. If testing indicates that the hypotheses, as formulated, are true, this affirmative finding provides some empirical verification of the theory. Failure to substantiate the hypotheses raises questions concerning the theory's validity.[2]

Of course, neither positive confirmation of the hypotheses nor failure to substantiate the hypotheses provide absolute proof of the theory's validity. Any number of factors may affect empirical testing, including the failure to develop adequate hypotheses, poor sampling, and unaccounted-for variables. Still, the testing of hypotheses provides some empirical linkage between theory and the real world. It is also true that, even following the best of procedures, the results of hypothesis testing rarely will provide complete verification or falsification of a theory. More likely, the testing will indicate the *circumstances* under which the theory seems to apply and those under which it may be less applicable. In any case, the formation and empirical examination of hypotheses is vital to theory evaluation.

The second important role of hypotheses in the research process is in providing guidance and direction for the data-collection stage. The hypotheses developed will dictate the nature of the data to be collected. Kaplan stated it well when he said that hypotheses "serve to guide and organize the investigation, providing us something to go on."[3] Suppose that you have proposed the following hypothesis as part of your research project: "Female state legislators are more likely than male legislators to support legislation aimed at limiting handgun possession." In the data-collection phase of your research, it is imperative that you collect information relating to legislators' gender, as well as their position, or voting record, on handgun legislation. You might gather a thousand other pieces of information on state legislators and their attitudes, but unless you have gathered information designed to measure both gender and attitude toward handgun possession, you cannot succeed in testing the original hypothesis.

A review of articles appearing in recent issues of any of the leading journals in political science will provide numerous good examples of hypothesis articulation. A 1995 issue of *The Journal of Politics,* for example, includes an article by Laura A. Reese and Ronld E. Brown entitled, "The Effects of Religious Messages on Racial Identity and System Blame Among African Americans."[4] There, Reese and Brown list the following several hypotheses about the relationship between religion, demographic characteristics, and political attitudes and behavior among African Americans.

H_1. Religiosity is affected by demographic factors such as gender, age, and income.

H_2. Increased attendance at a place of worship will lead to greater incorporation of particular messages.

H_3. African Americans hearing more political behavior and civic awareness messages at their place of worship will have higher levels of identity as belonging to a unique racial group.

H_4. African Americans with a stronger sense of group belonging or identity will feel closer to other members of minority groups than those with a lower sense of group identity.

H_5. African Americans who feel close to other minority group members will also perceive a distance between their racial group and other racial groups.

H_6. Respondents perceiving a distance or separation between their group and other groups are also more likely to perceive a power imbalance between the groups.

H_7. A stronger perception of power imbalance between groups will lead to higher levels of system blame as individuals externalize the sources of the imbalance.

H_8. Demographic factors such as gender, age, and income will also have direct effects on racial consciousness and system blame.

Another example is provided by de Mesquita, Siverson, and Woller's recent article, "War and the Fate of Regimes: A Comparative Analysis," which appeared in the *American Political Science Review.*[5] Their study, they say, is designed to test the following hypotheses about the relationship between war among nations and domestic turmoil within those nations:

H_1: The chances of a domestically instigated, violent change in regime increase with defeat in war.

H_2. Violent change in regime is least likely for winning initiators; the likelihood of violent overthrow of a regime increases for winning targets, losing targets, and losing initiators in that order.

H_3. The chances of a violent change in regime increase with the costs of war, irrespective of the nation's war outcome or initial conditions.

These hypotheses state with precision the issues to be pursued and the variables to be examined. Beginning researchers would profit from a personal examination of hypotheses presented in scholarly journals in their areas of interest.

The state of political science theory is such that it is not always possible to extract hypotheses as precise and elegant as those just presented. Some theories may lead to conflicting predictions, some areas of interest may even have little formal theory available or may offer theory that is too underdeveloped to be of much use. In such cases, it might be possible to borrow hypotheses from a related, and better estab-lished, area.

Frequently, too, in areas of weak or conflicting theory researchers will present their hypotheses in a less formal manner, substituting such terms as *assumptions, questions,* or *expectations.* In his study titled "Political Culture and State Develop-ment Policy," Keith Boeckelman used the following wording:

> We *expect* that policy in the moralistic states will focus on providing long-term gains of high-quality jobs. States with individualistic political cultures *may be more apt* to pursue business-oriented policies. In the traditionalistic culture [states] . . . we *expect* relatively low levels of economic development activity.[6]

Similarly, Hill posited his reseach issue in the form of a question, "Does the cre-ation of majority black districts aid Republicans?"[7]

Regardless, it is critical at this stage of the research process to give considerable thought to the questions that the research is intended to answer. Even experienced researchers sometimes forget to start each research project by carefully consider-ing the nature of the data that will have to be collected to address the issues of con-cern. This neglect almost automatically ensures project failure. The attempt, at least, to precisely set out hypotheses to be tested, *before* beginning the data-collection stage, will substantially reduce the probability of making this fatal research error.

VARIABLES AND CONCEPTS

Dependent and Independent Variables

The ultimate goal of any research effort is to determine the nature of the relation-ship between two or more variables. Although we postpone careful examination of the term *variable* until later chapters, we briefly introduce here the distinction be-tween dependent and independent variables. **Dependent variables** are those we are trying to explain, understand, or predict. **Independent variables** are those we are using to assist in our explanation, understanding, or prediction of the depen-dent variable.

Recall the preceding example hypotheses. In the first set of sample hypotheses, the investigator wanted to determine the effect of several independent variables (gender, age, and income) on the dependent variables (religiosity and racial consciousness); in the second set of example hypotheses, the researchers sought to measure the effect of several independent variables (defeat in war, costs of war, etc.) on the dependent variable (violent change in regime). Research design—a topic explored later in this chapter—helps clarify the extent to which observable change in the dependent variable (or variables) results from (1) the independent variables being manipulated—sometimes called the "treatment effects"; (2) other, unmeasured and perhaps unknown, variables—sometimes called "extrinsic effects"; or (3) the research design itself—sometimes called "intrinsic effects." Research design also can help us determine the extent to which results that we find in our study may be generalized to larger populations. All of these, of course, are important to the successful conduct of research. In this sense, developing an appropriate research design is as important as articulating the hypotheses, collecting the observations, analyzing the data, or any other phase of the research process.

Concepts: The Building Blocks

Hypotheses relate two or more concepts. **Concepts** are terms used to represent sets of characteristics. As Kenneth Bailey put it, "Concepts are . . . mental images or perceptions [that] may be impossible to observe directly, such as love or justice, or [that] may have referents that are readily observable, such as a tree or a table."[8]

Examples of concepts often used in political research are social status, power, influence, group cohesion, alienation, leadership, political efficacy, socialization, and political culture. To be useful for empirical analysis, concepts must be operational. As used here, **operational** means measurable; the concepts being used must be susceptible to measurement. The researcher must be able to translate the concepts being examined into observable and definable events. Satisfactory indicators of the concepts must be found or developed. This is the very important process of **concept operationalization.**[9]

Investigators typically will explain precisely how the concepts they are using have been operationalized. Sometimes this process is pretty straightforward, as is the case when using concepts that are relatively well understood or are frequently cited in the field. In their study of the factors affecting African American male employment in the United States,[10] Linda B. Stearns and Charlotte W. Coleman operationalized their variables according to the scheme shown in Table 3.1.

Operationalization of concepts can sometimes be quite complex, especially when the concepts themselves are complex or unusual. Sometimes, in fact, the task of concept operationalization can become a major focus of the study. An example is provided by Alexander M. Hicks and Duane H. Swank in their study of the relationships between various political institutions and welfare spending in 18 capitalist democracies.[11] The dependent variable, welfare spending, is operationalized for that study as "governmental spending relating to schemes, transfers, and services that (1) grant curative or preventive medical care, maintain income in case of involuntary diminution of earnings, or grant supplementary income to persons with family

TABLE 3.1

Illustration of Operationalization of Variables

Dependent Variables

1. *Percent prestigious white-collar employees:* The number of black male professionals and managers divided by the total number of male professionals.
2. *Percent skilled workers:* The number of black male technicians and craftspersons divided by the total number of technicians and craftsperons in each SIC manufacturing industry within each SMSA.
3. *Percent semiskilled/unskilled workers:* The number of black male operatives, laborers, and service workers divided by total number of male operatives, laborers, and service workers in each SIC manufacturing industry in each SMSA.

Independent variables

1. *Industry wages:* Annual payroll divided by the number of employees.
2. *Industry growth:* The difference in the number of employees between 1977 and 1982 divided by the total number of employees in 1977.
3. *Industry unions:* The percentage of unionized workers in an industry in 1980.
4. *Industry market concentration:* Eight-firm concentration ratio.
5. *Percent black in SMSA:* The number of blacks in the SMSA divided by the SMSA's total population.
6. *SMSA manufacturing growth:* The difference in the number of persons employed in manufacturing in the SMSA between 1977 and 1982 divided by the total number of manufacturing employees in 1977.
7. *SMSA manufacturing wages:* Annual payroll for all manufacturing industries within the SMSA divided by the total number of employees in manufacturing.
8. *Percent SMSA unionized:* The percentage of the SMSA's population belonging to a union in 1980.
9. *Residential segregation:* The index of dissimiliarity (*D*) for each SMSA for 1980.
10. *Region:* Coded as a dummy variable: South = 1; non-South = 0.

NOTE: "SMSA" refers to Standard Statistical Metropolitan Area. "SIC" refers to Standard Industrial Classification.

SOURCE: From Linda Brewster Stearns and Charlotte Wilkinson Coleman, "Industrial and Local Labor Market Structures and Black Male Employment in the Manufacturing Sector," *Social Science Quarterly* 71 (June, 1990), 291.

responsibilities; (2) are legislative sanctioned; and (3) are publicly or quasi-publicly administered." Their operationalization of one of the independent variables, governmental opposition, is defined as "the four year averages . . . of two annual measures of the strength of parties *not* leading governments: the year's average of the party type's proportion of legislative seats and the proportion of the popular vote in the last major election when the given party type did not govern."

In either case, the reader knows exactly how the concepts used in these studies have been measured. This process of operationalization is critical to the conduct of empirical research.

THE IMPORTANCE OF RESEARCH DESIGN

Prior to setting out on an unfamiliar journey, the traveler will consult a road map to select the route most desirable. Prior to conducting research, the investigator will develop the most desirable strategy for successfully completing the research. The strategy selected is the research design. A **research design** serves as the road map for conducting research. Like the map, the research design tells you how to get from here to there: how to get from articulation of a hypothesis to reaching conclusions. Research design, says Kenneth Bailey, "guides the investigator in the process of collecting, analyzing, and interpreting observations."[12]

Before looking at some typical research-design options, we consider more carefully some issues that arise when selecting a research design and when attempting to generalize from the findings of our study to probable relationships in larger populations. Commonly, these are called concerns of "internal and external validity."

We examine each of these validity threats in the context of the following illustrative hypothesis: Participation in a drug-education course will alter attitudes toward drugs and will reduce the use of alcohol and other drugs among high school students.

Here, our dependent variables are "*attitudes* and *use* of alcohol and other drugs," and our independent variable is "participation in a drug-education course." Following our discussion of validity, we use this same hypothesis to illustrate a variety of research-design options.

Internal Validity

Internal validity deals with the question of whether the independent variable or variables actually were related to observed changes in the dependent variable. This, as Donald Campbell and Julian Stanley have reminded us, is the sine qua non of research: It is the basic minimum criterion for interpreting results.[13] Unfortunately, a number of factors may threaten internal validity. Using as an illustration our hypothesis about the relationship between the participation in a drug-education course and the use of and attitudes toward alcohol and other drugs, we see how some of these threats might effect an actual research project.[14]

History. The historical factor relates to all of the events that occur between pre- and posttesting of subjects, in addition to their exposure to the experimental treatment variable. For example, assume that after initiation of a drug-education program in a particular high school, the local police conduct a major and highly publicized drug bust. A decline in student use of alcohol and other drugs that year might be related to the drug-education program, to the drug bust, or perhaps even to other—unknown—events.

Maturation. The maturational factor refers to those processes within the subjects (students, in this case) resulting in changes in attitude or behavior simply as a function of the passage of time. People naturally grow older, get hungrier, become more tired, and the like with the passage of time, regardless of exposure to any experimental variables. In the drug-education example, a decline in alcohol and other drug use, or perhaps even an increase in their use, might result normally simply from the process of growing older.

Test Reactions.   The testing process itself might affect scores on certain measures. Completing a survey might alter someone's opinion on a subject. Similarly, people might change their behavior as a result of knowing that they are being observed. Conceivably, inquiring about students' alcohol or other drug use might stimulate some students actually to use drugs; or it might scare other students away from experimenting with alcohol or other drugs. The risk that the test, or the instruments used, might effect results is known as **testing** or **instrument reactivity.**

Differential Loss of Subjects.   Occasionally, experimenters experience differential loss of subjects when some of the subjects selected to participate in a research project must drop out for one reason or another. Assume that students were selected to participate in the drug-education experiment because they *mirrored* (accurately reflected) the grade point distribution of all students in the high school. If for some reason all of the students with A averages had to drop out midway through the experiment, this differential loss of subjects would cast doubt on whether the final attitude and use scores of those who completed the course were affected by the course, by the fact that A students dropped out, or by a combination of both.

Selection Criteria.   If those subjects selected to participate in a research program are markedly different from those not participting, then any differences in behavior at the end of the program could not conclusively be attributed to the research program itself. If, for example, students participating in the drug-education program *elected* to take the course (rather than having been randomly selected), it is possible that factors other than those being examined may affect alcohol or other drug use. Students volunteering for a drug-education program may be less—or more—disposed to drug use, in the first place.

Subject Resentment.   Subjects in a study might sometimes grow to resent the fact that they either were or were not selected to receive a particular treatment. In either case, their observed behavior might be affected by their attitudes toward the study at least as much as by the treatment used in the study. Students required to sit through a drug-education course might indicate a level of alcohol or other drug use that more closely reflects their resentment at having to participate in the course than their response to the effects of the course.

Similarly, other factors also may influence internal validity.[15] To the extent that careful research design selection can minimize these threats, our conclusions about the effects of one or more independent variables on particular dependent variables are obviously stronger.

External Validity

External validity deals with the question of *generalizability:* To what extent may we conclude that whatever relationships we discover in our study hold true also for other population groupings, other situations, and other time periods? In our drug-education study, assuming that participation in the drug-education course was found to reduce substance use among students in that particular school, a question of immediate interest would be whether this finding also would also apply to future students, students in other schools, and students in other cities. A number of specific threats to external validity are discussed next.[16]

Interaction of Selection and Treatment.   The nature of the research project sometimes may influence the characteristics of those participating, so that results may be significantly biased. Cook and Campbell illustrate this biasing effect by reference to an experiment involving business executives, in which one of the treatment conditions takes a full day's time, as opposed to another treatment condition taking only 10 minutes. The experimental treatment requiring a whole day will be populated by executives having a lot of free time, a situation not very representative of the real world. A similar problem would befall our drug-education experiment, should it be decided to offer the program only *after* regular school hours. Students involved in extracurricular activities could not participate, and our ability to generalize to the student body would be hampered.

Interaction of Setting and Treatment.   The setting for the research might also affect our ability to generalize. Cook and Campbell asked, "Can a . . . relationship obtained in a factory be obtained in a bureaucracy, in a military camp, or on a university campus?" A drug-education program found to be effective in one particular high school setting, for example, would not necessarily be effective in other high schools, in elementary schools, or in colleges. The only way to find out the program's effectiveness is to conduct the research at various locations and to compare the results.

Interaction of History and Treatment.   Particular events might also affect people's behavior and attitudes so that results of some research projects might not be clearly applicable to future time periods. Cook and Campbell illustrate this by reference to studies conducted on very special days, such as when a U.S. president dies. Results of our drug-education experiment might not be generalizable to other settings if, unfortunately, a student from that school were to experience a severe drug overdose in the middle of our study.

Internal and External Validity: Concluding Thoughts

It is practically impossible for the political analyst to develop a research design that effectively eliminates all threats to internal and **external validity.** Frequently, in fact, a research design that is strong on controlling for one threat will be weak on controlling for another. It is important, nevertheless, that researchers be familiar with the issues of internal and external validity and that they always try to select the most effective research design for the problem at hand. It is important, also, to be aware of these threats when reviewing the works of others and to be able to evaluate available research in the light of how investigators have managed threats to internal and external validity.

SELECTING A RESEARCH DESIGN

There are numerous ways to categorize research design alternatives. Campbell and Stanley, in their classic study of research design, categorize all research designs as belonging to one of the following types: experimental, quasi-experimental, or correlational and ex post facto.[17] The following presentation distinguishes simply between designs that may be considered experimental from those that are basically nonexperimental. The key difference between these two is the degree to which the investigator *controls* both the subjects (voters, legislators, students, etc.) and the conditions (events and situations) to be studied. The final section of this chapter examines cost-benefit analysis, a technique designed to assess efficiency: whether program and policy benefits are worth their cost.

Experimental Research Design

Virtually everyone is familiar with the rudiments of experimental research. Results of such research are commonly presented even in daily newspapers. An article appearing in the *New York Times,* titled, "Magnesium Is Found to Aid Bypass Patients," reported on an experiment involving 100 patients at the New England Medical Center in Boston. Fifty of those patients received an injection of magnesium-chloride solution after bypass surgery, and fifty received a placebo. Those patients receiving the magnesium solution, according to the report, experienced a fifty percent reduction in heart-rhythm problems and also more speedy recoveries.

In another article, the *New York Times* reported the results of an experiment testing the effects of education, counseling, and social services on teenage mothers. In that study, one group of teenage mothers was selected to be "showered" with special education and social service programs, and a similar group received no services. After eighteen months, the study reported that the teenagers receiving special services were no more likely to be off welfare and in a job than the group receiving no services.[18]

The experimental method is sometimes used in political science research, and it is frequently used in policy and evaluation research. The problem facing investigators Terry R. Johnson and Daniel M. Geller was to determine whether basic reading and math skills of young workers participating in the federally funded Job Corps program could be improved by using computer-assisted instruction (CAI) teaching techniques rather than, or in conjunction with, the traditional (i.e., paper-and-pencil materials only) education programs. In order to determine which method was more effective, ten Job Corps centers around the country were selected to participate in a study whereby at each center, some participants were randomly selected to receive instruction via the new CAI teaching technique, and others were randomly selected to receive instruction via the traditional paper-and-pencil technique. In total, 5,396 young workers participated in the study, which extended over a period of about a year. At the conclusion, basic math and reading skill levels of those participating in each instructional method were compared, to determine, as Johnson and Geller put it, "whether students exposed to the CAI treatment experienced greater learning gains than students not exposed to CAI." While results were mixed, Johnson and Geller are able to conclude that, "there was some evidence that students with significant exposure to CAI experienced greater learning gains than did students [not exposed to CAI]."[19]

These examples illustrate many of the features of experimentation. Put formally, we may say that experimental research has the following basic characteristics:[20]

1. There is at least one group that is exposed to an experimental or test stimulus (termed the **experimental** or **treatment group**) and at least one group that is not (termed the **control group**).
2. Assignment of subjects to the experimental and control groups is determined by the investigator. Typically, subjects are assigned to control and experimental groups *randomly* (and sometimes assignment is made by *matching* processes), to preclude the likelihood of initial differences existing between the groups.
3. The investigator determines when and under what conditions the experimental group is exposed to the experimental variable—the treatment effect.
4. The investigator controls the setting of the experiment so that the influence of variables other than the experimental variable may be excluded.

If each of these conditions can be met, various threats to internal validity are largely controlled. However, this level of control is not always possible, and frequently we have to compromise our design to meet the conditions at hand. The following are some of the most frequently used **experimental research design** models.

The Classic Experimental Design. In the classic experimental design situation, at least two groups are selected. The one that is to be exposed to the treatment or stimulus representing the independent variable is the experimental group; the one that is not exposed to the treatment is the control group. Subjects should be randomly assigned to the two groups. Each group is measured on the dependent variable prior to introduction of the treatment effect (a process known as **pretesting**), and each group is measured following exposure to the treatment effect (called **posttesting**). Differences in the change occurring in the experimental and control groups provide a measure of the effect of the experiment.

The classic experimental design may be diagrammed as follows:

Random Assignment of Subjects to	*Pretesting of Positions on Dependent Variable*	*Exposure to Treatment Effect*	*Posttesting of Positions on Dependent Variable*
An experimental group	Yes	Yes	Yes
A control group	Yes	No	Yes

We might employ the classic experimental design as a means of evaluating the hypothetical drug-education program described previously. We could, theoretically, randomly select fifty students who would be assigned to a drug-education program (the experimental group), and fifty students who would receive no drug-education instruction (the control group). Members of each group would be pretested to determine their attitudes toward and behavior regarding alcohol and other drug use. Pretesting is important because it alerts us to any unusual differences in the groups, and it provides for each group a baseline for comparison.[21] Next, the experimental group would participate in the drug-education program, after which both groups again would be tested for attitudes and behavior toward substance use.

In this manner, a *change score,* representing the difference between pre- and posttest scores, is calculated for both the experimental and the control group. A comparison of change scores permits us to evaluate effects of the treatment variable—in this case, exposure to this particular drug-education program.

One problem with the classic experimental design is that the pretest itself might so sensitize both control and experimental groups to the issue being tested that posttest results are effected, independent of the treatment. This problem illustrates the issue of testing reactivity. Another problem common to all experimental designs relates to the ability to generalize results to larger populations. The experimenter can never be quite certain that results are representative of what would be found with other groups, in other situations, at other times. In addition, each of the techniques for dealing with these issues[22] has disadvantages of its own. Regardless, the classic experimental design, and especially the requirement that subjects be randomly assigned to experimental and control groups, takes care of most of the threats to internal validity and represents a very strong research design option.

The Posttest Only Design.   The posttest only design can be diagrammed as follows:

Random Assignment of Subjects to	*Pretesting of Positions on Dependent Variable*	*Exposure to Treatment Effect*	*Posttesting of Positions on Dependent Variable*
An experimental group	No	Yes	Yes
A control group	No	No	Yes

As can be seen, in this design situation, neither the experimental nor the control group is tested prior to introduction of the independent variable. This design might purposely be selected in order to avoid the problem of sensitizing subjects to the experiment through application of a pretest. Also, this design is frequently used because the researcher *is not in a position* to apply pretest procedures. As a program evaluator, you might be called in to evaluate the results of a drug-education program after students already had been assigned to the experimental and control groups and *after* the course had been completed. In such instances, pretesting obviously is not possible. The major problem with this design is that you cannot know whether any posttest differences between groups are the result of the treatment, or of differences that existed before the experiment.

Multiple Group Design.   A multiple group research design option might be diagrammed as follows:

Random Assignment of Subjects to	Pretesting of Positions on Dependent Variable	Exposure to Treatment Effect	Posttesting of Positions on Dependent Variable
Experimental group A	Yes	Yes	Yes
Experimental group B	Yes	Yes	Yes
Experimental group C	Yes	Yes	Yes
A control group	Yes	No	Yes

This design, it can be seen, is an extension of the classic experimental design option, with the exception that several experimental groups are involved here. The advantage of this design is that you can test the effects of different *levels* or *categories* of the independent variable. For example, students might be assigned to three different types of drug-education programs, and the experiment would be designed to tell us not only whether drug-education programs make a difference in attitudes and behavior, but also which types of programs make the *most* difference.

Solomon Four-Group Design.   The Solomon Four-Group Design option may be diagrammed as follows:

Random Assignment of Subjects to	Pretesting of Positions on Dependent Variable	Exposure to Treatment Effect	Posttesting of Positions on Dependent Variable
Experimental group A	Yes	Yes	Yes
Experimental group B	No	Yes	Yes
Control group A	Yes	No	Yes
Control group B	No	No	Yes

This is a very powerful design, considered by many to be the strongest for overcoming threats to both internal and external validity.[22] This technique controls for the problem of reactivity by removing two groups from the possible sensitizing effects of pretesting; and the use only of a posttest on the second control group provides a way to measure any effects of the experiment itself.

Factorial Designs.   **Factorial designs** may be used when you are interested in examining the effects of *more than one* independent variable on the dependent variable. The simplest factorial design involves two independent variables, each having only two values. Continuing with our example of concern about students' attitudes toward and behavior regarding drug use, we might want to examine the joint effects of students enrolling in a course designed to provide more information about drugs, *and* a course designed to increase self-esteem. Such a situation would produce four possible combinations, as illustrated by the following table.

Students Enrolled in Self-Esteem Course?	Students Enrolled in Drug-Education Course	
	No	Yes
No	1	2
Yes	3	4

Any of the designs previously discussed could be used to test the interactive effects of drug-education and self-esteem courses on drug use and attitudes. A sample design could be diagrammed as follows:

Random Assignment of Subjects to	*Pretesting of Positions on Dependent Variable*	*Posttesting of Positions on Dependent Variable*
Experimental group 1	No	Yes
Experimental group 2	No	Yes
Experimental group 3	No	Yes
Experimental group 4	No	Yes

Where group 1, group 2, group 3, and group 4 correspond to students placed in cells 1, 2, 3, and 4 of preceding table.

This design will tell us whether a drug-education program or a self-esteem course has greater impact on drug attitudes and use, and also whether the courses taken in combination have a greater effect than either alone. Typically, factorial designs do not require pretesting. They need not be limited only to two variables with two levels, as illustrated here; however with additional variables and values, the design becomes quite complicated, and complexity is the major deficiency of all factorial design options.

Follow-Up Testing

A question relevant to any experimental design is how much time should be permitted to pass before conducting the posttest. Possibly, the effects of an experiment might not be *immediate* but rather *delayed* for a period of time. A related issue is the *lasting effect* of the treatment. It might be desirable to know not only whether the experiment had any impact on behavior or attitudes but also whether such effect is short-term only or extends over a period of time. Conducting several posttests, a process known as **follow-up testing** can address both issues.

An experimental design incorporating a follow-up procedure might be diagrammed as follows:

Random Assignment of Subjects to	*Pretesting of Positions on Dependent Variable*	*Exposure to Treatment Effect*	*Posttesting of Positions on Dependent Variable*	*Follow-Up Testing of Positions on Dependent Variable*
Experimental group A	Yes	Yes	Yes	Yes
Experimental group B	Yes	Yes	No	Yes
Control group A	Yes	No	Yes	Yes

In this particular example, both experimental groups are to be tested over extended periods of time so that it can be determined whether results are immediate or are delayed, and whether effects extend over a period of some time (the difference between the dates of the posttest and follow-up test administrations). Additionally, this design calls for posttesting only one experimental group. This permits us to minimize, and also to evaluate, possible reactive effects of the posttest procedure.

Nonexperimental Research Designs

In a 1992 study, DeSantis, Glass, and Newell were interested in determining the factors associated with job satisfaction of city managers.[24] Specifically, this team of investigators wanted to know whether job satisfaction of city managers (the dependent variable) would be found to be related to managerial values, job tenure, relations with city council, and city size (the independent variables). Take just one of these independent variables, city size, and consider what would have been required if the researchers had applied the design of experimental research. The researchers would have had to select and assign managers to career positions in cities of varying sizes on a random basis, they would have had to pretest each manager on the dependent variable (job satisfaction) prior to the managers' commencement of their careers, and the researchers would have had to posttest the managers at staggered intervals for years after the managers began their jobs. Obviously, no researcher is in a position to have this much control over anyone's life. Application of the experimental research design was impossible.

Instead, DeSantis, Glass, and Newell conducted a *survey* of city managers, in which all respondents were asked to evaluate their level of job satisfaction and to provide information on the several independent variables (such as how long they had been on the job). Based on responses to the survey, and on known characteristics of the cities (e.g., population size) the researchers reached a number of conclusions about the relationships between the career satisfaction of city managers and the city size, managerial values, relations with city council, and job tenure of the managers.

Like DeSantis, Glass, and Newell, all political and policy researchers—students and senior researchers alike—frequently are interested in situations where it simply is not possible to meet the conditions required of experimental research designs. You may not be able to assign people to experimental and control groups, you may not be able to control exposure to the treatment effect, or you might not be in a position to pretest subjects. In such situations, other research designs—collectively called *nonexperimental* research designs are employed. Some of the most frequently used of these are discussed next.

Cross-Sectional Design. Probably the most frequently employed research design in political science is **cross-sectional research** (sometimes also called "correlational analysis" and used frequently in conjunction with surveys). Using this technique, an investigator typically will randomly select from a population of subjects (cities, nations, people, etc.) a sample that will serve as the single group to be studied. All members of the sample will be measured on the dependent variable (or variables) and the independent variable (or variables). Then, using some statistical testing procedures, inferences about the strength and the direction of relationships among the dependent and independent variables are made. Some of the differences between conclusions which can be reached using correlational and experimental research designs are illustrated in Box 3.1.

Using the drug-education situation as an example, an investigator might randomly select a group of students from the local high school and interview each student, inquiring as to (1) whether they had completed the drug-education course (the independent variable), and (2) their attitudes toward and use of alcohol and other drugs (the dependent variables). If testing indicated that those completing the drug-education course had significantly lower use of alcohol and other drugs than those students not completing the course, the investigator would conclude that a relationship exists between completing the drug- education course and drug use, and the investigator *might* be prone to infer that the drug-education course was responsible for the difference.

Notice, however, how much weaker is this design, in terms of concluding cause and effect, than is experimental research design. Students were not randomly assigned to experimental and control groups; no pretesting was conducted; the investigator had no control over the introduction of the treatment effect (the drug-education course); and no long-term follow-up testing was possible. While it was found that students completing the course used drugs less frequently than those not completing the course, any number of factors other than the drug-education course might have been responsible for the observed differences. Students less inclined to use drugs might have been more likely to enroll in the course in the first place.

BOX 3.1   Correlational versus Experimental Research: The Link between Smoking and Lung Cancer

The following article, taken verbatim from a June 16, 1994, article appearing in the *New York Times,* well illustrates the different conclusions that may be drawn from correlational versus experimental research designs.

'53 Experiment Found Cancer Link

In 1952, Dr. Richard Doll published a groundbreaking study on the health risks of smoking. The study linked the risk of developing lung cancer to the number of cigarettes smoked, with the risk rising in direct proportion to the number. One of the findings dealt with benzopyrene, an aromatic hydrocarbon that is found in cigarette smoke and is now widely considered to be one of tobacco's chief cancer-causing substances.

Although an exact relationship between dose and biological response, like that found by Dr. Doll, is a strong indication that a substance is a cause of disease, such studies do not conclusively demonstrate that cigarette smoking can induce malignant tumors in living animals; nor do they pinpoint the carcinogenic components of cigarettes.

Among the first proofs to do so came in 1953, with a paper published in the December issue of the journal Cancer Research by Dr. Ernst Wynder and his colleagues at the Sloan Kettering Institute. Dr. Wynder's group succeeded in experimentally producing cancers on the skin of mice by painting their backs with tobacco tars taken from cigarette smoke. Many similar experiments had failed, possibly because they had been too brief. But Dr. Wynder's study offered experimental proof that the contents of cigarette smoke could induce cancers in skin: 44 percent of the animals developed malignant tumors.

SOURCE: Philip J. Hilts, "Cigarette Makers Debated the Risks They Denied," *New York Times,* June 16, 1994.

Later chapters of this book show how the use of techniques for statistical control, in conjunction with cross-sectional designs, may reduce the confounding effects of these other factors. Still, it is impossible to control for every possible confounding variable, and cross-sectional designs can never conclusively demonstrate cause and effect relationships.

Cross-sectional designs are frequently used in conjunction with survey research, where random samples of a population are selected for study. This is the design technique, in fact, used by DeSantis, Glass, and Newell in the aforementioned study of career satisfaction among city managers. Because samples—if properly drawn—are highly representative, results may be very generalizable. Consequently, cross-sectional designs have the potential for being very strong on issues of external validity, as that term was defined and discussed previously herein.

Interrupted Time-Series Design.   Using a research option known as an **interrupted time-series design,** the investigator will measure positions on the dependent variable on several occasions *prior to* the introduction of some independent variable and then will measure positions on the dependent variable on several occasions *following* exposure to the independent variable. The measurements taken prior to introduction of the independent variable reveal a *pattern* of behavior, which can be compared with changes in this behavior following exposure to the independent variable. A time-series design typically is diagrammed as follows:

$$O_1 \quad O_2 \quad O_3 \quad O_4 \quad X \quad O_5 \quad O_6 \quad O_7 \quad O_8$$

Where O_1, O_2, O_3, and O_4 represent observations or measurements taken at various times before the introduction of the independent variable, X represents the independent variable (treatment effect), and O_5, O_6, O_7, O_8 represent observations or measurements taken at various times after the introduction of the independent variable.

In the drug-education example, an investigator employing a time-series design might survey a group of students on three or four occasions prior to their taking the drug-education course and might repeat the survey on three or four occasions following their completion of the course. This design will tell you not only whether the independent variable (in this case participation in the drug-education course) altered the pattern of behavior noted prior to the treatment, but also whether the effect was lasting or only temporary. Although this deisgn lacks a true control group, it does control for a wide variety of threats to internal validity. Its principal weakness centers on the lack of control for internal threats due to history and to testing re-activity, as these terms were defined above.

A use of the time-series design is provided by Stephen M. Rock's 1992 study of the impact of the seat-belt-use law enacted in Illinois in 1985. Rock collected information on a number of automobile-accident-related incidents—including deaths, serious injuries, moderate injuries, and minor injuries—for a period of 5 1/2 years prior to the passage of the act, and for a period of 5 years after the law took effect. Although he does not conclude that the act was associated with change in all accident-related variables, he reports that it was associated with change in some. One of his figures is reproduced in Figure 3.1, which shows that a noticeable drop in serious automobile-related injuries occurred after passage of the act.[25]

An additional interesting use of time-series design is provided by Robert Cameron Mitchell, in his examination of changing public opinion toward environmental protection legislation over the period of the 1980s.[26] Mitchell's time series chart is presented in Figure 3.2 (page 51).

In interpreting these trends, Mitchell makes the point that the American public reported increasing support for strong environmental protection legislation in the 1980s and that this position increased significantly following the highly publicized oil spill off the Alaskan coast, caused by the Exxon Valdez tanker. In Mitchell's words, "surveys in 1989 recorded an increase of an additional 15 percentage points for those who took the position [that environmental improvements should be made regardless of cost]—another effect of the Exxon Valdez oil spill."[27] Box 3.2 (page 52) illustrates some of the pitfalls of time-series analysis.

Panel-Study Design.   A design that combines some elements of cross-sectional with some elements of time-series analysis is known as **panel-study design.** Here,

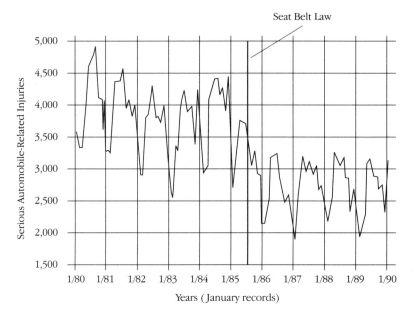

FIGURE 3.1

Illustration of Interrupted Time-Series Design: Monthly Automobile-Related Injuries in Illinois

SOURCE: Steven M. Rock, "Impact of the Illinois Seat Belt Use Law on Accidents, Deaths, and Injuries," *Evaluation Review* 16 (October, 1992), 497.

a researcher selects a sample of subjects to be studied, then the researcher takes measurements on the variables to be examined on several occasions. As in the cross-sectional design, the investigator collects measurements on the independent and dependent variables at the same time, and the researcher cannot control who is exposed to the independent variable. As in the time-series design, these measurements are taken at several times.

For example, suppose that a researcher wants to examine the effects of a presidential campaign on the relationship between partisanship and voting preferences. This researcher might select a group of voters and measure their attitudes and opinions on several occasions during a campaign. Note that only one group is selected, but this group is surveyed repeatedly. Two major difficulties are associated with the panel-design technique. One is *panel mortality:* Participants in the study may drop out during the course of the investigation, and those who do drop out may differ in significant ways from those who remain in the study.[28] Second, respondents may *react* to repeated surveying in such a way that the surveys, themselves, influence attitudes and behavior.

One-Group, Pretest–Posttest Design. The **one-group, pretest-posttest design** looks a lot like an experimental design, but it lacks many of the essential features of a true experiment. It may be diagrammed as follows:

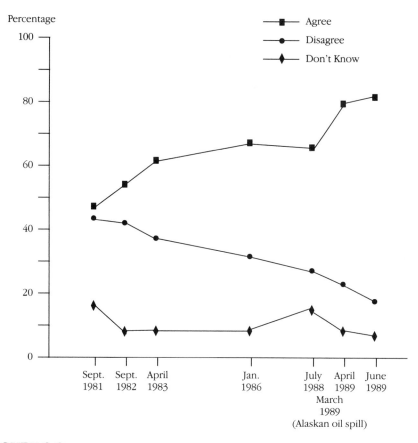

FIGURE 3.2

Illustration of Interrupted Time-Series Design: Views about Environmental
Protection Regardless of Cost

NOTE: The question asked was, "Do you agree or disagree with the following statement: Protecting
the environment is *so* important that requirements and standards cannot be too high, and continuing
environmental improvements must be made *regardless* of cost."

SOURCE: Robert Cameron Mitchell, "Public Opinion and the Green Lobby: Poised for the 1990s?" in
Environmental Policy in the 1990s eds., Norman J. Vig and Michael E. Kraft (Washington, DC:
Congressional Quarterly Press, 1990), 86. Data from national telephone surveys conducted by the
New York Times, July 2, 1989, 1.

	Pretesting of Positions on Dependent Variable	*Exposure to Treatment Effect*	*Posttesting of Positions on Dependent Variable*
Group A	Yes	Yes	Yes

Here, it can be seen, one group is compared with itself, before and after exposure to some independent variable. Unlike a true experiment, subjects may not have

BOX 3.2   Pitfalls of Time-Series Analysis

Time-series analysis can be a very useful tool of policy evaluation, but if used improperly, it also can be very deceptive, as illustrated in the following excerpted discussion by Donald T. Campbell.

The Connecticut Crackdown on Speeding

On December 23, 1955, Connecticut instituted an exceptionally severe and prolonged crackdown on speeding. Like most public reporting of program effectiveness, the results were reported in terms of simple before-and-after measures: a comparison of this year's figures with those of the year before. That is, the 1956 total of 284 traffic deaths was compared with the 1955 total of 324, and the governor stated, "With a saving of 40 lives in 1956 . . . we can say the program is definitely worthwhile. Figure 1 presents the data graphically. But this simple quasi-experimental design is very weak and deceptive. There are so many other possible explanations for the change from 324 to 284 highway fatalities. In attributing all of this change to his crackdown, the governor is making an implicit assumption that without the crackdown there would have been no change at all. A time series presentation, using the fatality records of several prior and subsequent years, adds greatly to the strength of the analysis. Figure 2 shows such data for the Connecticut crackdown. In this larger context the 1955–1956 drop looks trivial. We can see that the implicit assumption underlying the governor's statement was almost certainly wrong.

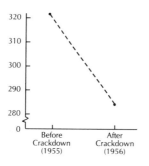

Figure 1

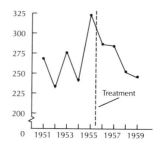

Figure 2

SOURCE: Donald T. Campbell, "Measuring the Effects of Social Innovations by Means of Time Series," in *Statistics: A Guide to the Unknown,* 3rd ed., ed., Judith M. Tanur (Pacific Grove, California: Wadsworth & Brooks/Cole Advanced Books, 1989), 94–95. [Originally appearing as: Campbell and H. L. Ross, "The Connecticut Crackdown on Speeding: Time-Series Data in Quasi-Experimental Analysis," *Law & Society Review* 3(1): 33–53.]

been randomly selected, and no control group is present. As applied to the drug-education research, a group of students might have been examined before taking a drug-education course and again at the conclusion of the course, and the students' differences in attitudes and use of drugs would be compared.

Even if change occurs between pre- and posttesting, there is no way of knowing whether the treatment (taking the drug-education course in this example) was responsible. This design suffers from many threats to internal validity, the most important of which are history, maturation, and test reactions, as these problems were described previously in this chapter.

Case-Study Design. A final non-experimental approach that may be identified is known as the **case-study design.** In the case-study approach, as defined by Robert K. Yin, (1) the researcher investigates a contemporary phenomenon within its real-life context; (2) the boundaries between phenomenon and context are not clearly evident; and (3) multiple sources of evidence are used.[29] Here a single group or a single phenomenon is studied on a single occasion, usually following exposure to some political or policy event. Yin argues that the case-study approach is preferred when examining contemporary events for which the relevant conditions cannot be controlled or manipulated. The case-study approach, he says, relies on many of the same techniques as history but it adds two additional sources of evidence: direct observation and systematic interviewing. The unique strength of the case-study approach, Yin argues, is "its ability to deal with a full variety of evidence—documents, artifacts, interviews, and observations."[30]

The case-study approach suffers from many of the threats to internal and external validity discussed previously. However there are some advantages to the technique. As Yin points out, case studies may be helpful in assessing whether an association discovered in a cross-sectional design study is causal, or simply spurious.[31] Case studies also can be helpful in examining extreme or very unusual situations, and also in "exploratory" research. Studies of cases can assist in developing appropriate questions, surveys, and testing materials to be used in experimental or cross-sectional studies.

An interesting use of the case-study design is provided by Ivy E. Broder's study of a federal regulatory agency, The Office of Noise Abatement and Control, which existed within the Environmental Protection Agency from 1972 to 1981. Based on intensive study of that agency, Broder was able to develop a framework predicting retention or elimination of regulatory agencies based on two criteria: interest group pressures and economic evaluations. In Broder's words, "Although [information] showing that a program is economically inefficient may be a necessary condition for ending that program, it clearly is not a sufficient condition. A large or important constituency almost always prevents an inefficient program from being eliminated."[32]

In some fields where a number of case studies are available, the results might be integrated into a single study. Such a technique sometimes is called *multiple case study design,* or *case-survey design.*

Cost-Benefit Designs. From the perspective of policy analysis and program evaluation, the above designs can be used to determine the impact of a program or policy. They are designed, essentially, to answer the question: "Is this program (or policy) working as intended?"

Cost-benefit designs, by contrast, are designed to answer the question: "Are the benefits of the program worth its costs?" Conceptually, cost-benefit analysis is a simple procedure. In theory, the researcher assesses all of the benefits provided by a particular policy or program and weighs these against all of the costs. If the benefits outweigh the costs, the program should be continued; otherwise it should be terminated.

But practically, the application of cost-benefit analysis is frequently very complex. It is often difficult to estimate benefits because, as Rossi and Freeman note, "one must ultimately place a value on human life in order to fully monetize program benefits."[33] In recognition of this basic problem, some analysts apply a technique called *cost-effectiveness* analysis where benefits are expressed in terms other than monetary.

There are other difficulties associated with applying cost-benefit analysis as well. Bingham and Felbinger alert us to several of these when they pose the following questions which must be answered in applying the technique:

As for costs: Do you include only the costs to a particular agency when more than one agency supports the program? How do you apportion overhead costs? What about the costs of in-kind contributions?

As for benefits: Do you consider short-term benefits or long-term benefits, or both? How do you divide programmatic benefits when a recipient participates in several related programs? How do you attach a dollar amount to [the benefits] or [costs]?[34]

But, in spite of these difficulties, cost-benefit analysis is a very powerful tool for policy analysis and has been used successfully in many contexts. Stokey and Zeckhauser present an ideal five-step procedure for applying cost-benefit analysis. Although it may seldom be possible to fully satisfy the requirements of each step, their model provides a good guide for program analysis. Those steps are:[35]

1. The project or projects to be analyzed are identified.
2. All the impacts, both favorable and unfavorable, present and future, on all of society are determined.
3. Values, usually in dollars, are assigned to these impacts. Favorable impacts will be registered as benefits, unfavorable ones as costs.
4. The net *benefit* (total benefit minus total cost) is calculated.
5. The choice is made: select the alternative that produces the greatest net benefit.

Cost-benefit and cost-effectiveness analysis procedures can be extremely useful tools for policy analysis. Like all tools, they have particular limitations and they must be used with care. The objectivity which the techniques appear to protray sometimes mask the more fundamental political and value issues which must be considered. Still, the techniques have been successfully utilized in many policy situations.

One such application of cost-benefit analysis is provided by Gray and Olson in their examination of alternative types of sentencing decision for burglars.[36] Based on a randomly selected group of burglars sentenced in Arizona, Gray and Olson es-

TABLE 3.2

Illustration of Cost-Benefit Analysis, Social Costs and Benefits Per Convict

	Incapac- itation Benefit	Rehabil- itation Benefit	Deterrence Benefit[a]	Social Costs	Net Social Benefits
Prison	$6,732	−$10,356	+$6,113	−$10,435	−$7,946
Jail	+774	−5,410	+5,094	−2,772	−2,315
Probation	0	−2,874	+5,725	−1,675	+1,176

[a] The savings per index crime prevented was estimated to be $2,274. Each condition prevented 6.59 crimes, or a total of $14,985. The benefit was distributed evenly over the 2.25-year study period and then was discounted.

SOURCE: Gray and Olson, "A Cost Benefit Analysis of the Sentencing Decisions for Burglars," 715. *Social Science Quarterly,* 70 (September, 1989).

timate the net social benefits (total social benefits – total social costs) for each of three different types of sentencing procedures—prison, jail, or probation. "Total social benefits" were calculated by summing for each convict their estimates of rehabilitation benefits, incapacitation benefits, and deterrence benefits for each sentence. "Total social costs" were calculated by summing their estimates of corrections costs and forgone earnings for each sentence. Their calculation of the "net social benefit" for each type of sentence is shown in Table 3.2

Interpreting their findings, Gray and Olson state: "For prison and jail, the net social benefits are negative. The relative value of the net social benefits, however, is more important than the absolute value. The net social benefits of probation exceed those of prison and jail by over $9,000 and $3,000, respectively."[37]

SUMMARY

Proper hypothesis formation, concept operationalization, and research-design selection set the stage for successful political and policy research. Hypotheses identify precisely what information must be collected. For concepts to be useful, they must be measurable, a process whch sometimes is very straightforward—as when a variable can be measured by a single indicator—but which sometimes is quite complex.

Considerable thought should be given to the research-design stage of the research process. It is important to select a research design suitable for answering the questions established for the study. Realizing that it is not always feasible to select the strongest design option, the researcher should select the best possible option, given time and resource limitations.

KEY TERMS

hypotheses

dependent variables

independent variables

concepts

operational

concept operationalization

research design

internal validity

testing (or instrument) reactivity

external validity

experimental or treatment group

control group

experimental research design

pretesting

posttesting

factorial design

follow-up testing

cross-sectional research

interrupted time-series design

panel-study design

one group, pretest –posttest design

case-study design

multiple case study (or case survey) design

EXERCISES

1. Formulation of hypotheses
   a. Discuss the functions served by hypotheses in the research process.
   b. Review three research articles appearing in recent issues of any political science journal, and list the hypotheses tested in each.
   c. On the basis of these hypotheses, discuss the theory (or theories) being tested by each researcher, and discuss the type of data each researcher must collect.
2. Operationalization of concepts
   a. Identify the dependent and independent variables, for each hypothesis listed in the preceding Item 1 of these exercises.
   b. For each of these hypotheses, list the concepts used, and discuss how each researcher operationalized these concepts.
   c. What are some alternative ways to operationalize these concepts?
3. Development of a research design
   a. Discuss the various research-design options frequently used in political and policy research, and discuss the situations in which each is most appropriate.
   b. Discuss the issues of internal and external validity, and discuss how each of the major research-design options deal with these issues.
   c. For each hypothesis developed in Item 1 of these exercises, identify the principal research design used by the researcher.
4. Nonexperimental research designs
   a. Describe the case study method of research design.
   b. Compared with the other research design options, what are some of the advantages and disadvantages of the case-study method?
   c. Identify at least three recent political science or policy research efforts (books or articles) that have used the case-study approach, and discuss how their approach and findings differ from what might be expected when using some other research-design approach.

NOTES

1. Julian L. Simon and Paul Burstein, *Basic Research Methods in Social Science,* 3rd ed. (New York: Random House, 1985), 29.
2. It should be noted that hypotheses may be developed from empirical observation, as well as deduced from theory. Also, empirical testing can never absolutely prove a hypothesis to be true, but such testing can at least lend support to a hypothesis. This support for the hypothesis, in turn, lends support to the theory from which the hypothesis is derived.
3. Abraham Kaplan, *The Conduct of Inquiry* (San Francisco: Chandler Publishing, 1964), 88.
4. Laura A. Reese and Ronald Brown, "The Effects of Religious Messages on Racial Identity and System Blame among African Americans," *Journal of Politics* 57 (February, 1995), 24– 43.
5. Bruce Bueno de Mesquita, Randolph M. Siverson, and Gary Woller, "War and the Fate of Regimes: A Comparative Analysis," *American Political Science Review* 86 (September, 1992), 638–646.
6. Keith Boeckelman, "Political Culture and State Development Policy," *Publius* 21 (Spring, 1991), 49–63 (emphasis added).
7. Kevin Hill, "Does the Creation of Majority Black Districts Aid Republicans? An Analysis of the 1992 Congressional Elections in Eight Southern States," *Journal of Politics,* 57 (May, 1995), 384–401.
8. Kenneth D. Bailey, *Methods of Social Research* (New York: Free Press, 1978), 33.
9. Charles O. Jones presents an interesting discussion of the importance of concept formation and argues that concepts serve the political scientist in three ways: (1) classification for general understanding, (2) classification of research expectations, and (3) classification of empirical findings. See "Doing before Knowing: Concept Development in Political Research," *American Journal of Political Science* 18 (February, 1974), 215–228.
10. Linda Brewster Stearns and Charlotte Wilkinson Coleman, "Industrial and Local Labor Market Structures and Black Male Employment in the Manufacturing Sector," *Social Science Quarterly* 71 (June, 1990), 285–298.
11. Alexander M. Hicks and Duane H. Swank, "Politics, Institutions, and Welfare Spending in Industrial Democracies, 1960–82," *American Political Science Reveiw* 86 (September, 1992), 658–674.
12. Bailey, *Methods of Social Research,* 191.
13. Donald T. Campbell and Julian C. Stanley, *Experimental and Quasi-experimental Designs for Research* (Chicago: Rand McNally, 1963), 5.
14. The discussion that follows relies heavily on Campbell and Stanley, *Experimental and Quasi-experimental Designs for Research;* and also on Thomas D. Cook and Donald T. Campbell, *Quasi-experimentation: Design and Analysis for Field Settings* (Boston: Houghton Mifflin, 1979).
15. For a more complete listing of threats to internal validity, see Cook and Campbell, *Quasi-experimentation,* 51–55.
16. This discussion relies principally on Cook and Campbell, *Quasi-experimentation,* 73.
17. Campbell and Stanley, *Experimental and Quasi-experimental Designs for Research.*
18. Jason DeParle, "Study Finds That Education Does Not Ease Welfare Rolls," *New York Times,* June 22, 1994.
19. Terry R. Johnson and Daniel M. Geller, "Experimental Evidence on the Impacts of Com-

puter-Assisted Instruction in the Job Corps Program," *Evaluation Review* 17 (February, 1992), 3–22.

20. See Paul E. Spector, *Research Designs* (Beverly Hills, CA: Sage Publications, 1981), 20–24.

21. Biases occurring in the pretesting stage will, obviously, affect a study's internal validity, and these are particularly likely to occur in studies relying on self-reports of attitudes, behavior, or opinion. For an exploration of this problem and some suggested solutions, see Leona S. Aiken and Stephen G. West, "Invalidity of True Experiments: Self-report Pretest Biases," *Evaluation Review* 14 (August, 1990), 374–390.

22. See David C. Leege and Wayne L. Francis, *Political Research: Design, Measurement and Analysis* (New York: Basic Books, 1974), 76–77.

23. Leege and Francis, *Political Research,* 78.

24. Victor S. DeSantis, James J. Glass, and Charldean Newell, "City Managers, Job Satisfaction, and Community Problem Perceptions," *Public Administration Review* 52 (September/October, 1992), 447–453.

25. Steven M. Rock, "Impact of the Illinois Seat Belt Use Law on Accidents, Deaths, and Injuries," *Evaluation Review* 16 (October, 1992), 491–507.

26. Robert Cameron Mitchell, "Public Opinion and the Green Lobby: Poised for the 1990's?" in *Environmental Policy in the 1990's* eds. Norman J. Vig and Michael E. Kraft (Washington, DC: Congressional Quarterly Press, 1990), 81–99.

27. Ibid., 85.

28. See S. G. Jurs and C. V. Glass, "The Effect of Experimental Mortality on the Internal and External Validity of the Randomized Comparative Experiment," *Journal of Experimental Education* 40 (1971), 62–66.

29. Robert K. Yin, *Case Study Research: Design and Methods* (Newbury Park, CA: Sage Publications, 1989), 23.

30. Ibid., 19–20.

31. Ibid., 16–19.

32. Ivy. E. Broder, "A Study of the Birth and Death of a Regulatory Agenda: The Case of the EPA Noise Program," *Evaluation Review* 12 (June, 1988), 291–309.

33. Peter H. Rossi and Howard E. Freeman, *Evaluation: A Systematic Approach,* 5th ed. (Newbury Park, CA: Sage Publications, 1933) 374.

34. Richard D. Bingham and Claire L. Felbinger, *Evaluation In Practice* (New York: Longman, Inc., 1989), 207.

35. Edith Stokey and Richard Zeckhauser, *A Primer for Policy Analysis* (New York: W. W. Norton and Company, 1978), 136.

36. Tara Gray and Kent W. Olson, "A Cost-Benefit Analysis of the Sentencing Decision for Burglars," *Social Science Quarterly,* 70 (September, 1989), 708–723.

37. Ibid., 714–715.

CHAPTER 4

Gathering Information:
Observational Techniques and Survey Research

Data collection is a fascinating phase of research, particularly in the case of political research. The collection of information often takes the student out of the classroom and into the field—the real world of politics. Here, the researcher may interview public officials, attend legislative sessions, examine public documents, talk to people about their political behavior, or simply trace public issues through newspaper sources. Through the collection and handling of information, the researcher begins to feel the actual excitement of politics and political behavior.

In setting out to collect the needed information, you may choose either of two options: (1) You may collect your own data, or (2) you may rely on data collected by someone else. When selecting one strategy over another, you base your decision on available resources and desired control. If your resources are limited, and if you are not greatly concerned about the conditions under which the data were collected, you probably will be content to rely on data collected by someone else or by some other organization. Fortunately, as the next chapter shows, many excellent sources of data are readily available to political researchers.

Sometimes, you may be interested in a topic for which no reliable information is available, and your only option is self-collection of data. Students of state and local politics, for example, often find themselves interested in issues pertaining to a *particular* locality (such as demographic characteristics of a city's school board, or participation by local citizens in neighborhood associations, or attitudes of city council members toward issues of local concern) for which no systematically collected data are available. Or, you may have been commissioned by some agency to assess the impact of a particular program or policy. In instances such as these, you must collect your own data.

Whether you decide to collect data yourself (sometimes called "primary data") or to rely on data collected by others (often called "secondary data" analysis), the process can be made more productive and more rewarding by following a few established procedures, discussed next.

SELF-COLLECTION: OBSERVATIONAL AND SURVEY RESEARCH

A number of strategies are available to researchers who decide to collect their own data. These include documentary search, experimental research, observational techniques, and survey research. Experimental research designs were discussed in the previous chapter, and documentary research is discussed in Chapter 5. We focus here on observational techniques and survey research. The primary distinction between these two is that when using **observational techniques,** the researcher *observes behavior as it occurs*; when using **survey techniques,** the researcher relies on *reports by individuals* regarding their own behavior or attitudes. Each of these techniques has particular advantages and disadvantages, as the following discussion shows.

Observation Techniques

Data sometimes may be collected while the behavior of interest is actually taking place. Although this method has been given various labels (e.g., *participant observation, field research, direct observation,* or *ethnography*), it is always distinguished by a single key feature: the *direct observation* of behavior by the researcher. In general, this technique is used more frequently in sociology, psychology, anthropology, and education research, but it has been used successfully in much of political research as well. Students interested in local politics, in political campaigning, in political party activity, in legislative and executive behavior, in judicial decision making, and in organizational behavior have made good use of observational techniques. (See Box 4.1.)

Danny L. Jorgensen concludes that observational techniques are especially appropriate for scholarly problems when[1]

1. Little is known about the phenomenon.
2. There are important differences between the view of insiders as opposed to outsiders.
3. The phenomenon is somehow obscured from the view of outsiders.
4. The phenomenon is hidden from public view.

As an observer of events, the researcher may assume a variety of strategies along a continuum of possible roles. Raymond L. Gold has identified the following four basic roles of observation:[2]

1. *The Complete Participant.* As complete participant, the "true identity and purpose" of the researcher "are not known to those whom he observes." The researcher in this role "interacts with [subjects] as naturally as possible in whatever areas of their living interest him and are accessible to him as situations in which he can play, or learn to play, requisite day-to-day roles successfully." An example of this

might occur when a student of political party conventions actually becomes an official delegate and collects data while attending one of the county, state, or national party conventions.

2. *The Participant-as-Observer.* In this role, the researcher participates fully with the group of interest, but it is clear to all that a study is taking place. This mutual awareness, says Gold, "tends to minimize problems of role-pretending." As in the preceding example, a student of political party conventions might become an official delegate to a national convention, but in this role, it would be clear to all that the delegate/student was also engaged in scholarly research.

3. *The Observer-as-Participant.* In this role the researcher interacts with the group being studied but makes no pretense of actually being a participant. This role is used, Gold says, primarily in "studies involving one-visit interviews." An example might be a student of legislative politics who interviews state legislators, visits them in their offices, and maybe even travels with them on visits to constituents, but who makes no attempt to actually become a legislator.

4. *The Complete Observer.* At this extreme, the researcher observers some social process but is removed entirely from interacting within that process. Frequently, according to Gold, the subjects of study will not even know that a study is taking place. An example of this role would be that of the student of local politics collecting data while observing a session of a city council meeting.

Regardless of the role assumed, observational techniques have one great advantage over any other means of data collection: The researcher is observing behavior *as it actually happens.* The researcher does not have to rely on respondents' ability to remember events that occurred at some time in the past; events are recorded as they take place. Furthermore, a number of political events that are of interest to students of politics are open to the public and readily accessible. Included are meetings of city councils, county commissioners, legislative committees, school boards, advisory committees, and the like.

On the other hand, observational techniques have several limitations that lessen their utility to political research. In the first place, many of the phenomena that are of interest to political researchers (such as voting behavior, public attitudes toward political issues, elite decision making) are not *directly* observable, and often the events that political scientists are interested in studying (revolutions, wars, or coups, for example) cannot be predicted. Observational techniques, in addition, frequently require a considerable amount of skill, training, and time. Access to situations that would be of interest (such as White House decision making) may be impossible, and the data generated from such observation are often difficult to quantify. Using observational techniques, the research also runs the risk of actually affecting the behavior that is being studied (this is especially true of the complete participant and the participant-as-observer roles), and under any circumstance, the researcher may become too closely identified with the subjects to remain a detached and objective observer.

In spite of these limitations, many very productive examples of research having political or policy implications and relying partly or wholly on observational techniques are available. Although conducted several years ago, Jeffrey L. Pressman's study of the relationships between federal programs and city politics—based on his experiences as an aide to the mayor of the City of Oakland—remains a seminal study in the area of federal/city relations. Describing his research methodology, Pressman said,

> The empirical basis for the study [was] drawn to a large extent from my experiences in—and observation of—the City of Oakland. [For five years] I participated in the Oakland Project, a group of graduate students and faculty members at the University of California, Berkeley, who were engaged in a program of participant-observation in Oakland. As a member of the project, I worked in the office of the mayor [For three years]. During that time, I concentrated both my work and my observation on relations between federal and city agencies.[3]

Another classic use of observational techniques is the study by Richard F. Fenno, Jr., of the relationship between members of the U.S. House of Representatives and their constituents. Fenno describes his research method in the following terms:

> I tried to observe and inquire into anything and everything these members did. I worried about whatever they worried about. Rather than assume that I already knew what was interesting I remained prepared to find interesting questions emerging in the course of the experience. The same with data. The research method was one of soaking and poking—or just hanging around.
>
> During nearly eight years of research, I accompanied eighteen individuals in their districts: fifteen sitting representatives, two representatives-to-be, and one representative-elect. I made 36 separate visits and spent 110 working (not traveling) days in the eighteen districts.[4]

More recent uses of observational techniques in political research include David M. O'Brien's 1990 study of decision making at the Supreme Court (based in part on his experiences there as a judicial fellow and a research associate).[5] Similarly, on a smaller scale, David M. Boje effectively used observational techniques in his 1991 study of how people use stories to gain political advantage in organizational settings.[6]

The preceding studies provide excellent examples of the use of observational techniques. These studies also illustrate the strengths and weaknesses of observational research. Each of these authors committed a considerable amount of time and effort in their study. These studies are limited to the time period, the localities, and the subjects selected for investigation. In a strict sense, generalizations to other times, other periods, or other situations are risky, at best. At the same time, these studies provide a depth of insight that could not be achieved using other techniques, and each has stimulated much additional research. Two journals of interest to political scientists, which frequently publish articles relying on observational techniques, are *Administrative Science Quarterly,* and the *Journal of Contemporary Ethnography.*

Observational techniques typically are classified as being structured or unstructured. When using **unstructured observational techniques,** participants are observed in their natural setting; the researcher does not attempt to manipulate the subjects or structure the research situation. Pressman's, Fenno's, and O'Brien's studies are examples of unstructured observation.

In contrast, when using **structured observational techniques,** the researcher may actually set the agenda and assign roles. For example, a scholar of municipal politics might ask a group of students to participate in a mock city council meeting, or a student of international politics might ask a group of students to participate in a simulated session of the United Nations. In either case, the researcher determines the rules, assigns the roles, and sets the agenda. The subjects are then asked to participate in a *simulated* decision-making situation, and the researcher observes the dynamics and the outcomes of the decision-making process under a variety of circumstances. While such simulated exercises are artificial in the sense that real policy is not being made, the method still is observational, and insightful results may be obtained.

SURVEY RESEARCH

In addition to the aforementioned list of limitations of observational techniques, one more should be mentioned: time. Observational techniques can be extremely time-consuming. All of the researchers mentioned as examples spent months—even years—in the collection of information for their studies. It is not unusual for a scholar using this approach to devote at least a year to the collection of data. Students, obviously, seldom have this much time to spend just on the collection of information.

A more expedient method of data collection is through use of a survey. A *survey* can be defined as a method of collecting information directly from people by asking them to respond to questions in writing, in person, or over the phone. In any case, when using survey techniques, behavior is not directly observed. Rather, respondents are asked to report on their own beliefs, feelings, attitudes, ideas, opinions, and desires.

An important issue in the use of survey techniques relates to respondents' ability and willingness to respond accurately and honestly. If behavior is not actually observed, how is the researcher to judge the validity of response? An extensive body of literature has focused on the question of *honesty* in response. Researchers have compared responses to survey questions with objective and known information in a variety of areas (such as economic status, education attainment, health conditions, and the like). While behaviors that may be embarrassing (such as alcohol consumption or bankruptcy) and/or illegal (such as fraud and drug use) are known to be consistently underreported in survey research,[7] researchers generally conclude that for the most part, people respond honestly to survey questions.[8]

It is also the case that racial, gender, and various demographic characteristics of interviewers can occasionally affect people's responses. It has been found, for example, that responses to questions dealing with feelings or opinions about a racial group are affected by the race of the interviewer. Respondents (of all races) are less

BOX 4.1   Participant Observation

Participant observation can be very time-consuming, but it also can be a very effective means of collecting political information. Carol M. Swain spent four years collecting information on African American congressional representatives and their districts. In the following excerpts from her resulting—and award-winning—book, *Black Faces, Black Interests,* Swain reveals some of the difficulties, but also some of the payoffs, of the participant observation technique.

Participant observation involves field research on subjects in their natural habitats . . . the "soaking and poking" approach of Richard Fenno, Jr., provided the model for this study. I traveled with, observed, and talked to several representatives as they worked in their districts.

Field research enabled me to gather individual perspectives on the ways politicians represent blacks. When I arranged my trips, I first mailed a letter to each black member of Congress and requested permission to travel with him or her. Next, for those representatives who responded positively, I made appointments with the staffers responsible for coordinating district trips. If my initial travel request was denied, I made an appointment directly with the representative. Usually I was able to persuade the representative to grant me a district visit. I followed a similar process with white members of Congress who represented districts with significant aggregate minority populations. Only two black members declined to participate at all, each giving a different reason for refusing the request.

Participant observation proved crucial for understanding typical constituent-member relationships: it allowed me to question and interview representatives personally about their views, policies, and tactical approach while they were actually "at work." In this practical aspect of my research I discovered links and connections that cannot easily be seen in statistics. I asked representatives and staffers very specific questions about how they decided on office locations and staff selection, and how they allocated time for their district and for work on the Hill. I tried to get them to talk about their supporting and opposing coalitions. I asked them how they saw their roles as representatives, and I asked them to describe how they spent their time. Field questions included: How did you decide on your office location(s)? What changes have you made over time in your views, campaign style, or voting behavior? Why? Who are your strongest supporters?

Source: Carol M. Swain, *Black Faces, Black Interests* (Cambridge, MA: Harvard University Press, 1993), 227–229. This book received the Woodrow Wilson Foundation Award as the best book published during 1993 on government, politics, or international relations.

likely to express critical or negative opinions of the group represented by the interviewer.[9] Fowler and Mangione recommend that "when the topic of a survey is very directly related to some interviewer characteristic so that potentially a respondent might think that some of the response alternatives would be directly insulting or offensive or embarrassing to an interviewer, researchers may want to think seriously about controlling those [interviewer] characteristics."[10] However, even in the worst case, such characteristics have not been found to greatly affect responses, and it probably is not fruitful to spend much time worrying about the effect of interviewer characteristics (e.g., race, ethnicity, or gender) on the quality of response.

Probably of greater concern is the issue of respondents' *ability* to accurately answer survey questions. Sometimes respondents do not *understand* the question asked, sometimes they cannot *recall* the answer, sometimes they simply do not *know* the answer. In each of these instances, various techniques can be applied that will enhance the validity of factual reporting of information. The most important of these techniques are described next. Regardless, some inaccuracies inevitably will result in survey research.[11] When using survey techniques, the researcher must proceed based on two assumptions: (1) Most people respond honestly and accurately most of the time; and (2) each individual respondent is in the unique position of being able to respond to questions dealing with her or his own attitudes, behavior, and opinion.

There are basically two types of survey techniques: questionnaires (usually mailed) and interviews (usually person-to-person, or telephone). In a **questionnaire,** subjects typically are asked to record their own responses to a prepared list of written items. In an **interview,** the researcher asks the questions and records the responses. Each of these techniques is discussed further next.

Questionnaires

The questionnaire is a very important data-collection instrument for political and policy researchers. Typically, the questionnaire is delivered through the mail or, on occasion, hand delivered. Compared with the interview technique, the questionnaire is much easier from the standpoint of the researcher. Questionnaires are less costly and frequently less time-consuming. Through use of the mail service, information can be solicited from anyone almost any place in the world. Because questionnaires generally are standardized (i.e., the same exact questions are asked of everyone in exactly the same order), they ensure uniform response patterns. Because questionnaires at least provide the appearance of anonymity and may be completed in the privacy of a person's home or office, subjects may be more likely to respond honestly and accurately to questions on sensitive topics. Research has shown that people frequently will respond more accurately to "impersonal" questionnaires than to personal interviews.[12] Questionnaires also pose less of an intrusion on each respondent's time, and because they may be completed and returned at the respondent's convenience, the responses received may be more thoughtful and accurate. Questionnaires offer one additional advantage: They provide a relatively simple and affordable means of collecting information over a long period of time.

On the other hand, questionnaires do not provide the opportunity for probing or in-depth questioning, which can take place in interview situations. Also, questionnaires do not permit respondents to ask for clarifications or explanations of difficult questions. Further, the major disadvantage of questionnaires is the *unpredictability of response.* The researcher does not know who or how many will

TABLE 4.1

Techniques for Increasing the Percentage of Mailed
Questionnaire Returns

Technique:	Possible Increase of Total Percent of Returns:	Comments:
Follow-up contacts		
a. By mail	30–50%	More than one follow-up may be needed. Researcher should find out whether respondent needs another copy of the questionnaire.
b. By phone	15–30%	
Nature of respondent and cover letter	17%	Sponsor and appeal for return are very important. The most prestigious and respected person to make the appeal can most influence returns. An altruistic appeal seems to get better results than the idea that respondent may receive something of personal value.
Length	22%	If a questionnaire is short, then the shorter the better.
Type of questions	13%	Questionnaires asking for objective information receive the best rate, and questionnaires asking for subjective information receive the worst.
Type of population surveyed	Varies	Response rates vary with education, income, and geographic location of respondents. Better educated and professionals are more likely to respond.
Salience of content	30–40%	Questionnaires are more likely to be returned if judged to be salient to the respondent.
Sensitivity of areas covered	Varies	Substantial drop in response if questions probe areas regarded by respondent as private and/or a threat.
Inducements	Varies	Monetary incentive probably increases return rate somewhat.
Method of return	Not known	A regular stamped envelope produces better results than a business reply envelope.
Time of arrival	Not known	If a questionnaire is sent to the home, it should arrive near the end of the week.
Format	Not known	Aesthetically pleasing cover, interesting title, attractive page format, easily readable size and style of type contribute to return rate.

SOURCE: Adapted from Delbert C. Miller, *Handbook of Research Design and Social Measurement,* 5th ed. (Newbury Park, CA: Sage, 1991), 144–155.

actually return the questionnaire. As a result, the sample may be biased: those who choose to respond to the questionnaire may differ in some significant way from those who do not answer. Because achieving a representative sample is really the important issue, the researcher must make every reasonable effort to ensure a high rate of return. Numerous studies of the factors associated with the return rate of mailed questionnaires have been conducted.[13] Table 4.1 summarizes the results of many of these.

The following discussion focuses on the general issues of questionnaire design and construction, and it explores many of the important techniques for encouraging respondents to complete and return a questionnaire.

Questionnaire Design and Construction

The Envelope.   Because the envelope in which the questionnaire arrives is the respondent's first introduction to you and your study, care should be taken to make this first impression a positive one. The envelope should be hand-addressed or typed personally for each respondent. Avoid using address labels (which give the impression of a mass-produced effort), and make every effort to address envelopes to individuals (rather than "occupant" or "Mayor"). The researcher should use first-class (even commemorative) postage stamps (rather than taking advantage of second-class rates). It is important that the respondent begin with a positive impression. If the envelope is not opened, the questionnaire will not be completed and returned. Although you may be sending out hundreds of questionnaires, each recipient should feel personally identified with, and important to, the study.

The Cover Letter.   The questionnaire will be accompanied with a cover letter that explains who you are, what the study is about, why and how each respondent was selected, why it is important for the respondent to complete and return the survey, and who is sponsoring the research. In general, the more prestigious and respected the person to appeal to the respondent, the higher the rate of return. As a student, for example, you might profit from having your professor, or department chair, or even the college dean sign the cover letter and make the appeal.

The cover letter should emphasize the social usefulness of the study and the importance of each individual respondent to the success of the study. The cover letter should also deal with the issues of confidentiality and anonymity. Respondents should be assured of the confidential nature of the study—you will not identify names with responses. If the survey is truly anonymous (i.e., the researcher is not able to identify people's names with their responses), this anonymity should be mentioned as well.

The Instructions.   Instructions for completing the survey will appear either separately or as part of the cover letter. In either case, the instructions should be as clear and as concise as possible. Remember, respondents to mailed questionnaires will not be able to ask questions about items that are confusing or unclear.

The Return Envelope.   It is assumed, of course, that questionnaires will be accompanied with a self-addressed, prepaid return envelope. It is not reasonable to ask the respondent to complete the survey, to take the time to address the return envelope, and to purchase postage for it.

The Questions and the Questionnaire.   Studies differ as to their findings regarding whether questionnaire length is related to response rate,[14] but it is evident that you should thoughtfully decide which questions are most important to your study, and you should eliminate extraneous questions. Long and tedious questionnaires do not contribute to high response rates. It is advisable to limit mailed questionnaires to about six pages or less.

It is also advisable to begin your questionnaire with easy questions, which the respondent will enjoy answering. Questions should be short; it is normally suggested that questions be presented in twenty words or less. Very personal questions (such as age, marital status, and income) should be left for the end. You should arrange your questions by topic so that they make sense to the respondent.

The questions must be presented clearly and simply. (See Box 4.2.) Care must be taken to avoid *double-barreled questions:* those that really ask about two issues in a single question. For example, the question "Do you support spending more money for public education and raising the state's income tax in order to accomplish this?" is really two questions. It would be preferable to determine first whether the respondent supports spending more for public education, then to determine what mode of taxation or revenue generation would be preferred.

One of the most effective techniques for judging question clarity and appropriateness is to *pretest* the questionnaire prior to its administration. It is *always* advisable to select a group of respondents roughly representative of those you wish to survey and to have them complete the questionnaire, calling to your attention any items that seem ambiguous, difficult, or confusing. This process almost always yields a better survey and, as a consequence, better data and better results.

Researchers generally agree that questions should be framed so as to offer a "no opinion" or "don't know" option. This filters for respondents who truly have no opinion on a particular issue. Additionally, offering several response alternatives is a good way to gauge both *direction* and *intensity* of opinion. As example, the following response set is frequently used in survey research:

Agree strongly   _____

Agree somewhat   _____

Uncertain   _____

Disagree somewhat   _____

Disagree strongly   _____

Researchers disagree as to whether the middle answer ("uncertain" in the preceding listing) should be included in the wording of responses. Some argue that such noncommittal answers are valid alternatives, which should be provided. Others argue that high proportions of the public will choose such a response when offered, even though they otherwise *would not* volunteer this response. Perhaps the

BOX 4.2   Even Experts Make Mistakes

Questionnaire construction remains part art and part science; even experts can make mistakes. An example occurred when the Roper polling organization was commissioned by the American Jewish Committee in 1992 and 1994 to assess the American public's attitudes toward the Nazi extermination of the Jews during World War II. One question on the surveys was designed *to determine* the extent to which Americans believe that the Holocaust happened. Because the question was poorly worded (in part because it contained a double negative) in the 1992 survey, it appeared that about 1 in 5 Americans doubted that the Holocaust happened at all! However, when this question was revised in 1994, results showed that only about 1 percent of Americans believe it possible that the Holocaust never happened.

   Both 1992 and 1994 versions of this question, and results of the national polls are shown in the accompanying figure.

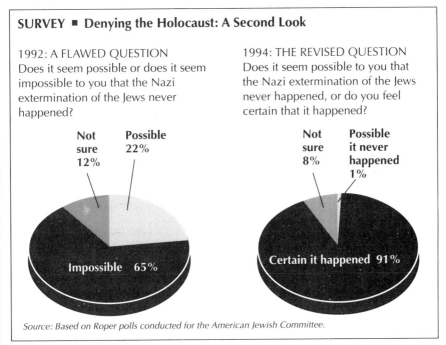

SURVEY ▪ Denying the Holocaust: A Second Look

1992: A FLAWED QUESTION
Does it seem possible or does it seem impossible to you that the Nazi extermination of the Jews never happened?

Not sure 12%   Possible 22%
Impossible 65%

1994: THE REVISED QUESTION
Does it seem possible to you that the Nazi extermination of the Jews never happened, or do you feel certain that it happened?

Not sure 8%   Possible it never happened 1%
Certain it happened 91%

Source: Based on Roper polls conducted for the American Jewish Committee.

SOURCE: Michael R. Kagay, "Poll on Doubt of Holocaust Is Corrected," *New York Times,* July 8, 1994.

best resolution is to first offer the question without a middle, noncommittal, response category, but then to follow this question with an intensity question.[15] As an example, the Inter-University Consortium for Political and Social Research (referenced to hereafter as ICPSR) in its 1994 American National Election Study survey

Some people have proposed that a woman on welfare who has another child not be given an increase in her welfare check. Do you favor or oppose this change in welfare policy?

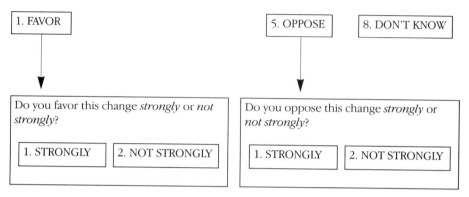

FIGURE 4.1

Illustration of Question about Welfare Reform

SOURCE: 1994 American National Election Study.

asked a question about attitudes toward welfare reform in the manner shown in Figure 4.1.

A final issue arising in questionnaire design relates to whether to use close-ended or open-ended questions. **Close-ended questions** (also called "fixed-alternative" or "forced-choice" questions) are those that state the question and provide the array of possible responses. The respondent simply has to place a check or some other mark in the appropriate space. Minimum response effort is required. As an example, the National Opinion Research Center (NORC), in its 1994 General Social Survey (GSS) study, included the following question:[16]

> Thinking about all the different kinds of governments in the world today, which of these statements comes closest to how you feel about Communism as a form of government?
>
> 1. It's the worst kind of all   _____
> 2. It's bad, but no worse than some others   _____
> 3. It's alright for some countries   _____
> 4. It's a good form of government   _____
> 5. Don't know   _____

Open-ended questions are those that ask the question but allow space for the respondent to record an answer in his or her *own words*. As an example, the GSS regularly asks the following question and provides about a third of a page for written response: "What are the most important problems that you and members of your household have had during the last 12 months?"

Open-ended questions do not force a preestablished response set and allow the respondent to answer as he or she really feels. Often, the responses generated have not been anticipated by the researcher. Thus, open-ended questions are especially useful in exploratory studies, which are to precede a larger study. Open-ended questions have been shown to generate more accurate responses when measuring sensitive or disapproved behavior (such as sexual or drinking activities).[17]

Closed-ended questions, on the other hand, are easier to code and analyze. From the perspective of the mailed questionnaire, they are also faster and easier to answer. The respondent need only place a mark in the appropriate space. In general, a carefully designed closed-ended survey is preferable. In developing closed-ended questions, it is helpful to conduct a few preliminary interviews with people representative of those to be included in the study. Another useful tactic, if space permits, is to present closed-ended questions but to follow each with an open-ended question such as, "Why do you feel that way?" or "Would you like to expand on your answer?" Adequate space would be provided for the respondent to comment. In this manner, the advantages of the closed-ended questionnaire are preserved, and the researcher has the benefit of longer answers from those finding the need and having the time to so respond.

Follow-Up Surveys.   Studies consistently show that follow-up mailings pay off in increased return rate for mailed questionnaires. A typical sequence is to send a postcard reminder about a week after having first mailed out the survey. After about three weeks, the first follow-up questionnaire is mailed to all nonrespondents, and—if necessary—a second follow-up questionnaire is mailed about three weeks after that.[18] According to Delbert C. Miller, the first follow-up yields an average response rate increase of about 20 percent. The second and, if necessary, third yield increases of about 12 percent and 10 percent, respectively.[19]

While these additional efforts add to the cost and time of conducting mailed surveys, studies have shown that the efforts pay off in terms of generating both higher numbers of respondents and, of far greater importance, a more representative sample. Bernick and Pratto have recently verified important differences to exist "between early and late respondents [to mailed surveys]." Those scholars who fail to use extra mailings, they say, "do so at the risk of losing valuable insight into how a broader segment of the population thinks."[20]

Assessing Response Bias

Careful attention to the foregoing techniques should result in questionnaires yielding useful and accurate results, and such attention should also contribute to achieving the highest possible rate of return. Although no strict guidelines exist, you should strive to achieve at least a 50 percent rate of return.[21]

Despite your best efforts, no matter how careful you are in designing and mailing the survey, it is certain that not *everyone* will respond, and it is always possible that those who do return the questionnaire may not accurately represent the population of interest. Thus, the sample may be biased, and this potential for bias is really the critical issue in questionnaire research. To the extent that any discrepancy exists between the characteristics, attitudes, and behaviors of those who return the questionnaire and the universe of possible respondents, the validity of the entire study is jeopardized.

Consequently, you should always make every effort to determine and report whatever biases in the sample may be known or suspected. Very often in research using questionnaires, some information about the population will be known. University officials will have some information pertaining to the characteristics of the entire student body (hometown, academic major, grade point average, etc.); city, county, and statewide demographic data will be available from census reports; various organizations, such as Congressional Quarterly, compile data on all Senate and House members (such as age, party affiliation, size of home district); the Republican and Democratic National Committees usually maintain some information pertaining to delegates attending the national conventions (age, sex, and race); and so on.

The point being made is that by matching known characteristics of the population to that of the sample returning the questionnaires, some indication of sample bias can be achieved. If severe bias exists—and especially if there is reason to believe this may affect responses—procedures are available for attempting to compensate for this bias. These processes, known as "weighting," are designed to adjust for noncoverage and nonresponses within the sample. In weighting, responses by some individuals are statistically given more or less weight than responses by others. As an example, if—in a particular survey—young people responded in much smaller proportions than older people, weights could be applied to make the sample conform to known age distributions of the population. In practice, the application of weights can be very complicated and should be used only with considerable caution. The best strategy, clearly, is to do everything possible to minimize nonresponse in the first place.[22]

Assessing the Cost of the Mailed Questionnaire

One of the major advantages of the mailed questionnaire is its low cost. Mailed surveys are the least costly means of collecting information, but the student should be warned that much more is involved than just the cost of the postage stamp. When considering costs of mailed questionnaires, be sure to include the expenses involved in purchasing supplies (envelopes, paper, stationery, etc.), printing, drawing the sample, coding and computer entry of data, providing postage for the return envelope, and so on. Also, remember that at least one follow-up (and, more likely, two or three) will be required to generate a sufficient response rate. Considering everything, you should count on the costs of a mailed questionnaire ranging from 2 to 5 dollars per respondent.[23]

The Interview

An alternative to the questionnaire is the interview survey technique. Using interview procedures—either *face-to-face* or by *telephone*—the researcher personally asks questions of the respondents and personally records the answers.

The advantages and disadvantages of the interview technique are, in many respects, the opposite of those pertaining to the mailed questionnaire. The interview process is usually more time-consuming and generally costs more money when paid interviewers are required. Interviews allow for a greater chance of *interviewer bias:* unintended effects of the interviewer on responses. Also, interviews largely remove the anonymity obtainable through mailed questionnaires.

One great advantage of the interview is that it almost always results in a higher response rate. Typical is the study of White House officials, congressional staff personnel, and Washington journalists by Mark Peterson, in which, 75 percent of those contacted agreed to complete the interview process. [24] People are often flattered to find that someone is actually interested in their opinions, experiences, and attitudes. Even very busy people will generally find the time to talk with the researcher. Of course, you have to be willing to conduct the interview *at the convenience of the subject.* This means that researchers who use interview techniques must schedule the data-collection stage during a period when their time is relatively unencumbered. For those conducting telephone surveys, it means much of the interviewing will take place after working hours and on the weekends. Regardless, interviews will almost always yield a sample more representative of the population and will therefore greatly reduce the aforementioned problems of nonresponse.

Interviews have many other advantages as well. The interview situation is more flexible, in that difficult or confusing questions can be explained thoroughly before responses are solicited. Interviews allow for a depth of exploration impossible with quick questionnaires. Interviews allow the respondents to answer in their own words—responses are not forced into some preconceived pattern. Additionally, the researcher can be sure that the person whom the researcher seeks to interview is actually responding (questionnaires addressed to mayors or other officials can easily be shuffled off to an assistant for completion).

Sometimes, the researcher will follow an **unstructured interview format.** That is, the researcher may be interested in obtaining general background information on a particular topic and will not have specific and identical questions to ask of each respondent. Often, an unstructured format is used in preparation for the development of a more structured interview schedule or in developing a questionnaire.

Sometimes, the researcher will follow a **structured interview routine.** That is, the same, or approximately the same, questions will be asked of each respondent, usually in the same order. In a structured interview the interviewer relies on an instrument called the "interview schedule" to guide the interview. The interview schedule will list the questions to be asked and the order in which they are to be pursued. As in developing the questionnaire, a considerable amount of thought—including ample opportunity for pretesting—should be given to devising the interview schedule.

The interview schedule may be highly structured. An example of one such interview is that used by the ICPSR in its American national election studies. Figure 4.2 shows the item used by the ICPSR national election studies to determine employment status.

Interviews of this nature are highly directed. Interviewers are extensively trained, and no deviations from the interview schedule are permitted. Precise instructions are provided to carry the interviewer from item to item.

When interviewing specialized segments of the population, such as elite public

We'd like to know if *you* are working now, temporarily laid off, or are you unemployed, retired, permanently disabled, (a homemaker), (a student), or what? (MARK ALL THAT APPLY)

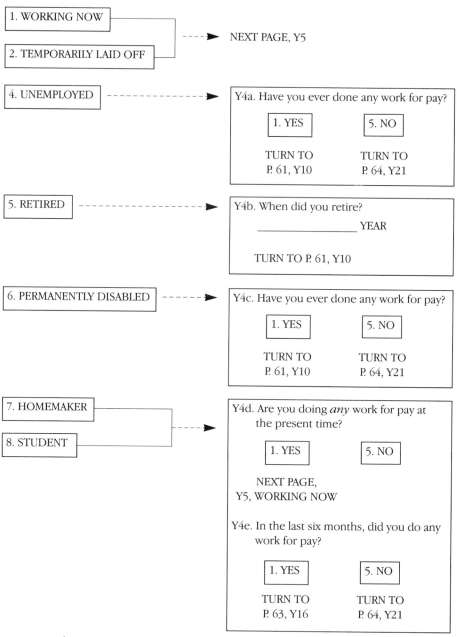

FIGURE 4.2

Measure of Employment Status as Used in the ICPSR American National Election Study

NOTE: Y's refer to particular questions.

SOURCE: ICPSR, The University of Michigan.

or private officials or executives, the interview procedure need not be as rigid as that used by national polling organizations, such as the SRC. In the process of conducting interviews, the researcher may find that some questions, which were previously deemed essential, are not now important and that other questions, which were not previously even considered, are now very important. One advantage of the interview technique, as compared with the mailed questionnaire, is that the interview permits the researcher to alter the set of questions in order to maximize its utility as a data-collection instrument.

Conducting Personal Interviews.   One of the earliest social scientists to systematically analyze the strengths and weaknesses of the personal, face-to-face, interview as a data-collection device was Lewis Dexter.[25] His observations for how best to prepare for and conduct personal interviews remain valid today. Dexter recommended that when conducting personal interviews, researchers should[26]

1. Always call or write for an appointment in advance of the interview. Don't just drop in.
2. Arrange the meeting at a time and place convenient for the interviewee. If possible, meet the respondent at his or her office.
3. Avoid interview situations of obvious distraction.
4. Explain at the beginning of each interview who you are, who sponsors the research, and what the project is about.
5. Begin the interview with more vague and general questions. More specific questions should be asked later.
6. Write up the notes on the interview as soon after it is completed as possible. When interviewing several individuals it is easy to confuse responses unless notes are prepared immediately.

Conducting Telephone Interviews.   Telephone interviewing has increased dramatically in recent years, especially because almost all Americans own phones and because the costs associated with other data-collection techniques have risen so dramatically. Further, response rates of telephone interviewing are competitive with those associated with personal interviews, especially in some larger urban areas where people are fearful of meeting and personally talking with strangers. Compared with other data-collection techniques, telephone interviewing is *fast.* Given adequate personnel and resources, it is possible to conduct 400 to 500 interviews in just a few days. Major polling organizations are set up so that they can conduct national surveys in just one or two days, and sometimes overnight. This speed of data collection makes telephone interviewing especially attractive to politicians and policy analysts who frequently want to immediately check the public pulse on some political or policy issue. Additionally, research has shown that in many instances, information collected from telephone interviews is as valid as information collected from face-to-face interviews or by using other techniques.[27]

Successful telephone interviewing depends heavily on adequate *training* of interviewers. The telephone interviewer must immediately establish credibility and rapport with the respondent. The interviewer must convince the respondent of the legitimacy and value of the study, must stimulate respondents to complete the interview process, and must be able to follow what sometimes are very complex instructions.

Through a process known as random-digit dialing, all working telephone exchanges in a particular area may be identified, and within these exchanges, a set of four-digit numbers can be randomly generated to produce a set of phone numbers for calling. Several private firms will now provide, for a relatively modest fee, randomly generated phone numbers guaranteed to connect with working residential phones for virtually any geographic area. These firms can provide phone numbers for targeted samples—such as age, income, or ethnic groups—as well

A problem with telephone interviewing is the increasingly large number of residents who have unlisted numbers (thereby reducing the utility of the published phone book as a source of phone numbers) and the escalating number of households using answering machines to screen calls. It is estimated that today roughly a fourth of all residences have unlisted numbers and that approximately 32 million households (one third) have telephone-answering machines.[28] Even more sophisticated advances in telephone service—such as the expanded use of videophones and the ability to identify the source of incoming calls—are rapidly becoming available for public consumption. It is now unclear how these technological advances will affect the quality of representative samples used in telephone interviewing, as well as how interview techniques should adapt to these changes.[29]

Choosing among Mailed Questionnaires, Face-to-Face Interviews, or Telephone Surveys

As the foregoing discussion has shown, each of the major data-collection techniques has particular advantages and disadvantages. The choice among these techniques involves the consideration of many factors, such as cost, speed, accuracy, ease of securing information, and confidentiality. The chart shown in Table 4.2 summarizes many of the important factors to consider when choosing among the mailed questionnaire, the face-to-face interview, or the telephone survey.

SAMPLE SELECTION

Political researchers very often deal with situations in which all units in a population of interest can be included in the study. If the focus of analysis is large American cities, or the fifty American states, or if the student is interested in congressional or United Nations voting behavior, or the American presidency, it typically will be feasible and desirable to collect information about all units (i.e., all cities, all states, all legislators, all presidents, and so forth). Gathering information on all elements of a population is known as a **census.**

On the other hand, students of politics are also often interested in situations in which a complete enumeration of the population is impossible, or nearly so. This is

TABLE 4.2

Choosing among the Mailed Questionnaire, Face-to-Face Interview, or Telephone Survey

Factors to Be Considered	Mailed Survey	Face-to-Face Interview	Telephone Survey
Cost	1	3	2
Time	3	2	1
Response rate	3	1	2
Accuracy of date collected	2	1	3
Completeness of data collected	3	1	2
Ease of date collection	1	3	2
Sample coverage (avoidance of selective nonresponse)	3	1	2
Reliability and validity	2	1	3
Sampling of special subpopulations	3	2	1
Confidentiality	1	3	2
Ability to ask sensitive questions	3	1	2
Ability to ask complex questions	3	1	2

Key: 1 = most favorable rating
        2 = intermediate rating
        3 = least favorable rating

SOURCE: Adapted from Delbert C. Miller, *Handbook of Research Design and Social Measurement,* 5th ed. (Newbury Park, CA: Sage, 1991), 168; and James H. Frey, *Survey Research by Telephone* (Newbury Park, CA: Sage Publications, 1989), 76.

especially true in the area of voting behavior (where the population may be the entire electorate), but it is also true whenever the population size is large and the information is difficult to collect. When it is not feasible to collect information on every unit, the researcher will have to be satisfied with studying a segment somewhat smaller than the total. This segment is known as a **sample.** Sampling is obviously a more economical way to collect data because gathering information from only a part of the population is less costly than gathering information from the whole. Sampling has other advantages, as well. Information can be gathered more rapidly, and results can be reported sooner. Because resources are concentrated on a part of the population, the quality of information gathered may be superior, and the results may be more accurate.[30]

The sample is useful to the political researcher to the extent that the sample facilitates the collection of information and is representative of the entire population. Two major issues must be addressed when deciding to select a sample: the *size* of the sample and the *method* by which the sample subjects will be selected. Although sampling theory is much too complex to be thoroughly examined here,[31] enough guidance can be provided to enable the researcher to deal confidently with each of these issues.

Method of Sample Selection

Many techniques for selecting a sample are available.[32] The procedure chosen will vary from situation to situation. For purposes of comparison with the more rigorous sampling techniques, consider the **convenient sampling technique,** for which the major criterion for sample selection is researcher convenience. You might pass out a survey to neighbors, friends, relatives, or classmates. You might stand in front of the student cafeteria and solicit opinions from those who pass. You might go to a shopping center on a Tuesday afternoon and interview anyone who is willing to take the time to respond. In all these situations, the selection process is more or less haphazard— people are included just because they are available and willing to cooperate. Two other methods are slightly more rigorous than the convenient sampling technique: (1) **judgment sampling,** in which the researcher attempts to evaluate and select those subjects judged to be representative of the population; and (2) **quota sampling,** in which subjects are selected in proportion to their distribution in the whole population (12 percent African American, 51 percent women, and so forth).

Convenient sampling, judgment sampling, and quota sampling are all **nonprobability sampling methods,** which can easily result in the selection of a sample that fails to represent the total population. The opinions of your friends, your relatives, or persons who shop on Tuesday afternoons may not accurately reflect the opinions of the broader community.

Probability sampling techniques have been developed in order to minimize the risks of drawing an unrepresentative sample. The risks of biased sampling can never be eliminated, but probability sampling techniques at least permit the researcher to state the probability of selecting a representative sample. The probability sample is drawn so that each element of the population has a known, nonzero, and typically equal chance of being selected.

One type of probability sample is the **simple random sample,** in which some method is used for selecting each subject at random. For example, a researcher might place the names of all 5,000 students of a college in a single pile, and from this pile, the researcher might draw a sample of 500. Instead, the researcher might assign sequential numbers to each of the 5,000 students and then select the sample of 500 by matching those numbers to 500 numbers selected from a table of random numbers. Yet another alternative is to rely on a computer programmed to generate a list of 500 random numbers. In any case, the sample is drawn so that the subjects are selected by chance, thereby avoiding selection biases and also permitting certain conclusions supported by statistical theory.

A variation on simple random sampling is known as **systematic sampling,** in which the sample is drawn so that, after a random start, every kth person is selected (where k equals some number). To use the preceding example, selecting 500 students from a population of 5,000 would yield a sample of 1 in ten (500/5,000). A systematic sample would be drawn by taking a random number between 1 and 10 to determine the first student to be selected, and taking every 10th student thereafter. If the random number were 6, then the students selected for the sample would be the sixth, sixteenth, twenty-sixth, and so on. This is a very convenient method of sample selection, as long as there is no reason to suspect that a bias might result from the selection of every tenth (or every *k*th) student.

Beginning researchers, especially, would more than likely use one of the aforementioned methods of sampling. In contrast, more sophisticated methods of probability sampling are used by professional polling organizations and those engaged in more elaborate research. These techniques are designed to produce more accurate samples, to ensure more adequate representation in the sample of various subgroups, or simply to reduce the costs and effort in large-scale sampling efforts.

Stratified sampling techniques break the population into important subtypes and then sample from each. In the preceding example, the researcher might first divide all 5,000 students into those coming from central cities, those coming from suburbs, and those coming from rural areas (assuming that this information were available). Samples could then be drawn from each of these subtypes, with the result being that the sampling error on this variable (location of hometown) would be reduced almost to zero—the sample distribution on this variable would perfectly (or almost perfectly) match that of the population. The student body could be further stratified to reduce sampling variation on other variables as well.

Disproportionate sampling techniques are used when the researcher wishes to ensure adequate representation of a subgroup. The researcher may know, for example, that out of the population of 5,000 students, only 250 are from rural areas. A 10 percent sample of the 5,000 would yield only about 25 students from rural areas. If location of hometown is an important focus of the study, this number would clearly include too few rural students for meaningful analysis. Using disproportionate sampling techniques, the researcher would intentionally oversample from the group of rural students. Perhaps 100 students could be drawn from this rural group, and the remaining 400 could be drawn from the rest of the student body. Comparisons could then be made between groups, and statistical weights could be applied to the nonrural sample to allow appropriate generalizations to the entire student body.

Cluster sampling techniques (either single stage or multistage) are designed to reduce the cost of large-scale sampling operations, by allowing the researcher to sample by clusters before selecting individuals. For example, a student of community voting behavior might randomly select a group of neighborhoods in a particular city and then randomly select interviews from only those neighborhoods. Because the student's interviews would be clustered in particular neighborhoods (rather than randomly spread throughout the city), time and effort should be reduced.

Multistage cluster sampling further extends this logic. A student of national voting behavior might randomly select a cluster of communities, and from these randomly select a cluster of neighborhoods, and from these randomly select a cluster of blocks. In addition to saving time and effort, cluster sampling also relieves the researcher of having to obtain a complete listing of the population. All that is needed is a list of the elements to be included in the clusters (communities, blocks, etc.).[33]

Most students will probably never use these more sophisticated methods of sampling during their college careers. The techniques can be quite costly and time-consuming and are designed to achieve a degree of precision typically not required or expected in undergraduate or even graduate research. Nonetheless, the student could profitably compare his or her sampling method with the probability sampling techniques, and every effort should be made to *approximate* the more sophisticated procedures. It should always be remembered that the more haphazard the sampling technique, the greater is the risk of drawing an unrepresentative sample. If generalizations to the population cannot be made without a degree of confidence, a question arises as to whether the research should be conducted in the first place.

SAMPLE SIZE

One of the questions most frequently asked in survey research is how large a sample is required to carry out the study. The answer depends on several factors. One is the *variance* (degree of dispersion in the values being measured) in the population, another is the amount of error in the sample judged to be tolerable, and a third is the degree of confidence the researcher wishes to have in generalizing from the sample to the populations.

Another factor that, on the surface at least, appears to be important is the size of the population surveyed. A sample of 20 students might reasonably be assumed to adequately represent a class of 40, but a much larger sample would be needed to adequately represent an entire student body of, say, 5,000 students. However, the relationship between population size and sample size is deceiving. After a certain point, increasing the sample size has a relatively small impact on the accuracy of the sample selected. Even for very large populations, a relatively high degree of accuracy can be achieved with a very small sample. The slight increase in accuracy that might result from doubling or tripling the sample size often is simply not worth the cost. Even national polling organizations with resources far outstripping most individual researchers typically draw samples of no greater than 1,200 to 1,500 individuals. Still, up to a certain point, increasing the sample size reduces the probability of selecting an unrepresentative sample.

A more important consideration is variability of opinion existing in the population. The greater the variance in the population, the greater the size of sample needed. To take an extreme example, if—in a particular election—*every* voter favored one candidate over the others, and *all* voters intended to vote according to their preference, a sample of only 1 would be required to accurately predict the outcome of the election. Similarly, the sample size needed to accurately predict the outcome of an election is less in a situation in which one candidate enjoys a ratio of 80 percent to 20 percent support over the opposition than in an election in which one candidate leads the other by a support ratio of only 51 percent to 49 percent.

Thus, population variance is an important factor in determining sample size. In practice, however, it is very difficult to know how much variance in the population actually exists. After all, if we knew the actual support ratios existing in the population for various candidates, it would be unnecessary to conduct a survey in the first place. Sometimes, educated guesses can be made about variance in the population. Informed judgment about the population may be sought. Results of surveys previously conducted on similar topics can be helpful, as can results of surveys conducted by different researchers. Any knowledge about the population variability can help in drawing a smaller and more efficient sample. However, in absence of such knowledge—and as a practical matter—it frequently is prudent to assume *maximum* variability and to select a sample size needed to accurately represent a population of evenly divided responses.

Other important factors to be considered in determining the size of a needed sample are (1) the extent of accuracy desired in predicting from the sample to the population and (2) the extent of confidence that can be placed in this prediction. Of course, all researchers want to be very confident that the sample values closely approximate the population values. However, greater accuracy and greater confidence require increasing the sample size, resulting in additional time and money. Based on available resources, the researcher may be willing to accept a sample size that 95 times out of 100 will be expected to vary 5 percent or less from the population rather than a sample that would be expected 99 out of 100 times to be accurate within 1 percent of the population. Again available resources is a key criterion in reaching these decisions.

Given these factors, the calculation of the required sample size is relatively straightforward. First, the formula for estimating proportional sample error at the 95 percent confidence level is presented:

$$SE = \pm 1.96 \sqrt{\frac{p(1-p)}{n}}$$

Several comments about this formula are in order. First, "SE" represents the degree of expected proportionate sample error. (*Note.* A proportion refers to the percentage of a sample that has a certain characteristic or that gives a certain response; proportion is discussed in greater detail in a later chapter.) This is the extent to which proportionate sample values would be expected to deviate from population values. The 1.96 value represents a Z score, which, when used in conjunction with the concept of the normal curve (both Z scores and the normal curve are described in a later chapter), represents a confidence level of 95 percent. This means that the researcher can be confident that 95 out of 100 samples drawn would not exceed the error range (i.e., SE). The p in the formula represents the estimated population variance. Because, as discussed previously, actual population variance is almost never known, maximum variance is assumed, and the value is recorded as 0.5. The n represents the sample size. So, for a sample of 600 drawn from an infinitely large population, the extent of error expected at the 95 percent confidence level would be calculated as follows:

$$SE = \pm 1.96 \sqrt{\frac{0.5(1-0.5)}{600}}$$

$$= \pm 0.04$$

It would be expected, in other words, that for every 95 out of 100 samples drawn, sample values would deviate from population values by no more than $\pm$ 4 percent.

Because we typically are more interested in estimating the sample size desired, the formula can be arranged as follows:

$$n = \left(\frac{1.96}{SE}\right)^2 \left[p(1-p)\right]$$

where n = sample size needed
         p = assumed population variance
         SE = tolerable error

Assuming an error tolerance of 5 percent at the 95 percent confidence level, the size of the sample needed is as follows:

$$n = \left(\frac{1.96}{.05}\right)^2 \left[.5(1-.5)\right]$$

$$= 384.16$$
$$= 385$$

Reader Note: In calculating sample size, it is customary to round all values up to the next larger integer to avoid fractional cases. Also, note that the preceding discussion assumes simple random sampling. Errors that might result from nonresponse or reporting errors are not reflected in this discussion, nor are errors that might occur as a result of sample design, poor questions, and the influence of interviewers, data entry, and other nonsampling sources of error.

For very large populations, Table 4.3 summarizes the various sample sizes required for varying degrees of error tolerance and confidence levels (assuming simple random sampling). Table 4.3 provides a good idea of the sample size needed for differing error and confidence ranges. Two additional points should be made. First, it is always a good idea to *oversample*. A researcher content with a 5 percent error tolerance at the 95 percent confidence level might be well advised to select a sample of 450 or so (rather than 385). The inclusion of additional cases, if selected without bias, increases the probable accuracy of the sample. More important, it is likely that for various reasons, information will not be collected from *every* element of the original sample. Some people will refuse to respond, some will not be at home, some will have moved away, and so forth. Oversampling by 10 or 15 percent adds a degree of protection.

TABLE 4.3
Sample-Size Requirements for Varying Degrees
of Error Tolerance and Confidence Levels

Error Tolerance	Confidence Levels	
(percent)	95 Percent	99 Percent
1	9,604	16,587
2	2,401	4,147
3	1,068	1,843
4	601	1,037
5	385	664
6	267	461
7	196	339
8	150	260
9	119	205
10	96	166

SOURCE: Adapted and extended from Charles H. Backstrom and Gerald D. Hursh, *Survey Research* (Evanston, Il: Northwestern University Press, 1963), 33.

Second, it should be noted that these sample sizes are appropriate only for generalizing from the entire sample. If the research focus shifts to *subgroups* in the sample, the error and confidence ranges associated with the total sample no longer apply. In selecting a sample size, care must be taken to ensure adequate numerical inclusion of the important subgroups to be analyzed.

SUMMARY

With the exception of topic selection, no phase of research is more important than is data collection. The quality of the data collected will have considerable bearing on the success of the entire project. Considerable care must be taken to assemble data of the highest possible quality.

It is also true that collection of data is one of the very exciting phases of social science research. It is out in the field that students really begin to gain a feeling for and an understanding of politics and political behavior. Collecting your own data allows for maximum creativity in research design and topic selection—your interests and imagination are not confined by the limitations of someone else's data.

In collecting your own data, remember that no analytic technique can compensate for poorly collected and assembled data. Considerable thought must go into the data-collection stage, and every reasonable precaution must be taken to collect data of the highest quality. Nothing is so critical as data collection for the achievement of an effort that is both satisfying to the researcher and of value to the broader academic, and policy-making, community.

KEY TERMS

observational techniques

survey techniques

unstructured observational techniques

structured observational techniques

questionnaire

interview

close-ended questions

open-ended questions

follow-up surveys

unstructured interview format

response bias

structured interview routine

census

sample

convenient sampling technique

judgment sampling

quota sampling

nonprobability sampling methods

probability sampling techniques

simple random sample

systematic sampling

stratified sampling techniques

disproportionate sampling techniques

cluster sampling techniques

EXERCISES

1. Observation techniques of data collection
   a. Identify and discuss three research situations in which observational techniques for collecting data might appropriately be employed.
   b. In each situation, describe difficulties that might arise in collecting information, and tell how these might be handled.
   c. Discuss the various roles that participant observers may assume, and identify which would be used in the situations you identify.
2. Observational techniques in political science research
   a. Review three political science and/or policy works (books or articles) using observational techniques as the sole or primary source of data collection.
   b. What data-collection difficulties did the authors of these studies encounter?
   c. How were these problems resolved?
3. Questionnaires used in survey research
   a. For a research topic of interest to you, develop a questionnaire that could be administered to a relevant sample of individuals. Include in your questionnaire at least three background questions (such as age, education, gender, etc.), three opinion questions (e.g., "What do you think about health care reform?"), and three knowledge items (e.g., "Name one senator from your state").
   b. Which of these items are best presented as open-ended, and which are best presented as closed-ended questions: Why is this so?
   c. Administer this questionnaire to at least 10 respondents, and ask them to evaluate the format of the survey and its ease of completion.
   d. On the basis of the responses you obtain, how would you alter your survey questions? Why?
4. Implementation options in survey research: Assume that the survey developed in Item 3 is to be administered to a sample of approximately 400 residents of your community.

a. Would you recommend using mailed survey or telephone interviewing to administer this survey?

b. What would be the advantages and disadvantages of each?

c. If you were to administer this questionnaire as a mailed survey, what techniques might be employed to ensure as high a response rate as possible?

d. What techniques might be used to assess the extent of response biases that might exist in the aforementioned mailed survey?

5. Interview techniques used in survey research

a. Develop and discuss a research situation in which the interview might be the most appropriate means of data collection.

b. Why is the interview the most appropriate mode of data collection in this situation?

c. What precautions might you take to maximize the benefits of the interview? What situations would you try to avoid?

6. Selecting a representative sample

a. Assume that your class has elected to conduct a survey of residents of your community concerning their attitudes toward some important local issue and that you have been assigned the task of selecting the sample. Discuss some of the issues that must be considered in drawing the sample, and recommend a method for the class to pursue. What factors are involved in your recommendation?

b. What should you report to the class concerning inferences about the entire community that can be drawn from the sample you will select?

c. Why is this so?

NOTES

1. Danny L. Jorgensen, *Participant Observation: A Methodology for Human Studies* (Newbury Park, CA: Sage Publications, 1989), 12.

2. Raymond L. Gold, "Roles in Sociological Field Observations," in *Issues in Participant Observation* eds. George J. McCall and J. L. Simmons (Menlo Park, CA: Addison-Wesley Publishing, 1969), 30–39.

3. Jeffrey L. Pressman, *Federal Programs and City Politics* (Berkeley, CA: University of California Press, 1975), 19–21.

4. Richard F. Fenno, Jr., *Home Style: House Members in Their Districts* (Boston: Little, Brown and Company, 1978), xiv.

5. David M. O'Brien, Storm Center: The Supreme Court in American Politics, 2nd ed. (New York; W. W. Norton, 1990).

6. David M. Boje, "The Storytelling Organization: A Study of Story Performance in an Office-Supply Firm," *Administrative Science Quarterly* 36 (1991), 106–126.

7. See W. Locander, S. Sudman, and N. Bradburn, "An Investigation of Interview Method, Threat and Response Distortion," *Journal of the American Statistical Association* 71 (1976), 269–275; and the discussion presented in Floyd J. Fowler, *Survey Research Methods,* 2nd ed. (Newbury Park, CA: Sage Publications, 1993), 89–90.

8. See Fowler, *Survey Research Methods,* 86.

9. H. Schuman and J. M. Converse, "The Effects of Black and White Interviewers on Black Responses in 1968," *Public Opinion Quarterly* 35 (1971), 44–68.

10. Floyd J. Fowler and Thomas W Mangione, *Standardized Survey Interviewing* (Newbury Park, CA: Sage Publications, 1990), 105.

11. In addition to those situations discussed here, error can result also from the sampling technique, as well as from coding and data-entry procedures.

12. See Roger Gates and Paul J. Solomon, "Research Using the Mail Intercept: State of the Art," *Journal of Advertising Research* 22 (1981/83), 43–49; Robert M. Groves and Robert L. Kahn, *Surveys by Telephone: A National Comparison with Personal Interviews* (New York: Academic Press, 1979); and Theresa F. Rogers, "Interviews by Telephone and in Person: Quality of Responses and Field Performance," *Public Opinion Quarterly* (40 (1976), 51–65.

13. See, for example, Thomas A. Heberlein and Robert Baumgartner, "Factors Affecting Response Rate to Mailed Questionnaires," *American Sociological Review* 43 (August, 1978), 447–462.

14. Ibid.

15. As suggested by Jean M. Converse and Stanley Presser, *Survey Questions: Handcrafting the Standardized Questionnaire* (Newbury Park, CA: Sage Publications, 1986), 37.

16. General Social Survey (GSS), National Opinion Research Center (NORC), 1994 survey.

17. N. Bradburn and S. Sudman, *Improving Interview Method and Questionnaire Design* (San Francisco: Jossey-Bass Press, 1979).

18. This procedure was described most completely by Dan A. Dillman, *Mail and Telephone Surveys: The Total Design Method* (New York: Wiley, 1978).

19. Delbert C. Miller, *Handbook of Research Design and Social Measurement,* 5th ed. (Newbury Park, CA: Sage Publications, 1991), 152.

20. E. Lee Bernick and David J. Pratto, "Improving the Quality of Information in Mail Surveys: Use of Special Mailings," *Social Science Quarterly* (March, 1994), 212–219.

21. However, Charles Mayer and Robert Pratt found a return of 23.5 percent to very closely represent the population in their study. See "A Note on Nonresponse in Mail Survey," *Public Opinion Quarterly* 30 (1966–1967), 637–646.

22. For an extended discussion, see Graham Kalton, *Introduction to Survey Sampling* (Newbury Park, CA: Sage Publications, 1983), 69–75; see also, Lewis Mandell, "When to Weight: Determining Nonresponse Bias in Survey Data," *Public Opinion Quarterly* 38 (1974), 247–252; and R. M. Groves, *Survey Errors and Survey Costs* (New York: Wiley, 1989).

23. For an excellent discussion, see Miller, *Handbook of Research Design and Social Measurement,* 636–639.

24. Mark A. Peterson, "The Presidency and Organized Interests: White House Patterns of Interest Group Liaison," *American Political Science Review* 86 (September, 1992), 612–625.

25. Lewis Anthony Dexter, *Elite and Specialized Interviewing* (Evanston, IL: Northwestern University Press, 1970).

26. Students will also profit from a review of Raymond Gorden's book, *Basic Interviewing Skills* (Itasca, IL: F. E. Peacock Publishers, 1991).

27. See James H. Frey, *Survey Research by Telephone,* 2nd ed. (Newbury Park, CA: Sage Publications, 1989), 27; Seymour Sudman and Norman M. Bradburn, *Asking Questions* (San Francisco: Jossey-Bass, 1982); and Miller, *Handbook of Research Design and Social Measurement,* 167.

28. For an interesting commentary, see Lena Williams, "Consumers vs. Callers: The Lines Are Busier," *New York Times,* June 20, 1991.

29. Some recent research indicates that households with answering machines are more likely to be contacted, more likely to complete the interview, and less likely to refuse to participate in telephone surveys than households without machines. Leaving messages on telephone answering machines—when they are encountered—prior to calling back, appears to have a positive impact on participation by potential respondents. See: Minghua Xu, Benjamin J. Bates, and John C. Schweitzer, "The Impact of Messages on Survey Participation in Answering Machine Households," *Public Opinion Quarterly* 57 (1993), 232–237.

30. The points also are made by Kalton, *Introduction to Survey Sampling,* 7.

31. Ibid.

32. See Miller, *Handbook of Research Design and Social Measurement,* 60–66.

33. A brief but informative overview of multistage cluster sampling techniques is provided in *Interviewer's Manual* (Ann Arbor, MI: Survey Research Center/Institute for Survey Research, 1976), 35–39. Also, an excellent review of all these, and other, sampling techniques is presented in Kalton, *Introduction to Survey Sampling.*

CHAPTER 5

Gathering Information:
Making Use of Available Data

Collecting your own data is fun. Self-collection of data also permits you to target your research precisely to the issue of interest to you, or—if you are working as a consultant—to your client. On the other hand, collecting your own data also is time-consuming and frequently very costly. It is not at all unusual for the data-collection stage of a research project to consume the greatest amount of time and money. Further, if—because of unforeseen circumstances—the data cannot be collected in a timely manner, the whole project may end in failure. Happily, many government and private organizations collect, store, and release information of interest to political and policy researchers at little or no cost.

In addition to economies of time and cost, there are other advantages to using data already available. Students of historical political events obviously are not in a position to collect original data on those events; utilization of data collected by researchers on the scene at that time is necessary. Additionally, researchers interested in change over time (e.g., changing public opinion on some issue—such as abortion) will probably use data collected by one—or even several—individuals or organizations at several different times.

One additional advantage of using existing data is *quality* of information. The major public and private data-collecting organizations—because of resources and skills available to them—are in a position to collect information of far higher quality and import than even most Ph.D. students. Many of these data sets provide the benefits of nationally representative samples, standardized items, standard indices, and—because many have been collected for years—means for permitting time-series analysis.[1]

Available data may be issued by government or private sources, or by university and university-related research organizations. Additionally, these data may be issued in print (hard-copy) format, on microformat (e.g., microfiche or microfilm), or in an electronic form such as compact disc or magnetic tape. A vast and growing body of data is available to any computer user via the Internet. (See Boxes 5.1 and 5.2). So many data are available, in fact, that researchers today have a difficult time simply

BOX 5.1   Political Information Available via the Internet

An enormous amount of information of interest to political and policy researchers—including much discussed in this chapter—is available to computer users on the **Internet**, and this body of available information is growing almost daily. Created in 1969 by the U.S. Department of Defense, primarily to serve university and government personnel, Internet access is available today to virtually all computer users. Students and faculty connected with universities have ready and easy access to the Internet. Others can gain access through relatively inexpensive service providers.

Travel around the Internet may be accomplished by access to a **Gopher**—a menu-based tool that searches the Internet for information on specific topics. Information available through the Gopher system is arranged hierarchically, from more general to more specific. Or, information may be accessed through the *World-Wide Web* (also known as WWW or "the Web"). The **Web** makes possible retrieval of information in graphic form, so that charts, images, sounds, as well as text may be obtained. And—since documents available through the Web are written in **hypertext**—the selection of certain key words within one document prompts access to other documents no matter where they are located on the Internet. Either through a gopher or the Web, once you find the information you want, you may view the information on the computer screen, or you may E-mail it to some specific address, or you may have it printed on "hard copy."

The American Political Science Association has developed a Gopher which directs users to much information of interest to political researchers. At this writing, both the University of Michigan and Northwestern University also have developed excellent Gopher sources of political information. Included among the information available through Northwestern University's American Government and Politics Gopher are the following main headings:

Elections, Campaigns and Speeches

Political Documents

Executive Branch

Judicial Branch

Legislative Branch

Political Parties

Political Communication and Public Opinion

Interest Groups and Social Movements

The States

Data Resources on U.S. Politics

Accessing the heading, **"Political Documents,"** one will find a number of sub-headings, including: U.S. Historical Documents, U.S. and World Constitutions, Clinton's Economic Plan, Republican 1994 "Contract with America," and Treaties and International Agreements.

Found under the sub-heading, "U.S. Historical Documents," is the full text of several documents of great historical interest to American government, including:

The Articles of Confederation, 1777

the Bill of Rights, 1791

the Constitution of the United States, 1787

the Declaration of Independence, 1776

the Emancipation Proclamation, 1862

the Gettysburg Address, 1863

Jefferson's First Inaugural Address, 1801

Martin Luther King's, "I have a Dream Speech," 1963

the Magna Carta, 1215

The Monroe Doctrine, 1823

Among the many sub-headings under the heading, "Data Resources on U.S. Politics," is one titled, "U.S. Census Bureau Gopher." Here, the researcher will find access to the *County and City Data Book* (top 77 cities rankings), *Financial Data from State and Local Governments, Population Data,* and selected information from the *Statistical Abstract of the United States.* Through the Statistical Abstract Gopher, one can obtain state-by-state data in such areas as population, health, education, employment, business, federal funds, crime, and income.

For a particularly useful guide to Internet use for students of politics see: Bruce Maxwell, *How to Access the Federal Government on the Internet* (Washington, DC, Congressional Quarterly Press, 1995). This book describes how to access texts of bills being considered by Congress as well as a wide range of information on current policy issues. Also useful, by the same author and publisher, is the book: *How to Access the Government's Electronic Bulletin Boards* (1994) which shows how to access over 200 computer bulletin boards operated by the federal government.

keeping abreast of the growing supply and sources of information. Those who specialize in particular areas soon become familiar with the sources of data most useful to their own research, but for beginning students, especially, the sheer quantity of data sources can seem overwhelming. Although it is not possible here to mention all the sources of data that political researchers find useful, a few of the major sources are listed and briefly annotated. Student may wish to review mainly those

BOX 5.2 Discussion Lists (or Listservers) Available via the Internet

Many discussion lists (sometimes called **listservers**) of interest to political scientists are available to those with access to the Internet. Listservers are computer centers that distribute electronic mail and files. Through subscribing to a particular list, you can receive updated information on that topic. You also can engage in discussion about particular issues, and you can add to the information on that topic. To subscribe to any list, the user just sends a message to the listserver of particular interest.

In most cases, subscription is accomplished in the following manner.

1. log on to your computer's electronic mail facility.
2. Address your message request to be sent to:

LISTSERV@*listserv.address* [where, "*listserv.address*" is taken from column 1 in the listing below]

3. In the body of the message type:

SUBSCRIBE *list* YOUR NAME [where, "*list*" is taken from column 2 in the listing below]

In order to remove yourself from a list,

1. log on to your computer's electronic mail facility.
2. Address your message request to be sent to:

LISTSERV@*listserv.address* [where, "*listserv.address*" is taken from column 1 in the listing below]

3. In the body of the message, type:

SIGNOFF *list* YOUR NAME [where, "*list*" is taken from column 2 in the listing below]

A sample of subscription lists of interest to students of politics and policy follows:

Listserv address:	*List:*	*Discussion Topic:*
UMCVMB.BITNET	afam-l	African American Research
KENTVM.KEN.EDU	afas-l	African American Studies
TEMPLEVM.BITNET	afroam-l	African American Issues
CS.ODU.EDU	animal-rights	Animal rights

Listserv address:	List:	Discussion Topic:
BUACCA.BU.EDU	arms-l	Arms Proliferation Issues
UMCVMB.BITNET	ashe-l	Higher Education Issues
UBVM.BITNET	BIOSPH-l	Biosphere Issues
MCGIL1.BITNET	canada-l	Canadian Politics
UBVM.BITNET	centam-l	Central America
PURCCVN.BITNET	chile-l	Chile
PUCC.BITNET	china	Chinese Studies
MIDWAY.UCHICAGO.EDU	dsa-1gb	Gay Dem Socialists
TRMETU.BITNET	ec	European Community
EMUVM1.BITNET	ecology	Politics & Environment
PCCVM.BITNET	elect-l	Running Political Campaigns
MACH1.BITNET	femisa	Feminism, Gender, etc.
SUVM.BITGNET	femjur	Feminist Thought & Law
VM.USC.EDU	grmnhist	German History
UICVM.BITNET	h-pol	Political History
UICVM.BITNET	h-urban	Urban History
UKCC.BITNET	healthre	Health Care Reform
VMS.CIS.PITT.EDU	hr-l	Human Rights
UCBVM.BITNET	hungary	Hungary
UMINN1.BITNET	int-law	International Law
ULKYVM.BITNET	islam-l	History of Islam
SUVM.SYR.EDU	pa-net	Public Administration
SHSU.BITNET	pol-econ	Political Economy
RPITSVM.BITNET	polcomm	Political Communication
UCF1VM.BITNET	politics	Political Discussion
UMINN1.BITNET	pubpol-l	Public Policy
MARIST.BITNET	repub-l	Republican Politics
VM.USC.EDU	rushist	Russian History
NUSVM.BITNET	seanet-l	Southeast Asia
VM.USC.EDU	sovhist	Soviet History
UMAB.BITNET	statepol	State Politics
TREARN.BITNET	urban-l	Urban Planning
UBVM.BITNET	vwar-l	Vietnam War
UMDD.BITNET	smst-l	Women's Studies
CSEARN.BITNET	wmun-l	World Model U.N.
UBVM.BITNET	wwii-l	World War II
SJUVM.BITNET	y-rights	Youth Rights

For an extended presentation of lists, see Gary M. Klass and Scott Cooley, "Internet Lists for Political Scientists," *Social Science Computer Review,* 12 (summer, 1994), 261–264.

sections of this chapter most directly related to their own research interests—such as Congress, or the presidency. Students would be well advised to personally locate and inspect these data sources in order to achieve a full appreciation of the richness and variety of the data contained therein.

DATA ARCHIVES

All political researchers should be familiar with the major social science archives, most of which have appeared since the early 1960s. These archives are organizations that specialize in the collection, storage, and dissemination of data, usually in a machine-readable form. A good way to get preliminary information on any one archive is to consult its entry in the *Research Centers Directory* (Karen Hill, ed., Detroit: Gale Research, 18th ed. 1994, two vols.).[2]

The most important data archives for political scientists is the Inter-University Consortium for Political and Social Research (ICPSR). Since 1962, the ICPSR—located at the University of Michigan and comprising more than 370 member universities from around the world—has collected, processed, and distributed data in machine-readable form. ICPSR is, today, the world's largest repository and disseminator of social science data. Included among ICPSR's vast holdings are data collections relating to community and urban studies; conflict, aggression, violence, and wars; education; elite and mass political behavior and attitudes; census records; health care and health facilities; social indicators; and election returns and legislative records. Information in some or all of these areas is available for more than 130 countries and is distributed via magnetic tape. Many collections also are available on diskettes, compact discs, and network file transfer. For scholars of American politics, particularly American voting behavior, the consortium's American National Election Studies, conducted every other year since 1952, provide the most detailed database on the political attitudes and behavior of the American public available.

Other influential data archives are held by the National Opinion Research Center (NORC), located at the University of Chicago. Since the early 1970s, NORC has annually conducted the General Social Survey (GSS), a very widely used and cited social survey. The GSS is a national cross-sectional sample of noninstitutionalized, English-speaking persons 18 years of age or older living in the United States. The GSS contains data on a wide variety of beliefs, attitudes, and behaviors toward work, sex roles, women's rights, abortion, civil liberties, personal happiness, job satisfaction, and so forth. These data easily lend themselves to time-series analysis because many of the same questions are asked each year.

Another useful archive is the Roper Center for Public Opinion Research, (University of Connecticut, Storrs, CT), which is concerned with public opinion on social and political attitudes and behavior, and with public policy matters. The Roper archives include actual survey response data for more than 10,000 surveys conducted in the United States and in 70 other countries.

UNITED STATES GOVERNMENT SOURCES

One of the largest creators and compilers of data in the world is the United States government. Under its mandate to provide information to the people, the federal government issues a wealth of publications, both statistical and narrative, every year. Much of this material provides very good data for political research papers. One reason for students to use government-issued data is that these data are readily available. Through the depository libraries program, the federal government deliberately provides information, in an organized fashion, in certain broad categories, for the use and information of the public. The categories include short publicity releases such as press releases, handbooks such as the *Statistical Abstract,* directories such as the *United States Government Manual,* proceedings, forms such as copyright forms and applications, maps and atlases, bibliographies, periodicals such as *Children Today* or *Dispatch,* laws, statistics, and even books.[3]

Department of Commerce: Bureau of the Census

The U.S. Bureau of the Census is a source of enormous amounts of information of interest to political researchers. The decennial census is one of the most impressive and useful compilations of data the government provides. It offers great potential for research. Historically, the census data have been released in print form; in recent times they have been made available on magnetic tape and—most recently—on compact disc. Much census data, as previously mentioned, is available through ICPSR.

Censuses have been compiled in this country since 1790, in a continuous sequence, once every decade. Additionally, the Bureau of the Census compiles information on many topics—including agriculture, government and the economy (trade, industry, manufacturing, and transportation)—every five years.

In order to come to terms with the vast body of material released by the Census Bureau, a researcher should use one of the many guides issued by the agency itself or by the private sector. The agency issues the *Census Catalog* and *Guide* annually, and for the population census, there is the very helpful *Subject Index to Current Population Reports.*

Demographic data obtainable from the census are an ideal database on which to base a research project. Consider the organization and level of detail of the print publications of the 1990 reports for housing and population:

1990 Census of Population and Housing Reports

Summary population and housing characteristics

Population and housing unit counts

Population and housing characteristics for census tracts and block numbering areas

Population and housing characteristics for congressional districts

Summary social, economic, and housing characteristics

1990 Census of Population Reports

General population characteristics

General population characteristics for American Indian and Alaskan Native areas

General population characteristics for metropolitan statistical areas

General population characteristics for urbanized areas

Social and economic characteristics

Social and economic characteristics for American Indian and Alaskan Native areas

Social and economic characteristics for metropolitan statistical areas

Social and economic characteristics for urbanized areas

Population subject reports

1990 Census of Housing Reports

General housing characteristics

General housing characteristics for American Indian and Alaskan Native areas

General housing characteristics for metropolitan statistical areas

General housing characteristics for urbanized areas

Detailed housing characteristics

Detailed housing characteristics for American Indian and Alaskan Native areas

Detailed housing characteristics for metropolitan statistical areas

Detailed housing characteristics for urbanized areas

Housing subject reports

The Current Population Survey (CPS), also from the U.S. census, is an important data set used by both the Bureau of the Census and the Department of Labor's Bureau of Labor Statistics. The CPS, a nationwide compilation of employment data, is conducted monthly by sampling 60,000 households.

While the printed census publications are available from the Government Printing Office (GPO) and can be identified through the *Monthly Catalog,* information in other formats is available from the Census Bureau itself from the Data Services Division, Customer Services. Machine-readable data are much more easily manipulated and have more powerful search and retrieval capabilities than their print counterparts. The Data Services Division provides information about the availability of the four *Summary Tape Files* (STF) which provide information from the *Census of Population and Housing.* The tapes provide population and housing data in more detail than can feasibly be provided in print format; they do not duplicate the print format publications. Online there are also the *Public-Use Microdata Samples* (PUMS), which in 1990, included for the first time a separate sample on the older population. PUMS are intended to provide sample long-form census records showing most population and housing characteristics, but with measures taken to protect confidentiality.[4] State-level demographic data from the census have also been compiled on compact laser disc (CD-ROM: compact disc—read-only memory) and are distributed through the depository library system. Perhaps the most exciting machine application from the census bureau is the TIGER maps. TIGER stands for topographically integrated geographic encoding and referencing. Because the geographic element of census data gathering is both crucial and error prone, the TIGER system was devised to make both the process and the product more accurate. The TIGER system enables researchers to combine map features with statistical data.

Nondemographic census data available on compact disc include the *1987 Census of Agriculture* and portions of the *1987 Economic Census,* which include retail trade, wholesale trade, the service industries, transportation, manufacturing, and construction.

The Census Bureau provides custom-made tape releases from its electronically compiled sources on request. The census publication *1990 Census of Population and Housing Tabulation and Publication Program* gives detailed information on how to request census data in nonprint format.

Another important Census Bureau publication is the *Historical Statistics of the United States: Colonial Times to 1970, in Two Parts* (Washington, DC: U.S. Department of Commerce, Bureau of the Census, for sale by the Superintendent of Documents, 1975). With historical coverage that extends back to 1610 when available, this two-volume compilation gives more than 12,000 times series describing the social, economic, and political development of the United States.

Many other agencies of the federal government collect and disseminate data. Some of the most important of these to political analyst are described next.[5]

Government Printing Office

The federal government's largest clearinghouse—the Government Printing Office—prints, binds, and distributes the publications of the U.S. congress, the executive branch, and many publications from other federal government agencies. It releases publications through the depository library system, and it runs the government bookstores that can be found in large cities nationwide. It also sells publications on a mail-order basis. Its *Monthly Catalog,* which started publication in 1895, has already been mentioned.

Another of its more important publications is *The Statistical Abstract of the United States* (Washington, DC: GPO, 1879–[present]). This important annual series (now available on compact disc as well as in print versions), compiled by the U.S. Bureau of the Census, has been in continuous publication for more than a century. The *Statistical Abstract* combines data from many government and private sources, as well as from unpublished documents. It includes information on a wide range of topics. Among those of most interest to political researchers are population, health, education, law enforcement, federal government finances and employment, national defense, state and local government finances and employment, and elections. Although the *Statistical Abstract* focuses primarily on the United States, it also includes a selection on comparative international statistics.

Department of Commerce: Other Bureaus

Not only does the commerce department include the U.S. Bureau of the Census, but it also provides information through other important subsidiary offices, such as the Bureau of Economic Analysis (BEA). The BEA issues the *Survey of Current Business* and its biennial accompanying *Business Statistics.* The department now offers the Commerce Department Economic Bulletin Board, an electronic mail service providing news about departmental activities and services. It now also issues on compact disc two new compilations, the *National Trade Data Base* (NTDB), and the *National Economic, Social, and Environmental Data Bank* (NESE).

NTDB is issued monthly and contains approximately 80,000 documents, tables, and time series from fifteen federal agencies. Major publications include the *World Factbook,* the *Basic Guide to Exporting,* and the *Foreign Trade Index.* NESE is released quarterly and contains the full text of several federal government publications, including the *Economic and Budget Outlook,* the *Annual Survey of Manufactures,* the *U.S. Industrial Outlook,* and *Toxins in the Community.* The NTDB also includes selected tables and data from the *Statistical Abstract,* the *Bureau of Justice Statistics,* and the *Survey of Current Business.* Although each contains publications that also exist in print, neither compact disc has a print equivalent.

Department of Education

Through its clearinghouse—the Educational Resources Information Center (ERIC)—this department issues a very large report series, the *ERIC Documents,* and two major interdisciplinary indexes to the education literature, the *Resources in Education,* and the *Current Index to Journals in Education.* Both indexes are available in print and in multiple electronic formats. Through the National Center for Education Statistics, the department also releases some important statistical publications: *Youth Indicators, The Condition of Education, The Digest of Education Statistics,* and *Projections of Education Statistics to 2006.* For the educational projections, the terminal year in the title changes with each edition of this annual publication.

Department of Health and Human Services

Several agencies of this department provide data of interest to researchers. For example, the Social Security Administration publishes the *Social Security Bulletin* and its annual *Statistical Supplement.* The Health Care Financing Administration issues the quarterly *Health Care Financing Review.* The Office of Human Development Services releases the well-known journal *Children Today.* The Public Health Service issues many publications through its subagencies the Substance Abuse, and Mental Health Administration; the Centers for Disease Control; the Food and Drug Administration; the Health Resources and Services Administration; the National Institutes of Health. These publications include the *Special Report to the U.S. Congress on Alcohol and Health,* the *Morbidity and Mortality Weekly Report, Vital Statistics, FDA Consumer,* and *Index Medicus.*

Department of Justice

This executive department also has important agencies that issue data of interest to researchers, including the Federal Bureau of Investigation, the Immigration and Naturalization Service, and the Drug Enforcement Administration. Important publications of these agencies include the *Uniform Crime Reports for the United States,* and the *Statistical Yearbook of the Immigration and Naturalization Service.* The Justice Department also issues the *United States Supreme Court Reports.* This body of material consists of the complete opinions delivered by the justices on cases heard by the Supreme Court.

Department of Labor

The labor department administers the following agencies: the Employment and Training Administration, the Office of Labor-Management Standards, United States Employment Service, the Bureau of Labor Statistics (BLS), and the Women's Bureau. The United States Employment Service is the agency that releases the *Dictionary of Occupational Titles.* This important source describes occupations held by people gainfully employed in the United States. The information is obtained by labor department personnel from private-sector professional organizations and from trade organizations. All occupations are defined as they most typically are encountered. A supplement, the *Selected Characteristics of Occupations Defined in the Dictionary of Occupational Titles,* is also published.

One of the most important agencies of the labor department for data-gathering and dissemination purposes is the BLS. Several BLS publications might be useful for political science research, such as *Employment and Earnings,* with its annual *Supplement;* the *CPI Detailed Report,* which tracks the consumer price index on a monthly basis; *Producer Price Indexes,* also issued monthly; the *Monthly Labor Review,* which includes articles and statistics and is considered authoritative; *Current Wage Developments;* the *Occupational Outlook Handbook; Earnings and Employment Statistics;* and the *Handbook of Labor Statistics.*

A 1993 flyer from the Bureau, "About BLS Data Diskettes," describes 18 data files that are available for sale from the bureau, on diskettes, in Lotus 1-2-3 and ASCII file format. Among the materials provided on diskettes are the *Consumer Expenditure Surveys,* the *Consumer Price Index, Labor Force Projections,* and *Import–Export Price Indexes.*[6]

Department of State

The state department is the ranking executive department, as it deals with American relations with the rest of the world. Included among its publications of special interest to political researchers are *Foreign Relations of the United States,* the *Amer-*

ican Foreign Policy Current Documents, the *Department of State Bulletin,* and its continuation of the *Dispatch,* the *United States Treaties and Other International Agreements,* and *Treaties in Force.*

Independent Federal Agencies

The researcher should especially consider the publications of the following independent agencies of the federal government: The General Services Administration (GSA), through its Information Resources Management Service, operates the federal information centers that are active nationwide. Many worthy publications are issued by the National Archives and Records Administration, through its Office of the National Archives, Office of Presidential Libraries, Office of Federal Records Centers, Office of the Federal Register, and National Historical Publications and Records Commission. The Office of the Federal Register alone issues the *United States Statutes at Large,* the *Federal Register,* the *Code of Federal Regulations,* the *Weekly Compilation of Presidential Documents,* the *Public Papers of the Presidents,* the *Codification of Presidential Proclamations,* and the *United States Government Manual.*

CONGRESSIONAL, EXECUTIVE, AND COURT INFORMATION

The Congress

For students of the U.S. Congress, the most important source of general information and data is the *Congressional Quarterly Weekly Report* (along with its companions the annual *Congressional Quarterly Almanac,* and the quadrennial *Congress and the Nation,* which is issued in conjunction with presidential terms of office), published by Congressional Quarterly Inc. (CQ), Washington DC. The *Congressional Quarterly Weekly Report* provides an up-to-date weekly review of congressional activities. All CQ publications report votes on key issues, in addition to a status review of major legislation, and provide analyses of key legislative areas (including, as appropriate, energy; national security; health, education, and welfare; transportation; law enforcement; consumer affairs; and agriculture). The weekly report is indexed quarterly and annually.

Five additional publications are especially useful for insights into Congress. For example, *Congressional Roll Call,* published annually, presents a member-by-member survey and analysis of congressional votes. Included is a section discussing key House and Senate votes, followed by analyses of important coalition voting patterns. These coalitions include what CQ calls the Conservative Coalition; Presidential Support Opposition; Voting Participation; North South Split; Party Unity; Bipartisanship; and Freshman Voting. This publication is an invaluable source of information and analysis for voting on key congressional issues.

The four other important CQ publications make up the guide series: *Congressional Quarterly's Guide to Congress, Guide to U.S. Elections, Guide to the Presi-*

dency, and *Guide to the U.S. Supreme Court.* These guides present comprehensive historical and contemporary overviews of the offices and bodies discussed, including chapters dealing with origins and development of these bodies, as well as useful appendixes that often offer a wealth of statistical data. The most recently published volume in the group is the *Guide to U.S. Elections,* which is in its third edition, published in 1994. The sections within it provide information and data dealing with the historical development of American political parties, highlights of the national party conventions (1831–1992), electoral and popular votes for presidential elections (1789–1992), gubernatorial elections (1789–1994), and all House and Senate elections from 1789 to 1994. An interesting section provides a narrative summary of important political and social events surrounding all U.S. elections following World War II. This guide is accompanied by 10 appendices, including those dealing with information on House and Senate leaders, changing methods of electing presidential electors, and constitutional provisions and amendments dealing with elections.

Students of Congress will find additionally useful the *Biographical Directory of the American Congress, 1774–1971.* This volume, compiled under the direction of the Joint Committee on Printing and published as Senate Document No. 92-8 (92nd Congress, first session), presents a paragraph-length biography of every member of the U.S. Congress. The paragraphs usually comment on early education, family occupation, military career, dates of congressional service, honors and distinctions received, other public offices held, and birth and death statistics. An updated biography of congressional members can be found in the *Congressional Directory* (published annually by the U.S. GPO, Washington, DC). A final biographical source that students of Congress might find helpful is the *Congressional Staff Directory* (published annually since 1959 by Charles B. Brownson and Ann L. Brownson, Mount Vernon, VA: Congressional Staff Directory). This volume presents biographical information of House, Senate, and joint congressional committee staff personnel. It provides photos and has indexes by personal name and keyword subject.

Because of the enormous and often unforeseen influence of political action committees (PACs) on the political process, they are a popular topic for research. Some compilations about the PACs that might be of interest are *Open Secrets: the Encyclopedia of Congressional Money and Politics* (Larry Makinson, ed., Washington, DC: Center for Responsive Politics, 1992) and *Open Secrets: the Cash Constituents of Congress* (Larry Makinson, Washington, DC: Center for Responsive Politics, 1992). The latter title deals specifically with campaign funds in the 1990 election. Also, the *Handbook of Campaign Spending: Money in the 1990 Congressional Races* (Sara Fritz and Dwight Morris, Washington, DC: Congressional Quarterly, 1992) should be examined.

One interesting approach to the study of Congress is through maps. There are now enough readily available map compilations so that this kind of graphic research is feasible. The most recently published volume in this series is the Atlas for the 103rd Congress. Information for the 104 Congress is available on compact disc from the customer services unit of the Census. In two large volumes, the atlas shows the congressional districts as based on the 1990 census. For most states (excluding those with only one voting member and those places with a nonvoting delegate) the maps are followed by extensive tables that link places, American Indian reservations, and counties with their congressional districts. This series is preceded by the magisterial *Historical Atlas of the United States Congressional Districts, 1789–1983* (Kenneth C. Martis, Ruth A. Rowles, and associates; New York: Free Press, 1982). For the first through 97th congresses for all congressional districts, this atlas provides maps showing all representatives for all districts in the House of Representatives, and it shows the boundaries of all districts. This work was originally started as a Works Progress Administration (WPA) project during the Great Depression. It has become the premier work graphically showing the influence of place on the activities of Congress. Any researcher interested in the effects of geography on the activities of Congress should also consider its companion sets, *The Historical Atlas of Political Parties in the United States Congress, 1789–1989* (Kenneth C. Martis, New York: Macmillan Publishing, 1989), and the *Historical Atlas of State Power in Congress 1790–1990* (Kenneth C. Martis and Gregory A. Elmes, Washington, DC: Congressional Quarterly, 1993).

There is a wealth of primary material on Congress, which the researcher should consider when planning a project. Some of the basic sources include the *Congressional Information Service Congressional Master File, 1789–1969* (Bethesda, MD: CIS, 1987), on compact laser disc, this master file, provides the *Congressional Committee Hearings Index 1822–1969,* the *Serial Set Index 1789–1969,* the *Congressional Committee Prints Index 1833–1969,* and the *Unpublished Senate Committee Hearings Index 1824–1964.* While the master file does not offer the full text of these congressional publications, it is a much more powerful index than any of its print counterparts. Depository libraries will have the materials themselves.

The researcher should also remember that mainstay of informational resources, the *Congressional Record.* The verbatim accounts of activities in Congress, along with supplementary material that members may include at their discretion, can be used in conjunction with any of the aforementioned sources.

The Presidency

For students of the presidency and the various executive departments, a very useful general source of information is the *National Journal,* published weekly by National Journal, Inc. (Washington, DC). This publication focuses on the White House and executive departments and agencies. Typically, features include articles on the presidency, politics, the economy, the bureaucracy, and urban affairs. Each issue includes an update feature, which discusses important political issues and the status of current legislation. The *National Journal* is indexed weekly and annually.

Students of the presidency also will find useful *The Budget of the United States Government,* which can be seen as a detailed statistical statement of executive policy. *Facts about the Presidents* (Joseph Nathan Kane, New York: H. W. Wilson Company, 6th ed., 1993), provides biographical and historical information on U.S. presidents (from Washington through Bush), including facts dealing with their parents and siblings, education, party affiliation, political careers, and cabinet and court appointments. Wide-ranging miscellaneous information on each president is included. What student of the presidency could rest comfortably in ignorance of the knowledge that the first asteroid named for an American President was Hooveria, that the "S" in President Harry S Truman's name has no special significance and is not an abbreviation of any name, or that George Bush was the first president to have served as director of the Central Intelligence Agency?

The Biographical Directory of the United States Executive Branch, 1774–1989 (Robert Sobel, ed., Westport, CT: Greenwood, 1990) provides brief sketches of the careers of all cabinet members, as well as of all presidents and vice presidents during this period.

The Weekly Compilation of Presidential Documents (Washington, DC: General Services Administration), published every Monday, contains texts of presidential statements, interviews, nominations, appointments, messages, and other presidential materials released by the White House during the preceding week. The volume is indexed semiannually. (An interesting analysis of Presidential decision making utilizing existing data is shown in Box 5.3, page 108.)

The Courts

The most important primary source of information on the U.S. Supreme Court is its set of opinions, as delivered case by case for each time the Court has met since 1789. The *United States Supreme Court Reports* is available at large depository libraries and is the official unexpurgated version of these opinions. There is a great deal of supporting literature on the high court and the cases it has heard. One index that a researcher might want to consult is *Supreme Court of the United States: An Index to Opinions Arranged by Justice* (Linda A. Blandford and Patricia Russell Evans, eds., Millwood, NY: Kraus International Publications, 1994). The index allows the researcher to search by known justice because it gives citations to the *United States Supreme Court Reports* by personal name. The index's arrangement is chronological, by date of service on the Court for each justice.

Another resource is the *Encyclopedia of the American Constitution.*[7] In four volumes, this encyclopedia gives articles, written by experts and accompanied by lists of further readings, within five general categories: "doctrinal concepts of constitutional law . . . people . . . judicial decisions . . . public acts . . . and historical periods." Supplement I, released in 1992, gives major developments and decisions since 1985 and has articles on such topics as abortion, creationism, the right of confrontation, executive prerogative, liberalism, and *torts* (lawsuits involving wrongful acts for which damages or an injunction is sought).

STATE AND LOCAL DATA

Students of state and local politics will find two publications prepared by interest groups especially useful. *The Municipal Year Book,* published annually since 1934 by the International City Management Association (Washington, DC), provides a wealth of data on cities, largely collected through questionnaire surveys of municipal officials. Information and analysis will be found dealing with administration, legislation, and judicial trends; employment; salaries; public services; and other municipal activities. Various topics are given priority in different issues. In 1995, for example, there was an interesting chapter called "Recent Supreme Court Cases Affecting Local Governments."

At the state level, *The Book of the States* (published biennially by the Council of State Governments, Lexington, KY) provides information and data (with brief analysis) for all states in the areas of state constitutions and elections, legislatures, the judiciary, administrative organizations, finance, intergovernmental relations, and the major state services (education, transportation, health and welfare, etc.). *The Book of States* is accompanied by supplements that may interest the researcher, including *State Administrative Officials Classified by Functions, State Elective Officials and the Legislatures,* and *State Legislative Leadership Committees and Staff.*

In addition to these publications, the researcher will find useful a number of special publications by the U.S. Bureau of the Census. The *Census of Governments,* published every year ending in 2 or 7 (1992, 1997, etc.), provides data for five major types of local governments—counties, municipalities, townships, school districts, and special districts—in the areas of government organization, number of elective officials, indebtedness, public employment, finances, school enrollments, retirement systems, and historical data.

The *County and City Data Book* (released most recently in 1994) provides selected data for all counties, for 952 incorporated cities with populations over 25,000, and for places of population 2,500 or more. Included is information dealing with population characteristics, education, labor force, income, housing, government finances, crime rates, manufacturing and trade, school services, and hospital care. The census publication, *U.S.A. Counties,* includes more than 2,500 variables on age, crime, education, elections, local governments, population, poverty, and other items for counties and county equivalents. Recent editions of the *County and City Data Book* and *U.S.A. Counties* are available on compact disc.

Additional U.S. census publications that may be useful are *City Government Finances, State Government Finances, County Government Finances,* and *Local Government Finances in Selected Metropolitan Areas and Counties,* followed by local government finances in *Major County Areas* (providing information for the nation's largest standard metropolitan statistical areas). These volumes, published annually, provide detailed financial information on sources of revenue, expenditures by function, and indebtedness for the respective jurisdictions.

Additionally, most states prepare and publish state statistical abstracts similar in content to the *Statistical Abstract of the United States,* described previously. A current list of state statistical abstracts (along with foreign statistical abstracts) is presented in Appendix 1 of each issue of the *Statistical Abstract of the United States.*

An additional source of interest to researchers of urban America is *Cities of the United States* (Deborah A. Straub and Diane L. Dupuis, eds., Detroit: Gale Research, 2nd ed., 1993). In four volumes—one for the South, the West, the Midwest, and the Northeast—this source discusses more than a hundred large and fast-growing cities.

For each city, information is compiled under the following categories: economy, convention facilities, recreation, history, geography and climate, education and research, and communications. Each article is accompanied by a map and by black-and-white photographs.

An important graphic resource for research on cities is the *Township Atlas of the United States,* prepared by Jay Andriot (McLean, VA: Documents Index). As a detailed accompanying source to compilations issued by the U.S. Bureau of the Census, Andriot's work fills an important gap. To quote from his Foreword on page i of the 1991 edition, the atlas provides

> maps of and indexes to the minor county subdivisions of the 48 conterminous United States. . . . This Atlas provides maps to show the relative size and location within the county of either the Minor Civil Divisions or Census County Divisions. The 48 individual State sections contain: a state map and corresponding county guide for locating each county within the state; an individual State index which lists all subdivisions alphabetically under each county; county maps (arranged alphabetically) showing the Census County Divisions and/or the Minor Civil Divisions; and state maps showing the individual townships resulting from the Public Land Survey for those states covered. In the first portion of the Atlas you will find a detailed explanation of the Public Land Surveys. And in the last portion, a complete index is included which identifies all subdivisions, followed by the County and State in which each is located.[8]

The *Index to Urban Documents* (Laura J. Kaminsky, ed., Westport, CT: Greenwood Publishing Group), published quarterly since 1972, provides citations to the publications released each year by the largest cities and counties of the United States and Canada. This index includes city council proceedings, planning department reports, financial statements, school district reports, information on crime, water supply, libraries, public health, and more. Of equal importance, most of the publications described in the index are available in microfiche from the publisher.

VOTING, ELECTIONS, AND PUBLIC OPINION DATA

Two publications are particularly useful as sources of election data. The first of these is *America Votes,* by Richard Scammon and (since 1976) Alice McGillivray, published since 1956 for each biennial election (Washington, DC: Congressional Quarterly). *America Votes* presents the results of (1) presidential primaries, (2) state-by-state election returns for presidential and senate races by county, (3) state-by-state congressional election returns by congressional districts, (4) results of state party primaries and party run-off elections, and (5) historical state voting profiles since 1946. Also included is a brief analysis of each election year.

The second major source of election information is Congressional Quarterly's *Guide to U.S. Elections,* mentioned earlier. This publication presents state-by-state election data for all major political offices. Included are data on political parties, presidential elections, Senate and House elections, and gubernatorial elections.

Three additional sources are likely to be helpful to students of elections and voting patterns. Svend Petersen's *A Statistical History of the American Presidential Elections* (New York: Frederick Ungar Publishing, 1963) presents presidential election statistics from 1787 to 1960. In compiling this information, Petersen relied on many varied sources, including the U.S. National Archives and newspaper files at the U.S. Library of Congress. For each election, the volume contains state-by-state results of electoral votes and popular votes for all candidates. For all the states, Petersen also lists votes by party for presidential contests. W. Dean Burnham's *Presidential Ballots, 1836–1892* (Baltimore, MD: Johns Hopkins Press, 1955) is a rich source of information for presidential elections during this period. Burnham provides state-by-state returns for presidential elections during this period, including (1) county-by-county party control, (2) county-by-county popular vote, and (3) state electoral vote. Richard Scammon's *America at the Polls: A Handbook of American Presidential Election Statistics, 1920–1964* (Pittsburgh, PA: University of Pittsburgh Press, 1965) presents a statistical history of presidential elections from the election of President Harding in 1920 to that of President Johnson in 1964. For each election, the publication includes state and county figures for total vote, party breakdown, pluralities, and percentages of total votes for Republican and Democratic candidates.

One of two more recent compilations is *Vital Statistics on American Politics* (Harold W. Stanley and Richard G. Niemi, Washington, DC: Congressional Quarterly Press, 1992, 3rd ed.), which deals with the media, interest groups, and economic issues, as well as such standard fare as elections, congress, and the presidency. The other compilation is *Political Parties and Elections in the United States: An Encyclopedia* (L. Sandy Maisel, ed., New York: Garland, 1991). In two volumes, the encyclopedia deals with political parties and elections in the United States. Signed articles are accompanied by references to the research literature so that the intrepid researcher can go from this useful starting point into more complex sources.

Scholars of voting behavior will also find useful the following national election studies, all available through ICPSR: United States (1948–1994), Argentina (1963, 1965), Australia (1967, 1969), Brazil (1960), Canada (1965–1988), Chile (1958), Denmark (1971–1981), Great Britain (several studies between 1963 and 1983), France (1958, 1967, 1968), Germany (several studies available from 1953 to 1990), Israel (1969), Italy (1968, 1972), Japan (1961, 1967), The Netherlands (several studies between 1967 and 1982), Norway (1957, 1965), Sweden (several studies between 1956 and 1982), and Switzerland (1972).

Students of public opinion will find most convenient the *Gallup Poll Monthly* (published monthly since 1965 by the Gallup Poll, Princeton, NJ). Each issue reports results of the Institute of Public Opinion's surveys of samples of the American public (1500-person sample) on wide-ranging domestic and international issues. For example, in the March, 1995, issue are reported results of questions dealing with deficit reduction, abortion, affirmative action, President Clinton, and major league baseball. These topics may not all be of equal interest to political scientists, but each is usually conveniently broken down by various descriptive characteristics (such as sex, race, education, and party preference). A useful feature is the reporting of trends when the same question has been asked on repeated occasions.[9] A great deal of longitudinal information can be obtained by looking at the Gallup compilations *The Gallup Poll: Public Opinion 1935–1971* (George H. Gallup, New York: Random House, 1972, three vols.), *The Gallup Poll: Public Opinion 1972–1975* (George H. Gallup, Wilmington, DE: Scholarly Resources, 1978), *The Gallup Poll: Public Opinion* (published annually from 1978 by Scholarly Resources), and the several international polls also released by Gallup. A more long-lived international poll publication is the *Index to International Public Opinion,* in annual publication since 1978 (Westport, CT: Greenwood). Latest volumes include material gathered in more than 145 countries and regions of the world. Box 5.3 shows an example of how interesting and valuable studies can be formulated from readily available, existing sources.

INTERNATIONAL AND COMPARATIVE DATA

Students of international and comparative politics may not enjoy the same variety of and accessibility to sources of data as do students of American politics. In international studies, newspapers, magazines, journals, and other similar materials may have to serve as a large component of the data sources. Some familiarity with the language or languages of the nations to be studied may be helpful or even essential. Still, many useful sources of statistical information are readily available. Some of the most important of these are listed herein.

The *Statistical Yearbook,* published annually by the United Nations, presents country-by-country data in such general categories as population, labor, agriculture, industrial production, manufacturing, energy, trade, consumption, finance, housing, health, and education.

The *Demographic Yearbook,* also published annually by the United Nations, presents country-by-country data in such areas as marriage, divorce, birth and death rates, and other general population characteristics.

Three commonly used handbooks may interest the political researcher: *The Europa World Year Book,* the *International Year Book and Statesman's Who's Who,* and the *Statesman's Year Book.* Published annually since 1926 (London: Europa Publications Limited), and appearing since 1960 as a two-volume set, the *Europa World Year Book* lists country membership in international organizations. For each country, the publication also provides data dealing with such topics as language, religion, recent history, economic affairs, social welfare, and education. For most countries, information is also provided regarding their constitutions, form of government, party system, and government leaders. Details of finance, press matters, radio and television, trade and industry, tourism, and university affairs are included as well. For scholars interested in world regions, Europa also publishes a handbook series, including the following titles: *Africa: South of the Sahara; South America, Central America, and the Caribbean, 1986; The USA and Canada; The*

BOX 5.3   Using Existing Data: The Relationship
between Presidential Character and Exercise
of Executive Clemency

As a review of virtually any issue of any political science or policy journal will indicate, students of politics can formulate very interesting and valuable studies from information readily available through *existing* sources and *existing* literature. P. S. Ruckman, Jr. illustrates this well in his recently published study of the relationship between presidential character and exercise of executive clemency.

The Office of Pardon Attorney for the U.S. Department of Justice compiles and maintains data on presidential clemency, according to three categories: **pardons** (used to "restore the reputation and civil rights of an individual), **commutations** (the "substitution of milder punishment than one imposed by the court), and **remissions** (forgiveness of fines and forfeitures). Ruckman examined the 71,205 requests for clemency in the administrations of the 17 Presidents between 1900 and 1993. Based on the well-known typology of presidential character posited by political scientist James David Barber (*The Presidential Character: Predicting Performance in the White House,* 4th edition, Englewood Cliffs, NJ: Prentice Hall, 1992), Ruckman grouped the issuance of clemency as follows:

Comparison of Presidential Type with Clemency Activity: 1900–1993

Presidential Type	Pardons (1)	Commutations (2)	Remissions (3)	Total Positive Actions (4)	Term Averages: Percent of Actions Positive (5)	Negative (6)
Active-positive	*6,672*	*1,092*	*542*	*8,306*		
T. Roosevelt	578	319	51	948	24%	76%
F. Roosevelt	2,721	491	475	3,687	28%	72%
Truman	1,911	120	13	2,044	42%	58%
Kennedy	472	100	3	575	39%	61%
Ford	382	27	0	409	35%	65%
Carter	534	32	0	566	22%	78%
Bush	74	3	0	77	5%	95%
Active-negative	*3,649*	*2,277*	*303*	*6,229*		
Wilson	995	1,403	152	2,550	37%	63%
Hoover	832	585	149	1,566	26%	74%
L. Johnson	959	227	1	1,187	25%	75%
Nixon	863	62	1	926	21%	79%

Presidential Type	Pardons (1)	Commutations (2)	Remissions (3)	Total Positive Actions (4)	Term Averages: Percent of Actions	
					Positive (5)	Negative (6)
Passive-positive	1,549	1,194	141	2,884		
McKinley	291	129	26	446	31%	69%
Taft	391	319	64	774	40%	60%
Harding	474	733	51	1,258	34%	66%
Reagan	393	13	0	406	13%	87%
Passive-negative	1,723	660	97	2,480		
Coolidge	613	613	97	1,323	21%	79%
Eisenhower	1,110	47	0	1,157	27%	73%

As a result, Ruckman states that "It is clear . . . that executive clemency policy is based on presidential character. Active presidents . . . account for a significant portion of executive clemency activity. A full 73 percent of the population of 'positive' clemency actions have been taken by active presidents . . . The 11 active presidents have an average of 1,321 'positive' clemency actions while the 6 passive presidents have an average of 894 'positive' clemency actions." Ruckman finds further that "active presidents have granted 65 percent of the total number of commutations and 78 percent of the remissions." Based on this analysis, Ruckman concludes that his study . . . "does provide evidence that presidential character is a critical factor in the clemency process . . . "

SOURCE: P. S. Ruckman, Jr., "Presidential Character and Executive Clemency: A Reexamination," Social Science Quarterly, Vol. 76 (March, 1995), 213–221.

Middle East and North Africa, 1948; The Far East and Australasia; and *Eastern Europe and the Commonwealth of Independent States.*

The *International Year Book and Statesman's Who's Who,* compiled by Robert M. Bradfield and published annually since 1953 (Kingston upon Thames, England: Kelly's Directories Limited), presents a brief country-by-country overview, including information pertaining to constitutions and government, the party system, local government, the legal system, and data dealing with such varied topics as population, birth and death rates, finance, communications, and education. Also included is a brief biographical sketch of state leaders of the world.

The *Statesman's Year Book* (Brian Hunter, ed. [since 1990], New York: St. Martin's Press) has been in publication since 1864 and thus offers a formidably long run of annual surveys of the nations of the world, providing a compact and consistent set of statistical and narrative information on each country. Of the aforementioned three handbooks, *Statesman's* has the longest run of information and is the least expensive, and it offers information at the regional level for major nations (e.g., a separate section on each American state). On the other hand, *International* has the unique biographical section, and *Europa* offers the most detail and the best coverage of international organizations.

For international information since the Second World War, another set of titles may be useful: the *Yearbook of the United Nations,* the *Latin American and Caribbean Contemporary Record,* and the *Political Risk Yearbook.* These three sources are more specialized than the handbooks. Published by Martinus Nijhoff (Dordrecht, The Netherlands) the *Yearbook of the United Nations* may be the best place to start for the researcher who wants to include United Nations coverage. It describes the previous year's work by the organization, as well as the activities of its major subagencies. The yearbook also reports on such issues as disarmament, peacekeeping, international economic relations and assistance, transnational corporations, the environment, human rights, and more. It includes the complete text of related documents. Although slow to reach publication, the yearbook is a very informative source on the regions of the world and major international concerns.

Latin American and Caribbean Contemporary Record (New York: Holmes and Meier) is an annual providing a good overview of the Western Hemisphere, from Mexico to Chile. It offers articles on major topics of concern in the region, a separate article on each nation, the full text of important documents concerning the region, and relevant statistics. *The Political Risk Yearbook* (New York: Frost and Sullivan) can be compared to *Europa* for much of its content, but it also offers political and economic forecasts for each nation and is much more detailed. It is issued in separate volumes for the regions covered: Western Europe, Eastern Europe, Asia and the Pacific, the Middle East and North Africa, North and Central America, and South America.

Thomas T. Mackie and Richard Rose's work, the *International Almanac of Electoral History* (New York: Free Press, 1974), provides a rich source of electoral information for those Western industrial societies conducting competitive elections regularly since the end of World War II. Data are provided for 23 countries, including Australia, Canada, Germany, Japan, the United Kingdom, the United States, France, Italy, and Finland. For each country, the evolution of the electoral system and franchise laws are described, a list of political parties is presented, election results are presented, giving the total numbers and percentage for each party, and the number and percentage of seats won by each party are listed. This publication represents a very useful source of data, especially for students of comparative electoral patterns.

International Historical Statistics is a series now in its third edition. Prepared by Brian R. Mitchell, *International Historical Statistics: 1750–1988* (New York: Stockton Press, 1992, 1993) is in three volumes, subtitled *Europe* (1992), *The Americas* (1993), and *Australasia, Asia and Africa* (1993). The series presents a variety of statistical information for each nation, including climate, population, labor force, agriculture, industry, trade, transportation and communications, finance, and education.

The *Statistical Abstract of Latin America* (annual publication, James W. Wilkie, ed., Los Angeles: UCLA Latin American Center Publications) presents geographic, social, socioeconomic, economic, and trade statistics for the Latin American countries.

For researchers interested in the former Union of Soviet Socialist Republics, now the Commonwealth of Independent States, the *1989 USSR Census* contains a vast body of material that can be used to conduct demographic research on these nations. Written in Russian and available on microfiche from East View Publications of Minneapolis, it is being released in 12 volumes, incorporating within them 23 books dealing with population size and distribution, vital statistics, housing, education, employment, mobility, and ethnic and national composition of the population.

A series of data sets available through ICPSR will also be of special interest to students of international and comparative politics. For one, *The World Handbook of Political and Social Indicators III* (assembled by Charles Lewis Taylor and David A. Jodice) features data for 155 countries, dealing with various social, political, economic, and demographic indicators. Most data are from the 1950–1982 period. *The World Handbook of Political and Social Indicators, II* (assembled by Charles Lewis Taylor and Michael C. Hudson) consists of data for 136 countries, including indicators of population size, communications, education, culture, economics, and politics for the four base years of 1950, 1955, 1960, and 1965. *The Cross Polity Survey, 1963* (assembled by Arthur S. Banks and Robert B. Textor) features data for 115 countries, including indicators of economics, demography, political modernization, and interest articulation. *The Cross-National Time Series, 1815–1973* file (assembled by Arthur S. Banks) consists of longitudinal national data for 167 nations. Included are data dealing with demographic, social, political, and economic topics. A series of surveys (known as the Euro-Barometer studies), conducted between the years 1974 and 1992 (originally under the direction of Jacques-Rene Rabier and Ronald Inglehart, with later studies also headed by Helene Riffault, Karlheinz Reif, and Anna Melich), provides a wide variety of information on respondents from a variety of European countries. Included in the Euro-Barometer studies are data dealing with respondents' attitudes toward community goals, personal and environmental situations, European unification, regional development, status of women, consumers, poverty, and standard of living, along with standard demographic information. Though dated, *The Civic Culture Study* (compiled by Gabriel Almond and Sidney Verba) provides interesting and useful basic political attitudinal and demographic data on respondents from five countries (Germany, Italy, Mexico, the United Kingdom, and the United States) collected in 1959 and 1960.

Another data set is available from the ICPSR, which offers impressive data files of domestic public opinion polls commissioned by large news distributors such as *ABC News* and the *Washington Post*. For these two news agencies, the files consist of the results of polls conducted by telephone from 1981 to 1991; the polling process is ongoing. These polls are in three categories: the monthly polls, the special topics polls, and the election polls. The polls are concerned broadly with public opinion on politics and on a broad range of other issues, such as foreign affairs, the economy, terrorism, personal finances, and the presidency.

In addition to the more general sources just listed, it should be noted that many countries prepare yearbooks presenting a variety of useful data. Although it is not possible here to discuss each of these yearbooks, these publications typically are the most complete and most reliable for Western industrialized countries and are less regularly published for developing countries. *Official Publications of Foreign Countries* (Bethesda, MD: American Library Association, Government Publications

Round Table, 1990) describes each nation's official yearbooks and statistical yearbooks, as well as other publications from the nation. It also indicates the lack of a publication for a given action. Students should be familiar with these publications in their own particular areas or countries of interest.

Other sources on international affairs include the *World Press Review,* which reprints news stories from the press outside of the United States. Another source for internationalists to consider is the *Foreign Broadcast Information Service* (FBIS), a federal government publication issued daily by the Superintendent of Documents. The FBIS monitors broadcasts, news agency transmissions, newspapers, periodicals, and government statements. It then offers translations of this material in its FBIS Daily Reports. The reports are released by region for Asia and the Pacific, China, Eastern Europe, Latin America, the Middle East and Africa, South Asia, the Commonwealth of Independent States, and Western Europe.

OTHER SOURCES

A few additional general sources of news and statistics are of interest to all political researchers. News sources for political research include major newspapers such as the *Times, London;* the *New York Times;* the *Christian Science Monitor;* and important newspapers from the region or nation being studied, such as the *Toronto Globe and Mail* or the *Seattle Post-Intelligencer.* Finding stories in these sources is not necessarily difficult, as newspaper indexing is commonplace; several of the aforementioned papers even issue their own indexes, and much of this information can be retrieved electronically.

The Almanac of American Politics (New York: originally published by E. P. Dutton) is organized by state and issued annually. It is a good general source and starting point for researching domestic political activity. It presents a summary of important political issues in each of the American states, followed by important state census data (population size, percentage urban population, median income, median education, etc.), information on each state's share of federal outlays and economic base, state voter information (percentage of registered voters, mean voting age, employment profiles, ethnic group breakdowns), and ratings for all senators and members of congress by various rating organizations (including Americans for Democratic Action, COPE, Ripon Society, and Consumer Federation of America). The *Almanac* is an excellent quick source of information on American politics.

There are many additional compilations of data with broad application to political scientists. *American Statistics Index* (ASI) (Bethesda, MD: Congressional Information Service) is a private-sector published index to statistics compiled by the federal government. It is issued annually with monthly supplements. It can be used to locate statistics on any topic, provided the data were compiled by a government source. Three cumulative indexes simplify research on earlier years. The data are also available on compact disc. There is a companion set to ASI for the private sector, the *Statistical Reference Index* (SRI) (Bethesda, MD: Congressional Information Services). On a monthly basis, with annual updates, and four year cumulations, this set indexes statistics not issued by the federal government, including statistics on finance, business, and the economy; on social concerns such as education and health care; and on politics, the environment, and the population. This material is also included on the *Statistical Masterfile*. In addition to the index, researchers can buy the statistics themselves, as issued by the publisher, on microfiche from Congressional Information Services (CIS), if the original publisher has given CIS permission to reissue the material.

SUMMARY

The observations made at the outset of this chapter deserve to be repeated at this point. There are, today, many public and private organizations that compile and release information of interest to political and policy researchers. Although it may be fun to collect your own data, there are many reasons to look first to available data. An individual scholar, with limited time and money, simply cannot match the skills and resources of the professional data-collecting organizations discussed herein. Use of available data is strongly advised. Not only will it normally save considerable time, but also the data available almost certainly are superior to those that most individuals, in a short time and with limited resources, can assemble.

KEY TERMS

Internet	hypertext
gopher	political documents
web	listservers

EXERCISES

1. Data archives
   a. Ask your instructor, or your librarian, to direct you to the major data archival holdings available to you at your university (such as the Inter-University Consortium for Political and Social Research, and the National Opinion Research Center).
   b. Examine the guide to resources and services accompanying each of these archives, and identify a few data sets that would be of most interest to you in conducting your own research.
   c. Explore the process and feasibility of ordering data sets from these archival holdings.
2. Locate the population census and housing census reports in your library, and familiarize yourself with the data presented therein. Prepare a report on the various ways information contained therein could be used in political and policy research.

3. Locate the latest edition of *The Statistical Abstract of the United States* (compiled by the U.S. Bureau of the Census), and examine its contents. Develop a set of 10 hypotheses that could be tested from the data available there.

4. In your library, locate the (a) *Congressional Quarterly Weekly Report;* (b) *Congressional Quarterly Almanac;* and (c) *National Journal.* Select any major policy topic (education, housing, health care reform, etc.), and discuss the varying focus given that topic by these publications.

5. Locate in your library (a) *The Book of the States,* (b) *The County and City Data Book,* and (c) *The Municipal Year Book,* and report on the format and variety of data presented on state and local governments. Develop hypotheses regarding state and local issues, which could be tested by information contained in each of these.

6. Locate in your library the United Nations publications, *Statistical Yearbook* and *Demographic Yearbook.* Compare the information contained in these two publications, and develop a set of hypotheses that could be tested with the data available there.

NOTES

1. For additional advantages and disadvantages of secondary data analysis, see K. Jill Kiecolt and Laura E. Nathan, *Secondary Analysis of Survey Data* (Newbury Park, CA: Sage Publications, 1985); and David W. Stewart and Michael A. Kamins, *Secondary Research Information Sources and Methods,* 2nd ed. (Newbury Park, CA: Sage Publications, 1993).

2. Karen Hill, ed., *Research Centers Directory* (Detroit: Gale Research, 1994, 18th ed., 2 vols.).

3. Joe Morehead and Mary Fetzer, *Introduction to United States Publications Sources* (Englewood, CO: Libraries Unlimited, 1992, 4th ed.).

4. For more information on PUMS, see page 25 of the *1990 Census of Population and Housing Tabulation and Publication Program* (Washington, DC: U.S. Department of Commerce, Bureau of the Census, July, 1989).

5. Ibid.

6. The publication, "About BLS Data Diskettes," names and describes the contents of all the diskettes and gives purchase and availability information (Washington, DC: U.S. Department of Labor, Bureau of Labor Statistics, Superintendent of Documents number L2.2:D26/2/FLYER).

7. Leonard W. Levy, ed., *Encyclopedia of the Constitution* (New York: Macmillan, 1986).

8. Jay Andriot, *Township Atlas of the United States* (McLean, VA: Documents Index, 1991).

9. For a review and critique of many of the data sources mentioned in this section, as well as of other data sources, see Edward R. Tufte, "Political Statistics for the United States: Observations on Some Major Data Sources," *American Political Science Review* 71 (March, 1977), 305–314.

CHAPTER 6

Measurement Strategies:
Data Processing, Data Entry, Index and Scaling Techniques

Having collected a set of data, the researcher's attention is now directed to the assembling, storing, and processing of such information and to the issues of data measurement.

DATA PROCESSING

After the researcher has collected the information or has found an appropriate source of information, the data must be assembled in a manner that facilitates analysis. In some instances, the analysis may be performed manually, taking information directly from the questionnaire, survey schedule, or some other source. This is especially true if the number of cases is small (say, less than 100) and the amount of information collected on each case is relatively limited. In such situations, the researcher may perform the desired analytic tasks with a desk calculator.

Today, however, it is more often the case that the researcher will want to collect and store the gathered information in a manner permitting computer analysis. Computer storage is much more convenient and permanent than manual storage. Further, data prepared for computer analysis is much more easily transferred from one location or one researcher to another. Most important, however, when computers are used in conjunction with statistical and graphic software programs, they permit rapid and sophisticated statistical analysis of data, as well as the creation and imaginative display of data in all manner of charts, graphs, figures, and other pictorial forms. Modern statistical and graphical packages permit a speed and sophistication of data analysis and presentation almost impossible to otherwise achieve. Computers have become indispensable in all phases of the research process, from gathering information, to analyzing data, to writing the research report. Students of political and policy analysis must be familiar with at least the basic computer-based statistical and graphical tools.

Use of Microcomputers

It is typical to classify computers as "micros," "minis," or "mainframes," based largely on their computing speed, storage capacity, and ability to accommodate multiple users. However, as Madron, Tate, and Brookshire point out, it is more useful simply to distinguish between *personal computers* (PCs) and all others.[1] All students are familiar with the personal computer, which, in its simplest form, consists of a central processing unit, memory storage devices (hard disks and/or floppy disks), a keyboard (and possibly a mouse system) for input, and a monitor (and possibly a printer) for output. Virtually all universities, and many political science departments, have computer laboratories where personal (micro) computers are available for student use. Personal computers may be linked to others in a multiuser network of systems, but their distinguishing feature is that they are self-contained computing systems, designed to be used by one person at a time. Micros have become so popular that many relatively low-cost versions of software packages—offering word processing, database management, spreadsheet, statistical, and graphical capabilities—have been designed specifically for their use.

Student Statistical Packages

With the proliferation of microcomputers has come the availability of powerful relatively low-cost, statistical packages suitable for student use. The best of these perform standard descriptive statistics (mean, median, mode, etc.), correlation and regression analysis, scatter plots, crosstabs, *t*-tests, chi-square tests, and a variety of variable-transformation options. Some of the most widely utilized include SPSS/PC+, SAS PC, BMDP/386, MicroCrunch, Stat View, Data Desk, Systat, STATA, MicroCase, and Minitab. Many of these programs are available in both MS-DOS and Macintosh versions.[2]

Since the early 1990s, a new capability in microcomputer statistical processing has appeared: a development that Weisberg and Smith call "dynamic graphics statistical computing."[3] In addition to simply computing statistics, packages offering this option facilitate considerable interaction between the researcher and the program. Dynamic computing capabilities provide the researcher the ability to (1) identify data points in graphical displays; (2) add additional statistical analysis to a graph without executing the commands that generated the original graph; (3) move from statistical results and graphs directly to related analysis and displays, without returning to the original command entry mode; and (4) modify the data and see the effect of such modifications on the current results. Among the best of these dynamic programs currently available, according to Weisberg and Smith, are Data Desk for the Mac, and NSDstat+ for the MS-DOS platform.[4]

Data Entry: Codesheets

Information can sometimes be transferred from the survey or data source directly into computer storage through the use of software programs designed especially to accomplish this transfer. Most professional telephone polls, for example, are conducted so that the interviewers input answers directly into the computer as the interview is taking place. This, of course, greatly speeds the research process because the data are ready for analysis immediately upon conclusion of the survey. It can be argued, further, that direct data entry contributes to greater accuracy because several handling steps are eliminated.

An alternative to direct data entry is first to record the information on codesheets. A **codesheet** is a sheet of paper having several columns and several rows. Each row on the codesheet represents one case (i.e., voter, city, state, etc.). Typically, each case will be assigned a distinct identification number, and this number will be coded as well (usually in the first or last several columns). **Coding** is the process of assigning numbers to all possible responses to all questions or items.

An Example

The use of coding will become much clearer by reference to an example. Suppose that the researcher has collected some fiscal and political information on the American states. From appropriate sources, the researcher may have assembled for each of the fifty American states a set of information pertaining to per capita revenue, per capita expenditures, party affiliation, and total numbers of state senate and house members. This information might be recorded on a codesheet, as shown in Figure 6.1.

Figure 6.1 illustrates several important points about the preparation of codesheets. First, it can be seen that for each state, the same information is coded in the same columns. The same columns are consistently used for ID, per capita revenue, and so forth. This is called "fixed-field" formatting and describes the situation when variables are recorded in the same order and same location for each case. "Free-field" formatted data, by contrast, occurs when variables are recorded in the same order for each case, but not necessarily in the same column location. You need to make sure you know which formatting procedure is most convenient for the software programs you will be using to analyze your data.

Figure 6.1 shows also that the amount of column space assigned to any variable is equal to the *largest* value for that variable. In the preceding example, three column spaces are allotted to "Total House Members," even though only Alabama required this many columns. Also, note that the variables are entered into the columns so that the units position of each variable is recorded in the extreme right column; blank spaces are positioned in the left columns and are interpreted by the computer as zeros. This method is called "right-justified" fields. Once all data are recorded on codesheets, the information can then be entered directly into hard disk storage, placed on floppy disks, or stored in some other manner.

Preparation of the Codebook

Prior to conducting the analysis, the researcher usually will want first to prepare a **codebook,** which serves the researcher much as a road map serves a motorist. That

		1 2 3 4 5 6 7 8 9 10 11 12 13 14		15 16 17 18 19 20 21 22 23 24			25 26 27 28 29 30 31 32 33		
State	ID	Revenue per Capita	Expenditures per Capita	Senate Dem.	Rep.	Total	House Dem.	Rep.	Total
ALABAMA	0 1	1 9 9 8	1 9 6 8	2 8	7	3 5	8 2	2 3	1 0 5
ALASKA	0 2	9 9 5 3	7 8 8 3	1 0	1 0	2 0	2 3	1 7	4 0
ARIZONA	0 3	2 0 1 3	1 9 4 4	1 7	1 3	3 0	2 7	3 3	6 0
WISCONSIN	4 9	2 3 8 6	2 2 8 8	1 4	1 4	3 3	5 8	4 1	9 9
WYOMING	5 0	3 7 8 5	3 5 6 0	1 0	2 0	3 0	2 2	4 2	6 4

FIGURE 6.1

Example of a Codesheet

SOURCE OF DATA: *The Book of the States, 1992–1993;* and *Significant Features of Fiscal Federalism* (Advisory Commission on Intergovernmental Relations: Washington, DC), September, 1993.

is, the codebook tells the researcher the precise location of each variable in the data set. For a small set of data (such as the set illustrated in Figure 6.1), the codebook may be only one page in length, or it may not be necessary at all (the codesheet can, in effect, serve as the codebook). For larger sets of data, a codebook is essential.

Codebooks normally describe each variable, indicate response possibilities, and present the values assigned to each response. As an example, the section of the codebook for the Inter-University Consortium for Political and Social Research: (ICPSR) 1994 American National Election Survey dealing with party identification is reproduced here:

Var #

652   Generally speaking, do you usually think of yourself as a Republican, a Democrat, an Independent, or what?

1. REPUBLICAN
2. INDEPENDENT
3. NO PREFERENCE
4. OTHER PARTY
5. DEMOCRAT
8. DK
9. NA

This section of the 1994 American National Election Study codebook (which exceeds 350 pages) indicates the number assigned to this variable (#652), the precise question that was asked, the possible response categories (Republican, Democrat, etc.), and the numerical value assigned to each response category. When conducting surveys, it is common to assign values (in this case 8 and 9) to those who do not know answers to questions or who refuse to answer.

VARIABLES AND VALUES

We have been using the term *variable* in several different contexts; it is time now to examine this term more closely. **Variables** are empirical terms having two or more values. Sex, party identification, years of education, age, annual income, and race are all examples of variables often used in political research. Variables that may vary by magnitude (more than, less than, higher than, lower than, etc.) are **quantitative variables;** those that vary by attributes are **qualitative variables.** Age and education are examples of quantitative variables; sex, party identification (when coded as Democrat, Republican, or Independent), and religion are qualitative variables.

Variables may also be distinguished according to the number of values they may assume. Some variables are *dichotomous,* taking only either of two values. Sex is an example of a dichotomous variable, as is employment status defined as employed or unemployed, as well as race defined as white or nonwhite. Some variables may take on several values (such as social class, party identification, and education); still others may have a range of values, almost equivalent to the size of the population (such as income).

Three classifications of variables are referred to at several junctures in this text. **Dependent variables** are those we are trying to explain, understand, or predict. **Independent variables** are those we are using to assist in our explanation, understanding, or prediction of the dependent variable. **Control variables,** explained more fully in later chapters, are those assisting in more clearly defining the relationship between the independent and the dependent variables. It should also be understood that the terms independent, dependent, and control variables are situationally defined. A variable considered to be the independent variable in one study may be taken as the dependent variable in another. One researcher may be interested in the effects of "strength of party identification" (taken as the independent variable) on political behavior; another may be interested in those factors that predict or are correlated with "strength of party identification" (taken as the dependent variable).

LEVELS OF MEASUREMENT

Coding, as mentioned previously, is the process of assigning numbers to represent the values of variables. Coding is an important stage in the research process. Research could proceed without assigning numbers to all variables (party identification could be labeled simply "Democrat," "Republican," "Independent," or "Other"), but the assignment of numbers greatly facilitates the analysis process. At the same time, it is clear that the numbers assigned to particular classifications of data cannot all be manipulated in the same way. We know that assigning a 1 to the Protestant category of religion, a 2 to the Catholic, and a 3 to the Jewish is not to imply any particular ordering among those categories. Numbers can be used in several different ways. Sometimes, numbers can be used only as convenient labels for categories of variables; sometimes, they can be used to rank order categories of variables; and sometimes, they can be used to specify the distance or interval between categories of variables. It is essential that the student distinguish among these levels of measurement. Various analytic techniques are designed to be applied to specific levels of measurement.

Nominal Measures

Nominal measures are those that simply attach numeric labels to various categories of variables. In this instance, numbers are assigned to categories of variables simply as a convenient means of classification. Symbols other than numbers could be used, but numbers facilitate analysis with electronic data-processing equipment. Many examples of nominal measures are available in political and policy research. When assigning to the variable "religion" the value of 1 for all Protestants, 2 for all Catholics, 3 for all Jews, and 4 for all other religions, the researcher has developed a nominal measure of religious preference. Sex, party identification (when coded as Democrat, Republican, or Independent), region of the country, nationality, race, and college major are typical examples of nominal variables. Numbers that are assigned to categories of nominal measures do not show order or distance; they only classify.

The important point about numbers assigned to categories of nominal variables is that they be *mutually exclusive* (no case can be assigned to more than one category) and that they be *exhaustive* (all cases are assigned to one of the categories). The selection of numbers assigned to the categories is arbitrary. Protestants could be assigned the number 1, 5, or 20; it makes no difference (as long as different distinct numbers are assigned to Catholics, Jews, and other religious preferences).

Ordinal Measures

Ordinal measures not only classify but also rank (or order) the assigned values along some characteristic or property. Ordinal measures, then, indicate positioning—a higher number may indicate "more than," "greater than," or "more likely than" a lower value. Socioeconomic status—when categorized as working class, middle class, or upper class—would be considered an ordinal scale. If the numbers 1, 2, and 3 were assigned to the various values of socioeconomic status, individuals assigned a 3 are defined as having a higher value on this scale than are those assigned a 1 or a 2. An example of an ordinal scale is the measure of liberalism–conservatism used by the ICPSR in its American national election surveys. That question, as asked in the 1994 survey, is presented in Figure 6.2.

We hear a lot of talk these days about liberals and conservatives. Here is a 7-point scale on which the political views that people might hold are arranged from extremely liberal to extremely conservative. Where would you place yourself on this scale, or haven't you thought much about this?

1	2	3	4	5	6	7
Extremely Liberal	Liberal	Slightly Liberal	Moderate, Middle of Road	Slightly Conservative	Conservative	Extremely Conservative

FIGURE 6.2

Survey Research Center's Measure of Liberalism–Conservatism

SOURCE: 1994 American National Election Study.

Ordinal measures indicate degrees of difference but do not represent equivalence of interval difference. In the example of the liberalism–conservatism measure, a 7 is a more conservative response than a 6, but we do not know *how much more* conservative. The difference between a 6 and a 7 may not be equivalent to the distance between a 5 and a 6, and indeed, the distance between a 6 and a 7 may not be the same even for any two people. However, ordinal measures do permit comparisons, and statements of "greater than," "more than," and the like are appropriate.

Interval and Ratio Measures

Interval measures are those for which the properties of a variable can be ranked or ordered with exact and constant distances between the rankings. Interval measures not only position and categorize phenomena, but they also indicate the extent of difference between values. Income, education, temperature, and age are examples of interval measures. **Ratio measures** have all the properties of interval measures, and they also have a natural "zero" point. Properties such as weight, time, and length can be measured at the ratio level.

In political and policy science, many of our measures are of the nominal or ordinal variety. Many also are interval in nature. Such information as population size, gross national product, voting turnout, and revenue and expenditure data could all be measured at the interval level. Even data that clearly are nominal may be transferred into metric-level measurement by conversion to percentages, when this is appropriate. The researcher might measure religion as percentage Catholic, Protestant, or Jewish; party identification might be measured as percentage Democrat or Republican; and so on. Frequently, it is desirable to use the highest level classification scheme possible because higher level measures permit more sophisticated and interesting analysis.

INDEXES AND SCALES

Scaling techniques are helpful to political and policy research for several reasons. Scaling techniques often aid in the measurement and operationalization of very complex concepts. Concepts such as alienation, racial prejudice, and political activism may be too complex to be adequately measured by reference to a single item. Several items designed to measure the various dimensions of these concepts might be included on a survey, and the combined responses to these items would be said to form a scale of alienation, racial prejudice, or political activism.

A similar point was made by Robert F. DeVellis, when he argued that scales are used to measure "theoretical," as opposed to "atheoretical" concepts.[5] **Atheoretical concepts** (i.e., those readily **observable**) such as age, race, and sex can be measured by simple observation or by just asking respondents to reveal this information. Scales are used, however, "when we want to measure phenomena that we believe to exist because of our theoretical understanding of the world, but which we cannot assess directly."[6]

Scales also may be used in an attempt to develop higher level measures of a particular concept. Scales may be used to develop ordinal or even interval-like level measures. "Finally, scales may be viewed as efficient means of summarizing information. A survey might include several items designed to measure self-esteem, political activism, or levels of political information. Analyzing each separate indicator might be tedious and repetitious; combining the items into a single scale of self- esteem, political activism, or political information might be a preferable way to present the information.[7]

For these reasons, the topic of scaling is important to political and policy research. Sometimes, the term *scale* is used to describe items measured by only one item or only one question. As an example, the ICPSR in its 1994 American National Election Study, asked the question shown in Figure 6.3. This item can be considered a women's rights scale. Respondents indicate that they are more or less in favor of equal roles for women and men.

More generally, scales are thought of as **composite measures** formed by combining scores or answers to two or more items. *Scaling* is defined here as a technique combining two or more measures in order to form a single score that is assigned to each individual or case. Some of the most often used of these techniques are discussed next.

Index Construction

The easiest, and perhaps the most common, form of scaling might simply be termed *index construction*. The words *index* and *scale* are used almost interchangeably in the literature, but as used here, an *index* refers to assigning scores based simply on the combined response to two or more items assumed to be related. Scaling techniques are also designed to achieve a single score based on responses to two or more items, but the selection, ordering, and weighting of items is accomplished in a more sophisticated manner.[8]

Recently there has been a lot of talk about women's rights. Some people feel that women should have an equal role with men in running business, industry, and government. Suppose these people are at one end of a scale, at point 1. Others feel that a woman's place is in the home. Suppose these people are at the other end, at point 7. And, of course, some other people have opinions somewhere in between at points 2, 3, 4, 5, or 6. Where would you place yourself on this scale, or haven't you thought much about this?

1	2	3	4	5	6	7

Women and
Men Should   A Woman's
   Have an   Place Is in
Equal Role   the Home

FIGURE 6.3
Women's Rights Scale
SOURCE: 1994 American National Election Study.

Researchers Sidney Verba, Kay Lehman Scholzman, Henry Brady, and Norman H. Nie created an index of citizen activity based on whether respondents participated in a number of political acts.[9] Relying on responses from a sample of 15,000 Americans, their measure was constructed as follows:

Did respondent report	Yes	No
1. voting?	____	____
2. working in a political campaign?	____	____
3. making a campaign contribution?	____	____
4. contacting a government official in the past year?	____	____
5. attending a protest, march, or demonstration within the past two years?	____	____
6. working informally to deal with some community issue?	____	____
7. serving in a voluntary capacity on a local governing board or attending meetings of such a board?	____	____

Assigning a code of "1" for each positive or "yes" response, and a "0" for each "no" response, scores on their scale of citizen activity could range from 0 to 7. The average score for the entire sample was reported by Verba et al. to be 1.75.

Index construction, it can be seen, is very simple. However, some disadvantages of the technique are obvious also. First, it is difficult to know how to weight the various components of the index. In the preceding example, all items were assigned equal weights; however, some researchers might assign greater importance—and thus might weight more heavily—some activity items (such as making political contributions) than others. The decision as to how weights are to be assigned, if at all, is left largely to the individual researcher.

Another problem of index construction is the interpretation of scores other than the highest and lowest values. In the preceding example, a score of "0" indicates participation in none of the listed activities, and a score of "7" indicates participation in all, but how are scores 1 through 6 to be interpreted? A score of 3, for example, could be achieved through participation in several different combinations of activities, but it is not apparent which items would be combined to achieve this score for any particular respondent. Most important, perhaps, is the fact that when we create indexes, we frequently have no way of empirically knowing whether the components of the index are really interrelated. Are the items all tapping the same dimension of activity or attitude, or are they tapping other dimensions as well? More elaborate means of scale construction have been developed to address such issues. These are discussed in the following sections.

Likert Scaling

The **Likert scaling technique** is designed to provide some empirical justification for selecting which items to include on the scale.[10] Assume that the researcher wants to construct an index of domestic liberalism. Briefly stated, the steps in Likert scale construction are as follows:

1. The researcher assembles a large number of questions (perhaps 50 items or more), which he or she believes tap the dimension of domestic liberalism.
2. Possible responses to each item so selected are ordered on a continuum indicating intensity of feeling (such as from strongly agree to strongly disagree, or strongly favor to strongly disapprove). Usually, this is a five-point response continuum (with responses such as strongly agree, agree, uncertain, disagree, strongly disagree), with the middle category reserved as a "no opinion" or "uncertain" response category. However, a continuum of seven, nine, or more responses is possible.
3. Each response to each question is assigned a score value. A response of "strongly agree" may be assigned a score of 4 and a "strongly disagree" response may be assigned a score of "0." It is important that scores are assigned to questions in a consistent manner. If the answer considered to be most conservative to one question is assigned a score of "0," all most-conservative responses must be assigned the score of "0." The scoring scheme is not revealed to respondents.
4. The researcher then selects a sample of respondents believed to be representative of the group to which the scale is to be administered. If the researcher were attempting to construct a scale to measure domestic liberalism of the elementary and secondary school population, this sample might consist of schoolchildren. All items that have been selected for possible scale inclusion are then administered to the sample.

5. Based on the answers to these questions, each respondent is assigned a total score. If the researcher has assembled 50 questions designed to measure domestic liberalism, and the most liberal response to each question is assigned a score value of 4 and the most conservative is assigned a score value of 0, any individual's *total* score could range from 200 (most liberal) to 0 (most conservative) and any individual's *average* score could range from 4.0 to 0.0.

6. Based on their total scores, the sample subjects are then divided into groupings. For items measuring liberalism, the sample might be broken into quartiles: the 25 percent with the most liberal scores, the 25 percent next most liberal, the 25 percent who are even less liberal, and the 25 percent with the most conservative scores.

7. Each item on the original list of 50 is then separately evaluated, and those found to best discriminate between the highest quartile of scores (in this example the most liberal respondents) and the lowest quartile (here, the most conservative respondents) are selected for inclusion in the final scale.[11]

If, for example, the weighted mean score of the most liberal quartile on the first question were found to be 3.5, and the weighted mean score of the most conservative were found to be 1.5, the difference would be 2.0. For each item in the scale, this difference is known as the **discriminative power** of the item. If the difference in weighted mean scores between the most liberal and most conservative quartiles on the second question were found to be only 0.5, it would be concluded that the first question better discriminates between liberal and conservative respondents. The researcher might then apply more rigorous tests to distinguish differences of means between the items. Nonetheless, the point is that items having the greatest mean difference are assumed to best discriminate among those to whom the index is to be administered, and those questions are selected for inclusion in the final index.

The Likert technique can be criticized on two grounds: (1) There is no way to determine whether the items finally selected to comprise the index really do measure the concept of interest (in the preceding example, domestic liberalism); and (2) because of its obvious reliance on the selection of extreme items, the Likert technique may not be able to satisfactorily distinguish between more moderate respondents. Still, the technique provides a relatively rational basis for item selection; it is relatively quick to apply and administer; and it provides a range of alterative responses to each question. For these reasons, the Likert technique is widely used in political and policy research.

One example of the use of the Likert technique is Thompson and Browne's study of urban bureaucratic responses to the hiring of minorities. The authors wanted to develop a scale of attitudes toward minority hiring, which was to be administered to a sample of urban personnel management officials. According to the authors, "In order to measure commitment to hiring minorities, [we] solicited the advice of a panel of personnel experts and subsequently devised a set of eight Likert items. These items are designed to measure the degree to which officials believe that government should seek out and employ minorities where these groups suffer from underrepresentation in the public bureaucracy."[12] The personnel management officials were asked to indicate their extent of agreement or disagreement with the following items from Thompson and Browne's scale:

Scale of Attitudes toward Hiring Minorities

1. That the government should make a special effort to advertise job vacancies in the minority community.
2. That minorities should receive preference where minority and white applicants are of equal ability and minorities are underrepresented on a department's work force.
3. That government has a responsibility to recruit members of disadvantaged groups.
4. That government employers are *not* placing too much emphasis on affirmative action.
5. That special committees of minority leaders should be set up to make recommendations to improve hiring.
6. That government should at times hire a minority applicant even if there is a more competent white one who wants the job.
7. That where minorities are underrepresented, consideration should be given to hiring only minorities until they attain adequate representation.
8. That public agencies should establish hiring targets for racial minorities and timetables for obtaining them.[13]

In constructing the final Likert-type scale, it is important that the items selected be varied so that (in the case of liberalism, for example) the extreme responses at one end of the continuum are not always those in agreement with each statement, and the extreme responses at the other end of the continuum are not always in disagreement. The questions should be presented so that agreement sometimes indicates a response at one extreme and sometimes indicates a response at the opposite extreme. This counterbalancing helps to prevent respondents from falling into what is known as a *response-set* pattern—simply selecting the same responses for each item without thoroughly considering each question. In their survey, Thompson and Browne reversed three of the items in their minority hiring scale so that positive responses did not always indicate a favorable attitude toward minority hiring.

Thurstone Scales

A number of methods were devised by Louis Thurstone in his attempts to develop scaling techniques resulting in scales that more clearly possess interval properties. These techniques are variously known as the methods of *paired comparisons, equal-appearing intervals,* and *successive intervals.*[14] Although each method cannot be described in detail here, the general procedure for the equal-appearing interval method is as follows:

1. The researcher selects a large number of items possibly measuring the dimension being examined (liberalism, prejudice, alienation, etc.).
2. A large number of judges (50 or more) are asked to sort these statements into several piles (usually 7 or 11), ranging from those most favorable for the dimension being examined to those most unfavorable.[15]

3. Each statement is assigned a score equivalent to its mean (sometimes median) position in the various groups. If 25 of 50 judges placed the first statement in the first pile, and 25 placed it in the second pile, its score would be 1.5.
4. Statements that receive widely diverse pile placements are discarded. If, for example, 10 judges placed the third statement in the first pile, 10 place it in the third grouping, 10 place it in the fifth pile, 10 place it in the seventh pile, and 10 place it in the eleventh grouping, the statement probably should be discarded as being too ambiguous.
5. From the remaining items, the researcher selects a set that is evenly spread along the various points on the continuum.

When the Thurstone scale is administered, respondents are asked to indicate whether they agree or disagree with each statement (each of which has been assigned a score according to the aforementioned procedure). Of course, the value assigned to each item is not revealed to the respondents, and respondents' total scores are calculated as the mean value of the statements to which they agree.

An example of the use of the Thurstone technique is provided by Balogh and Mueller, in their development of a scale they call the "Attitude toward Capital Punishment Scale."[16] First, Balogh and Mueller developed a pool of 100 statements they considered to be relevant to capital punishment, collected from magazine articles and books. Next, they presented these items to 15 criminology students, who were asked to place each statement in one of seven piles, indicating the degree of each statement's favorability toward capital punishment. Items indicating a very favorable attitude toward capital punishment were placed in the first pile; items indicating the least favorable attitude toward capital punishment were placed in the seventh pile. Items considered neutral toward capital punishment were placed in the fourth pile. As with Likert technique, Balogh and Mueller performed an analysis of each item to select those that best discriminated among the group of students. The 15 items selected to compose their scale of attitudes toward capital punishment, along with each item's scale value (with a lower score indicating a more favorable attitude toward capital punishment), are presented in Figure 6.4.

The advantage of the Thurstone technique is its presumed achievement of an interval (or at least an interval-appearing) scale. A number of problems are also associated with the technique. The selection of judges may have a biasing influence on the assignment of scale values. Judges from differing backgrounds may rate items differently. Also, because scale scores are calculated as the mean or median of the value of those items agreed to, the same score on the scale may represent different attitudinal dimensions. That is, the same score may be achieved by those responding differently to different questions.

Techniques are available that may assist in minimizing the preceding problems. Perhaps the principal reason that the technique is not used more often is due simply to the cumbersome and time-consuming procedures required. In proportion to the amount of effort involved, the results have not been shown to be clearly superior to those obtained by the Likert procedure. As DeVellis put it, "Thurstone scaling is an interesting and sometimes suitable approach . . . [however] the practical

Item	Scale Value
1. Capital punishment is not morally right or wrong; it is merely just one method of punishment.	4.0
2. A murderer deserves to die.	1.1
3. Murderers are social misfits and are useless to society; therefore it is best to execute them.	1.3
4. Society does not have the right to take a human life no matter what the circumstances.	6.7
5. The public would feel less secure if capital punishment were abolished.	2.6
6. When a murderer is sentenced to death, society is just as bad as the condemned.	6.7
7. Since capital punishment has not prevented murders, society should abolish it.	5.1
8. Murder is a sin and should be punished by death.	1.2
9. Statistics show that a person will only kill once; therefore, the murderer should be allowed to live and prove himself.	5.6
10. Since murderers can be rehabilitated, they deserve the chance to become useful citizens	6.1
11. Capital punishment will do until something better is found.	3.4
12. Society should make murderers work for the state rather than execute them.	5.5
13. Capital punishment seems to have proven to be a fairly effective deterrent to murder.	2.9
14. When society sentences a murderer to death, we ourselves become murderers.	6.8
15. Rather than execute a murderer, society should try to help him through treatment.	6.0

FIGURE 6.4

Scale of Attitudes toward Capital Punishment

NOTE: When administering this scale, respondents are asked to place a check mark beside each item with which they agree. A total score is obtained by summing the scale values of all items to which a respondent agrees. *High* scores indicate *negative* attitudes toward capital punishment.

SOURCE: J. Balogh and M.A. Mueller, "A Scaling Technique for Measuring Social Attitudes toward Capital Punishment," *Sociology and Social Research* 45 (1960), 24–26.

problems associated with the method often outweigh its advantages unless the researcher has a compelling reason for wanting the type of calibration it provides."[17]

Guttman Scaling Techniques

All the aforementioned techniques share one common problem. They can provide no assurance that the items selected to compose the scale all actually measure the same dimension. Consider the following hypothetical "scale of campaign participation," constructed from items asked in the ICPSR 1994 American National Election Study.

During the campaign this year, did you	Yes	No
1. talk to any people and try to show them why they should vote for or against one of the parties or candidates?	_____	_____
2. wear a campaign button, put a campaign sticker on your car, or place a sign in your window or in front of your house?	_____	_____
3. go to any political meetings, rallies, speeches, dinners, or things like that in support of a particular candidate?	_____	_____
4. do any other work for one of the parties or candidates?	_____	_____
5. give money to an individual candidate (or political party) during this election year?	_____	_____

Following the aforementioned techniques, a scale of campaign activity might be constructed simply by summing each individual's response to these five items, so that scores would range from 0 (for those participating in none of the activities) to 5 (for those participating in all activities). Constructed in this manner, however, many of the same scale scores—1, 2, 3, 4—could be achieved through several different combinations of responses. As it stands, there would be no way to determine from these scale scores whether the same score is tapping identical or different dimensions of campaign activity. A score of 2 achieved through contributing money and working for a candidate may denote a degree of activism and campaign commitment different from a score of 2 achieved from talking to someone (such as a spouse or roommate) about the election and wearing a campaign button. Some indication of whether the scale items are measuring a single dimension (i.e., are unidimensional) is clearly desirable. The Guttman technique attempts to provide such a measure.[18]

The **Guttman technique** begins by ordering potential scale items according to the degree of difficulty assumed to be associated with responding positively to each item. According to the logic of the Guttman technique, if the scale that has been developed really is unidimensional, it would be expected that individuals responding positively to the more difficult items would also respond positively to the less difficult items. For purposes of illustration, assume that the researcher has ranked the aforementioned campaign activity items in order of difficulty and that six individuals have been asked whether they participated in the various activities. The distribution of answers to these questions might appear as shown in Figure 6.5.

In Figure 6.5, a distribution is observed that is said to be perfectly unidimensional. As such, any individual's answer to each campaign activity can be predicted with complete accuracy from knowledge of that person's total score. Knowing that individual D received a score of 2, the researcher also knows the activities in which this person participated (talking and wearing a button) and those in which he or she did not participate. The researcher is thus able to *reproduce* each individual's

	More Difficult ◄ - ► Less Difficult					Scale Score
Person:	Give money?	Work for candidate?	Go to meetings?	Wear button?	Talk to anyone?	
A	Yes	Yes	Yes	Yes	Yes	5
B	No	Yes	Yes	Yes	Yes	4
C	No	No	Yes	Yes	Yes	3
D	No	No	No	Yes	Yes	2
E	No	No	No	No	Yes	1
F	No	No	No	No	No	0

FIGURE 6.5
Illustration of Unidimensionality

answers to each question by knowing each individual's total score. Of course, it almost never would be the case that a scale would achieve 100 percent reproducibility, as in the preceding simplified example. More likely, there will be a number of **error responses,** which deviate from the expected pattern. If in the preceding example, person E had responded "yes" to wearing a button but "no" to talking about the election, this would be considered one deviation or error from expected unidimensionality. The ratio of these error responses to the total number of possible responses, known as the **coefficient of reproducibility,** provides one criterion for judging the unidimensionality of a set of scale items. The coefficient of reproducibility (CR) is calculated as:

$$CR = 1 - \frac{\text{number of errors}}{\text{total number of responses}}$$

where the total number of responses is equal to the total number of cases (or respondents) times the total number of scale items.

A second criterion for evaluating a Guttman scale, known as the **coefficient of scalability,** is essentially a measure of how much the scaling routine actually improves reproducibility over what would have been expected simply by reference to the marginal totals of responses for each item. Although there are no absolute standards, it is recommended that a coefficient of reproducibility of at least .90, and a coefficient of scalability of at least .60 should be achieved. If, in the original evaluation of potential scale items, either coefficient is below the recommended level, the scale can often be improved by dropping some items.

An interesting use of the Guttman technique was provided by Judy A. Andrews and her co-authors, in their construction of a scale of "Adolescent Substance Use."[19] As they describe their process, 756 adolescents were recruited from a moderate-sized northwestern urban area and were asked to complete a survey dealing with their use of cigarettes, marijuana, alcohol, and "hard drugs" (including barbiturates,

TABLE 6.1

Scale of Adolescent Substance Use

	Totals	**Percent**
Pure scale types	682	90.2
Abstainers	159	21.0
Alcohol	162	21.4
Cigarettes	121	16.0
Marijuana	145	19.2
Hard drugs	95	12.6
Error types	74	9.8
Cigarettes only	36	4.8
Cigarettes and marijuana	7	.9
Alcohol and marijuana	16	2.1
Alcohol, cigarettes, and hard drugs	8	1.1
Other error types	7	.9
CR = .961		

SOURCE: Andrews et al., "The Construction, Validation and Use of a Guttman Scale of Adolescent Substance Use."

cocaine, hallucinogens, and opiates). The progression of response tested by the Guttman routine was (a) had never used any substance, (b) had used alcohol, (c) had used cigarettes, (d) had used marijuana, and (e) had used at least one hard drug. The results of their scaling, showing numbers of adolescents classified as "pure" scale types and numbers classified as "error" types, is shown in Table 6.1.

Like the other scaling techniques, the Guttman technique is not without problems. One of these is that the Guttman technique typically is applied ex post facto. That is, the test is applied to a set of data after the data have been collected. Even if the items meet the suggested criteria for one set of individuals, there is no assurance that the same items will form an acceptable scale for another group. Thus, the researcher designing a scale meeting the criteria necessary for unidimensionality must evaluate the items of that scale with every administration.[20]

Factor Analysis

A final scaling technique discussed here is factor analysis, a statistical routine having many applications, one of which is the construction of scales. In general, **factor analysis** describes a statistical technique used to identify a relatively small number of underlying factors ("dimensions") that can be used to represent relationships among sets of many interrelated variables. Responses to many questions might be submitted to a factor analysis, and the results would (a) indicate the most important underlying dimensions among that set of questions, and (b) show which questions were most highly related to which dimensions.

For example, in a survey of students at your university, you might ask respondents to rate how important they believe to be a number of potential problems facing the United States. Dozens of items might be rated. Various students probably would rate as very important issues relating to health care, employment, housing, environment, abortion, law and order, women's rights, national defense, waste in government, and so on. In all probability, some underlying patterns of response would occur, so that those students rating as important an issue such as pollution would also rate highly issues such as disposal of radioactive waste, conservation of natural resources, development of alterative sources of energy, and so forth. However, these patterns might not be obvious through casual inspection alone. Factor analysis makes such patterns clear.

Factor analysis begins by computing a correlation matrix for all variables. The correlation matrix becomes the input for the factor analysis, which extracts the factors (sometimes called "latent variables") necessary to represent the matrix. The extent to which each item is related to each factor is measured by a score known as a **factor loading.** Factor loadings range from 0 to 1.0. Items having high loadings on particular factors are highly related to the underlying dimension or concept represented by that factor. In this manner, scales may be developed by selecting variables that are shown to load highly on particular factors (normally, a factor loading of 0.500 or higher would be required for the identification of variables to comprise a particular scale).

Lee Ann Banaszak and Eric Pultzer used factor analysis to assist in their construction of a "Profeminism Scale."[21] Based on national surveys from a number of European countries (including Belgium, France, Germany, Ireland, Italy, Luxembourg, The Netherlands, and the United Kingdom), they applied factor analysis to a set of questions to identify items measuring attitudes toward feminism. The six items selected for measuring this concept, along with the factor loadings on the feminism dimension, are shown in Table 6.2.

Factor analysis is a very useful tool in scale development. It is especially helpful when trying to reduce a large number of variables to a few that are most representative of underlying dimensions or concepts; these underlying dimensions may then be most appropriate to serve as scale items for that concept.

RELIABILITY AND VALIDITY

A final consideration in the development of scales concerns the issues of reliability and validity. To be useful, scales should be both reliable and valid. Measures are **reliable** to the extent that the same individual achieves identical (or nearly identical) scores on repeated administration of the measure. Measures are **valid** to the extent that the measures really reflect the actual activity or behavior that is being studied. As Carmines and Zeller put it, "reliability focuses on a particular property of empirical indicators—the extent to which they provide consistent results across repeated measurements . . . validity concerns the crucial relationship between concept and indicator."[22] As an example, a measure of alienation is said to be reliable if the same

TABLE 6.2

Profeminism Scale

Item	Factor Loading
1. What is your opinion of movements which have come about recently whose aim is the liberation of women?	.652
2. Do you agree with the aim to fight against prejudiced people who would like to keep women in a subordinate role both in the family and in society?	.647
3. Do you agree with the aim to obtain true equality between women and men in their work in careers?	.752
4. Do you agree with the aim to persuade the political parties to give women the same chances as men of reaching responsible positions in the parties and of becoming candidates in elections?	.714
5. Do you agree with the aim to arrange things so that when a child is unwell it could be either the father or the mother who stays home to care for it?	.638
6. Do you agree with the aim to organize women into an independent movement to achieve a radical transformation of society?	.520

SOURCE: Banaszak and Pluzer, "Contextual Determinants of Feminist Attitudes: National and Subnational Influences in Western Europe."

individuals receive approximately the same scores on repeated testing, or if individuals having similar levels of alienation receive similar scores. An indicator of alienation is said to be valid if it is really measuring the concept of alienation and not some other concept.[23]

Reliability

Reliability is a reflection of stability, dependability, and consistency in measurement. It is assumed that any individual's score on some scale is a result of that individual's true position on the concept being measured (alienation, racial prejudice, or campaign activity, for example), plus an error component. Error may be caused by any number of factors, including those relating to the inadequacy of the measuring instrument. Lack of reliability, in essence, is a function of this error component for any individual's or any group's score. The greater the variation in total score attributable to error, the less reliable is the measure.

A number of techniques are available for estimating the reliability of a particular measure. Using the **test–retest method** of estimating reliability, the researcher simply administers the same test to the same group on more than one occasion. The correlation between the scores on the different administrations is said to be the measure of reliability. The higher the correlation between the sets of scores, the more reliable is the measure. The test–retest method has some obvious limitations. In the first place, researchers often are not able to obtain measures at several times. Costs, availability of respondents, and time constraints all limit our ability to retest individuals. Also, as Carmines and Zeller correctly pointed out, different scores at different times may not mean that the measure is unreliable. It may mean, instead, that the people's attitudes about a particular issue have, in fact, changed.[24] Another problem with the test–retest method is that repeated administrations of the same test to the same individuals may influence their scores.

The **alternative-form method** of estimating reliability is similar to the test–retest method in that it requires testing a group of individuals on at least two occasions. It differs, however, in that the same test is not used in each situation; rather, an alternative form of the test is administered. It is assumed that each test is measuring the same concept and, indeed, the tests should not differ from each other in any systematic way. Correlation between scores on the alternative forms provides the measure of reliability. The most obvious difficulty with this procedure is in developing alternative test forms that are identical in every way except for the wording of questions.

The **split-half method** of estimating reliability splits or divides an original scale into two or more subscales. Each subscale is administered to a group of individuals, and the average difference among the obtained scores is said to be a measure of test reliability. If the scores on one subscale deviate from the scores on a second subscale by an average of 5 percent, the split-half reliability would be said to be 0.95 (1.0 minus 0.05). A score of 0.90 or higher is considered acceptable evidence of a reliable scale.

An alternative assessment of split-half reliability is known as the Spearman–Brown prophecy formula.[25] In using this formula, when the total test is twice as long as each split part (if, for example, a 10-item measure were divided into two 5-item scales), the formula can be presented as follows:

$$p_{xx}'' = \frac{2 p_{xx}'}{1 + p_{xx}'}$$

where p_{xx}'' = the reliability coefficient for the whole test
p_{xx}' = the split-half correlation

The topic of correlation is dealt with more formally in later chapters. Here, it can be said that correlation is a measure of the strength of relationship or association between variables (or items in a scale). Correlation coefficients generally range from 0.0 (in the case of no linear relationship between variables), to 1.0 (in the case of perfect linear relationships). If the correlation between scores on two halves of a scale were found to be 0.75, for example, the reliability for the total test applying the Spearman–Brown technique would be

$$pxx'' = \frac{[(2)\,(.75)]}{1 + .75}$$

or

$$pxx'' = 0.857$$

Because this score can range from between 0.0 to 1.0, higher scores are considered to indicate greater reliability.

The Spearman–Brown procedure is criticized because of its lack of uniqueness: The procedure yields different coefficients, depending on which items are grouped when the test is split into two parts. Accordingly, other methods of reliability testing have been developed. Known collectively as tests of **internal consistency,** these procedures measure the correlation among all of the scale items simultaneously rather than in any particular split. The most widely used of these tests today is known as Cronbach's alpha (α).[26] The formula for Cronbach's α can be presented as follows:

$$\alpha = \frac{N\bar{p}}{[1 + \bar{p}(N - 1)]}$$

where N = number of items in the scale
$\bar{p}$ = the average interitem correlation.

If for example, the average interitem correlation of a seven item scale is .40, then α would be calculated as:

$$\alpha = \frac{7\,(.40)}{[1 + .40\,(7 - 1)]}$$

or

$$\alpha = 0.823$$

Cronbach's α ranges from 0.0 to 1.0, with higher values indicating greater reliability. For the Profeminism Scale presented in Table 6.2, Banaszak and Pultzer report an α of 0.72.[27]

Validity

Validity refers to whether the measuring instrument actually measures what it purports to measure. A valid measure of intelligence measures intelligence and not something else. The determination of validity is more important, and more difficult, than the determination of reliability. A measure that is valid would have to be reasonably reliable, but a reliable measure (one producing the same scores on repeated administrations) may not be valid (it may be measuring unknown properties). Measurement validity is very difficult to establish, especially in political and policy science. If "true" positions on the construct of interest were known, validity could be directly assessed simply by comparing scale scores with known positions. However, because true positions are almost never known, validity can only indirectly be estimated by reference to other relevant indicators.

Content validity refers to whether the scale reflects the full range of issues about the concept being measured. A test of arithmetic, for example, would not be content valid if it included only addition problems, ignoring subtraction, multiplication, and division. A test of campaign participation would not be content valid if it included only giving money to a candidate and ignored other activities, such as going to meetings, talking to people about the campaign, and so forth. In order to ensure content validity, the researcher must carefully search the literature to make sure that all the ways in which the construct is used are measured by items on the scale. While there is no single statistical test that can be used to make sure that content validity has been established, procedures can be followed that assist in this regard. As Bohrnstedt suggested, these procedures include (1) sampling from the full construct domain being examined; (2) stratifying the concept into its major components, and selecting items to measure each; (3) writing scale items to be sure to capture the shades of meaning associated with each stratum; and (4) analyzing the items after data have been collected, to determine whether items in a stratum correlate more highly with each other than they do with other items on other strata.[28]

Criterion validity is ascertained by comparing the scale being developed with another direct measure of the characteristic being investigated. A scale of religious orthodoxy, for example, could be evaluated by comparing responses with church attendance. College entrance exams could be evaluated by comparing with success (e.g., grades) in college. A statistical measure of criterion validity can be generated simply by calculating the correlation between the scale and the criterion. This coefficient is taken to be the "validity coefficient."[29] Probably the most apparent problem in ascertaining criterion validation is that for many political measures, there exist no obvious criterion variables. Concepts such as political trust, political efficacy, and political alienation, as examples, are difficult to assess by reference to direct, objective criterion measures.

Construct validity attempts to logically relate scale items within a theoretical context. Basically, construct validity deals with the extent to which a particular measure relates to other measures in a manner that would be theoretically suggested from hypotheses concerning the concept being examined. It would be expected that measures of civil rights attitudes would correlate with measures of welfare attitudes, measures of conservatism would correlate with measures of candidate preference, measures of self-esteem would correlate with participation in civic activities, and so forth. Of course, perfect congruency among the various measures is not required, but the expectation is that if the underlying assumptions are correct, some congruence should result if the measures are indeed valid.

SUMMARY

This chapter has reviewed the assorted topics of managing, processing, and measuring information. It has been noted that the computer, and especially the PC, is today an indispensable tool of political and policy research. Recently developed, affordable versions of PC-compatible sophisticated word-processing, database management, statistical, and graphical software packages have greatly facilitated the tasks of data processing, analysis, and presentation. Data-management capabilities, which only a few years ago could be achieved only by the most advanced computing systems at a relatively few universities, are today available to virtually everyone. It is reasonable to assume that the next few years will witness even more advances in computing capabilities and corresponding increases in our dependence on electronic data-processing equipment and facilities.

Nonetheless, it should always be remembered that the computer is capable only of analyzing whatever information is fed into it. The computer does not ask whether hypotheses have been clearly developed, information has been appropriately collected, concepts have been adequately operationalized, data have been properly coded and measured, or the research is worth pursuing. All these decisions (and many more) still must be made by the human researcher. The old programming adage, "garbage in/garbage out" is as true today as ever. The quality of output is determined by the quality of input, not by the sophistication of the computer or its programs.

This chapter also reviewed the techniques of index and scale construction and discussed the many ways in which scales can enhance the quality of measurement in research. One final word of caution is in order here. Prior to setting out to construct scales, the researcher should always thoroughly review the literature to determine whether adequate scales already exist in the area of interest. Thousands of scales have been developed in the social sciences in the past several years. The process of ensuring validity and reliability often is long and arduous. It almost always is the case that the effort devoted to searching for existing scales—those that already have been shown to meet the various tests of reliability and validity—is well worth the time.[30]

KEY TERMS

codesheet	nominal measures
coding	ordinal measures
codebook	interval measures
variables	ratio measures
quantitative variables	scaling
qualitative variables	altheoretical concepts
dependent variables	composite measures
independent variables	Likert scaling technique
control variables	test–retest method

discriminative power
Guttman technique
error responses
coefficient of reproducibility
coefficient of scalability
actor analysis
factor loading
reliability

validity
alternative-form method
split-half method
internal consistency
content validity
criterion validity
construct validity

EXERCISES

1. Visit your department's data laboratory, and familiarize yourself with the computing options available to you. Find out which statistical, graphical, and word-processing packages are available for your use. Find out also which—if any—of these may be made available to you at no cost, or at student-discounted rates.

2. Coding of variables
   a. In your own area of interest, and from the sources of data available to you, select a small number of cases (cities, states, nations, etc.), and for each case compile information on five or six variables. Be sure that at least one of these variables is measured at the nominal, one at the ordinal, and one at the interval, or ratio, level.
   b. Place this information on a codesheet.
   c. Using the microcomputing options available to you, then transfer and store this data onto a PC file.

3. Indexes and scales
   a. For any area of political research of interest to you, develop five questions that might be used to form an index of some concept in that area.
   b. Discuss the circumstances under which such an index might be useful and the reasons, in general, for developing scales.
   c. What are some of the problems of index construction, as revealed in this chapter?

4. Index and scale construction
   a. Compare and contrast the various methods of index construction as discussed in this chapter.
   b. Under what circumstances might the various techniques be most appropriate?
   c. Discuss the issues of reliability and validity, and identify the techniques used to evaluate each.

5. Research applications of scales
   a. From recent political science and policy literature, identify three studies that construct and use scales in their analysis.
   b. What methods of scaling were used?
   c. What techniques of reliability and validity are reported?

NOTES

1. Thomas W. Madron, C. Neal Tate, and Robert G. Brookshire, *Using Microcomputers in Research* (Newbury Park, CA: Sage Publications, 1990), 10.

2. For a review of some of the best of these, see Sheryl Canter, "Stat of the Art," *PC Magazine* 12(9) (May 11, 1993) 227– 287. For a review focusing especially on a political science perspective, see Anne Permaloff and Carl Grafton, "Student Statistical Packages," *PS: Political Science and Politics* (December, 1989), 821–831; Grafton and Permaloff, "Microcomputer Statistical Packages," *PS: Political Science and Politics* (Winter, 1988), 71–83; Permaloff and Grafton, "Top of the Line: SPSS, SAS, and SYSTAT," *PS: Political Science and Politics* (Summer, 1988), 657–666. For a general review of the use of microcomputers in the classroom, see Permaloff and Grafton, "Using the Microcomputer in the Classroom: Initial Considerations," *PS: Political Science and Politics* (December, 1991), 689–693.

3. Herbert F. Weisberg and Charles E. Smith, "The Advent of Dynamic Graphics Statistical Computing," *PS: Political Science and Politics* (June, 1993), 228–232.

4. Ibid.

5. Robert F. DeVellis, *Scale Development: Theory and Applications* (Newbury Park, CA: Sage Publications, 1991), 7–9.

6. Ibid., 9.

7. For a thorough review of many of the indexes and scales used in the social sciences, see Delbert C. Miller, *Handbook of Research Design and Social Measurement,* 5th ed. (Newbury Park, CA: Sage Publications, 1991), 323–582.

8. DeVellis offered another useful distinction between scales and indexes. Scales, he said, consist of "effect indicators"—items having values that are caused by an underlying construct. Indexes, on the other hand, consist of "cause indicators"—items that determine the level of an underlying construct. As an example, a *scale* measuring optimism would comprise responses to items presumably caused by levels of optimism: More optimism would cause higher item scores. An *index* of socioeconomic status would comprise items such as education. More education would result in higher SES scores, but high levels of SES do not cause higher levels of education. See DeVellis, *Scale Development,* 9.

9. Sidney Verba, Kay Lehman Scholzman, Henry Brady, and Norman H. Nie, "Citizen Activity: Who Participates? What Do They Say?" *American Political Science Review* 87 (June 1993), 303–318.

10. See Rensis Likert, "A Technique for the Measurement of Attitudes," *Archives of Psychology* 22 (1932), 1–55.

11. Those desiring more rigorous criteria might select the top and bottom 40 and 50 percent for item evaluation.

12. Frank J. Thompson and Bonnie Browne, "Commitment to the Disadvantaged among Urban Administrators: The Case of Minority Hiring," *Urban Affairs Quarterly* 13 (March, 1978), 355–378.

13. Ibid., 361.

14. See Louis Thurstone, "The Method of Paired Comparisons for Social Values," *Journal of Abnormal and Social Psychology* 21 (1927), 384–4000; Louis Thurstone, "A Theory of Attitude Measurement," *Psychological Bulletin* 36 (1929), 221–241; and Louis Thurstone and E. J. Chave, *The Measurement of Attitude* (Chicago: University of Chicago Press, 1929).

15. The terms *favorable* and *unfavorable* are used only for convenience. The piles could be representative of liberal to conservative, trusting to alienated, prejudiced to tolerant attitudes, and so forth.

16. J. Balogh and M. A. Mueller, "A Scaling Technique for Measuring Social Attitudes toward Capital Punishment," *Sociology and Social Research* 45 (1960), 24–26.

17. DeVellis, *Scale Development,* 62.

18. See Louis Guttman, "A Basis for Scaling Quantitative Data," *American Sociological Review* 9 (1944), 139–150; and Louis Guttman, "The Basis of Scalogram Analysis," in Samuel A. Stouffer et al., eds., *Measurement and Prediction* (Princeton, NJ: Princeton University Press, 1950), 60–90.

19. Judy A. Andrews, Hyman Hops, Dennis Ary, Edward Lichtenstein, and Elizabeth Tildseley, "The Construction, Validation and Use of a Guttman Scale of Adolescent Substance Use: An Investigation of Family Relationships," *Journal of Drug Issues* 21 (Summer, 1991), 557–572.

20. DeVellis, *Scale Development,* 62–63. An especially troubling feature of the Guttman technique is its *deterministic* approach: the assumption that observations will be completely determined by the assumed positions of respondents on an underlying latent scale. A number of more realistic techniques have been developed. Collectively called "latent-trait models," the most widely used of these—named after their authors—are the Mokken model, the Rasch model, and the Birnbaum model. For a review of the approach these models take, see: Kees Niemoller and Wijbrandt van Schuur, "Stochastic Models for Unidimensional Scaling: Mokken and Rasch," in David McKay, Norman Schofield, and Paul Whiteley, eds., *Data Analysis and the Social Sciences* (London: Frances Pinter, 1983), 120–170.

21. Lee Ann Banaszak and Eric Plutzer, "Contextual Determinants of Feminist Attitudes: National and Subnational Influences in Western Europe," *American Political Science Review* 87 (March, 1993), 147–157.

22. Edward G. Carmines and Richard A. Zeller, *Reliability and Validity Assessment* (Newbury Park, CA: Sage Publications, 1979), 12.

23. An excellent discussion of the reliability and validity issues is presented in George W. Bohrnstedt, "Reliability and Validity Assessment in Attitude Measurement," in Gene F. Summers, ed., *Attitude Measurement* (Chicago: Rand McNally, 1970), 80–99.

24. Carmines and Zeller, *Reliability and Validity Assessment,* 39.

25. See C. Spearman, "Correlational Calculated with Faulty Data," *British Journal of Psychology* 3 (1910), 271–295; and W. Brown, "Some Experimental Results in the Correlation of Mental Abilities," *British Journal of Psychology* 3 (1910), 296–322.

26. Lee J. Cronbach, "Coefficient Alpha and the Internal Structure of Tests," *Psychometrika* 16 (September, 1951), 297–334.

27. Banaszak and Plutzer, "Contextual Determinants of Feminist Attitudes," 150.

28. Bohrnstedt, "Reliability and Validity Assessment in Attitude Measurement," 91–92.

29. Ibid., 94.

30. A point made by Miller, *Handbook of Research Design and Social Measurement,* 323.

CHAPTER 7

Data Presentation:
Charts, Graphs, Measures of Central Tendency and Dispersion

Having completed the often lengthy process of collecting, coding, and processing information, the researcher is ready to begin the process of data analysis. For many researchers, this is the most exciting phase of the research process. The pace quickens as the computer begins to generate results, as gross patterns that have been obscure begin to come into focus, and as the researcher begins to receive the first hints of whether the data appear to substantiate his or her initial expectations. It is at this stage that the political researcher can really sense the excitement of discovery—a thoroughly invigorating and stimulating intellectual experience shared by all scientists.

At this early stage of data analysis, the researcher usually will want to begin by examining and describing in summary fashion the information that has been collected. Having spent a considerable amount of time among the trees, the researcher is anxious now to step back and begin to comprehend the whole forest. Sometimes, in fact, the data-analysis stage may *end* at this point. Having interviewed a sample of voters from your community, for example, you may simply be interested in discovering and reporting the *proportion* that voted in the most recent mayoral election, the *distribution* of party preferences among the sample, or the *average* amount of time devoted by each individual to community affairs. After examining all 50 states, the political scientist may be interested in determining the *typical* length of state constitutions, the *mean* salary paid to legislators, and the job held most *frequently* by individuals before being elected governor. A student of urban politics might be interested in finding the *variation* of income levels among America's largest 100 cities, or the *proportion* of these same cities experiencing high levels of unemployment.

In each of these instances, we have emphasized such terms as "typical," "proportion," and "average"; and in each instance, the researcher is interested only in making summary statements about the group being examined. To repeat a previously made point, these descriptive summaries may be the extent of the data analysis needed. Summary information such as this may be all that is required for the task at hand. Because only one variable at a time is being examined, the category of methods used in such analysis is termed **univariate analysis.**

141

TABLE 7.1

General Format for the Frequency Distribution

Category	Frequency	Proportion (or percentage[a])
A	f(A)	f(A)/N
B	f(B)	f(B)/N
C	f(C)	f(C)/N
D	f(D)	f(D)/N
E	f(E)	f(E)/N

Total N

where A, B, C, D, E = categories of the variable
$f(A)$ through $f(E)$ = number of
observations in each category
N = sum of frequencies in all categories
$f(A)/N$ through $f(E)/N$ = number of
obesrvations in each category, divided by
the total number of observations.

[a] The proportion multiplied by 100 yields the percentage. Also useful is a *cumulative distribution,* which shows for each frequency or percentage category the number or percentage of cases in that *and all preceding categories.*

In organizing and presenting distributions of single variables, the researcher may want to use frequency or percentage distributions, graphs and charts, measures of central tendency, measures of dispersion, and indications of the shape and the form of distributions. Beginning students are probably most familiar with frequency presentations and use of charts and graphs; however, all these measures are useful, as this chapter shows.

FREQUENCY DISTRIBUTIONS AND GRAPHIC PRESENTATIONS

One of the first steps in organizing and presenting information often is the construction of frequency distributions and/or graphic displays of the variables of particular interest. Frequency distributions and graphs help summarize large amounts of information and—when well constructed—facilitate rapid visual interpretation of data.

Frequency Distributions

The **frequency distribution** refers to a tabulation of data according to the important categories of those variables of interest. A frequency distribution of age, for example, refers to the listing of the number of individuals assigned to each age cat-

TABLE 7.2

Frequency Distribution of Liberalism–Conservatism Responses of American Electorate, 1994

Value	Value Label	Frequency	Percentage	Cumulative Percentage
1	Extremely liberal	25	1.8	1.8
2	Liberal	113	8.1	9.9
3	Slightly liberal	138	9.9	19.8
4	Moderate (middle of the road)	476	34.1	54.0
5	Slightly conservative	260	18.7	77.7
6	Conservative	323	23.1	95.9
7	Extremely conservative	57	4.4	100.0
	Total	1392	100.0	

SOURCE: 1994 American National Election Study.

egory (or interval). A frequency distribution of party identification refers to the listing of the number of individuals assigned to each category of party identification.

The general format for the presentation of a frequency distribution might appear as shown in Table 7.1. As Table 7.1 indicates, in presenting a frequency distribution, the researcher begins by listing each category of the variable to be examined, presents the number of observations (frequencies) assigned to each category, calculates the total number of observations for the variable, and generally presents the proportion or percentage of frequencies falling into each category (this statistic typically is called the "relative frequency"). When examining nominal data (as discussed in Chapter 6), such as sex, race, or party identification (coded as Democrat, Republican, or Independent), the researcher may present these categories in any reasonable order. When examining ordinal data, such as socioeconomic status, the researcher will present the data in order from the lowest to the highest (or vice versa) scale categories.

When examining interval data, such as age or income, the researcher will also present the data in ordered fashion, but—because of the large number of categories that may be involved—the researcher may also want to group the data according to meaningful categories. Age, for example, might be grouped into ten-year categories, such as 20–29, 30–39, 40–49, and so forth. When grouping data, you should be careful to avoid constructing groups that include either too few or too many cases, and the intervals of the groups should be the same size (or almost so).

An example of a frequency distribution is shown in Table 7.2, where responses of a 1994 sample of the American electorate to a measure of liberalism–conservatism are presented. As is indicated in Table 7.2, of the 1,392 people responding to this question, 25 (or 1.8%) considered themselves "extremely liberal," 113 (or 8.1%) considered themselves "liberal," and so forth. Table 7.2 illustrates another feature often presented in frequency distributions: the **cumulative percent.** The cumulative percentiles presented in Table 7.2 show the percentage of the sample responding

---

 BOX 7.1   Deciding Authorship: Use of
Descriptive Statistics

Skillfully used, descriptive statistics—such as rates, frequencies, and averages—can assist in answering very interesting political questions. This is illustrated in the classic study by Mosteller and Wallace examining the authorship of 12 disputed *Federalist Papers*. The *Federalist Papers* were a series of essays published in 1787–1788 by Alexander Hamilton, John Jay, and James Madison, to persuade citizens of New York to support the newly drafted Constitution. Today the *Federalist* is an extremely important work in political philosophy, and it serves as the leading source of information for interpreting the intent of the authors of the Constitution. Although the papers were originally published anonymously, over the years, general agreement regarding authorship of most of the papers was reached. However, dispute continued over authorship of a few papers. By comparing the frequency of the use of certain words in essays known to have been authored by Hamilton, Jay, and Madison with the frequency of the use of these same words in the disputed *Federalist* papers Mosteller and Wallace assign authorship of all 12 disputed papers to James Madison. The following is excerpted from their study.

Deciding Authorship

There is general agreement on the authorship of 70 [of the 85 Federalist] papers—5 by Jay, 14 by Madison, and 51 by Hamilton. Of the remaining 15, 12 are in dispute between Hamilton and Madison, and 3 are joint works to a disputed extent. . . . The political content of the essays has never provided convincing evidence for authorship.

. . . we can take the *rate* or *relative frequency* of the use of [specific words] as a measure pointing toward one or the other author. . . . one word showed up early as a powerful discriminator, sufficient almost by itself. When should one write *upon* instead of *on*? Even authoritative books on English don't provide good rules. Hamilton and Madison differ tremendously. Hamilton writes *on* and *upon* almost equally, about

---

at levels equal to or less than each particular value. For example, 19.8% of the sample reported a value of 3 ("slightly liberal") or 2 ("liberal"), or 1 ("extremely liberal"). Arrayed in this manner, the table is said to be cumulative in *ascending order,* which is the normal pattern for presenting cumulative percentiles or cumulative frequencies. (Box 7.1 presents an intriguing use of frequency distribution to address a question unresolved by other means.)

Graphic Display

The relatively recent development of sophisticated software packages designed especially to produce graphs and charts has greatly simplified the use of such meth-

3 times per 1,000 words. Madison, on the other hand, rarely uses *upon*. [The accompanying table] shows the distribution for *upon* [in known Madison and Hamilton papers, and in the 12 disputed papers]. In 48 papers, Hamilton never failed to use *upon*; indeed, he never used it less than twice. Madison used [upon] in only 9 of 50 papers, and then only with low rates. The disputed papers are clearly Madisonian with *upon* occurring in only 1 paper.

[We conclude that] Madison is extremely likely, in the sense of degree of belief, to have written the disputed [12] Federalist papers.

Frequency Distribution of Rate per 1,000 Words in 48 Hamilton, 50 Madison, and 12 Disputed Papers for *upon*

Rate per 1,000 Words	Hamilton	Madison	Disputed
0 (exactly)[a]		41	11
0–0.4		2	
0.4–0.8		4	
0.8–1.2	2	1	1
1.2–1.6	3	2	
1.6–2.0	6		
2.0–3.0	11		
3.0–4.0	11		
4.0–5.0	10		
5.0–6.0	3		
6.0–7.0	1		
7.0–8.0	1		
Totals	48	50	12

[a] Each interval, except 0 (exactly), excludes its upper endpoint. Thus a paper with a rate of exactly 3 per 1,000 words would appear in the count for the 3.0–4.0 interval.

Source: Frederick Mosteller and David L. Wallace, "Deciding Authorship," in Judith M. Tanur, ed., *Statistics: A Guide to the Unknown,* 3rd ed. (Wadsworth & Brooks/Cole Advanced Books: Pacific Grove, CA, 1989), 115–125. This was originally published as Mosteller and Wallace, *Inference and Disputed Authorship: The Federalist* (Reading, MA: Addison-Wesley, 1964).

ods in the analysis and reporting of political and policy data. A number of excellent, and relatively low-cost, products—many of which have been designed especially for PC use—are available.

Graphs can be very effective means of presenting data. Compared with frequency distributions, graphs often are much more visually appealing and call attention rapidly to important characteristics of the data. There are many different ways to graphically display information; a few of the most common of these are discussed in this section.

When dealing with nominal or ordinal data, the information may be presented as a **bar graph.** As such, bars (which may be displayed horizontally or vertically) are drawn for each category of the variable in a manner so that the height (or length)

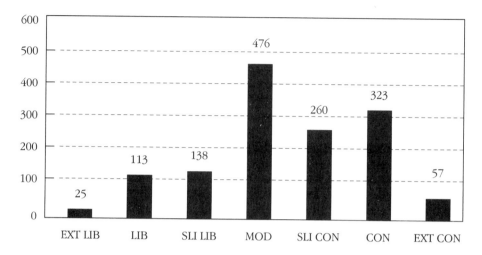

FIGURE 7.1

Illustration of Bar Graph (liberalism–conservatism)

NOTE: EXT = extremely; SLI = slightly; LIB = libreal; MOD = moderate; and CON = conservative.

SOURCE: 1994 American National Election Study.

of the bars represents the number of cases (frequency) for each category. Usually, the bars of a bar graph are separated and, although the widths of the bars have no significance, usually they are made the same width.

Figure 7.1 presents the data considered in Table 7.2 in a bar-graph format. The visual advantage of the data presented in this manner is obvious. The observer can see immediately that the largest number of respondents consider themselves to be "moderate," and smaller numbers consider themselves to identify with the remaining categories of liberalism and conservatism.

When constructing a graph of interval or continuous data, the bars of such a graph are not separated, and the resulting figure is called a **histogram.** The height of the bars of a histogram are proportional to the frequencies of each category, and the width of the bars are proportional to the size of each interval. Because of this, the *area* of each bar—not just its height—represents the frequencies of each interval. For this reason, histograms normally are drawn so that all intervals have the same width. Having a somewhat more pleasing visual appeal is a **frequency polygon**, which is a graph connecting the midpoints of the top of each bar of a histogram with a solid line.

William G. Jacoby makes good use of the frequency polygon in his recent study of the consistency in political views existing among the American electorate.[1] From various questions asked in the American National Election Studies, Jacoby develops a scale showing the proportion of respondents consistently liberal or conservative in their responses. Figure 7.2 shows a portion of Jacoby's findings.

Based on this analysis, Jacoby concludes that, "the score distributions are highly skewed (a term to be discussed later in this chapter) with the vast majority of respondents falling in the lower half [of the scale] . . . the modal score is 0: . . . 16.3%

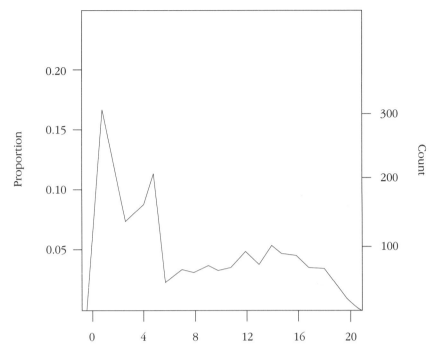

FIGURE 7.2

Illustration of a Frequency Polygon (ideological thinking in American electorate)

Source: William G. Jacoby, "The Structure of Ideological Thinking in the American Electorate," *American Journal of Political Science,* 39 (May, 1995), 325.

of the . . . respondents display *no* ideologically consistent judgments across *any* of the 19 [items] that are included in their scale." Jacoby points out, too, that over 20 percent of respondents display scale scores ranging between 11 and 15, meaning that they are ideologically consistent on this many political questions. According to Jacoby, these people ". . . can identify the ideological positions of political actors; they take on nonneutral ideological positions themselves; and they also display ideological consistency on some issues . . . there is a sizable minority of people who do appear to use liberal-conservative ideas to structure most of their political orientations."

Histograms and polygons provide quick and easy visual interpretation of data. They also tell us something about the *shape of the distribution*.

In the case of Jacoby's study of the ideological distribution of the American electorate, we see a highly asymmetric shape—most respondents had scores falling in the lower half of the scale. The significance of such shapes is discussed more fully later in this chapter.

Another commonly used graph is a **pie chart** (sometimes called a "pie diagram"), which is a graph made by dividing a circle into segments so that each segment shows the proportion of the whole pie represented by each classification. Pie

Where it Comes From . . .

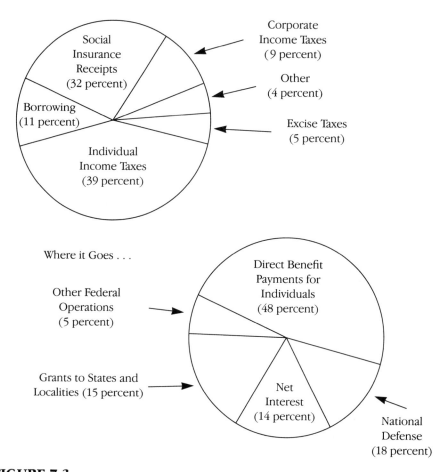

Where it Goes . . .

FIGURE 7.3
Illustration of Pie Charts (the 1995 federal budget)

Source: *Budget of the United States Government* (Washington, DC: U.S. Government Printing Office, 1994), 12.

charts are used to show the relationship of various parts of a distribution to the whole, and they are very frequently used to illustrate budget sources and allocations. For example, the 1995 budget of the United States was approximately $1,518.3 billion. The pie charts presented in Figure 7.3 show where that money came from and how it was spent.

An extension of a pie chart is a graphic in which stylized pictures of the variables being presented are used in the graph. Commonly called **pictograms,** such charts are used frequently by newspapers, magazines, and other more popular sources of information. An example of a pictogram is presented in Figure 7.4, which shows unemployment rates in a number of European countries.

Unemployment: A Burden on Youth

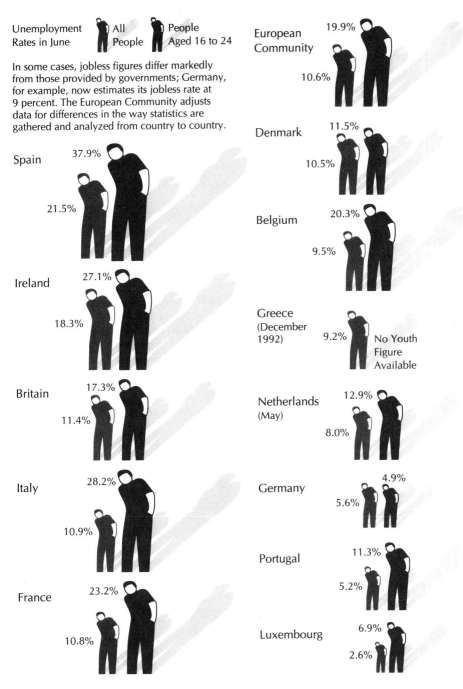

Unemployment Rates in June — All People — People Aged 16 to 24

In some cases, jobless figures differ markedly from those provided by governments; Germany, for example, now estimates its jobless rate at 9 percent. The European Community adjusts data for differences in the way statistics are gathered and analyzed from country to country.

Spain — 37.9% — 21.5%

Ireland — 27.1% — 18.3%

Britain — 17.3% — 11.4%

Italy — 28.2% — 10.9%

France — 23.2% — 10.8%

European Community — 19.9% — 10.6%

Denmark — 11.5% — 10.5%

Belgium — 20.3% — 9.5%

Greece (December 1992) — 9.2% — No Youth Figure Available

Netherlands (May) — 12.9% — 8.0%

Germany — 4.9% — 5.6%

Portugal — 11.3% — 5.2%

Luxembourg — 6.9% — 2.6%

FIGURE 7.4

Illustration of a Pictogram (unemployment in various European countries)

SOURCE: *New York Times* August 12, 1993; data source, Eurostat (Statistics office of the European Community).

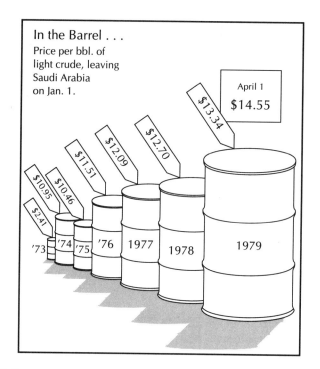

FIGURE 7.5
Pictogram Showing Price of Oil Increase

SOURCE: *Time,* April 9, 1979, p. 57; cited in Edward R. Tufte, *The Visual Display of Quantitative Information* (Cheshire, CT: Graphics Press, 1983), 62.

Pictograms must be used with extreme caution. Because the pictures may represent area and volume, as well as numbers, they can inadvertently present grossly distorted information. Edward R. Tufte has written extensively on the distortion effects often associated with pictograms.[2] An example used by Tufte to illustrate this point is presented in Figure 7.5, which purports to show the changing price of oil from 1973 to 1979. Although the dollar amount of $13.34 shown in that graph is 454 percent larger than the dollar amount $2.41, the area of the last barrel shown is 4,280 percent larger than the first barrel!

A final form of graph discussed in this chapter is a **line diagram** (sometimes called a "line graph"). A line diagram simply connects all points of a graph with a continuous line. Typically, such graphs are used to show *trends,* or change over time. Figure 7.6 is a line diagram showing the changing percentage of the eligible electorate voting for the U.S. president from 1880 through 1992. It can be seen there that significantly larger proportions of Americans took part in presidential elections prior to the turn of the century.

Political scientists Jan E. Leighley and Jonathan Nagler used line diagrams as a way to show differential voting turnouts by socioeconomic status in the United States in

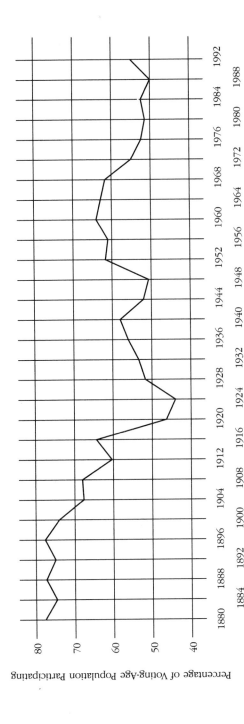

FIGURE 7.6

Illustration of Line Diagram (voter participation in presidential elections, 1880–1992)

NOTE ALSO: A true zero point is not shown on this graph.

SOURCE: This graph is reproduced from Milton C. Cummings, Jr., and David Wise, *Democracy under Pressure*, 7th ed. (Ft. Worth, TX: Harcourt Brace Jovanovich Publishers, 1993), 309. Data source: Figures for 1880 to 1916 in Robert E. Lane, *Political Life* (New York: The Free Press, 1965), p. 20. Reprinted with permission of Macmillan Publishing Co. Inc. from *Political Life* by Robert E. Lane. Copyright © 1959 by the Free Press. Figures for 1920 to 1948 in *Statistical Abstract of the United States 1969*, 368. Data for 1952 to 1980 from *Statistical Abstract of the United States: 1984*, p. 262. Data for 1984 from *Washington Post*, January 8, 1985, p. A3. Data for 1988 from *New York Times*, November 13, 1988, p. 32, and data for 1992 provided by the Committee for the Study of the American Electorate, Washington, DC.

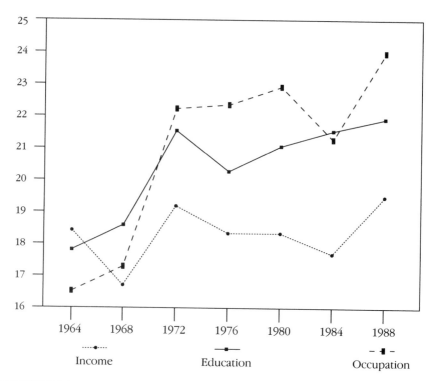

FIGURE 7.7

Illustration of Line Diagrams (trends in class bias, using various measures of socioeconomic status)

NOTE: Income bias is the difference in turnout rates between the top and bottom halves of the income distribution. Education bias is the difference in turnout rates between high school graduates and non-high school graduates. Occupation bias is the difference in turnout rates between white-collar and blue-collar workers. A true zero point is not on this graph.

SOURCE: Computed from the Current Population Surveys, 1964–1988. Cited in Jan E. Leighley and Jonathan Nagler, "Socioeconomic Bias in Turnout 1964–1988: The Voters Remain the Same," *American Political Science Review* 86 (September, 1992), 730.

recent national elections. Figure 7.7 charts the trend in class bias (measured in terms of income, education, and occupational status) in voting turnout in the United States from 1964 to 1988. Leighley and Nagler conclude, based on this, that socioeconomic biases in voting have generally increased over this period, and that this is especially true for voting bias associated with occupation status.[3]

The Leighley and Nagler chart also illustrates the use of a line diagram to report data on several variables at once (in this case, income, education, and occupational status voting differentials). When using this technique, be sure that the lines representing different variables are distinctively marked (by color, style, shading, etc.).

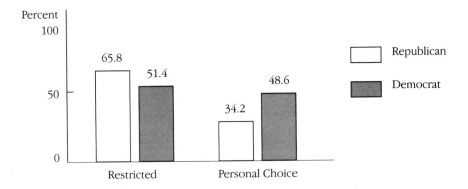

FIGURE 7.8

Clustered Bar Chart Showing Democratic and Republican Attitudes toward Abortion

The question asked in the 1994 survey was, "There has been some discussion about abortion during recent years. Which one of the following opinions best agrees with your view?"

1. By law, abortion should never be permitted.
2. The law should permit abortion only in the case of rape, incest, or when the woman's life is in danger.
3. The law should permit abortion for reasons *other than* rape, incest, or danger to the woman's life, but only after the need for the abortion has been clearly established.
4. By law, a woman should always be able to obtain an abortion as a matter of personal choice.

SOURCE: 1994 American National Election Study

In constructing this chart, the first three responses were collapsed into one category: "Restricted."

Selecting Charts and Graphs: Some Words of Caution

The various graphic options discussed in this chapter all are designed to illustrate various aspects of the information of interest. It would be unusual for all of these options to be presented for any single variable; rather, it is important to carefully consider what aspect of the variable you most want to illustrate and to use the chart or graph best designed to achieve that goal. While none of the charts and graphs discussed here is designed *exclusively* to accomplish one or the other of these objectives, each is better able to achieve some objectives than others. Polygons and histograms are best used to show what is most *typical* about a set of data (the feature of *central tendency*). Bar charts are used to show *comparisons* among categories of data, and pie charts are best used to *illustrate parts of a whole* at a given time. Line graphs are used to show *change over time.* Clustered bar charts (presented sometimes as overlapping bars, and sometimes as stacked bars) can assist in comparing subcategories on some variable. Figure 7.8 compares attitudes of identified Democrats and Republicans toward the abortion issue, as reflected in the ICPSR 1994 American National Election Study. Presented in this manner, it can be seen quickly that greater proportions of Republicans believe that abortion options

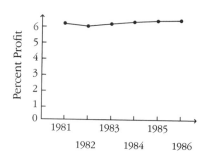

(a) Company Profits 1981–1986
(distorted graph)

(b) Company Profits 1981–1986
(correct graph)

FIGURE 7.9

Illustration of Graphic Distortion

SOURCE: Donald R. Byrkit, *Statistics Today* (Menlo Park, CA: Benjamin/Cummings Publishing Company, 1987), 25.

should be "restricted," greater proportions of Democrats believe that the issue should be a matter of "personal choice."

While graphs and charts are highly instructive, it should be remembered that poorly constructed graphs can be confusing and—worse—can even distort information. Graphs should be constructed carefully and used with prudence and caution. In the first place, the use of too many charts and graphs can quickly clutter and overburden a report. A graph or chart should be used to highlight the *most important* variables or relationships in the study; other statistics can be used to quickly summarize supporting or less important information.

Graphs can quickly lose their effectiveness if they are forced to show too much information. As general rules-of-thumb, use no more than six slices for pie charts, no more than four bars per cluster for bar charts, and no more than four or five lines for line graphs. Use of color, of course, greatly enhances graphic performance. When using color, be sure to be consistent from graph to graph: Don't use blue for Democrats in one chart, and red in another.

The ease with which pictograms can project false impressions was discussed previously. Another very common error occurs when researchers are not careful in constructing the vertical and horizontal scales of a graph. The units represented on each scale should be uniform—that is to say distances that are numerically equal should be equal in length on each scale (the distance from 1985 to 1986 should be the same as the distance from 1986 to 1987 and so forth). Normally, the vertical scale of a graph should begin at zero. Donald R. Byrkit presents a good illustration of the distortion that can result when this rule is not followed (see Figure 7.9).

The first graph in this illustration might falsely convey the impression of sharply increasing company profits over this period. The second graph, where the vertical scale begins at zero, shows a more realistic picture of generally stable profits. When it is not feasible to start the vertical scale at zero, this fact should be brought obviously to the reader's attention by use of broken lines indicating a lapse in distance.

One of the most thorough studies of those factors related to graphical excellence and integrity is Edward R. Tufte's book, *The Visual Display of Quantitative Information.*[4] Tufte finds that graphical excellence

1. is the well-designed presentation of interesting data—a matter of *substance,* of *statistics,* and of *design.*
2. consists of complex ideas communicated with clarity, precision, and efficiency.
3. is that which gives to the viewer the greatest number of ideas in the shortest time with the least ink in the smallest space.
4. is nearly always multivariate [i.e., more than one variable is illustrated].
5. requires telling the truth about the data.[5]

All political and policy researchers would be well advised to review Tufte's study and to carefully consider the suggestions for graphic presentation provided therein.[6]

MEASURES OF CENTRAL TENDENCY AND MEASURES OF DISPERSION

Charts and graphs greatly assist in the description and understanding of information, but the researcher often wishes to present his or her findings in a still more convenient fashion. As previously mentioned, any report dealing with more than just a few variables would soon become quite unwieldy if reliance were solely on the presentation of charts, graphs, and frequency distributions. Also, the researcher may desire more convenient measures for *comparing* characteristics of differing populations or subsets of a population (such as Democrats versus Republicans, high- versus low-income families, men versus women). One such measure is a **measure of central tendency,** which is a number calculated to tell what is most representative, or most typical, about a set of data. Another measure is a **measure of dispersion,** which is a number calculated to tell something about the spread, or variability, of a set of data. Both of these measures are extremely useful.

Measures of Central Tendency

The Mode.   The **mode** is that category of a variable having the largest number of instances. It is used as a measure of central tendency mainly for nominal-level data. In its 1994 American National Election Study, the ICPSR asked respondents to indicate their party preference. The responses to that question are presented in Table 7.3, where it can be seen that the modal party preference for this sample is Democrat.

The Median.   The **median** is a measure of central tendency, which may be used with ordinal data. The median may also be used with a distribution of interval-level data when a few extremely low or a few extremely high values would render an alternative measure, the mean statistic, unrepresentative. The median is defined as that value dividing a distribution into two groups of equal size. An easy way to find the median is simply to arrange the cases in ascending or descending order and

TABLE 7.3

Party Identification of a Sample of the American Electorate, 1994

Category	Frequency	Percentage
Republican	541	30.3
Independent	514	28.8
No preference	113	6.3
Other	5	0.3
Democrat	614	34.4
Total	1787	100.0 (rounded)

SOURCE: 1994 American National Election Study.

Reader Note: Strictly speaking, the category of a variable having the largest number of observations (In Table 7.3, Democrat) is the mode; but it is comon to label a distribution having two pronounced categories as bimodal and one having several pronounced categories as multimodal. If all categories have equal numbers of cases, any category can be said to represent the mode, or, more often, it will be said that the distribution has no unique modal value.

to count to the middle case—which will be the median if the number of cases is odd. Hence, if the number of cases is odd, the median is defined by the formula: $(N + 1)/2$ where N is the total number of cases.

If the number of cases is even, the median is the value of the two middle cases if these cases are tied; it is the value halfway between these two when they are not tied. As an example, assume that a political science student has administered a scale of attitudes toward abortion to seventeen classmates. The distribution of scores ranging from 1 (least permissive) to 10 (most permissive) might appear as shown in Table 7.4. In this example, the score of the ninth student is the median: 4.

Had the seventeenth student not been included in this sample, there would be no middle case. In such situations, the median falls halfway between the two middle cases, in this case between the eighth and the ninth students. Because the eighth student reported a score of 5 on the attitudes toward abortion scale, the median would be reported as 4.5.[7]

The Mean. For interval-level data, the *arithmetic mean*—or, simply, the **mean**—is the most often used measure of central tendency. The mean is operationally defined as the sum of all scores divided by the total number of cases. The formula used to calculate the mean is defined as

$$mean = \frac{\Sigma X}{N}$$

where ΣX = sum of all scores
N = total number of observations

TABLE 7.4
Hypothetical Distribution of Scores for Attitudes toward Abortion Scale

Student	Score	Student	Score
1	10	10	4
2	9	11	3
3	9	12	3
4	8	13	2
5	7	14	2
6	6	15	2
7	5	16	1
8	5	17	1
9	4		

Reader Note: Often, in the chapters that follow, the symbol Σ is used. This symbol, the Greek capital letter sigma, means to sum or to add. It simply is a shorthand way of saying, "add the following." Σ, as used in the preceding formula, means to add all observations of that category of observations known as X.

Note also that statisticians frequently use different symbols to distinguish between statistics calculated for data representing a *population* and those calculated for data representing a *sample*. The symbol $\overline{X}$ is generally used to represent the mean score for sample data; the Greek letter μ (mu) is frequently used to represent the mean score for population data.

As an illustration, a researcher interested in the mean annual income of 20 families selected for study would simply total the annual income for each family and divide the sum by 20. The result is the mean annual income for the group.

While the calculation of the mean is simple and easily understood, you should make note of two important properties of the statistic. First, the calculation of the mean has the algebraic property that the sum of the deviations of each score from the mean will equal zero. That is, if we subtract the mean from each score and add the results, the sum will be zero. The significance of this property is discussed in later chapters.

Additionally, the mean can be affected by a few very large or a few very small scores. If, in the preceding example, one of the 20 families selected for the study happened to have had an annual income of $10,000,000, this would obviously greatly distort the mean annual income score for this set of families (assuming, of course, that the other 19 families reported more normal incomes). Statisticians use the term *resistance* to describe the extent to which a particular statistic can be significantly affected by changes in one or a few cases.[8] The mean is one of those statistics that is not very resistant to change of this sort (especially when the number of cases is small), and it therefore can sometimes present a distorted picture of the data. It is for this reason that the median—a statistic that *is* fairly resistant to change—is sometimes a better measure of central tendency for interval-level data.

An interesting example of the use of the mean score is provided in the 1994 study

TABLE 7.5

Mean Comparisons: Differences between White and Black Childbearing Women and Differences between All White and Black Respondents by Survey Year

| | Childbearing Women | | | | | Total Sample | | | | |
| | Whites | | Blacks | | | Whites | | Blacks | | |
Year	Mean	(N)	Mean	(N)	Difference	Mean	(N)	Mean	(N)	Difference
1972	4.09	(279)	3.61	(49)	.48	4.01	(1,109)	3.07	(207)	.94
1973	4.20	(344)	3.93	(44)	.27	4.27	(1,178)	3.33	(161)	.94
1974	4.51	(356)	4.09	(53)	.42	4.30	(1,135)	3.61	(147)	.69
1975	4.29	(346)	4.09	(44)	.20	4.19	(1,148)	3.66	(135)	.53
1976	4.41	(361)	4.07	(27)	.34	4.20	(1,212)	3.32	(111)	.88
1977	4.33	(339)	3.92	(63)	.41	4.23	(1,183)	3.47	(156)	.76
1978	3.96	(384)	3.84	(64)	.12	3.96	(1,202)	3.39	(144)	.57
1980	4.17	(340)	4.22	(46)	−.05	4.19	(1,162)	3.51	(117)	.68
1983	4.49	(417)	3.98	(161)	.51	4.27	(1,413)	3.39	(431)	.88
1984	4.31	(371)	3.47	(60)	.84	4.02	(1,114)	3.25	(150)	.77
1985	4.00	(353)	3.80	(41)	.20	3.85	(1,199)	3.45	(132)	.40
1987	4.09	(393)	3.73	(175)	.36	3.95	(1,342)	3.43	(455)	.52
1988	4.01	(215)	3.81	(47)	.20	3.82	(696)	3.53	(115)	.29

NOTE: Abortion attitude scale values range from 0 (for opposition to abortion in every case) to 6 (when respondencts approve abortion in every case). Results are based on 1972 to 1988 General Social Survey data. Original authors did not report data for all years. Also, indicators of level of statistical significance, as reported by authors, have been deleted from this presentation.

SOURCE: Lynxwiler and Gay, "Reconsidering Race Differences in Abortion Attitudes," *Social Science Quarterly* (March, 1994), 73.

by Lynxwiler and Gay, examining differences in attitudes toward abortion of childbearing European American and African American women and of European Americans and African Americans in general. Relying on responses to the 1972 through 1988 General Social Survey (GSS) data (where, on a scale of 0 to 6, the higher the mean score, the more prochoice the attitudes), these researchers demonstrate that European Americans are generally more prochoice than African Americans, that the differences are less pronounced for childbearing women than for the total samples, and that over time, the "pro-choice gap between whites and blacks is decreasing."[9] Their results are shown in Table 7.5.

To illustrate further, assume that the researcher is interested in examining the salaries paid by states to their governors and in comparing these salaries by regions. Table 7.6 shows the annual salaries of the governors of each of the 50 states (as of 1992); the mean gubernatorial salary of each of the several regions, calculated according to the formula for the mean; and the mean compensation for all 50 states (also calculated according to this formula). This table illustrates several important properties of the mean.

First, it can be seen that when presented in this fashion, mean scores assist in comparing different groupings. We can tell at a glance that the mean gubernatorial compensation of the middle Atlantic region is higher than the mean for any of the other regions and that on the average, the states of the mountain region provide the lowest salary for their governors.

These data also illustrate the impact that a few deviant cases can have on the mean score. Consider the border-states region. It can be seen that the gubernatorial salary of Maryland is considerably higher than the salary of the other states in that region. Had Maryland not been included in this region, the mean annual compensation of these governors would have been calculated as $76,564. The actual mean income for this region ($85,251) is greatly affected by the inclusion of Maryland. Similarly, the state of Arkansas, with a gubernatorial compensation considerably lower than any of the other states in the southern region, may be said to affect the mean for that entire region. In using and reporting mean scores, then, it is necessary to consider the effects of highly deviant cases on these scores and to consider the appropriateness of other measures of central tendency, which may not be so sensitive to extreme cases.

Table 7.6 can be used to illustrate another point about the calculation and use of the mean with *grouped* data. The researcher could average the mean scores of each of the eight regions, the result being the mean *regional* gubernatorial compensation. However, because of unequal frequencies in each region, this figure of $86,334 (not shown in Table 7.6) is not equivalent to the mean score for *all* 50 states (shown to be $84,906). The first score ($86,334) is known as the *unweighted mean* and may be the appropriate measure to calculate if the researcher is, in fact, interested in the mean regional annual compensation of governors. However, if the focus is to be on the mean annual compensation of all 50 states, and if this figure is to be derived from regional groupings, the *weighted mean* must be calculated. In this case, the weighted mean would be derived by weighting all regions by their respective number of states before calculating the mean. This is easily done, as illustrated in Table 7.7. The weighted mean is thus equivalent to the mean of the entire group of 50 states.

All of this is to say, in conclusion, that in calculating and reporting measures of central tendency (and, indeed, all statistical measures), it is important (1) to have a firm idea of the questions to be answered, and (2) to be thoroughly familiar with the data being analyzed. The choice of which statistical measure to apply will be largely dictated by these concerns.

MEASURES OF DISPERSION

Although measures of central tendency are extremely helpful in identifying important trends within an array of data, it should be obvious from the preceding discussion that some measure of the *deviation* from the average or typical is also needed. Measures of central tendency will more accurately reflect the actual values of all members of a distribution when the data are closely grouped about the central values. Conversely, measures of central tendency will less accurately reflect the actual

TABLE 7.6

Annual Compensation of Governors, Grouped by Region

Region	Annual Salary	Region	Annual Salary
New England		Pacific and external	
Connecticut	$78,000	California	$114,286
Maine	70,000	Oregon	80,000
Massachusetts	75,000	Washington	112,000
New Hampshire	79,541	Alaska	81,648
Rhode Island	69,900	Hawaii	94,780
Vermont	80,730	Mean	96,543
Mean	75,529		
		South	
Middle Atlantic		Alabama	81,151
Delaware	80,000	Arkansas	35,000
New Jersey	85,000	Florida	103,909
New York	130,000	Georgia	91,080
Pennsylvania	105,000	Louisiana	73,440
Mean	100,000	Mississippi	75,600
		North Carolina	123,000
East north central		South Carolina	98,000
Illinois	97,370	Texas	93,301
Indiana	74,100	Virginia	105,882
Michigan	106,690	Mean	88,036
Ohio	99,986		
Wisconsin	92,283	Border states	
Mean	94,086	Kentucky	79,255
		Maryland	120,000
West north central		Oklahoma	70,000
Iowa	76,700	Tennessee	85,000
Kansas	74,235	West Virginia	72,000
Minnesota	109,053	Mean	85,251
Missouri	88,541		
Nebraska	65,000	Mountain states	
North Dakota	67,800	Arizona	75,000
South Dakota	60,890	Colorado	70,000
Mean	77,460	Idaho	75,000
		Montana	54,254
		Nevada	82,391
		New Mexico	90,692
		Utah	72,800
		Wyoming	70,000
		Mean	73,767

NOTE: Mean annual compensation for all 50 states = $84,906 (rounded).

SOURCE: *The Book of the States, 1992–93.*

TABLE 7.7
Calculation of the Weighted Mean

Region	Regional Mean ($\overline{X}$)	×	Number of States (f)	=	$f\overline{X}$
New England	$ 75,529		6		$453,174
Middle Atlantic	100,000		4		400,000
East north central	94,086		5		470,430
West north central	77,460		7		542,220
Pacific and external	96,543		5		482,715
South	88,036		10		880,360
Border states	85,251		5		426,255
Mountain states	73,767		8		590,136
Total			50		$4,245,290

$$\text{weighted mean} = \frac{\$4,245,290}{50}$$

$$= \$84,906 \text{ (rounded)}$$

values of all members of a distribution that is heavily skewed in one direction (*skewness* is a term discussed later in this chapter), or for distributions in which the data are widely dispersed. For this reason, measures of dispersion are a useful tool for a more complete understanding of a distribution of values. Many measures of dispersion have been developed for the several levels of measurement. Some of the most frequently used of these are discussed next.

The Variation Ratio: A Measure Useful with Nominal Data

The **variation ratio** (v) is a simple-to-calculate and easy-to-understand measure of variation for nominal data.[10] As this section shows, v is a function of the proportion of cases falling in the modal category. The general formula for v is

$$v = 1 - \frac{\text{number of cases in the modal category}}{\text{total number of cases}}$$

Examining this formula, it can be seen that if *all* cases fell in the modal category (i.e., if in a distribution of religion every individual happened to be classified as Protestant), v would be calculated as 0. From this, it can be inferred that the *lower* the v score, the *more* suitably the mode represents all cases.

As an illustration, consider the distribution of religion by region as revealed in the 1994 American National Election Study. These data are presented in Table 7.8. It can be seen from the information in this table that the mode is a better repre-

TABLE 7.8

Distribution of Religion by Region of the Country

Religion	Region			
	Northeast	North Central	South	West
Protestant	41	126	202	90
Catholic	64	81	55	44
Jewish	6	4	5	4
Total	111	211	262	138
$v =$	$1 - 64/111$	$1 - 126/211$	$1 - 202/262$	$1 - 90/138$
$v =$	0.423	0.403	0.229	0.348

SOURCE. 1994 American National Election Study.

sentation of religion in the south (in this case, Protestant) than is the modal religious category for any other region. The variation ratio also shows that the mode is a less satisfactory summary of all religious categories in the northeastern states than for any other region. Put another way, the northeastern respondents were more varied in their religious affiliations.

Another measure of dispersion sometimes used with nominal data is known as the *index of qualitative variation* (IQV), developed by Mueller, Schuessler, and Costner.[11] The IQV provides an *overall* index of heterogeneity, and therefore, it presents a somewhat better summary description of the data than the statistic *v*. However, IQV is more tedious to calculate, and in most cases, *v* is a satisfactory measure of dispersion for nominal data.

The Range: A Measure Useful with Ordinal Data

A simple measure of variation, useful when data are ordered or ranked, is known as the **range**. The range measures the distance between the highest and lowest values of a distribution: the smaller the range, the more accurate or representative of all values of the distribution is the median score.

In Table 7.4, we presented a hypothetical distribution of student scores to a measure of attitudes toward abortion, with values varying from 1 (least permissive) to 10 (most permissive). The range for this variable would be calculated as 9 (10 − 1 = 9).

While the range is simple to calculate and certainly useful as a measure of dispersion, the range suffers from the obvious problem of being totally influenced by extreme values (the highest and lowest scores of a particular distribution). In situations where only one or a very few cases are actually assigned the highest or lowest possible values, the range may provide a misleading impression of variation. For this reason, a variety of other measures of the range have been developed. All of these, essentially, are designed to eliminate extreme cases from consideration. The **decile range** (symbolized as *d*), for example, calculates the range over the middle

80 percent of the data (eliminating the extreme highest and lowest 10 percent of the cases). The **interquartile range** is equal to the difference between the 75th percentile and the 25th percentile values, measuring the spread over the middle half of a distribution.[12] A statistic known as the **median absolute deviation** is derived by calculating the median of the absolute values of deviation of all cases from the median. When the distribution is skewed by a few extreme cases, these other measures will probably provide a more accurate reflection of variance. Still, the simple range remains the most often used measure of dispersion for ordinal data.

The Mean Deviation, Variance, and the Standard Deviation: Measures Useful with Interval Data

One measure of dispersion useful when the data are interval is the **mean deviation,** which is calculated by taking the difference between each observation and the mean, summing these deviations (ignoring negative signs, which otherwise would result in a sum of zero), and dividing this sum by the total number of observations. Arithmetically, the mean deviation is expressed as:

$$\text{Mean deviation} = \frac{\Sigma \mid X - \bar{X} \mid}{N}$$

where X = each observation
$\bar{X}$ = mean of all observations
N = total number of observations
$\mid \mid$ = absolute difference (ignoring positive and negative signs)

Table 7.9 illustrates the calculation of the mean deviation for salaries of governors of the southern states, as presented earlier in Table 7.6. It can be concluded that on the average, the salary of each governor in the southern states in 1992–93 deviated from the mean salary for all governors in the southern states by $17,391.

The mean deviation is a helpful measure of dispersion mainly because of its ease in calculation and interpretation. However, more useful measures have been developed. One of these, based on calculations similar to the mean deviation, is the mean-squared deviation—more commonly known as the **variance.** The formula for calculation of the variance is

$$\text{variance} = \frac{\Sigma (X - \bar{X})^2}{N}$$

where X = each observation
$\bar{X}$ = mean of all observations
N = total number of observations

TABLE 7.9

Annual Salaries of Governors of the Southern States: Calculation of the Mean Deviation

State	Salary (X)	$|X - \bar{X}|$
Alabama	$ 81,151	$ 6,885
Arkansas	35,000	53,036
Florida	103,909	15,873
Georgia	91,080	3,044
Louisiana	73,440	14,596
Mississippi	75,600	12,436
North Carolina	123,000	34,964
South Carolina	98,000	9,964
Texas	93,301	5,265
Virginia	105,882	17,846
Total		$ 173,909
Average salary =	$ 88,036	
Mean deviation = $\dfrac{\$173,909}{10}$		
= $17,391 (rounded)		

Rather than taking the absolute difference between each observation and the mean, ignoring the sign, as was the case when calculating the mean deviation, the variance squares these differences, sums the squares, and divides the sum by the total number of cases. The lower the variance, the more accurately does the mean represent all the scores of all cases in a distribution of interval-level data. However, the variance is not often reported as a measure of dispersion; it is more often used in conjunction with more advanced statistical tests, as described in later chapters.

The **standard deviation** is probably the most widely used measure of dispersion for interval-level data. It provides a powerful summary statistic, as discussed later in this chapter. The standard deviation is obtained by taking the square root of the variance, and it is expressed as

$$\text{Standard deviation} = \sqrt{\frac{\Sigma (X-\bar{X})^2}{N}}$$

where X = each observation
$\bar{X}$ = mean of all observations
N = total number of observations of a population

Reader Note: The preceding formulas show the calculation for the variance and the standard deviation for *population* data. The symbol usually used for population variance is σ^2, and the symbol used for population standard deviation is σ.

When calculating the variance and standard deviation for sample data, the quantity $n - 1$ (where n = sample size) is used as the denominator in each formula, in order to achieve unbiased population estimates. The symbol used for sample variance is s^2, and the symbol used for sample standard deviation is s.

Again considering the 1992–1993 salary of governors in the southern states, the standard deviation is found to be $23,938. Unlike the mean deviation (found for this same example to be $17,391), the standard deviation is not easily interpretable. It is when we consider the standard deviation in terms of the normal curve that the utility of the measure becomes apparent.

The Coefficient of Variation

Prior to a discussion of the normal curve, one final measure of dispersion must be discussed: the **coefficient of variation,** used when the researcher wishes to compare the dispersion of two or more groups about their respective means. If the mean score for each group were exactly the same, the standard deviation would serve this purpose. If the means are different (as will most often be the case), a comparison of standard deviation scores alone might be misleading. A standard deviation of 3.3 for a group having a mean score of 5.0 on a particular variable would have a different interpretation than a standard deviation of 3.3 for a group having a mean score of 50.0 on this variable. That is, in the first instance, the standard deviation of 3.3 would indicate a considerable amount of spread about the mean; in the second instance, the standard deviation of 3.3 would indicate a group more homogeneously group about the mean. The coefficient of variation is used to compare differences of this nature, and its formula is

$$CV = s / \bar{X}$$

$$\text{where} \quad CV = \text{coefficient of variation}$$
$$s \quad = \text{standard deviation}$$
$$\bar{X} \quad = \text{mean}$$

For the two aforementioned cases, the coefficient of variation for the first group (mean of 5.0, standard deviation of 3.3) is 0.66. For the second group (mean of 50.0, standard deviation of 3.3), the coefficient of variation is 0.066. Again, the *lower* the coefficient of variation, the *greater* is the homogeneity of the group.

SHAPE OF THE DISTRIBUTION

In addition to measures of central tendency and dispersion, distributions can be considered in terms of their shape. We noted previously that the shape of a distribution can be revealed by connecting with a solid line the midpoints of the top of each bar of a histogram. The resulting shape will be a function of the original frequency distribution. Distributions having large proportions of cases with scores

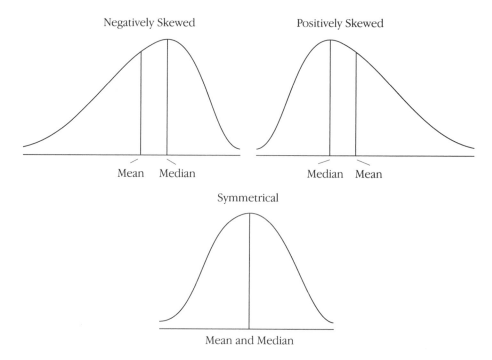

FIGURE 7.10
Some Possible Shapes of Frequency Distributions

above the mean will take on different shapes from those having large proportions of low scores or those having a large proportion of scores clustering close to the mean.

Of the many possible shapes, three common shapes are depicted in Figure 7.10. The first two shapes presented in this figure are said to be **skewed;** this means that in both instances, there are more extreme scores in one direction or the other. In the first instance, there are more extremely low scores; the distribution in this case is said to be *negatively skewed.* It can also be seen here that the mean is pulled in the direction of the lower scores. In the second shape, there are more extremely high scores, and the distribution is said to be *positively skewed.* In a positively skewed distribution, the mean is pulled in the direction of the higher scores.

The third shape is said to be *symmetrical.* In such a distribution, an equal number of cases fall on each side of the curve, and the mean, median, and mode will coincide. As we noted earlier, it is apparent that in reporting measures of central tendency, the shape of the distribution is a factor to be considered. For distributions that are highly skewed in one direction or the other, the mean may present a distorted image of the distribution. In such instances, the median or the mode may be a more representative measure, even though the mean might otherwise be appropriate.

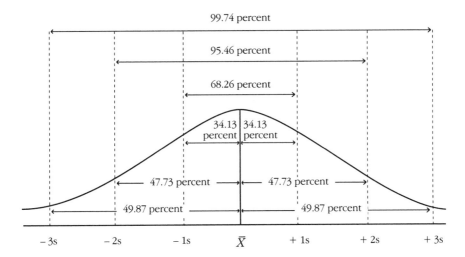

FIGURE 7.11
Areas under the Normal Curve

A special type of symmetrical distribution is known as the **normal curve,**[13] which is a distribution that has the properties of being *unimodal* (having exactly one mode) and symmetrical, and that has equivalent mean, median, and mode scores. Another property of the normal curve is that a constant proportion of cases will lie between the mean and a distance from the mean, defined in unit of standard deviation.

It is the latter characteristic of the normal curve that is most useful to researchers. Figure 7.11 illustrates the areas of the normal curve, defined in units of standard deviation. As shown, in a normal distribution, approximately 34.13 percent of all cases can be found within an area of 1 standard deviation greater than the mean, and an equal proportion are found to lie within an area of 1 standard deviation less than the mean. Thus, slightly over 68 percent of all cases in a normal distribution can be expected to lie within 1 standard deviation (plus or minus) of the mean. Similarly, over 95 percent of all cases can be found within 2 standard deviations (plus or minus) of the mean, and practically all cases (over 99%) will fall within 3 standard deviations (plus or minus) of the mean.

In this manner, the standard deviation—used in conjunction with the normal curve—becomes an extremely important tool for data evaluation. Assume, for example, that the public's rating of a particular presidential candidate on a scale of 0 (very negative) to 100 (very positive) is normally distributed with a mean of 50.0 and a standard deviation of 15. We can conclude from this that about 68 percent of the public assigns this candidate a rating between 35 and 65 (± 1 standard deviation from the mean) and that more than 95 percent of the public assigns the candidate a rating between 20 and 80 (± 2 standard deviations from the mean).

It is useful to think of frequency distributions in political research as approximating a normal curve. This is especially true when considering distributions of sample statistics, discussed in Chapter 8. The properties of the normal curve become especially useful in interpreting the nature of data, and, in fact, many distributions in the political and social sciences do approximate normality.

The z Score

We also might be interested in estimating the proportion of the public assigning the candidate a rating between 50 (the mean) and 75. This can be accomplished by calculation of the z score (sometimes called the *standard score*), the formula for which is

$$z = \frac{X - \bar{X}}{s}$$

where X = any proportionate distance (score) of any observation
we wish to estimate
$\bar{X}$ = mean
s = standard deviation

The **z score** tells the number of standard deviations that the score lies above or below the mean. Applying the formula to the aforementioned situation, the score is found to be

$$z = \frac{75 - 50}{15} = 1.67$$

In this instance, we find that score of 75 is 1.67 standard deviation units greater than the mean.

We know, from our discussion of the normal curve, that 34.13 percent of the cases lie between the mean and one standard deviation above he mean and that 47.43 percent of the cases lie between the mean and 2 standard deviations above the mean. Because the rating of 75 is 1.67 standard deviation units above the mean, the proportion of the public assigning the candidate a score of 50 to 75 must be somewhere between 34.13 and 47.42 percent.

Tables have been developed to allow rapid interpretation of the z values. One such table is shown in appendix B. To use this table, find the first two digits of the z value presented in the leftmost column (in this case 1.6) and the third digit as presented in the column headings. For a z score of 1.67 we find the value to be .4525, which means that 45.25 percent of the public has assigned the candidate a rating of between 50 and 75. Had the z score been 1.43, we would conclude that 42.36 percent of the public rated the candidate between these two scores. If we had wished to determine the proportion of the public assigning the candidate a rating between 0 and 75, we simply would have added 0.50 to the z value obtained (0.4525) because

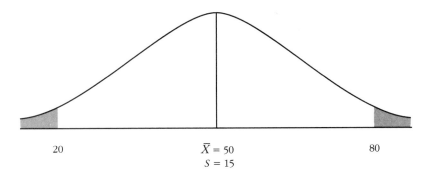

FIGURE 7.12
Normal Curve, with Emphasis on Both Ends of the Curve

in the normal curve, it is assumed that 95.25 percent of the public would rate the candidate from 0 to 75.

As a final illustration of the normal curve and the use of the z score, assume that we are interested in finding the proportion assigning the candidate very high and very low scores. For some reason, we may be interested in knowing the proportion of the public assigning the candidate a score of 80 or higher and 20 or less. Such an interest is illustrated in Figure 7.12.

To calculate this proportion, we would first find the proportion assigning the candidate a score of 50 to 80, then we would *subtract* this total from 0.50 (because, again, it is assumed that 50 percent of all cases fall on the positive side of the mean). Because the same proportion of cases are assumed to assign the candidate a score of 80 to 100 as would assign the candidate a score of 0 to 20 (because, by definition, this is a normal curve), we then only need to double this score to find the total proportion rating the candidate at both extremes. This is accomplished in the following manner:

$$z = \frac{80 - 50}{15} = 2.00$$

Returning to our table of z values presented in Appendix B, it can be seen that for a z score of 2.00, 47.73 percent of the cases fall between the mean value of 50 and the rating of 80. Thus only 0.0227 (0.50 – 0.4773) of the public gives the candidate a rating of 80 or above. Doubling this number to account for the proportion of the public assigning the candidate a score of 20 or less we find that 0.0454 (or less than 5%) of the public assigns the candidate a highly positive or a highly negative score. Such information might be of interest not only to the political researcher but also to the candidate, who may value an image of appealing to a wide spectrum of the public without raising intense levels of feeling (either positive or negative) among the voters.

SUMMARY

This chapter has examined some of the important ways of describing single variables.[14] A frequency distribution can be constructed, showing numbers of cases percentages, or proportions per category. Charts and graphs provide rapid visual interpretation of data, and measures of central tendency can be used to describe the average characteristics of a group. Measures of dispersion can be calculated, showing the extent to which the distribution varies from the typical value. Used in conjunction with the normal curve, the standard deviation can be used to estimate the proportion of cases falling within certain distances from the mean.

All of these techniques assist in describing and understanding distributions. However, these techniques do not, in themselves, reveal *relationships* that may exist among variables. Often, it is the discovery or measuring of relationships that is of central concern to the political analyst. We turn to this issue in the next chapter.

KEY TERMS

univariate analysis	mean
frequency distribution	variation ratio
cumulative percent	range
bar graph	decile range
histogram	interquartile range
frequency polygon	median absolute
pie chart	deviation
pictograms	mean deviation
line diagram	variance
measure of central	standard deviation
tendency	coefficient of variation
measure of dispersion	skewed
mode	normal curve
median	z score

EXERCISES

1. In its 1992 American National Election Study, the Inter-University Consortium for Political and Social Research (ICPSR) asked respondents to place themselves on a seven-point "women's rights scale," from 1 ("Women and men should have an equal role in running business, industry, and government") to 7 ("A woman's place is in the home"). Responses were as follows:

Value	Value Label	Frequency of Response
1	Women and men should have an equal role	295
2		78
3		59
4		101
5		38
6		27
7	A woman's place is in the home	30

NOTE: All responses other than the preceding have been deleted.

    a. Prepare a frequency distribution for this set of data, showing the *total number of cases in the distribution,* the *percentage of case falling in each category,* and the *cumulative percentage for each category.*

    b. What measure(s) of central tendency would be most appropriately reported for this set of data? Why? What would this (these) measure(s) be in this instance?

    c. What measure(s) of dispersion would be most appropriate to report in conjunction with this set of data? Why? What is the value of this (or these) measure(s) in this instance.

    d. Discuss this distribution by reference to the measures of central tendency and dispersion reported in the preceding subitem. How do these measures assist in understanding this distribution?

2. In its 1992 survey, the ICPSR asked respondents to place themselves on seven-point "government services scale," including spending on health and education, ranging from 1 ("Government should provide many fewer domestic services") to 7 ("Government should provide many more services"). Responses were as follows:

Value	Value Label	Frequency of Response
1	Government should provide many fewer services	54
2		93
3		165
4		340
5		206
6		147
7	Government should provide many more services	147

NOTE: All responses other than the preceding have been deleted.

    a. Construct a *bar graph* for the preceding set of data.

    b. How does graphic presentation assist in understanding a distribution such as that presented here? Why?

    c. What other graphic options might be used to present this set of data? Which are most appropriate, and why?

3. Federal budgetary outlays in 1993, by major category, were estimated to be as follows:

Category	Outlay (in millions)
National defense	$ 289,299
Human resources	837,865
(including social security, Medicare, health, education)	
Physical resources	94,877
(including transportation and housing)	
Net interest	202,771
Other	87,336
Total	1,512,148

SOURCE: *Statistical Abstract of the United States, 1993,* 330. All categories other than those shown have been deleted.

a. Calculate the percentage of expenditures for each category.
b. Present this information in pie-chart format.
c. How does graphic presentation aid in understanding this set of data? Why?
d. Discuss some of the conditions under which pie charts are appropriate, and some conditions under which they are inappropriate for the presentation of data.

4. Rates of crime, per 100,000 in the United States for various offenses for the years 1982 to 1991 are shown in Table 7.10.
   a. Prepare a *line diagram* for the data presented in Table 7.10. Note. Separate graphs may be constructed for each category of crime (murder, theft, robbery, etc.), or graphs may be constructed for each major type of crime (violent crime or property crime), or *all crime rates* may be shown in one graph.
   b. Discuss how line diagrams assist in presenting and understanding data such as that shown here.
   c. What techniques might be used to enhance the visual presentation of line diagrams?

5. Measures of central tendency and of dispersion: For each category of crime reported in the preceding item,
   a. Calculate the *mean score* for this period of time.
   b. Calculate the *mean deviation,* the *variance,* and the *standard deviation* for each category of crime, and discuss the interpretation of each.

6. Research applications of data organization and presentation
   a. Review articles in any recent issues of several political science and policy journals, and discuss the use of frequency distributions and graphs in those articles.
   b. In each instance, report the type of graph or chart used and how that graph or chart enhanced the author's presentation.
   c. Report also how, in your opinion, each presentation might have been enhanced or improved.

TABLE 7.10

Rates of Crime from 1982 to 1992

	Violent Crime				Property Crime		
Year	Murder	Rape	Robbery	Aggravated Assault	Burglary	Larceny/ Theft	Motor Vehicle Theft
1982	9.1	34.0	239	289	1,489	3,085	459
1983	8.3	33.7	217	279	1,338	2,869	431
1984	7.9	35.7	205	290	1,264	2,791	437
1985	7.9	37.1	209	303	1,287	2,901	462
1986	8.6	37.9	225	346	1,345	3,010	508
1987	8.3	37.4	213	351	1,330	3,081	529
1988	8.4	37.6	221	370	1,309	3,135	583
1989	8.7	38.1	233	383	1,276	3,171	630
1990	9.4	41.2	257	424	1,236	3,195	658
1991	9.8	42.3	273	433	1,252	3,229	659

SOURCE: U.S. Federal Bureau of Investigation, "Crime in the United States," for years shown, as reported in *Statistical Abstract of the United States,* 1993, 192.

NOTES

1. William G. Jacoby, "The Structure of Ideological Thinking in the American Electorate," *American Journal of Political Science,* 39 (May, 1995), 314–335. Emphasis in original.
2. Edward R. Tufte, *The Visual Display of Quantitative Information* (Cheshire, CT: Graphics Press), 1983.
3. Jan E. Leighley and Jonathan Nagler, "Socioeconomic Class Bias in Turnout, 1964–1988," *American Political Science Review* 86 (June, 1992), 725–736.
4. Tufte, *The Visual Display of Quantitative Information.*
5. Ibid., 51.
6. See also Edward R. Tufte, *Envisioning Information* (Cheshire, CT: Graphics Press), 1990.
7. Some researchers prefer to report the median in the same units as the data, and they do not include decimal places if the original values do not include decimal places. Whatever seems to provide for greatest clarity would be appropriate.
8. See Frederick Mosteller and John W. Tukey, *Data Analysis and Regression* (Reading, MA: Addison-Wesley), 1977.
9. John Lynxwiler and David Gay, "Reconsidering Race Differences in Abortion Attitudes," *Social Science Quarterly* (March, 1994), 67–84.
10. As discussed in Linton C. Freeman, *Elementary Applied Statistics* New York: John Wiley & Sons, 1965), 40–43.

11. See John Mueller, Karl Schuessler, and Herbert Costner, *Statistical Reasoning in Sociology* (Boston: Houghton Mifflin, 1970), 174–179.
12. See also Ibid., 154–155.
13. A special type of normal curve is one with a mean of zero and a standard deviation of 1.0. Such a distribution is known as the standard normal curve.
14. It should be noted that many of the formulas presented in this chapter, as well as elsewhere in this text, are *definitional formulas*. Often *computational formulas*, which are less tedious to apply and which reduce the risk of computational error, can be employed.

CHAPTER 8

Searching for Relationships:
Contingency Tables and Tests of Statistical Significance

Measures useful for summarizing and describing single variables—such as those discussed in Chapter 7—play an important role in the conduct of political research. Students of politics and policy obviously will be interested in such information as the *variation* of voting turnout among various racial and ethnic groups, the *proportion* of Democratic congresspersons supporting a Democratic president's proposed legislation, the *extent* of crime in particular neighborhoods, and the *frequency* of drug and alcohol use among adolescents. Information such as this, systematically collected and accurately reported, is essential to the informed political observer and policy analyst.

However, political and policy analysts generally are more interested in establishing **relationships** among variables. As a rule, political scientists want to discover factors *associated with* voting turnout, congressional voting patterns, criminal behavior, and illicit drug use. Put another way, political scholars and policy analysts are interested in establishing **predictive relationships** among variables. We want to know the extent to which knowledge of one variable assists in predicting the appearance of another. Also, when dealing with information collected from *samples,* we want to know whether these relationships truly reflect the relationships existing within the **population.**

The ultimate design of science, *any* science, is the establishment of causal relationships among variables. As Hubert M. Blalock puts it, "One of the basic aims of any science . . . is to establish causal relations . . . it is extremely difficult to think theoretically in any other terms."[1] Political scientists, like all scientists, want to establish cause and effect relationships among variables important to our areas of concern. An important first step in establishing causation is demonstrating a predictive relationship, or a correlation. Clearly, no causal relationship can exist among variables that are not correlated.

Even in the "hard" sciences, where rigorous control is possible, it is debatable whether undisputed causal laws ever can be found.[2] Certainly, many obstacles exist to the development of causal relationships in the policy sciences. Still, the first step

175

in establishing such relationships is discovering predictive associations among variables. If we find one variable useless in predicting another, then we can at least conclude that no causal relationship exists between the two.

Relationships, then, are the *sine qua non* of science. In addition to serving as a criterion for establishing causality, a more practical reason for establishing and measuring relationships exists. If we are concerned about a problem and want to do something effective about that problem, then we must know what factors actually are related to the issue of concern. If we want to address the problem of substance abuse among high school students, as an example, an important first step is to determine what factors are related to adolescent drug use. If we want to do something about homelessness in our cities, it is important to assess those factors related to homelessness. If we want to encourage greater recycling activities among residents of a particular community, it is important that we know which factors impede and which encourage recycling efforts. In the absence of such knowledge, it is impossible to develop meaningful, cost-effective programs to address issues of public concern.

THE NATURE OF ASSOCIATION

Establishing and measuring relationships, then, is an important step both to developing our theoretical understanding of political phenomena and also to helping policy makers make better decisions. When we say that two variables are associated or related to one another, we are saying that knowledge of one variable assists in understanding or predicting another. As discussed in Chapter 3, the variable that we seek to understand or predict is the *dependent variable.* The variable that we are using for making this prediction is the *independent variable.* The degree to which we can predict the dependent variable from a knowledge of the independent variable indicates the strength of the *association* between the two.

Even strong relationships can be deceiving, however. Sometimes what appears to be a strong relationship between two variables is actually caused by the confounding influences of one or more additional variables. The policy analyst must eliminate as many of these potentially confounding variables as possible before concluding that a strong association between the two variables of interest actually does exist. For the moment, however, our concern is with establishing the initial relationship between the independent and dependent variables.

CONTINGENCY-TABLE ANALYSIS

When both independent and dependent variables are nominal- or ordinal-level data, relationships are usually presented in tabular form. As a general rule, tables are easier to read and interpret if the *independent variable* is arrayed as the *columns* of the table, and if the categories of the independent variable are presented so as to sum to 100 percent. The sums of each column are the **column marginals,** and the sums of each row are the **row marginals.**

TABLE 8.1

Frequency Distributions of Attitudes toward Federal Aid to Big Cities, and Type of Community in which Respondent Lives

Attitudes toward Federal Aid to Big Cities	Frequency	Percentage
Increase	487	20.7
Stay the same	1174	49.8
Decrease	696	29.5
Total	2357	100.0

Type of Community in which Respondent Lives		
Central city	600	25.5
Suburb	1000	42.4
Nonmetropolitan	757	32.1
Total	2357	100.0

NOTE: Type of community variable has been recoded from original values.

SOURCE: 1992 American National Election Survey.

Suppose that we are interested in people's attitudes toward federal aid to big cities, and we want to know what factors might be associated with such attitudes. It might be supposed that where people reside—in central cities, in suburbs, or in nonmetropolitan areas—would be one such variable affecting their attitudes toward federal aid to cities. In its 1992 American National Election Study, the ICPSR asked people to indicate the type of community in which they reside (central city, suburb, or non-metropolitan area), and also asked whether they believed federal aid to big cities should be increased, decreased, or should remain about the same. Table 8.1 presents the *frequency distributions* for these variables.

It can be seen from the frequency distributions presented in Table 8.1 that more respondents said federal aid to cities should "stay the same" than selected either of the other responses, and also that higher proportions of respondents lived in suburbs than in central cities or in nonmetropolitan areas. Of course, this distribution says nothing about the possible relationship between attitudes to federal aid to big cities and place of residence. Frequency distributions alone will not reveal relationships, but cross-tabulation procedures tables may. Table 8.2 presents a cross-tabulation of these two variables.

It can be seen in Table 8.2 that a relationship between attitudes toward federal aid to big cities and type of community in which people reside indeed does exist. Of those living in the central cities, 32.5 percent supported increases in such aid, and in neither of the other community types did such a large proportion support increases in aid to big cities. Thirty-eight percent of those living in nonmetropolitan areas supported *decreases* in aid to big cities, and in neither of the other community types did such a large proportion support decreased aid. Knowledge of type of

TABLE 8.2

Attitudes toward Federal Aid for Big Cities, by Type of Community in which Respondent Lives

Attitude toward Federal Aid to Big Cities	Type of Community			
	Central City	Suburbs	Non-metropolitan	Totals
Increase	195 [a]	184 [b]	108 [c]	487
	(32.5)	(18.4)	(14.3)	(20.7)
Stay the same	279 [d]	534 [e]	361 [f]	1174
	(46.5)	(53.4)	(47.7)	(49.8)
Decrease	126 [g]	282 [h]	288 [i]	696
	(21.0)	(28.2)	(38.0)	(29.5)
Total	600	1000	757	2357
	(25.5)	(42.4)	(32.1)	(100.0)

NOTE: Numbers in parenthesis are percents. Cell identification letters (A, B, C, etc.) are inserted to assist with the calculation of the chi-square, as demonstrated in Table 8.4.

SOURCE: 1992 American National Election Study.

community in which people live, in other words, helps in predicting their attitudes toward federal aid to big cities. We have discovered a relationship.

Table 8.2 also helps to illustrate another point important to all political and policy research. The relationship between type of community in which people live and their attitudes toward federal aid to big cities is by no means perfect. Many people living in the central cities supported *decreased* aid to big cities (21.0%), and a significant proportion living in suburbs supported *increased* aid (18.4%). Thus, other factors must be associated with attitudes toward federal aid to big cities: Type of community in which people live is only one such variable, and we do not yet know how strong this association is. To thoroughly understand attitudes toward federal aid to big cities, we would clearly want to examine other variables also.

Another example of contingency-table analysis is provided by John Harrigan and his examination of the relationship between form of local government in the United States and city size.[3] Harrigan's tabular analysis of this relationship is shown in Table 8.3.

Presented in this manner, it can be seen that some noticeable relationships exist between city size and form of local government preferred. As Harrigan concludes, "a majority of all cities in the 25,000 to 250,000 range have the manager form of government . . . the mayor form is most popular in large cities and small towns.[4]

In the following chapters, we examine statistics designed to tell us with some degree of precision how *strong* are relationships such as those shown in Tables 8.2 and 8.3. Here, we first consider the important question of whether relationships found using data drawn from a sample (as is the case in the information presented in Table 8.2) are likely to reflect relationships actually existing in the population.

TABLE 8.3

Form of Local Government by Population Group

Form of Government	Population Group					
	Over 1,000,000	500,000 – 1,000,000	250,000 – 499,999	25,000 – 249,000	10,000 – 25,000	2,500 – 9,999
Mayor council	6 (75%)	13 (81%)	16 (41%)	407 (36%)	676 (42%)	2192 (58%)
Council-manager	2 (25%)	3 (19%)	22 (56%)	681 (60%)	751 (47%)	1240 (33%)
Commission	0 (0%)	0 (0%)	1 (3%)	22 (2%)	52 (3%)	73 (2%)
Town meeting	0 (0%)	0 (0%)	0 (0%)	27 (2%)	123 (8%)	287 (8%)
Total	8	16	39	1137	1602	3792

NOTE: Harrigan's presentation has been rearranged so as to array population characteristics as the columns of this table.

SOURCE: John J. Harrigan, *Politics and Policy in States and Communities*, 5th ed. (New York: HarperCollins, 1994), p. 169. Original data calculated by Harrigan from *The Municipal Year Book*, 1993 (Washington, DC: International City and County Management Association, 1993), Table 2, p. xi.

STATISTICAL SIGNIFICANCE

When dealing with *sample data,* as we said earlier, one important question to be asked is this: How confident can we be that whatever relationship is discovered truly reflects a relationship in the population? It is, of course, the population that is of central interest to the researcher. Findings based on sample data are of little utility unless they can be generalized with some degree of confidence to the entire population. Although it appears in our earlier example that type of community in which people reside is related to their opinions about federal aid to big cities, our analysis obviously is not based on information collected from the entire population, only from those people who compose the sample responding to the 1992 American National Election Survey.

Sample values, as discussed in Chapter 4, may deviate from population values and, in all probability, values of repeated samples drawn from the same population will deviate from each other. This deviation of values is known as **sampling error.**[5] Because of sampling error, there is a risk that the researcher may incorrectly infer—from the sample data—that a relationship exists in the population. On the other hand, there is a risk that the researcher may incorrectly infer from the sample data that no relationship exists in the population. The former are **Type I errors;** the latter are **Type II errors.** Research using sample data can never eliminate these risks. In fact, procedures that may be taken to reduce one type of risk increase the probability of making the other. It is possible, however, to state with some degree of precision the risks of making either error. In practice, researchers most often measure only the risk of making a Type I error, but it always should be kept in mind that in minimizing Type I risks, the chance of making a Type II error increases. As research scholars, we want to minimize the risk of falsely reporting a relationship which, in the population, really does not exist (a Type I error). Thus, the significance level reported in political and policy research can be thought of as the probability of making a Type I error. While there are many tests of significance, among the most useful for political research are the chi-square, single-sample and two- sample difference of means tests, and analysis of variance. These are discussed in the remainder of this chapter.

Using Tests of Significance

Before examining any of these tests, it is useful to consider the factors involved in selecting and interpreting tests of significance. Among the most important of these are

1. Specifying a null and a research hypothesis
2. Specifying a significance level
3. Selecting one-tailed or two-tailed tests
4. Deciding whether to accept or reject the hypotheses

Specifying Hypotheses.   In Chapter 3, hypotheses were defined as "testable statements relating two or more concepts or variables." Here, we can be more precise and note that in the research situation, *two* hypotheses are actually being tested. The first is called the "research hypothesis" (in fact several hypotheses may be tested); the second (implied but often not stated) is called the "null hypothesis." The **research hypothesis,** symbolized as H_1 (H_2, H_3, H_4, and so on if more than one alternative is tested) makes an assertion. A hypothesis expressed in Chapter 3 was that, "Female state legislators are more likely than male legislators to support legislation aimed at limiting handgun possession." This is a research hypothesis; a relationship is asserted to exist between gender and support for handgun legislation.

The **null hypothesis** (symbolized as H_0), on the other hand, assumes *no* relationship to exist. For the preceding situation, the null hypothesis might be stated, "No difference exists between men and women state legislators in terms of their support of handgun legislation."

What is the purpose of stating hypotheses in this fashion? Null hypotheses are necessary because it never is possible to prove an assertion to be true beyond any doubt. The researcher may find that women legislators are more supportive of handgun legislation, but this is not *proof* that it is gender that makes the difference. Any number of other factors—such as age, education, religion, income, race, ethnicity, and so forth—may be related to support for handgun legislation, and additional research may find these to be far more important than gender. However, null hypotheses can be *disproved* if a hypothesis of no relationship can be shown to be false. By testing the null hypothesis, and finding some relationship to exist, it can be said that it would be wrong to conclude that gender is not possibly related to support for handgun legislation. In so doing, support is lent to the research hypothesis.

Therefore, it can be said that in the research situation, it actually is the null hypothesis that is tested. To accept the null hypothesis (of their being no relationship between the two variables) is to conclude that whatever difference may have been evidenced in the sample could have occurred just by chance. The relationship in this case is said to be *not statistically significant.* To reject the null hypothesis (of there being no relationship between two variables) is to conclude that whatever difference may have been evidenced in the sample are unlikely to have occurred just by accident or by chance. In this case, the relationship is said to be *statistically significant.*

The research hypothesis (or hypotheses), then, makes an assertion but is not directly tested. The null hypothesis is tested, and from the results, substantive inferences about population characteristics are made.

Specifying a Significance Level.   The level of significance used to accept or reject a null hypothesis is based largely on the extent of variation between the hypothesized and actual sample values and the values that could have occurred just by chance. If the difference between these two values (for example, a hypothesized correlation of zero and a sample correlation of some nonzero value) is so great that the researcher is not willing to attribute this just to chance or to sampling error, the relationship is said to be *statistically significant,* and the null hypothesis is rejected.

What level of significance must be reached for the researcher to confidently reject the null hypothesis? The more stringent the criteria set, the less the risk of making a Type I error (falsely reporting a relationship that does not exist in the population). However the precise magnitude of the difference sought is arbitrary. Although some research situations may require more stringency than others, conventions have developed. In political science and policy research, it is typical to see the ".05 level" used as the level of significance. This means that in rejecting the null hypothesis, the researcher knows that 5 percent of the time, a sample difference as large as the one obtained would be expected to occur *just by chance* even if the null hypothesis is true. More rigid standards may be set by selecting a significance level of .01, or .001, or some more remote probability level. Having established the .001 level, for example, the researcher would not reject the null hypothesis unless the sample correlation were so large as to occur by chance in only 1 out of every 1,000 samples. In reducing the risk of falsely reporting a population relationship to exist, however, it should be remembered that the risk of failing to reject a false null hypothesis increases.

One-Tailed and Two-Tailed Tests. An issue that arises in significance testing is whether to apply one-tailed or two-tailed tests. Actually, the question being asked is whether the hypothesis is directional or nondirectional. A **directional hypothesis** specifies the direction of the relationship. The research hypothesis, "Lower educated citizens will have a lower rate of voter turnout than higher educated citizens," is directional. A **nondirectional hypothesis** does not specify direction of the relationship. The research hypothesis, "Voting turnout will vary by levels of education," is nondirectional. In the latter example, the researcher is suggesting a relationship between education and voting participation but is unsure of the direction of that relationship.

When hypothesizing a directional relationship, the **one-tailed test** is used. When hypothesizing a nondirectional relationship, the **two-tailed test** is used. The "tail" in these instances refers to the extremes of the theoretical sampling distribution. In a directional hypothesis, a sample value is said to be statistically significant if it falls in a region of the sampling distribution significantly greater (or lower if this had been the direction of the hypothesis) than the expected value (represented by the null hypothesis). In a nondirectional hypothesis, a sample value is said to be statistically significant if it falls in a region that deviates significantly in *either* direction from the expected relationship (it may, in other words, fall in regions at either end of the sampling distribution). The determination of which to use is based on the nature of the hypothesis: Directional hypotheses call for a one-tailed test; nondirectional hypotheses require a two-tailed test.

Summary So Far

Statistical tests of significance are applicable with sample data. The question to be answered is whether the relationships that may have been found in the sample actually reflect true relationships within the population. This question can never be answered with certainty, but the level of risk taken in generalizing from the sample to the population can be stated. In so doing, the researcher sets out a research hypotheses and a null hypothesis. The research hypothesis, which asserts a relationship to exist, can never be proven, but the null hypothesis, which assumes no relationship, can be rejected (thus lending support to the research hypothesis). The null hypothesis is rejected (and the relationship is said to be statistically significant) when it can be shown that the sample statistic probably did not occur by chance. This is accomplished by comparing the sample statistic with a theoretical sampling distribution, indicating the probability of obtaining such a sample value, or one more extreme. The following section examines some of the more commonly used tests of significance.

SIGNIFICANCE TESTING WITH CONTINGENCY TABLES: THE CHI-SQUARE DISTRIBUTION

One of the most common situations faced in all of political research occurs when the researcher has prepared a contingency table of two variables and wishes to determine whether, in the population, the two variables are independent of each other. The appropriate test of statistical significance for this situation is the Pearson's chi-square (or, simply, chi-square). Symbolized as χ^2 the test has many applications and is often used in problems involving the cross-tabulation of nominal or ordinal variables. In general terms, the χ^2 test is used to determine the extent to which the actual (or observed) values in a particular table deviate from the values that would have been expected *if the two variables are not related to one another.* (See Box 8.1, page 187.)

By way of illustration, consider again the information previously provided in Tables 8.1 and 8.2, concerning type of community in which people reside, and people's attitudes toward federal aid to big cities. We know, from the frequency distributions presented in Table 8.1, the proportions of the entire sample supporting "increased," "decreased," and "no change" in aid to big cities. It is shown there that 20.7 percent of all respondents supported increased federal aid, 29.5 percent supported decreased federal aid, and 49.8 percent said federal aid to big cities should remain about the same. If there were no relationship between attitudes toward aid to cities and where people reside, it would be expected that these same proportions would be reflected among respondents residing in each category of type of community. If residence is not related to attitudes toward aid to cities, then we would expect 20.7 percent of those living in central cities to support increased aid, 20.7 percent of those living in the suburbs to support increased aid, and 20.7 percent of those living in nonmetropolitan areas to support increased aid. Likewise, we would expect identical proportions to support decreased aid, and identical proportions to favor aid remaining about the same, regardless of type of community in which they live. We can calculate the expected frequency for any cell by application of the following simple formula:

Expected cell frequency = column total × row percentage

This formula yields the frequency expected to fall in any cell, assuming the two variables (in this case, attitudes toward aid to big cities and type of community) are independent of each other.

Because we already have examined the actual table cross-tabulating attitudes toward aid to cities with type of community in which people live (Table 8.2), we know that some relationship between these variables exists. The observed (or actual) entries in each cell of that table deviate somewhat from those that would have occurred if attitudes toward federal aid to cities were truly independent of community of residence. Thus, attitudes toward aid to cities and type of community residence cannot be said to be independent of each other; there is some degree of dependency. As is true with all tests of significance, χ^2 tells us whether we could have expected respondents in our sample (in this instance, the 2,357 respondents to the 1992 American National Election Survey) to display this degree of dependency if, in the population as a whole, attitudes toward aid to cities and type of community residency are, in fact, not related. The general χ^2 formula is

$$\chi^2 = \sum \frac{(f_o - f_e)^2}{f_e}$$

where f_o = observed frequency for each cell
f_e = expected frequency for each cell
(and where f_e is calculated as the product of the
row and column marginals for each cell divided by
the total number of cases in the table)

Verbally, the formula states that the χ^2 value is obtained by first subtracting the expected value for each cell from the observed value and squaring the result (squaring eliminates negative differences, which would cancel the positive values in the summation process). This squared value is then divided by the expected value for each cell (a process that standardizes for different-sized cell entries), and each of these values is then summed. The total summed value is the χ^2.

As an illustration of the calculation of the χ^2 value, consider again the relationship between respondents' attitudes toward federal aid to big cities and type of community in which they reside, shown in Table 8.2. We have already noted that some relationship between these two variables seems to exist: Larger proportions of respondents living in central cities support increased federal aid to big cities, and larger proportions of those living in nonmetropolitan areas support decreased federal aid. The question is this: Could differences such as these within the sample have occurred just by chance, or do they probably reflect true differences in the population of all Americans? In calculating the χ^2, it is helpful to follow the steps illustrated in Table 8.4.

TABLE 8.4
Calculation of the Chi-Square Value

Cell	Observed Frequency (f_o)	Expected Frequency (f_e)	$f_o - f_e$	$(f_o - f_e)^2$	$\dfrac{(f_o - f_e)^2}{f_e}$
A	195	123.97	71.03	5045.26	40.70
B	184	206.62	-22.62	511.66	2.48
C	108	156.41	-48.41	2343.53	14.98
D	279	298.85	-19.85	394.02	1.32
E	534	498.09	35.91	1289.53	2.59
F	361	377.06	-16.06	257.92	0.68
G	126	177.17	-51.17	2618.37	14.78
H	282	295.29	-13.29	176.62	0.60
I	288	223.54	64.46	4155.09	18.59
Total	2357	2357.00			96.72 (i.e., χ^2)

NOTE: Cell identification letters (A, B, C, etc.) correspond to cell labels presented in Table 8.2. The expected value for each cell is calculated as either: the product of that cell's column total and row percent; or as the product of the row and column marginals for that cell divided by the total number of cases. For cell A, using the second formula, this becomes $(600 \times 487) / 2357 = 123.97$.

In this manner, the χ^2 for the data presented in Table 8.2 is found to be 96.72 (rounded). In deciding whether this value of χ^2 is to be considered significant, we make use of the distribution of χ^2 values presented in Appendix C, showing the distribution of chi-square values. One additional step is required prior to interpreting the chi-square value: calculation of the degrees of freedom. Larger tables, it should be apparent, are likely to produce larger chi-square values. The aforementioned cell-by-cell summation process will naturally yield larger chi-square values as the number of rows and columns—and consequently cells—increases. We need a way, then, to account for varying table sizes, and this accounting is accomplished by calculating the degrees of freedom. **Degrees of freedom** refer to the number of values in a distribution, which are free to vary, after imposing certain constraints.[6] When dealing with tables, the degrees of freedom refer to the number of cells of that table that can be filled before the entries in all remaining cells are determined. The formula for determining degrees of freedom for any table is

$$df = (\text{Number of columns} - 1) \times (\text{Number of rows} - 1)$$

For Table 8.2, the degrees of freedom are calculated as $(3 - 1) \times (3 - 1) = 4$.

It will be noted from an examination of the chi-square table (Appendix C) that several distributions of the chi-square value are presented. Having calculated the degrees of freedom, the researcher must select an acceptable level of risk. As discussed previously, the .05 level means that only 5 out of 100 times would we have selected a sample having the characteristics of those reported if these characteris-

TABLE 8.5

Community Opinion of Saturn by County, June 1990 and June 1991 (percentages)

	1990			1991		
	Maury	**Williamson**	**Total**	**Maury**	**Williamson**	**Total**
Extremely favorable	12.8%	15.9%	14.3%	11.4%	15.4%	13.4%
Favorable	35.9	52.3	43.8	33.5	53.6	43.4
Not sure	13.5	15.9	14.7	20.3	21.9	21.1
Unfavorable	25.7	9.6	17.9	19.0	7.3	13.2
Extremely unfavorable	12.1	6.3	9.3	15.8	1.8	8.9
	Chi-square = 51.49			Chi-square = 83.36		
	Sig. = .0000			Sig. = .0000		

SOURCE: David Folz et al., "Saturn Comes to Tennessee: Citizen Perceptions of Project Impacts," *Social Science Quarterly* (December, 1993), 797.

tics are not truly reflective of the population. The .01 level means that such a sample would be expected to occur just by accident 1 out of 100 times, and so forth.

Assuming that the .05 level has been selected, the chi-square distribution indicates that for 4 degrees of freedom, we need a value of 9.488 *or higher* to reject the null hypothesis of no significant relationship and to conclude, instead, that significant differences do exist. In this case, the chi-square value of 96.717 is considerably greater than that needed at the 0.05 level. In fact, it can be seen that this value is even greater than that needed for acceptance at the 0.001 level. We can conclude, then, that the differences in attitudes existing between those living in different types of communities in this sample are statistically significant; that is, they probably are reflective of true differences in the population. We can also say that the likelihood is less than 1 out of 1,000 that we would have obtained a χ^2 of this magnitude if, in the population, there actually are no differences in attitude by type of community.

An interesting application of the chi-square test is provided in the 1993 study by researchers Folz, Gaddis, Lyons, and Scheb. In their study, they were seeking to determine differences in community attitudes to the decision by General Motors to locate its Saturn auto assembly plant in Tennessee.[7] In order to test for possible differences, they interviewed (by telephone) residents of two communities: One was Maury County, where the plant was actually located, and the other was Williamson County, which adjoins Maury County. One hypothesis being tested by the authors was that because the plant failed to live up to the economic and job-enhancement expectations that preceded the plant's arrival, the disappointing outcomes might result in more negative attitudes toward the Saturn plant in the community (Maury County) where the plant was actually located. A portion of their analysis is shown in Table 8.5.

BOX 8.1   Importance of the Chi-Square Test

In 1984, *Science* magazine previewed what its editors believed to be this century's twenty most significant discoveries in science, technology, and medicine. Among those discoveries so identified was Karl Pearson's chi-square test. The following is excerpted from that article.

Trial by Number

Our world is inundated with statistics. Every medical fear or triumph is charted by a complex analysis of chances. Think of cancer, heart disease, AIDS: The less we know, the more we hear of probabilities. This daily barrage is not a matter of mere counting but of inference and decision in the face of uncertainty. No committee changes our school or our prisons without studies on the effects of busing or early parole. Money markets, drunken driving, family life, high energy physics, and deviant cells are all subject to tests of significance and data analysis.

This all began in 1900 when Karl Pearson published his chi-square test of goodness of fit, a formula for measuring how well a theoretical hypothesis fits some observations. . . . Pearson's chi-square test gives one measure of how well theory and data correspond.

The chi-square test can be used for hypotheses and data where observations naturally fall into discrete categories that statisticians call cells. If, for example, you are testing to find whether a certain treatment for cholera is worthless, then the patients divide among four cells: treated and recovered, treated and died, untreated and recovered, and untreated and died. If the treatment is worthless, you expect no difference in recovery rate between treated and untreated patients. But chance and uncontrollable variables dictate that there will almost always be some difference. Pearson's test takes this into account, telling you how well your hypothesis—that the treatment is worthless—fits your observations.

The chi-square test was a tiny event in itself, but it was the signal for a sweeping transformation in the ways we interpret our numerical world. Now there could be a standard way in which ideas were presented to policy makers and to the general public.

SOURCE: Ian Hacking, "Trial by Number," *Science* (November, 1984), 69–70.

It can be seen that, in fact, attitudes in Maury County—where the plant was located—were more negative, in both the 1990 and the 1991 surveys. These differences are shown by the **chi-square test** to be statistically significant, and to have actually increased from one year to the next. As the authors put it, "A significant and enduring difference emerged between the residents of Maury and Williamson Counties in their evaluations of Saturn. A significantly larger proportion (69 percent) of Williamson County citizens had at least a favorable opinion of Saturn while only about 45 percent of residents in Maury County thought favorably of Saturn."[8]

TABLE 8.6

Cross-Tabulation of Discussing Politics by Gender

Does Respondent Discuss Politics with Family or Friends?	Gender		
	Male	**Female**	**Totals**
Yes	662	717	1379
	(79.2)	(74.8)	(76.9)
No	174	241	415
	(20.8)	(25.2)	(23.1)
	836	958	1794
	(46.6)	(53.4)	(100.0)

NOTE: Numbers in parentheses are percentages.

SOURCE: 1994 American National Election Study.

Modifications of the Chi-Square

Before concluding our discussion of the Chi-Square test, two modifications of the formula should be mentioned. First, when the researcher has a 2×2 table (i.e., two rows and two columns), a special formula for the calculation of χ^2 may be applied. Consider Table 8.6, which examines the relationship between gender and whether people discuss politics with family and friends (as reflected in responses to the 1994 American National Election Study).

In the case of such a 2×2 table, the χ^2 can be calculated by the following formula:

$$\chi^2 = \frac{n\,(AD - BC)^2}{(A + B)(C + D)(A + C)(B + D)}$$

where A, B, C, and D are the number of cases falling in each cell, and n is the sample size

In the example presented in Table 8.6, the χ^2 is calculated as follows:

$$\chi^2 = \frac{1794(159{,}542 - 124{,}758)^2}{(1379)(415)(836)(958)}$$

$$\chi^2 = 4.74 \text{ (significant at the 0.05 level)}$$

Second, whenever some or all of the cell entries are small, the χ^2 value, as calculated by either of the formulas presented here, may provide a poor estimation of the actual χ^2 distribution. To correct for this, in 1934, F. Yates suggested a modification that is still widely used. Applying Yates's modification, the researcher reduces the distance between the observed and the expected frequencies by 0.5 prior to calculating χ^2. In a 2×2 table, whenever any cell entry is less than 5, the correction developed by Yates should be used.[9]

Further, when the total sample size is small, an alternative test, known as *Fisher's exact test,* is frequently used. For any 2×2 table of fewer than 20 cases, this test should be used instead of the Chi-Square.

DIFFERENCE-OF-MEANS TEST

Sometimes, a researcher has obtained a *single sample* and wishes to know whether the mean of that sample differs significantly from the mean of the population. Even more commonly, the researcher has obtained *two samples* (or has subdivided one randomly drawn sample into *two subsamples*) and wishes to know the likelihood of the samples having been drawn from populations having different mean scores. When testing hypotheses about difference of means, either of two sampling distributions may be appropriate. One of these is known as Student's *t*, (or the *t* distribution); the other is known as the normal (or standard) distribution. Because the two-sample test situation is generally more interesting, single-sample tests are only very briefly considered here.

Single-Sample Difference-of-Means Test

Occasionally, a researcher wishes to compare some characteristic of a sample (usually some measure of central tendency such as the mean) with that same characteristic in the population, to determine whether differences exist between the sample and the population. As an example, a researcher may want to know whether less-senior members of the House and Senate spend more money, on average, in their campaigns for re-election than do all House and Senate members. Another researcher may want to know whether average test scores of high school students from suburban areas differ from test scores of all high school students. Yet another may seek to determine whether the level of political information of political science students differs from that of all students in a particular university. In each of these cases, it is assumed that the researcher has obtained random samples from the groups being examined (less senior House and Senate members, suburban high school students, and political science students) and is comparing the characteristics of these samples with known values of each population group (all House and Senate members, all high school students, and all students). In situations such as these, when the population sampled is normally distributed,[10] and the population standard deviations are known, the normal distribution is used. This appropriate test statistic becomes

$$z = \frac{}{\sigma / \sqrt{n}}$$

$$\text{where } \bar{X} = \text{mean score of the sample}$$
$$\mu = \text{population mean}$$
$$\sigma = \text{population standard deviation}$$
$$n = \text{sample size}$$

As the table in Appendix B shows, at the 0.05 level of statistical significance for a one-tailed test, a z score of 1.65 or higher must be obtained to reject the null hypothesis of no difference between the sample mean and the population mean. For a two-tailed test, a score of 1.96 or higher must be obtained at the 0.05 level.

Generally, it is unrealistic to assume that the standard deviation of the population will be known. In such cases, the standard deviation of the sample can be used to estimate the standard deviation of the population (assuming that the population is normally distributed), and the appropriate formula becomes

$$t = \frac{}{s/\sqrt{n}}$$

$$\text{where } \bar{X} = \text{sample mean}$$
$$\mu = \text{population mean}$$
$$s = \text{standard deviation of the sample}$$
$$n = \text{sample size}$$

An examination of the table of t values (Appendix D) shows that there are several distributions for t corresponding to the size of the sample. These sample sizes are expressed in terms of degrees of freedom, which must be calculated before the application of the table of t values. In the case of t distribution, the degrees of freedom needed to provide the most unbiased estimate of the population variance are calculated according to the formula $n - 1$, where n = sample size. For a sample size of 25 (and thus 24 degrees of freedom) the t value needed to conclude statistical significance at the 0.05 level for the one-tailed test is shown in Appendix D to be 1.711. The two-tailed test at the 0.05 level requires a t value of 2.064 or higher for a sample size of 25. For larger samples (120 and over), the t values approximate the z values.

Two-Sample Difference-of-Means Test

A more complex—but generally more likely—situation arises when the researcher is interested in comparing the mean difference of two samples. Here, the concern is not with assessing the values of the population means, but with comparing the magnitude of differences between them.[11] The null hypothesis in this situation is that there is no difference between the magnitude of the means of the population sampled.

If the sample sizes are relatively large (and therefore the sampling distribution of the difference of means between the samples will be normally distributed), the z test to be applied is expressed as follows:

$$z = \frac{(\bar{X}_1 - \bar{X}_2) - (\mu_1 - \mu_2)}{\sqrt{\sigma_1^2/n_1 + \sigma_2^2/n_2}}$$

where $\bar{X}_1, \bar{X}_2$ = sample means
μ_1, μ_2 = population means
σ_1, σ_2 = standard deviation of populations
n_1, n_2 = sample sizes

Compared with the z formula discussed for single-sample tests, it can be seen that the numerator of $\bar{X} - \mu$ is replaced by $(\bar{X}_1 - \bar{X}_2) - (\mu_1 - \mu_2)$ (the mean difference of the two subgroups, minus the mean difference of the two populations), and the denominator of $\sigma\sqrt{n}$ is replaced by $\sqrt{\sigma_1^2/n_1 + \sigma_2^2/n_2}$ (an estimate of the standard deviation, or estimated standard error, of the difference of the sample mean scores).

Because our hypothesis is that $\mu_1 - \mu_2 = 0$, the $\mu_1 - \mu_2$ expression can be eliminated from the two sample z test, and the numerator simply becomes $(\bar{X}_1 - \bar{X}_2)$. Because σ_1 and σ_2 (standard deviations of population means) are presumed unknown, these must be estimated by reference to the standard deviations of the samples. In instances where sample sizes are relatively large σ_1 and σ_2 may be replaced with s_1 and s_2 (standard deviations of each sample). Thus a simplified formula for the two-sample difference-of-means test becomes

$$z = \frac{\bar{X}_1 - \bar{X}_2}{\sqrt{s_1^2/n_1 + s_2^2/n_2}}$$

where s_1 and s_2 are the standard deviations of each sample

As an example of the use of the z test in the two-sample case, assume that a researcher is interested in comparing the attitudes held by various subsamples of women toward what the researchers called "feminists." It might be expected that younger women, those who affiliate with the Democratic Party, and those who live outside of the South are more favorable toward feminists than their counterparts who are older, non-Democratic, or Southern.

In order to test for these differences, two sets of hypotheses are established for each situation. The *research hypotheses* assert that younger women, those who affiliate with the Democratic party, and those who live outside of the South will be more favorable toward feminists ($H_1 : \mu_1 > \mu_2$). The *null hypotheses* assume no population differences ($H_0 : \mu_1 = \mu_2$). Table 8.7 tests these hypotheses, relying on data provided by the 1992 American National Election Survey.

Turning first to the expectation that women not from the South would be more favorable toward feminists than those from the South, the data presented in Table

TABLE 8.7

Women's Attitudes toward Feminists

	Region		Party Identification		Age (in years)	
	South	**Non-South**	**Democrat**	**Republican**	**Less than 40**	**40 or Over**
Mean Scores	55.29	54.00	61.63	45.99	55.18	53.78
N	375	736	423	263	523	588
Standard Deviations	22.28	23.44	20.09	23.69	22.34	23.64

NOTE: For these and a number of other people and groups, respondents were asked to indicate their "feeling" on a scale of from "0"—very negative—to "100"—very positive. Shown in this table are mean scores, sample size, and standard deviations for the responses of women to the item "Feminists."

SOURCE: 1992 American National Election Study.

8.7 show that this research hypothesis can be rejected without *reference to the difference of means test.* It is found, in fact, that the mean score of women from the South was somewhat more *positive* than that for women not from the South (55.29 to 54.00).

Considering partisanship (affiliation with the Democratic or Republican Parties) and age (less than 40 years or 40 and above), the data presented in Table 8.6 show that Democrats and younger women are more positive toward feminists than their counterparts. These are the sorts of relationships anticipated by the research hypotheses, and the question now becomes, Are these differences statistically significant? Applying the **z test** to these mean differences, the results are found to be

$$z = \frac{61.63 - 45.99}{\sqrt{\dfrac{20.09^2}{423} + \dfrac{23.69^2}{263}}} \qquad \frac{55.18 - 53.78}{\sqrt{\dfrac{22.34^2}{523} + \dfrac{23.64^2}{588}}}$$

$$z = 8.91 \qquad\qquad z = 1.01$$

Because each original hypothesis was directional, the 1.65 z score is used as the critical value of significance. Considering partisanship, the z score of 8.91 is greater than the critical value; therefore, the null hypothesis of there being no difference in the populations of Democratic and Republican women is rejected, and, instead, support is lent to the research hypothesis. It appears that partisanship is, indeed, a factor significantly related to women's attitudes toward feminists.

Considering age, the z score of 1.01 is not equal to the critical value (1.65). Therefore, we cannot conclude from this analysis that, in the population, younger and older women differ in their attitudes toward feminists.

TABLE 8.8
t-Tests of Environmental Concerns between Richer and Poorer Nations

Question	Low/Middle Income (N = 11)		Advanced Industrialized (N = 11)		t
	Mean	**SD**	**Mean**	**SD**	
Very serious for nation	55	9.8	42	15	2.50*
Personal concern	71	21	69	14	0.36
Air pollution and smog	67	10	56	11	2.40*
Water pollution	65	13	66	12	−0.25
Contaminated soil	55	16	48	9	1.18
Loss of species	61	16	55	9	1.10
Loss of rain forest	63	17	72	10	−1.36
Global warming	51	4.1	55	12	−0.64
Loss of ozone	61	16	64	8.6	−0.57

* Statistically significant at the .05 level.

NOTE: High means indicate agreement with the item. All tests consisted of 11 countries in each group. The values of *t* and the $p > |t|$ were computed assuming equal variance, which is appropriate here.

SOURCE: Steven R. Brechin and Willett Kempton, "Global Environmentalism: A Challenge to the Postmaterialism Thesis?" *Social Science Quarterly* (Fall, 1994), 253.

In cases where the sample size is small, the standard normal curve is inappropriate, and the *t* distribution is used instead. In the two-sample case, the formula for the *t* test (when it cannot be assumed that the two population variances are equal) becomes

$$t = \frac{\bar{X}_1 - \bar{X}_2}{\sqrt{s_1^2/(n_1 - 1) + s_2^2/(n_2 - 1)}}$$

When discussing the single-sample **t test**, it was mentioned that the researcher must calculate degrees of freedom before using the table of *t* values (Appendix D). This is also true in the two-sample case, where the degrees of freedom are calculated as $n_1 + n_2 - 2$.

An example of the use of the two-sample difference-of-means test is provided by Steven R. Brechin and Willet Kempton, in their examination of differences in attitudes toward environmental issues, as held by people living in rich versus poor nations.[12] Brechin and Kempton hypothesize stronger support for such concerns among wealthier nations. Using surveys conducted in a number of nations, Brechin and Kempton reported the data presented here in Table 8.8.

Contrary to their expectations, the authors conclude, "Of the nine tests performed, only two were statistically significant; on both the poorer nations demonstrated *greater* environmental concern, the opposite direction from the common Western belief."[13]

Multisample Test: Analysis of Variance

Political researchers often encounter situations where differences between more than two samples are examined. Studying differences in political attitudes by region (e.g., northern, southern, midwestern, or western) for example, requires examination of differences among four samples. Examining differences among religions (e.g., Protestant, Catholic, Jewish, or other), also requires testing of multiple samples. So, too, would an examination of attitudinal differences among residents of central cities, suburbs, and nonmetropolitan areas. In cases such as these, one approach would be to apply two-sample difference-of-means testing to all combinations of sample pairs. One problem with this, however, is that this process becomes very tedious as the number of groups increase. Seven groupings, for example, would require twenty-one separate tests. More importantly, if we conduct many *t*-tests, the probability increases that—by chance—one of these will reach a level of apparent statistical significance, even if all means in the population are equal. Multiple-comparison procedures, such as the procedure discussed in this section, adjust for the number of comparisons being made and therefore protect from accidentally concluding that differences exist when, in actuality, they do not.

An appropriate comparison procedure, when testing for differences among multiple samples or categories, is an **analysis of variance *F*-test.** A well-developed formal mathematical theory underlies analysis of variance testing, and the presentation of that theory is beyond the scope of this text.[14] Stated briefly, analysis of variance is based on the assumption that each observed value of the dependent variable can be thought of as a sum of three terms: (1) the mean score for all observations, (2) the deviation of that observation's group mean from the overall mean, and (3) the deviation of that observation from that observation's group mean. The deviation of a group mean from the overall mean is assumed to represent the effect on each observation that is due to being a member of that group. The deviation of any observation from that observation's group mean is assumed to represent the effect of all other factors. The *F*-test is calculated to answer the following question: Are there significant differences between groups, as measured by a ratio of variability between groups (adjusted for numbers of groups) to variability within groups (adjusted for numbers of observations).

The first step in computing the *F* statistic is the calculation of a value known as **within-groups sum of squares.** This value is derived by multiplying the square of the standard deviation of each group by one less than the number of cases in the group and summing the results. This number is then divided by the within-groups degrees of freedom, a value that is derived simply by summing the number of cases, minus one, for each group. The resulting value is known as the **mean squares within groups.**

TABLE 8.9

Attitudes toward Homosexuals, by Region

Region	Number of Cases	Mean score	Variance
Northeast	266	42.36	789.46
Midwest	478	31.82	784.85
South	625	32.23	904.79
West	364	41.64	844.19
Total	1733	35.65	862.40

NOTE: Respondents were asked to indicate their "feeling" on a scale of from "0"—very negative—to "100"—very positive toward "Gay men and lesbians; that is, homosexuals." Shown in this table are mean scores and variance for respondents from each of the four major regions and mean score for the total sample.

SOURCE: 1994 American National Election Study.

The next step in computing the *F* statistic is the calculation of a value known as the **between-groups sum of squares.** This value is derived by subtracting the overall mean from the mean of each group, squaring each difference, multiplying the squared value by the number of observations in its group, and summing the results. This number is divided by the between-groups degrees of freedom, a value that is derived by summing the number of groups and subtracting one. The resulting value is known as the **mean squares between groups.**

These two values, the within-groups and the between-groups mean squares, represent two independent estimates of the population variance. If the populations sampled have different means, the numerator will be larger than the denominator, resulting in an *F*-ratio larger than 1.0. The null hypothesis (which assumes no differences in the population among the various groups) will be rejected when the *F*-ratio exceeds 1.0 by an amount greater than can be attributed to chance fluctuations in sampling.

These calculations will be made clear by reference to an example. The 1994 American National Election Survey asked respondents to rate their feelings toward a number of groups and people on a scale of from 1 (very negative) to 100 (very positive). Out of those groups which respondents were asked to rate was homosexuals, gay men and lesbians. Table 8.9 presents the mean score and the variance for answers to this question for respondents from *each of the four major regions,* and also for *all* respondents in the survey.

It can be seen in Table 8.9 that, for this sample, some regional differences exist in attitudes toward homosexuals. The mean scores indicate that respondents from the Northeast and from the West are somewhat more positive than are respondents from the Midwest or the South. Are these differences enough to conclude that similar regional differences exist in the population?

With the information provided in Table 8.9, we can test the *null* hypothesis that in the population, attitudes toward homosexuals (as measured by mean scores to this question) do *not* vary by region. Table 8.10 presents the results of the analysis

TABLE 8.10

Analysis of Variance Table

| Source of Variation | Homosexuals on the Feeling Thermometer* | | | | |
	Sums of Squares	Degrees Freedom	Mean Square	F-Ratio	Significance of *F*
Between groups	39,358.75	3	13,119.59	15.598	.000
Within groups	1,454,298.20	1,729	841.12		
Total	1,493,656.95	1,732			

* For homosexuals, the exact item to which the sample was asked to respond was; "Gay men and lesbians; that is, homosexuals."

SOURCE: 1994 American National Election Study.

of variance test applied to the information presented in Table 8.9. As can be seen in Table 8.10, for this set of data, an *F*-ratio of 15.609 is obtained. The calculation and interpretation of this ratio are described in the next section.[15]

Computing Within-Group Variability

The first step in obtaining the *F*-ratio is calculating the within-groups sum of squares. This is done by multiplying the variance in each group by one less than the number of cases in each group and then summing the results. For the information provided in Table 8.9, this is

$$(789.46 \times 265) + (784.85 \times 477) + (904.29 \times 624) +$$
$$(844.19 \times 363) = 1,454,298.20$$

This number is listed in Table 8.10 as the within-groups sum of squares.

The next step in computing within-group variability is to divide the sum just obtained by the within-group degrees of freedom, a number obtained by summing the number of cases in each group, minus one 1. In our example, this is

$$(266 - 1) + (478 - 1) + (625 - 1) + (364 - 1) = 1729$$

This number is shown in Table 8.10 as *within-groups degrees of freedom*.

The final step in calculating within-group variability is to divide the sum of squares by the degrees of freedom, to obtain the value for the *within-groups mean squares*. This is 1,454,298.20 divided by 1729, or 841.12.

Computing Between-Group Variability

The between-groups sum of squares is obtained by subtracting the overall mean (35.65 in this case) from each group mean, squaring the difference, multiplying the square by the number of cases in each group, and summing the results. In our example this is

$$266 \times (42.36 - 35.65)^2 + 478 \times (31.82 - 35.65)^2 + 625 \times (32.23 - 35.65)^2 +$$
$$364 \times (41.64 - 35.65)^2 = 39{,}358.75$$

Between-group degrees of freedom are calculated simply as the number of groups (here, four) minus one. So, in this example, the between-groups degrees of freedom is 3 (4 − 1).

The between-groups sum of squares divided by its degrees of freedom yields the between-groups mean square. Here, that is 39,538.75 divided by 3, or 13,119.59.

The *F-ratio*

These two scores—the within-groups mean square and the between-groups mean square—represent two estimates of the variability in the population. The within-groups mean square is an estimate of how much the cases within each group (here, respondents within each region) vary, the between-groups mean square is an estimate of how much variance exists between groups. If the null hypothesis is true (that in the population, attitudes toward homosexuals do not vary by region), then these two numbers should be close, and the ratio of the two (that is, one divided by the other) should be close to 1.0. This ratio is the *F*-ratio and is calculated as

$$F = \frac{\text{Between-groups mean square}}{\text{Within-groups mean square}},$$

which, in this case becomes

$$F = \frac{13{,}119.59}{841.12}$$

$$F = 15.598$$

The *F*-ratio for this set of data, then, is found to be 15.598. Is this number great enough to reject the null hypothesis of no difference among the various regions? The distribution of *F* values is shown in Appendix E. It can be seen there that in order to use this table, degrees of freedom need to be calculated for the numerator (n_1) and denominator (n_2). For the numerator, degrees of freedom are calculated as $k - 1$ (where k = number of groups); for the denominator, degrees of freedom are calculated as $n - k$ (where n = sample size). Because in this case our sample size is 1,733 and we are examining 4 groups, the respective numerator and denominator degrees of freedom are 3 and 1,729, respectively. Examining the table of *F* val-

TABLE 8.11

Support for Presidential Civil Rights Proposals

	Civil Rights Act of 1975	Voting Rights Act of 1965
Overall average score	11.90	16.43
Party identification		
Democrat	−.05	9.00
Republican	26.93	31.99
F-scores	48.805	56.524
Regional party identification		
Northern Democrat	36.48	24.71
Southern Democrat	−43.44	−25.85
Eastern Republican	31.94	40.51
Noneastern Republican	23.40	28.48
F-scores	271.954	161.513
Region		
Nonsouth	32.55	29.95
South	−43.04	−23.38
F-scores	1000.666	595.907
Percentage African-American population (by state)		
Less than 10%	32.09	30.18
Between 10 and 20%	−7.36	11.54
Greater than 20%	−43.82	−37.07
F-scores	242.48	347.469

* All *F*-scores are reported by authors to be significant at the .001 level. For a definition of presidential support on civil rights score, see text.

SOURCE: James D. King and James W. Riddlesperger, Jr., "Presidential Leadership of Congressional Civil Rights Voting," *Policy Studies Journal* 21 (3) (1993), 548.

ues (see Appendix E), it can be seen that for these degrees of freedom, a value of 2.60 is needed at the .05 level (3.78 is needed at the .01 level, as shown in the second of the three tables in Appendix E), to reject the null hypothesis that there are no differences among the populations sampled (the four regions). Because our *F*-score is well above this threshold, we conclude, instead, that people in the various regions do differ in their attitudes toward homosexuals.

Another example of the use of analysis of variance is provided in the 1993 study by James King and James Riddlesperger, in which they look at factors associated with United States Congress members' support of civil rights initiatives that resulted in passage of the Civil Rights Act of 1957 and the Voting Rights Act of 1965.[16] After examining members' votes on various roll-call votes related to these initiatives, the authors developed a "Presidential Support on Civil Rights" score, which serves as their

TABLE 8.12
Analysis of Variance for Voting Technologies ($n = 265$)

	Sum of Squares	df	Mean Square	F	Significance
Between groups	56.35	2	28.18	5.67	.0039
Within groups	1302.31	262	4.97	—	—

SOURCE: Peter A. Shocket, Neil R. Heighberger, and Clyde Brown, "The Effect of Voting Technology on Voting Behavior in a Simulated Multi-Candidate City Council Election," *Western Political Quarterly* (June, 1992), 531.

dependent variable. Their independent variables include party identification, region, and percentage of state population having African American ancestry. The result of their analysis of variance is shown in Table 8.11.

These data show, according to King and Riddlesperger, that "both Eisenhower and Johnson were most successful in attracting support from the dominant faction of the opposition party . . . [and that both presidents] failed to attract the support of southern Democrats."[17]

Another interesting application of analysis of variance is provided in an experiment conducted by Shocket, Heighberger, and Brown, who were looking at the impact of voting technology on voting behavior.[18] Simulating elections of nine city councilpeople, these researchers asked three randomly selected groups to cast votes for nine candidates, using (1) punch-card, (2) paper, or (3) direct electronic balloting. The average number of votes cast by those using each technique were punch-card (6.8), electronic system (7.8), and paper ballot (7.7). Clearly, those using punch-card techniques, on average, cast ballots for fewer candidates than those using the other techniques. Analysis of variance was used to determine whether these differences were statistically significant, and the results are shown in Table 8.12.

The results, it can be seen, are significant ($F = 5.67$). The authors concluded, "Analysis of variance indicates that there is a statistically significant difference between the three groups. From the means it is obvious that the punch-card group is the source of difference between the three groups.[19]

SUMMARY

This chapter has examined some of the most often used tests of statistical significance. Tests of significance, it should be obvious, are important tools in the conduct of political and policy research. These techniques allow the researcher to state with some degree of assurance (as measured by the level of risk) that relationships found in the sample actually do (or do not) represent population differences. When dealing with sample data, this consideration is very important.

At the same time, the limitations of these tests should be clearly understood.[20]

In the first place, tests of significance are appropriately applied only to samples of the population. That is, tests of significance have no meaning when applied to the total universe of cases because, if the researcher is in possession of data for the total population, there is no possibility of making a sampling error when reporting observed differences. Thus, if one is using as the unit of analysis all 50 states, or all units of local government in the United States, or all nations in the world, and data have been drawn from each unit in the population, tests of significance would not be used.

A related question concerns the universe from which the sample is drawn. An obvious point, but one that is often overlooked, is that tests of significance are applicable only to the universe from which the sample is selected. For example, a researcher selecting a random sample of counties from the southern states would be limited to making generalizations only regarding the counties in that region. It would not be appropriate to generalize from such a sample to other counties in other regions or to all counties in the United States.

Also, tests of significance assume *random sampling.* Tests of significance are appropriate used only when all cases in the universe have an equal chance of being selected in the sample. Samples that are drawn by any other method should not be used with tests of significance.[21]

Finally, and this is *most important,* tests of statistical significance are not equivalent to measures of strength. That is, tests of significance are not designed to tell us how strong a relationship is, only whether the relationship is likely to reflect the true population relationship. As mentioned previously, tests of significance are sensitive to the size of the sample. The larger the sample, the more likely are these tests to indicate significant relationships. This effect only makes sense because these tests are designed to determine whether characteristics of a sample are likely to deviate from the characteristics of the population. Intuitively, we are likely to have more faith in results obtained from large samples, but with large samples, even trivial differences are often statistically significant.

A simple example illustrates this last point. Suppose that we have two samples: one sample of 100 individuals, and the other of 10,000. Suppose further that the distributions of the two samples appear as shown in Table 8.13.

It can be seen in the table that, although Sample B includes 100 times more observations than Sample A, the *proportion* of cases falling in each cell has not changed from sample to sample. However, the χ^2 value for the first sample is found to be not significant, whereas the χ^2 in the second sample is found to be 100 times greater and is "very" significant. This is the case even though the strength of the relationship is shown to be the same in both cases (i.e., equivalent proportions of cases fall in equivalent cells of both tables). Thus, although the strength of the relationship in each case has not altered, one is found to be statistically significant, but the other is not.[22]

Significance, then, is not equivalent to strength, and such tests should not be used or interpreted as measures of strength. Schroeder, Sjoquist, and Stephan make this point well when they say, "Statistical significance does not necessarily imply political, social, or economic significance. The relationship found may be so

TABLE 8.13
Illustration of Chi-Square with Differing n's but with Proportionately
Equivalent Cell Entries

	Sample A (n = 100) Characteristic A				Sample B (n = 10,000) Characteristic A		
Characteristic B	**1**	**2**	**Total**	**Characteristic B**	**1**	**2**	**Total**
1	27	23	50	1	2,700	2,300	5,000
2	23	27	50	2	2,300	2,700	5,000
Total	50	50	100	Total	5,000	5,000	10,000
$\chi^2 = 0.64$ (not significant)				$\chi^2 = 64.00$ (significant at 0.001 level)			

small—even though statistically significant—that the variable is of little consequence."[23]

Measures of association—which do assess strength—are discussed in the following chapters. Tests of significance and measures of association *complement,* but
do not *replace* each other. In a given research situation, the researcher should use
whichever is most appropriate for the questions being asked and for the nature of
the data being analyzed.

KEY TERMS

relationships
predictive relationships
population
column marginals
row marginals
sampling error
Type I errors
Type II errors
research hypothesis
null hypothesis
directional hypothesis
nondirectional hypothesis

one-tailed test
two-tailed test
degrees of freedom
chi-square test
z-test
t-test
analysis of variance F-test
within-groups sum of squares
mean squares within groups
between-groups sum of squares
mean squares between groups

EXERCISES

1. Following is a table presenting the relationship between party identification and
   approval of Bill Clinton's performance as president, as revealed in the 1994 American National Election Study.

| | Party Identification | | | |
Approval Rating	Republican	Independent	Democrat	Totals
Approval	106	239	462	807
Disapproval	412	245	125	782
Total	518	484	587	1589

NOTE: All responses other than those shown have been deleted.

    a. In the preceding table, which are the *independent* and the *dependent* variables?

    b. Calculate the percentage value for each cell, and report the results.

    c. Considering the cell frequencies and percentages, what can be said about the apparent *direction* and *strength* of this relationship?

2. Tests of statistical significance

    a. Calculate the *chi-square* value for the preceding table.

    b. Determine the *degrees of freedom* for this table.

    c. Using the table of chi-square values presented in Appendix C of this book, determine whether the relationship presented here is *statistically significant.*

    d. Explain (a) what is meant by the term *statistical significance,* and (b) how it would be interpreted in this instance.

3. Assume that a researcher is interested in examining the beginning salaries of those college graduates majoring in political science and in economics and in testing for the possibility that a statistically significant difference exists between the two. A random sample of 250 political science majors is drawn, and mean first-year salary is found to be $34,000, with a standard deviation of $1,000. A random sample of 150 employed economic majors is drawn and the mean first-year salary is found to be $34,250, with a standard deviation of $2,000.

    a. State the likely null and research hypotheses for the testing of these mean differences.

    b. Apply the one-tailed z test of statistical significance to test for the difference between these income levels.

    c. What conclusions can be drawn based on this test concerning the null and research hypotheses you just stated?

    d. Assume that the sample size for the sample of employed economic majors had been 400 (rather than 150). Recalculate the difference-of-means test, and compare this result with the one previously obtained. What does this indicate about the effect of sample size on the z score, and on our use and interpretation of tests of statistical significance in general?

4. From recent issues of political science and policy journals, locate researchers' use of the chi-square, *t*-test, and analysis of variance statistics. Discuss both the conditions under which these tests were used and the conclusions that these tests support.

NOTES

1. Hubert M. Blalock, Jr., *Social Statistics,* 2nd ed. (New York: McGraw-Hill, 1979), 469.
2. For an extended discussion, see Julian L. Simon and Paul Burstein, *Basic Research Methods in Social Science,* 3rd ed. (New York: Random House, 1985), 431–441.
3. John J. Harrigan, *Politics and Policy in States and Communities,* 5th ed. (New York: HarperCollins, 1994), 169.
4. Ibid., 168.
5. As used here, sampling error is contrasted with nonsampling error attributable to the various sources of error associated with data collection, coding, entry, and measurement.
6. As discussed in Ramon E. Henkel, *Tests of Significance* (Beverly Hills: Sage, 1976), 89.
7. David H. Folz, Linda Gaddis, William Lyons, and John M. Scheb, II, "Saturn Comes to Tennessee: Citizen Perceptions of Project Impacts," *Social Science Quarterly* (December, 1993), 793–803.
8. Ibid., 796–797.
9. However, for discussion of the controversy surrounding the merits of this correction, see W. J. Conover, "Some Reasons for Not Using the Yates Continuity Correction on 2 × 2 Contingency Tables," *Journal of the American Statistical Association* 69 (1974), 374–376; and N. Mantel, "Comment and a Suggestion on the Yates Continuity Correction," *Journal of the American Statistical Association* 69 (1974), 378–380.
10. Actually, with large samples, the assumption of a normally distributed population can be relaxed.
11. As explained in Henkel, *Tests of Significance,* 61.
12. Steven R. Brechin and Willett Kempton, "Global Environmentalism: A Challenge to the Postmaterialism Thesis?" *Social Science Quarterly* (Fall, 1994), 245–269.
13. Ibid., 252 (emphasis added).
14. For a review, see Gudmund R. Iversen and Helmut Norpoth, *Analysis of Variance,* 2nd ed. (Newbury Park, CA: 1987).
15. The explanation here follows closely that presented in Mariga J. Norusis, *The SPSS Guide to Data Analysis* (Chicago: SPSS, 1988), 253–270.
16. James D. King and James W. Riddlesperger, Jr., "Presidential Leadership of Congressional Civil Rights Voting," *Policy Studies Journal* 21(3) (1993), 544–555.
17. Ibid., 549.
18. Peter A. Shocket, Neil R. Heighberger, and Clyde Brown, "The Effect of Voting Technology on Voting Behavior in a Simulated Multi-Candidate City Council Election: A Political Experiment of Ballot Transparency," *Western Political Quarterly* (June, 1992), 521–537.
19. Ibid., 531.
20. See Henkel, *Tests of Significance,* 78–92.
21. In practice, this requirement is often relaxed, as in the case with samples drawn by use of multistage cluster techniques.
22. Hubert M. Blalock has shown that if we multiply each frequency in a contingency table by some constant value, the value of chi-square is multiplied by the same constant. See Hubert M. Blalock, Jr., *Social Statistics,* 2nd ed. (McGraw-Hill: New York, 1979), 299–303.
23. Larry D. Schroeder, David L. Sjoquist, and Paula E. Stephan, *Understanding Regression Analysis* (Newbury Park, CA: Sage Publications, 1986), 53.

CHAPTER 9

Measuring Strength of Relationships:
Two Variable Situations

Tests of statistical significance, as discussed in Chapter 8, are used to determine the probability that a relationship exists in a population. However, concluding that a relationship in the population probably exists is not the same as saying that the relationship is a *strong* or an *important* one. A number of **measures of association** have been developed to assess strength of relationship.

Most (but not all) tests of association for *linear relationships* (i.e., straight line) in use today have been developed so as to range in value from –1.0 to +1.0 (in the case of nominal relationships, the scores range from 0.0 to +1.0). This expression permits us to rapidly assess the strength of *any* relationship and also to *compare* the strengths of *several* relationships. The closer a relationship is to 0.0 the weaker is the association. A relationship of 0.0 implies *no* linear relationship between two variables at all; knowledge of one variable is of no use in predicting values of another. The closer is a relationship to 1.0, on the other hand, the stronger is the association. A relationship of 1.0 is a perfect relationship; every value of the dependent variable is associated with a particular value of the independent variable. Perfect relationships rarely are found in political and policy research, but this scale permits convenient comparison of degree of association. An association between two variables of .50 is stronger than an association of .25 and weaker than an association of .75. Although it is not always easy to give a verbal interpretation to these values, James Davis has provided some appropriate phrases to describe the various ranges of values for one measure of association, known as "Yule's Q."[1] Davis's scheme is shown in Table 9.1.

In general, Davis's terms—or some similarly worded descriptors—can appropriately be applied to measures of strength used in the political and policy sciences. However, in applying these phrases to describe the level of association, one must still be cautious. In the first place, as the following section shows, the magnitude of the different correlation coefficients can vary, even for the same set of data. So it is important to select the correlation coefficient appropriate to the model, hypotheses, and nature of data being tested, not just the "strongest" or "weakest" that might

TABLE 9.1

Suggested Verbal Interpretations of Correlation Coefficients

Correlation Values	Appropriate Phrases
+0.70 or higher	Very strong positive association
+0.50 to +0.69	Substantial positive association
+0.30 to +0.49	Moderate positive association
+0.10 to +0.29	Low positive association
+0.01 to +0.09	Negligible positive association
0.00	No association
−0.01 to −0.09	Negligible negative association
−0.10 to −0.29	Low negative association
−0.30 to −0.49	Moderate negative association
−0.50 to −0.69	Substantial negative association
−0.70 or higher	Very strong negative association

SOURCE: Adapted from James A. Davis, *Elementary Survey Analysis* (Englewood Cliffs, NJ: Prentice-Hall, 1971), 49.

be generated for a particular set of data. Also, although it generally is true that a correlation of, say, .70 represents a very strong relationship, if a researcher were attempting to identify variables that could be used to construct a *scale* (such as social class, or domestic liberalism), correlations of even higher values might be sought. Thus, the interpretation of the values of correlation coefficients depends to some extent, on the purposes of the analysis and on the underlying assumptions being tested.

The remainder of this chapter discusses some of the most frequently used measures of association, as well as the conditions under which each is appropriate. (Box 9.1 illustrates an interesting use of correlation as a diagnostic tool.)

MEASURES OF ASSOCIATION FOR NOMINAL DATA

A number of tests are available when variables are both measured at the nominal level. Before discussing these, however it is appropriate to ask, why not use the chi-square test—which we reviewed in Chapter 8—as the measure of the association? The reason not to do so is that the chi-square statistic is affected both by the size of the sample (as we saw in Chapter 8) and by the size of the table. Changing either sample size or table dimensions will alter chi-square values, even if the underlying strength of relationship has not changed. Further, because chi-square is based on differences between expected and observed frequencies, equivalent chi-square values can be obtained for many different types of tables. The chi-square tells us nothing about the strength of the relationship.

Nevertheless, a number of measures *based* on the chi-square value have been developed. These attempt to normalize the chi-square so that it falls within a range between 0 and 1, and also to remove its sensitivity to sample and table size.

BOX 9.1   Correlation as a Diagnostic Tool

Even when it is clear that no cause-and-effect relationship exists, knowing one variable is correlated with another—or that scores on one variable can help predict scores on another—can be a very important diagnostic tool for policy analysts and scientists. This is illustrated in the following report excerpted from an article appearing in the *New York Times,* February 24, 1993:

A Bald Spot on Top May Predict Heart Risk

Younger men with bald spots on top of their heads may have reason to protect their hearts as well as cover their scalps.

In a study of men under 55, a bald patch in that position was found to be correlated with a slight but definite increase in the risk of heart attack, according to a study being reported today in *The Journal of the American Medical Association.*

The more extensive the baldness on top, called vertex baldness, the higher the risk. For men with mild or moderate vertex baldness, the risk was about 40 percent greater than that for men with a full set of hair, raising to 340 percent for those with severe vertex baldness, the authors of the Boston University study said.

The researchers said they did not know why baldness might be linked to heart attacks, but speculated that a hormone might be a factor. The authors and other experts said that it would be prudent for men with vertex baldness to follow standard recommendations to control other risk factors for heart disease like diet, weight, exercise, smoking and high blood pressure.

SOURCE: Lawrence K. Altman, "A Bald Spot on Top May Predict Heart Risk," *New York Times,* February 24, 1993.

The Phi Coefficient

The **phi coefficient** (ϕ) is a simple modification of the chi-square statistic, suitable when both independent and dependent variables are dichotomous (i.e., each has only two values). To calculate phi, simply divide the chi-square value by the sample size and then take the square root, as shown in the formula:

$$\phi = \sqrt{\frac{\chi^2}{N}}$$

The phi coefficient has two advantages: It is (1) easy to calculate, and (2) identical to the widely used Pearson correlation and the tau-b coefficients (both discussed subsequently) in a dichotomous situation. The disadvantage of phi is that its value can exceed 1.0 for tables greater than 2 × 2.

As an example of the use of the phi coefficient, consider Table 9.2, showing the relationship between gender and whether people discuss politics, as revealed in the

TABLE 9.2

Illustration of the Phi Coefficient

Does Respondent Discuss Politics with Family or Friends?	Gender		Totals
	Male	**Female**	**Totals**
Yes	662	717	1379
	(79.2)	(74.8)	(76.9)
No	174	241	415
	(20.8)	(25.2)	(23.1)
	836	958	1794
	(46.6)	(53.4)	(100.0)

$$\chi^2 = 4.736$$

$$\phi = \sqrt{\frac{4.736}{1794}}$$

$$\phi = .051$$

NOTE: Numbers in parentheses are percentages.

SOURCE: ICPSR 1994 American National Election Study.

1994 American National Election Study. Based on the phi coefficient of .051, it would be concluded that only a negligible relationship exists between gender and whether people discuss politics.

Cramer's V

Cramer's V is a modification of phi, which can be used for any size of table. The formula for Cramer's V is similar to phi except that in the denominator, the sample size is multiplied by the term $k - 1$, where k represents the smaller of either the number of rows or the number of columns in the table. This correction results in a measure that can achieve, but will not exceed, 1.0:

$$v = \sqrt{\frac{\chi^2}{N(k-1)}}$$

Charles Davis used the Cramer's V statistic in his examination of the relationship between "religious" and "secular" attitudes and party loyalty among the general public, and among a subsample of workers, in Mexico.[2] Davis distinguished between secular and religious attitudes on the basis of frequency of attending mass. His results are shown in Table 9.3.

Davis concludes that, "the PRI draws more support from religious workers than from secular workers, though the differences are less pronounced than [findings from an earlier study]."[3] The Cramer's V scores (.09 for workers, and .14 for the na-

TABLE 9.3
Religiosity and Partisan Loyalty: 1986 *New York Times* Survey

	Workers Subsample (*n* = 207)		National Subsample (*n* = 1867)	
	Religious	**Secular**	**Religious**	**Secular**
Percentage loyal to				
PR1	50.4%	41.7%	50.5%	39.5%
Leftist parties	.5	.5	1.3	4.7
Rightist parties	20.7	22.2	17.9	19.0
Independent	28.1	34.7	30.3	36.8
N	135	72	1,280	595
		Cramer's V = .09 .14		

Source: Charles L. Davis, "Religion and Partisan Loyalty: The Case of Catholic Workers in Mexico," *Western Political Quarterly* (March, 1992), 285.

tional sample) indicate that for both groups, the relationship between religious and secular attitudes and party identification is not very strong.

The Contingency Coefficient

A final chi-square-based measure of association is known as the **contingency coefficient** and is symbolized by the letter *C*. The formula for the contingency coefficient is

$$C = \sqrt{\frac{\chi^2}{\chi^2 + N}}$$

The measure *C* can be used on any size of table; however, it never reaches a value of 1.0, even when the relationship is perfect. Further, the value of *C* depends on the number of rows and columns in the table. For this reason, *C* is most appropriate when comparing tables of the same size.

Further Illustration of Cramer's *V* and the Contingency Coefficient

As an illustration of Cramer's *V* and the contingency coefficient, Table 9.4 presents the relationship examined in Chapter 8 (in Table 8.2) between attitudes toward federal aid to big cities and where people reside. The chi-square value, the Cramer's *V*, and the contingency coefficient statistics are presented at the bottom of this table. The chi-square value of 96.71682 permits us to reject the null hypothesis that there is no relationship between place of residency and attitudes toward federal aid for

TABLE 9.4

Attitudes toward Federal Aid for Big Cities, by Type of Community in which Respondent Lives

Attitude toward Federal Aid to Big Cities	Type of Community			Totals
	Central City	Suburbs	Nonmetropolitan	
Increase	195	184	108	487
	(32.5)	(18.4)	(14.3)	(20.7)
Stay the same	279	534	361	1174
	(46.5)	(53.4)	(47.7)	(49.8)
Decrease	126	282	288	696
	(21.0)	(28.2)	(38.0)	(29.5)
Totals	600	1000	757	2357
	(25.5)	(42.4)	(32.1)	(100.0)

$$\chi^2 = 96.71682$$
$$V = .143$$
$$C = .198$$

NOTE: Numbers in parentheses are percents.

SOURCE: ICPSR 1992 American National Election Study.

big cities (for 4 degrees of freedom, we need a chi-square value of only 5.991 at the .05 level). The Cramer's V and the contingency coefficient statistics permit us to assess the strength of this relationship. The value for V, as can be seen, is .143, and the value of C is shown to be .198. Although not equivalent, these values are of roughly the same magnitude. On a scale of 0.0 to 1.0, the relationship would be said to be not very strong.

Proportionate Reduction-of-Error Measure: The Lambda Statistic

All of these chi-square-based measures of association lack an intrinsic meaning: We only can conclude that a relationship appears to be low, moderate, substantial, or some other description. We can only say that an association between two variables of 0.60 is stronger than one of 0.59 and weaker than one of 0.61.

The *lambda* statistic (symbolized as λ) is one of a group of statistics based on the notion of **proportionate reduction of error.** These statistics tell us how well we can predict values of the dependent variable, once we know values of the independent variable. They permit us to answer the question, How much can the error in predicting values of the dependent variable be reduced, once we know the values of the independent variable? A lambda value of 0.37 means that knowledge of the independent variable reduces by 37 percent errors in predicting values of the dependent variable. It is this direct interpretation that makes lambda such a useful statistic.

TABLE 9.5
Distribution of Party Identification

Party Identification	Total	Percentage
Democrat	689	38.9
Independent	598	33.8
Republican	484	27.3
Total	1,771	100.0

SOURCE: ICPSR 1992 American National Election Study.

In practice, lambda may be used as an *asymmetric* (directional) or a *symmetric* (nondirectional) statistic. As an asymmetric statistic, lambda is used when predicting the direction of a relationship. When used in an asymmetric sense, lambda is usually symbolized as λ_a. As a symmetrical statistic, lambda may be used when the direction of a relationship is unknown or cannot be predicted. Lambda in the symmetrical sense may be symbolized simply as λ.

By way of illustration, consider the frequency distribution of party identification as, reflected in the 1992 American National Election Study presented in Table 9.5. If we were asked to individually predict the party identification for each of the 1,771 respondents, knowing no other information but the distribution presented in this table, we would predict a Democratic identification for each respondent. We know from the data presented that the modal category is Democrat and that, by definition, more cases fall in this classification than in either of the other two. We also know that, in predicting Democrat for everyone, we would make 1,082 errors (total number of non-Democrats). Still, no other category would generate as high a percentage of successful predictions as Democrat—we are assured of 689 (38.9%) correct predictions.

Suppose, then, that additional information concerning party choice is provided. It might be suspected that each respondent's mother's party choice has an impact on each respondent's own party identification. Relying on information provided by the 1992 American National Election Study, Table 9.6 shows the relationship between mothers' and respondents' party choices.

Provided with this information, mothers' party choices, we now are in a position to more accurately predict respondents' choices. If we are told that a respondent's mother is a Republican, we would predict that the respondent would also be a Republican (because this is the modal partisan choice for all respondents whose mothers were Republican). Similarly, we would predict all respondents whose mothers are Independents to be Independents and all whose mothers are Democrats to be Democrats.

By proceeding in this fashion, we will still make a number of errors. We will mistakenly classify 427 respondents whose mothers were Democrats, 88 respondents whose mothers were Independents, and 229 respondents whose mothers were Republicans. These are respondents who deviate from each modal category of mothers' party choice. In all, using mothers' party choice as an aid in predicting, we will still make a total of 744 errors (the total number of respondents whose party choice differed from their mothers). Recalling that we would have made 1,082 errors in predicting partisan choice only on the basis of the distribution of respondents' party identification (Table 9.5), we have reduced by 338 the total number of errors in prediction once we know each respondent's mother's party choice. Lambda is a summary statistic that tells us proportionately the extent of error reduction. The formula for lambda (asymmetric) can be thought of as

$$\lambda_a = \frac{\text{amount of error reduction}}{\text{amount of original error}}$$

For Table 9.6, asymmetric lambda would be calculated as

$$\lambda_a = \frac{1082 - 744}{1082}$$

$$= 0.312$$

Interpreting this coefficient, it would be said that knowledge of mothers' party choice (the independent variable) reduces by 31.2 percent the error in predicting respondents' party choice (the dependent variable). It is this intrinsic interpretation that gives lambda its distinctive advantage over a chi-square-based measure of association such as phi.

A somewhat more convenient formula for calculating asymmetric lambda is the following:[4]

$$\lambda_a = \frac{\Sigma f_i - F_d}{N - F_d}$$

where f_i = largest (modal) frequency for each value of the independent variable

F_d = largest (modal) frequency found among the marginal totals of the dependent variable

N = total number of cases

For Table 9.6, according to this formula, asymmetric lambda would be calculated as

$$\lambda_a = \frac{(576 + 153 + 298) - 689}{1771 - 689}$$

$$= \frac{338}{1082}$$

$$= 0.312$$

TABLE 9.6

Respondents' Party Identification by Mothers' Party Identification

Respondents' Party Identification	Mothers' Party Identification*			
	Democrat	**Independent**	**Republican**	**Totals**
Democrat	576 (57.4)	42 (17.4)	71 (13.5)	689 (38.9)
Independent	287 (28.6)	153 (63.5)	158 (30.0)	598 (33.8)
Republican	140 (14.0)	46 (19.1)	298 (56.5)	484 (27.3)
Total	1003 (56.6)	241 (13.6)	527 (29.8)	1771 (100.0)

* As reported by respondent.

NOTE: Numbers in parentheses are percentages.

SOURCE: ICPSR 1992 American National Election Study.

In those instances when the researcher is not assuming a directional relationship among the data, the symmetrical lambda will be the appropriate statistical test. The symmetrical lambda is interpreted as the proportionate amount of prediction error in both variables, which can be reduced from a knowledge of the values of each variable. The computational formula for symmetrical lambda is

$$\lambda_a = \frac{\Sigma f_r + \Sigma f_c - (F_r + F_c)}{2N - (F_r + F_c)}$$

where f_r = largest (modal) frequency occurring in each row
f_c = largest (modal) frequency occurring in each column
F_r = largest (modal) frequency occurring in the row marginals
F_c = largest (modal) frequency occurring in the column marginals
N = total number of cases

As an example of λ, consider the relationship between fathers' and mothers' party identification, as reported by respondents in the 1992 American National Election Survey. Those data are presented in Table 9.7. It can be concluded that the knowledge of fathers' and mothers' party identification (as reported by survey respondents) reduces by 70.6 the amount of error in predicting one from the other.

Another illustration of use of the lambda statistic is provided by Renu Khator's study of the factors related to recycling activities among the American states.[5] Based on the extent of their commitment to recycling efforts, Khator classifies all states into three groups: "aggressive," "conformist," and "dormant." The relationships between this classification and various political, economic, and physical characteris-

TABLE 9.7

Fathers' Party Identification by Mothers' Party Identification

Fathers' Party Identification	Mothers' Party Identification*			
	Democrat	Independent	Republican	Totals
Democrat	889 (90.9)	29 (11.7)	56 (11.0)	974 (56.1)
Independent	34 (3.5)	187 (75.4)	17 (3.3)	238 (13.7)
Republican	55 (5.6)	32 (12.9)	436 (85.7)	523 (30.1)
Totals	978 (56.4)	248 (14.3)	509 (29.3)	1735 (100.0)

$$\lambda = \frac{(889 + 187 + 436) + (889 + 187 + 436) - (974 + 978)}{2\,(1735) - (974 + 978)}$$

$$= \frac{10.72}{1518}$$

$$= .706$$

* As reported by respondent.

NOTE: Numbers in parentheses are percentages.

SOURCE: ICPSR 1992 American National Election Study.

tics of the states are shown in Table 9.8 (Khator explains that interval-level independent variables were transformed into dichotomies for this analysis).

Khator presents the lambda statistic only for those relationships found to be statistically significant. He concluded, based on this, that "economic variables have little explanatory power . . . with the exception of Per Capital Income. The Lambda value of 0.16 for the income variable can be interpreted as the likelihood of a 16% reduction in the error of predicting Recycling Commitment with the knowledge of Per Capita Income."[6]

TESTS OF ASSOCIATION FOR ORDINAL DATA

A number of tests of association appropriate for ordinal-level data have been developed. These range in value from –1.0 (perfect negative relationship) to +1.0 (perfect positive relationship), and the most frequently used of these rely on comparisons of paired relationships in the data.

The strength of a relationship in a *positive* direction increases with increasing numbers of paired relationships for which one member of the pair has a higher

TABLE 9.8
Contingency Table Analysis for States' Recycling Efforts

Variable	Chi-Square Values	Level of Significance	Lambda Coefficient
Political model			
Party control	7.01	0.030*	0.13
Public participation	2.88	0.236	
Policy participation	2.33	0.128	
Innovation	11.99	0.017*	0.30
Local government discretion	3.12	0.200	
Economic model			
Per capita income	6.74	0.036*	0.16
Financial difficulty	2.24	0.327	
Expenditure per capita	0.94	0.624	
Policy-perpetuation model			
Environmental commitment	29.80	0.000*	0.41
Per capita environmental expenses	2.61	0.270	
Environmental policy innovativeness	6.07	0.049*	0.13
Environmental bureaucratic strength	13.59	0.001*	0.30
Physical-factor model			
Density	8.86	0.011*	0.16
Region	26.49	0.047*	0.38

* Significant at 0.05 level.

NOTE: Measures of association are reported only for statistically significant relationships, and for ordinal relationships Khator reports the tau-b coefficient, discussed later in this chapter.

SOURCE: Renu Khator, "Recycling: A Policy Dilemma for American States?" *Policy Studies Journal* 21 (Summer, 1993), 217.

ranking on both variables being considered than does the other member. Similarly, the strength of a relationship in a *negative* direction increases with increasing numbers of paired relationships for which one member of the pair has a lower ranking on one variable and a higher ranking on the second variable.

Paired Relationships

As an illustration, consider Table 9.9, which presents a hypothetical relationship between two variables. In order to calculate the various ordinal statistics, we must determine the possible pairings of cases in this table.

P Pairs.   It is conventional to label all pairs in the table for which one member of the pairs is ranked higher on both variables than the other member of the pair as *P pairs*. These are also called "concordant pairs." In Table 9.9 these are the pairs formed by the observations falling in cells A and D, and the product of these two

TABLE 9.9

Hypothetical Relationship between Two Dichotomous Ordinal Variables

Dependent Variable, Y	Independent Variable, X		
	Low	High	Total
Low	ᴬ4	1ᴮ	5
High	ᶜ2	3ᴰ	5
Totals	6	4	10

cells (A × D) yields a total of 12 concordant pairs. In any table, the greater the pro-portionate number of concordant pairs, the stronger will be the relationship in a *positive direction*. If all observations fell in cells A and D (the *main diagonal*), the correlation would be +1.0.

Q *Pairs*. It is conventional to label all pairs in the table for which one member of the pair is ranked higher on one variable and lower on the other variable, as com-pared with the other member of the pair as Q *pairs*. These also are called "discor-dant pairs." In the preceding example, these are the pairs formed by the observations falling in cells B and C, and the product of these two cells (B × C) yields a total of 2 discordant pairs. The greater the proportionate number of discordant pairs in any table, the stronger will be the relationship in a *negative direction*. If all observations fell on these discordant pairs (the *minor diagonal*), the correlation would be –1.0.

T$_x$ *Pairs*. Those pairs of observations in a table tied on the x (independent) vari-able may be symbolized as the T_x *pairs*. These are those pairs having the same value on the X variable but different values on the Y variable. In the preceding example, these are the pairs formed by the observations falling in cells A and C and those falling in cells B and D. The product of cells A and C (4 × 2), added to the product of cells B and D (1 × 3), yields a total of 11 pairs tied on the X variable.

T$_y$ *Pairs*. Those pairs of observations in a table tied in the Y (dependent) variable may be symbolized as the T_y *pairs*. These are those pairs having the same value on the Y variable but different values on the X variable. In the preceding example, these are the pairs formed by the observations falling in cells A and B and those falling in cells C and D. The product of cells A and B (4 × 1) added to the product of cells C and D (2 × 3) renders a total of 10 pairs tied on the Y variable.

Tests of Association

Having calculated the possible categories of paired relationships in the table, the various ordinal tests can be calculated and applied. These various tests, named for the people who developed them, are *Goodman and Kruskal's gamma, Kendall's tau,* and *Somers' d.*[7] The choice of which test to use is based on underlying assumptions of the relationships being examined. An asymmetrical relationship posits one variable as the independent variable and the second as the dependent variable. It is assumed that variation in the independent variable is a least one possible cause of variation in the dependent variable. Strength of relationship is also a factor to be considered. Some measures assume their highest values in situations that might be considered weak perfect associations, others assume their highest values only in cases of strong perfect associations.[8]

Gamma.   Gamma (γ) is used as a symmetrical (nondirectional) test for a table of any size. Referring to the aforementioned symbols for paired relationships, gamma is calculated as

$$\gamma = \frac{P - Q}{P + Q}$$

Gamma is a very useful statistic, in that, like lambda, it has a proportionate reduction-in-error interpretation.[9] Gamma's weakness, however, is that in emphasizing discordant and concordant pairs, it ignores pairs that are tied. As a result, the gamma coefficient may include in its calculation only a comparatively small number of a table's paired observations and also will yield the highest value of any of the ordinal coefficients (except in those instances when all the coefficients result in a value of 1.0 or 0). This can become especially troublesome in the case of a 2 × 2 table, where any vacant call will result in a gamma of 1.0.

Kendall's t_b and t_c.   Tau-*b* and tau-*c* are symmetrical measures that account for ties on each variable in a pair separately. Referring to the aforementioned symbols for paired relationships, τ_b is calculated as

$$\tau_b = \frac{P - Q}{\sqrt{(P + Q + T_y)(P + Q + T_x)}}$$

For the example presented in Table 9.7, τ_b would be

$$\tau_b = \frac{12 - 2}{\sqrt{(12 + 2 + 10)(12 + 2 + 11)}}$$

Tau-*b* will achieve a maximum value of ± 1.0 only in the case of perfectly symmetrical tabular dimensions (equal number of rows and columns). If the table being examined is perfectly square (2 × 2, 3 × 3, etc.), τ_b will achieve a ± 1.0 if a perfect relationship exists. However, τ_b will not reach 1.0 when calculated with any other shape of table. Tau-*c* corrects for this deficiency, and its formula is

$$\tau_c = \frac{P - Q}{\frac{1}{2}N^2[(m-1)/m]}$$

where N = total number of cases
 m = smaller of rows or columns (in a 3×5 table, $m = 3$)

Tau-c, then, should be used as a substitute for τ_b when considering tables of unequal numbers of rows and columns; however, in practice, the actual magnitude of the differences between the values of τ_b and τ_c is typically very slight.[10]

An interesting example of the use of both the gamma and tau coefficients is presented by Bryan Jones, Frank Baumgartner, and Jeffrey Talbert in their article titled, "The Destruction of Issue Monopolies in Congress."[11] Here, the authors were interested in determining whether a relationship exists between U.S. congressional committee jurisdictions and the policy positions of witnesses who tend to be invited to testify before the committees. One of their tables is reproduced in Table 9.10, where they examine the "tone" of witnesses testifying about pesticides (1900–1988) and civilian nuclear power (1944–1986), as well as the relationship of this tone to the venue of the congressional committees receiving testimony, arrayed according to the committees' presumed favoritism to these industries.

In both cases, the reported gamma and tau-b coefficients are positive, indicating

TABLE 9.10

The Correspondence between Tone and Venue in Congressional Hearings on Pesticides and Civilian Nuclear Power (percentages)

	Tone				
Venue	**Positive**	**Neutral or Uncodable**	**Critical**	**Total (N)**	
Pesticides hearings, 1900–1988*					
Agriculture committees	17.6	3.9	78.5	100.0	(102)
Neutral or uncodable committees	11.2	6.3	82.5	100.0	(63)
Health or environmental committees	1.8	5.0	93.2	100.0	(220)
Total	7.5	4.9	87.5	100.0	(385)
Civilian nuclear power, 1944–86†					
Booster committees	20.0	28.0	52.0	100.0	(611)
Neutral or uncodable committees	6.3	52.0	41.7	100.0	(352)
Critical committees	8.8	7.7	83.5	100.0	(274)
Total	13.6	30.3	56.1	100.0	(1,237)

* Gamma = .48; tau-$_b$ = .20; chi-squared (4 d.f.) = 26.9 ($p < .001$).

† Gamma = .30; tau-$_b$ = .18; chi-squared (4 d.f.) = 190.5 ($p < .001$).

SOURCE: Jones, Baumgartner, and Talbert, "The Destruction of Monopolies in Congress," *American Political Science Review* 87 (September, 1993), 663.

a tendency for witness tone to be affected by committee jurisdiction. According to the authors, "In general, this is the pattern that we have found for all our issues. . . . congressional committees are strongly biased. Proindustry committees do not often schedule critical hearings; and when they do they hear from proindustry representatives. Similarly, critical venues tend to schedule witnesses that provide unfriendly testimony."[12]

When examining a lot of variables and a lot of relationships, scholars sometimes will delete the actual cross-tabulations and present just the ordinal correlation coefficients. An example of this is J. David Gopoian and Sissie Hadjiharalambous's study of those factors related to the timing of voters' decision on presidential candidates. Examining the relationships between a number of political variables and the timing of voting decisions for a number of presidential elections, these authors present their results as shown in Table 9.11. There, it can be seen that *only* the tau-b coefficients are presented; for efficient presentation, the actual tabular cell entries are deleted.[13]

TABLE 9.11

Political Characteristics of Voters by Time of Decision: Kendall's Tau-*b* Coefficients for the Relationships between Political Characteristics of Voters and Time of Decision (early, middle, late)

	Year				
	1972	**1976**	**1980**	**1984**	**1988**
Party ID	.16***	.05	.00	.13***	.05
1 = Republicans					
2 = Pure Independents					
3 = Democrats					
Strength of partisanship	−.12***	−.24***	−.22***	−.18***	.23***
1 = Pure Independents					
2 = Weak and leaning					
3 = Strong partisans					
Carryover effect for Democratic identifiers	.01	.19***	.12***	.08	.08
0 = Prefer nominee					
1 = Prefer rivals					
Carryover effect for Republican identifiers	—	.16***	—	—	.20***
0 = Prefer nominee					
1 = Prefer rivals					
Participated in one or more political activities	−.06*	−.05*	.13***	.06*	−.12***
0 = Not active					
1 = Active					

TABLE 9.11 *(continued)*

	Year				
	1972	**1976**	**1980**	**1984**	**1988**
Follow government	.02	.00	.06*	.10**	.09**
1 = Most of time					
2 = Somewhat					
3 = Little/very little					
See differences between					
Democrats and Republicans —		.09**	.08*	.12***	.19***
1 = Yes					
2 = No					
Interest in the campaign	.09**	.07*	.06*	.14***	.11***
1 = High					
2 = Medium					
3 = Low					
Care about outcome					
of election	.18***	.18***	.25***	.17***	.21***
1 = A good deal					
2 = Not much					
Efficacy scale	.03	.05	.07*	.02	.00
1 = Low					
2 = Middle					
3 = High					
Trust scale	.03	.00	.02	.01	−.02
1 = Low					
2 = Middle					
3 = High					

   * Significant at .001.

  ** Significant at .01.

*** Significant at .05.

SOURCE: J. David Gopoian and Sissie Hadjiharalambous, "Late Deciding Voters in Presidential Elections," *Political Behavior*, 16 (1994), 64–65. Data source, computed from ANES data sets for appropriate years.

Somers' d.   Gamma and the tau coefficients are symmetrical in their treatment of the variables. That is, no distinction is made between independent and dependent variables. Robert Somers suggests a refinement of these coefficients, which is asymmetrical in interpretation.[14] Somers' *d* is considered appropriate for the test of an asymmetrical relationship. (Somers also argues that *d* is the ordinal analog of the ordinary regression coefficient, a topic discussed later in this chapter.) Thus, when distinguishing between the independent and dependent variables, or specifying one variable as the cause of another, Somers' d would appropriately be used. Referring again to the symbols for paired relationships presented previously (and remembering especially that the symbol, T_y, refers to those pairs of observations tied on the *dependent* variable), the formula for d becomes

$$\text{Somers' } d = \frac{P - Q}{P + Q + T_y}$$

For the hypothetical relationship presented in Table 9.9, d would be calculated as follows:

$$\text{Somers' } d = \frac{12 - 2}{12 + 2 + 10}$$

TESTS OF ASSOCIATION FOR INTERVAL-LEVEL DATA

Interval-level data permit a degree of precision in stating relationships that is not possible with nominal or ordinal data. Statistical techniques designed for use with interval data indicate the magnitude and the direction (positive or negative) of the relationship between two variables. These techniques also permit the mathematical expression of the dependent variable as a function of the independent variable. Using these techniques, we are able to predict with a certain degree of accuracy (to be measured by the correlation coefficient) the effect of unit changes in the independent variable on changes in the dependent variable.

In a **linear model** (this term is discussed more thoroughly subsequently), the relationship between two interval variables is defined by the **regression equation** $Y = a + bX$, where X is a given value of the independent variable and Y the predicted value of the dependent variable. The values of a (**intercept**) and b (**slope**) are constants to be calculated. The **correlation coefficient** is a measure of the extent to which the regression equation accurately predicts all values of Y.

By permitting the expression of one variable as a function of another and thereby enhancing our ability to *predict* the values of one variable, given the values of another, interval-level tests are considered to be much more powerful than the tests of nominal and of ordinal data discussed previously. Additionally, interval-level techniques greatly facilitate examination of the relationship between two variables, *controlling for* the influence of one or more additional variables.

The Regression Equation

Regression analysis is used to improve our ability to predict the values of a particular variable. In our previous discussion of nominal data, it was seen that given the distribution of a single variable, the best prediction for any value of that variable is

TABLE 9.12

Voting Turnout, 1992 Presidential Election by State (including difference from mean scores)

State	Turnout (%) (Y)	(Y − Ȳ)	(Y − Ȳ)²
Alabama	55.2	−3.1	9.61
Alaska	65.4	7.1	50.41
Arizona	54.1	−4.2	17.64
Arkansas	53.8	−4.5	20.25
California	49.1	−9.2	84.64
Colorado	62.7	4.4	19.36
Connecticut	63.8	5.5	30.25
Delaware	55.2	−3.1	9.61
Florida	50.2	−8.1	65.61
Georgia	46.9	−11.4	129.96
Hawaii	41.9	−16.4	268.96
Idaho	65.2	6.9	47.61
Illinois	58.9	0.6	0.36
Indiana	55.2	−3.1	9.61
Iowa	65.3	7.0	49.00
Kansas	63.0	4.7	22.09
Kentucky	53.7	−4.6	21.16
Louisiana	59.8	1.5	2.25
Maine	72.0	13.7	187.69
Maryland	53.4	−4.9	24.01
Massachusetts	60.2	1.9	3.61
Michigan	61.7	3.4	11.56
Minnesota	71.6	13.3	176.89
Mississippi	52.8	−5.5	30.25
Missouri	62.0	3.7	13.69
Montana	70.1	11.8	139.24
Nebraska	63.2	4.9	24.01
Nevada	50.0	−8.3	68.89
New Hampshire	63.1	4.8	23.04
New Jersey	56.3	−2.0	4.00
New Mexico	51.6	−6.7	44.89
New York	50.9	−7.4	54.76
North Carolina	50.1	−8.2	67.24
North Dakota	67.3	9.0	81.00
Ohio	60.6	2.3	5.29
Oklahoma	59.7	1.4	1.96
Oregon	65.7	7.4	54.76
Pennsylvania	54.3	−4.0	16.00
Rhode Island	58.4	0.1	0.01
South Carolina	45.0	−13.3	176.89
South Dakota	67.0	8.7	75.69
Tennessee	52.4	−5.9	34.81
Texas	49.1	−9.2	84.64

State	Turnout (%) (Y)	($Y - \overline{Y}$)	($Y - \overline{Y}$)^2
Utah	65.1	6.8	46.24
Vermont	67.5	9.2	84.64
Virginia	52.8	−5.5	30.25
Washington	59.9	1.6	2.56
West Virginia	50.6	−7.7	59.29
Wisconsin	69.0	10.7	114.49
Wyoming	62.3	4.0	16.00
	Mean turnout = 58.3%		Variance = 53.40

Note: The mean and variance scores reported here are as calculated by SPSS/PC$^+$.

Source: *Statistical Abstract of the United States,* 1993, 285.

the *mode.* If most of our respondents in a sample of 1,000 are Democrats, the best guess of the values of any member of that distribution would be Democrat.

Similarly, with interval data, the best guess of the values of a single distribution is the *mean* of that distribution. In a statistical sense, the mean score of a distribution of interval data minimizes the variance of error in estimating all values of the distribution.

As an example, suppose we are interested in examining voting turnout among the 50 states in the 1992 presidential election. This information is presented in Table 9.12. Table 9.12 also shows that the average turnout for all states was 58.3 percent and that the variance for this array of data is 53.40 (both scores rounded).

We saw in Chapter 7 that the variance of a distribution may be defined as the average squared deviation from the mean. This score, as it turns out, is less than the mean of the squared deviations of all observations from any other value. Stated another way, having no other information, the mean of a distribution is the most efficient predictor of all the values of that distribution. The extent of error in guessing values based on the mean is represented by the variance, but no other *single* predicted value will result in as small an error factor. The mean, then, becomes the standard by which we gauge the predictive ability of other variables. To be useful, predictive variables must be at least as efficient in estimating values of the dependent variable as is the dependent variable's own mean. Regression analysis is a technique that seeks to minimize the error factor by reference to knowledge of another variable.

The mean percentage of voting turnout among all states in the 1992 presidential election, then, is 58.3, and the variance is 53.40. Can we reduce this variance (error) factor by reference to another variable? Assume that we also have collected information on the percentage of each state's population having completed 12 grades or more of education. We might, in fact, be testing the hypothesis that voting turnout at the state level is, in part, a function of state educational levels. We might expect states with higher proportions of more highly educated citizens to experience higher levels of voter turnout. In a formal sense, the question we are asking is whether educational status (measured here as the percentage completing 12 or more grades of school) is a better predictor of voter turnout (here measured as per-

TABLE 9.13

Voting Turnout, 1992 Presidential Election, and Percentage of Population
Completing 12 Years of School, by State

State	Turnout (%)	Percentage Completing 12 Years or More of School
Alabama	55.2	66.9
Alaska	65.4	86.6
Arizona	54.1	78.7
Arkansas	53.8	66.3
California	49.1	76.2
Colorado	62.7	84.4
Connecticut	63.8	79.2
Delaware	55.2	77.5
Florida	50.2	74.4
Georgia	46.9	70.9
Hawaii	41.9	80.1
Idaho	65.2	79.7
Illinois	58.9	76.2
Indiana	55.2	75.6
Iowa	65.3	80.1
Kansas	63.0	81.3
Kentucky	53.7	64.6
Louisiana	59.8	68.3
Maine	72.0	78.8
Maryland	53.4	78.4
Massachusetts	60.2	80.0
Michigan	61.7	76.8
Minnesota	71.6	82.4
Mississippi	52.8	64.3
Missouri	62.0	73.9
Montana	70.1	81.0
Nebraska	63.2	81.8
Nevada	50.0	78.8
New Hampshire	63.1	82.2
New Jersey	56.3	76.7
New Mexico	51.6	75.1
New York	50.9	74.8
North Carolina	50.1	70.0
North Dakota	67.3	76.7
Ohio	60.6	75.7
Oklahoma	59.7	74.6
Oregon	65.7	81.5
Pennsylvania	54.3	74.7
Rhode Island	58.4	72.0
South Carolina	45.0	68.3
South Dakota	67.0	77.1
Tennessee	52.4	67.1
Texas	49.1	72.1
Utah	65.1	85.1
Vermont	67.5	80.8

State	Turnout (%)	Percentage Completing 12 Years or More of School
Virginia	52.8	75.2
Washington	59.9	83.8
West Virginia	50.6	66.0
Wisconsin	69.0	78.6
Wyoming	62.3	83.0
	Mean = 58.3%	76.3%
	Variance = 53.40	

NOTE: The mean and variance scores represented here are as calculated by SPSS/PC$^+$.

SOURCE: *Statistical Abstract of the United States,* 1993, 285 and 155.

centage voting in the 1992 presidential election) at the state level than is simply the mean percentage of voting turnout for all states.

Adding the information to our distribution of states, the results appear as shown. A casual inspection of Table 9.13 indicates that educational status (as measured here) indeed *may* be related to voting turnout. It can be seen there that some states with very high proportions of citizens completing high school experience relatively high voting turnout rates (such as Montana, Maine, and Minnesota), and some states with relatively low proportions of citizens completing high school experience relatively low turnout rates (such as West Virginia, South Carolina, and Mississippi).

The Scatterplot

Relationships such as that presented in Table 9.13 are often displayed graphically in the form of a **scatterplot** (sometimes called a "scattergram"). A scatterplot depicts the relationship between the two variables by plotting on intersecting axes the points representing the X and Y observations for each case (here, states). Maine, for example, has an X (educational status) coordinate of 78.8 and a Y (percentage of voting turnout) coordinate of 72.0. Moving out along the horizontal (X) axis to 78.8 and up the vertical (Y) axis to 72.0, we locate the point representing these coordinates. This point for Maine may be written as $X = 78.8$, $Y = 72.0$, or more simply as (78.8, 72.0). Similarly the points representing the X and Y values for all states could be plotted, and the resulting scatterplot would appear as shown in Figure 9.1. The plotted positions of all 50 states for these two variables are shown in this figure.

It always is a good idea to examine the scatterplot of any relationship before proceeding with the techniques of analysis discussed later in this section. The scatterplot itself will provide a rough indication of the *nature* of the relationship. If the general flow of the plotted points is upward and to the right, the relationship is *positive*—as one variable increases in value, so does the other. If the plotted points appear to be randomly spread, there is little or no relationship between the variables. Also, the scattergram indicates the *shape* of the relationship. If the plotted points are distributed so that the values of the dependent variable appear to increase or decrease in relation to the independent variable at a more-or-less consistent and constant rate, a **linear relationship** is said to exist. If a nonlinear relationship is discovered, the techniques discussed in this chapter would be inappropriate.

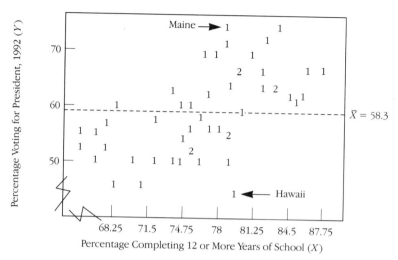

FIGURE 9.1

Scatterplot of Relationship between Percentage of Voting Turnout in 1992 Presidential Election and Percentage of Population Completing 12 or More Years of School

NOTE: In this scatterplot each number represents the coordinates of particular states. The number "2" means that two states had approximately the same coordinate values.

SOURCE: *Statistical Abstract of the United States,* 1993, 285 and 155.

When constructing scatterplots, it is customary, as illustrated in Figure 9.1, for the vertical axis to represent the dependent (or Y) value and for the horizontal axis to represent the independent (or X) variable. Examining Figure 9.1, it can be seen that for this scattergram, the mean percentage of voting turnout for all 50 states (58.3) is represented by a single horizontal line. As discussed previously, this mean score provides the best guess for all values of Y (the dependent variable), when no other information is provided. Although there is considerable variation on either side of this mean score (i.e., the line comes close to the scores of some states but is far from the scores of some others), no horizontal line would result in as small a variance score.

Now, however, we have additional information regarding each state: percentage of the population completing 12 grades of education. The question that regression seeks to answer is this: Can this new information be used to construct a new line, which will be closer to all points plotted in Figure 9.1 than is the line representing the mean? Put another way, can knowledge of educational status help construct a line that will reduce the variation in percentage of voter turnout?

The regression equation, as discussed previously, defines such a line and (in the case of linear relationships) can be presented as follows:

$$Y_p = \alpha + \beta X$$

Reader Note: Recall that Greek letters are typically used to present formulas when using a population data, but lowercase Roman letters are used when presenting formulas for sample data. Hence, for sample data, the regression formula would be presented as: $Y_p = a + bX$.

In this equation, X refers to values of the independent variable and Y_p to predicted values of the dependent variable. In this instance, the X values are the *actual* values of the independent variable (educational status) for each state. The Y_p values represent the *predicted* values of the dependent variable (percentage of voting turnout) for each state for each value of X. The constant α (or a when using sample data) is called the "Y intercept" because it defines the location where the new line will intercept the Y axis. The symbol β (or b when using sample data) is called the "slope" (or "regression coefficient") and is interpreted as the average change in the dependent variable associated with a one-unit change in the independent variable.

After calculating α and β, we can insert in our scatterplot the new *least squares line*—the straight line that will minimize the variation in the dependent variable. One formula for calculating β is as follows:

$$\beta = \frac{N(\Sigma XY) - (\Sigma X)(\Sigma Y)}{N(\Sigma X^2) - (\Sigma X)^2}$$

The value of α may be calculated by application of either of the following two formulas:

$$\alpha = \frac{\Sigma Y - b\,\Sigma X}{N}$$

or

$$\alpha = \bar{Y} - b\,\bar{X}$$

For the data on state educational status and percentage of voting turnout in the 1992 presidential election presented in Table 9.13, β and α would be calculated as presented in Table 9.14.

Selecting any two values of X and calculating the expected values of Y using this equation will permit us to insert the regression line in our scatterplot. If X is 65, for example, the predicted value of Y is 50 (rounded). For an X value of 75, the predicted value of Y is 57.4 (rounded). Connecting these two points yields the regression line shown in Figure 9.2.

The regression routine provides a powerful predictive tool. We are using information on one variable (in this case, percentage of population completing 12 or more grades of education) to predict expected scores on another variable (percentage of voting turnout). We know, of course, the precise turnout for each of

TABLE 9.14

Calculating the Simple Regression Equation

State	Turnout (%) (Y)	Percentage Completing 12 Years or More of School (X)	$X \times Y$	X^2
Alabama	55.2	66.9	3692.88	4475.61
Alaska	65.4	86.6	5663.64	7499.56
Arizona	54.1	78.7	4257.67	6193.69
Arkansas	53.8	66.3	3566.94	4395.69
California	49.1	76.2	3741.42	5806.44
Colorado	62.7	84.4	5291.88	7123.36
Connecticut	63.8	79.2	5052.96	6272.64
Delaware	55.2	77.5	4278.00	6006.25
Florida	50.2	74.4	3734.88	5535.36
Georgia	46.9	70.9	3325.21	5026.81
Hawaii	41.9	80.1	3356.19	6416.01
Idaho	65.2	79.7	5196.44	6352.09
Illinois	58.9	76.2	4488.18	5806.44
Indiana	55.2	75.6	4173.12	5715.36
Iowa	65.3	80.1	5230.53	6416.01
Kansas	63.0	81.3	5121.90	6609.69
Kentucky	53.7	64.6	3469.02	4173.16
Louisiana	59.8	68.3	4084.34	4664.89
Maine	72.0	78.8	5673.60	6209.44
Maryland	53.4	78.4	4186.56	6146.56
Massachusetts	60.2	80.0	4816.00	6400.00
Michigan	61.7	76.8	4738.56	5898.24
Minnesota	71.6	82.4	5899.84	6789.76
Mississippi	52.8	64.3	3395.04	4134.49
Missouri	62.0	73.9	4581.80	5461.21
Montana	70.1	81.0	5678.10	6561.00
Nebraska	63.2	81.8	5169.76	6691.24
Nevada	50.0	78.8	3940.00	6209.44
New Hampshire	63.1	82.2	5186.82	6756.84
New Jersey	56.3	76.7	4318.21	5882.89
New Mexico	51.6	75.1	3875.16	5640.01
New York	50.9	74.8	3807.32	5595.04
North Carolina	50.1	70.0	3507.00	4900.00
North Dakota	67.3	76.7	5161.91	5882.89
Ohio	60.6	75.7	4587.42	5730.49
Oklahoma	59.7	74.6	4453.62	5565.16
Oregon	65.7	81.5	5354.55	6642.25
Pennsylvania	54.3	74.7	4056.21	5580.09
Rhode Island	58.4	72.0	4204.80	5184.00
South Carolina	45.0	68.3	3073.50	4664.89
South Dakota	67.0	77.1	5165.70	5944.41
Tennessee	52.4	67.1	3516.04	4502.41
Texas	49.1	72.1	3540.11	5198.41
Utah	65.1	85.1	5540.01	7242.01
Vermont	67.5	80.8	5454.00	6528.64

State	Turnout (%) (Y)	Percentage Completing 12 Years or More of School (X)	X × Y	X²
Virginia	52.8	75.2	3970.56	5655.04
Washington	59.9	83.8	5019.62	7022.44
West Virginia	50.6	66.0	3339.60	4356.00
Wisconsin	69.0	78.6	5423.40	6177.96
Wyoming	62.3	83.0	5170.90	6889.00
$\Sigma y = 2915.10$	$\Sigma x = 3814.30$	$\Sigma xy = 223{,}530.92$	$\Sigma x^2 = 292{,}531.31$	

SOURCE: *Statistical Abstract of the United States,* 1993, 285 and 155.

$$\beta = \frac{50(223{,}530.92) - 3814.30(2915.10)}{50\,(292{,}531.31) - 14{,}548{,}884}$$

$$\beta = \frac{57{,}480}{77{,}682}$$

$$\beta = .739$$

$$\beta = .74 \text{ (rounded)}$$

$$\alpha = \frac{2915.10 - .739(3814.30)}{50}$$

$$\alpha = \frac{2915.10 - 2818.7677}{50}$$

$$\alpha = 1.85 \text{ (rounded)}$$

or

$$\alpha = 58.3 - 0.74(76.3)$$
$$= 1.85 \text{ (rounded)}$$

Thus, $y_p = 1.85 + .74\,(x)$

these 50 states, but the regression analysis permits us to state with a new degree of precision the effect on voting turnout associated with changing levels of educational status. For this group of states, it can be said that for every increase of 1 percent of the state's population having completed 12 years of education, there was, on average, an associated increase of voting turnout in the 1992 presidential election of 0.74 percent (rounded). Further, the sign of the slope provides important information about the nature of the relationship between the variables. A *positive slope* (such as this one) indicates that as one variable increases in value, so does the other. A *negative slope* tells us that as one variable increases, the other variable decreases.

Further, if we were dealing with data drawn from a sample (rather than from the entire population, as is the situation in this example), regression can be used to predict the expected values of any case based on results found when analyzing the sample cases. When using regression to predict, remember that the predictions are only expected values. Actual values are likely to deviate somewhat.

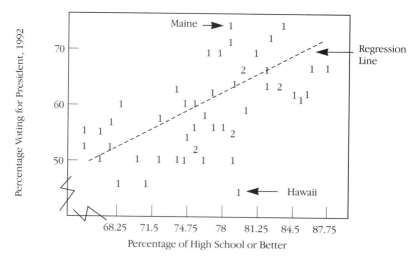

FIGURE 9.2

Plotting the Regression Line for the Data in Figure 9.1

Reader Note: The regression line does not extend byond the minimum and maximum values of the independent variable (X axis), illustrating one of the important points of regression analysis. The regression equation is to be used to summarize a relationship only within the given range of values. It would not be safe to predict percentage of voting turnout for educational status scores either higher or lower than those included in the analysis.

The Correlation Coefficient

The question that then arises is this: How accurate is our prediction equation? That is, how effectively can we predict the percentage of voting turnout, based on the percentage of persons in each state having completed 12 or more years of school? One gauge of accuracy can be provided simply by inspecting the regression line that has been inserted onto the scatterplot (Figure 9.2). The closer that all or most of the points representing actual X and Y values cluster on or near the expected values represented by regression line, the more accurate is the predictive equation. In this case, it can be seen that some plotted values do fall on, or very close to, the regression line, but it also can be seen that many of the plotted points are off the line.

The correlation coefficient is a statistic designed to measure how closely our regression line fits the actual distribution of data. The closer the fit, the higher the correlation coefficient, and the more confident we can be in predicting values of the dependent variable, based on the values of the independent variable.

As is the case with most of the statistics discussed in this text, the actual calculation of the correlation coefficient is a relatively simple and straightforward (if sometimes tedious) task. However, prior to illustrating one of the typical ways to calculate the correlation coefficient, it may be helpful to consider for a moment what this statistic actually measures. In fact, a number of interpretations can be given to the correlation coefficient. One of these is the correlation coefficient as a reduction-of-vari-ance ratio. As such, the coefficient to be described first is known as the **coefficient of determination** and is symbolized as r^2. For positive relationships, the **simple correlation coefficient** (r) is obtained by taking the square root of r^2.

Returning to the notion of variance, it will be recalled that relying on the mean score, the total variance for the distribution of state voting turnout in the 1992 presidential election was shown to be 53.40 (Table 9.12). It was also noted that no other *single value* would render a lower variance score than that given by the mean. Having now generated a predicted score for *each* value of Y (voting turnout for each state), we can calculate the amount of variance in Y that remains unexplained after accounting for the independent variable (educational status) by substituting for $\bar{Y}$ in the variance formula the predicted values of Y (Y_p). The resulting formula appears as

$$\sigma_p^2 = \frac{\Sigma(Y - Y_p)^2}{N}$$

The resulting sum is known as the **unexplained variance,** and this value, together with the total variance, can be used to calculate r^2. Applying the preceding formula, the unexplained variance is found to be 36.05. For the 50 states, then, the total variance has been reduced from 53.40 to 36.05. The difference between these two values is known as the **explained variance,** and the ratio of explained variance to the total original variance provides the measure for the coefficient of determination and can be expressed for this set of data as

$$r^2 = \frac{\sigma^2 - \sigma_p^2}{\sigma^2}$$

$$= \frac{53.40 - 36.05}{53.40}$$

$$= 0.33 \text{ (rounded)}$$

where σ^2 = variance
σ_p^2 = unexplained variance

It can be concluded, then, that about 33 percent (or one third) of the variance in the percentage of voting turnout in the 1992 presidential election is accounted for by reference to educational status (measured as the percentage of state population having completed 12 grades of school). Because r^2 ranges from 0 to 1.0, this is a moderate amount of variance explained (1.0 would indicate 100% of explained variance), and it suggests that educational status is a moderately good predictor of voting turnout. An r^2 of 1.0 implies perfect predictability, in which all coordinate points representing X and Y observations would lie on the regression line; all the variance would have been explained. An r^2 of 0.0 indicates that the unexplained variance is equivalent to the total variance and that the independent variable is of no assistance in predicting values of the dependent variable (again, assuming a linear relationship).

To repeat, the coefficient that has just been described (r^2) is known as the coefficient of determination, and it measures the proportionate amount of variance in the dependent variable explained by the independent variable. The value represented by $1 - r^2$ is known as the **coefficient of nondetermination,** which is a measure of the amount of variance left unexplained by reference to the independent variable.

A Computational Formula for *r*

For positive relationships, the simple correlation coefficient (r) can be obtained by taking the square root of r^2. In actual research situations, the simple correlation coefficient (alternatively known as the "zero-order correlation coefficient," the "product-moment correlation coefficient," the "Pearson correlation coefficient," or simply as r) is often calculated prior to the calculation of r^2. The definitional formula for r can be presented as

$$r = \frac{\Sigma(X - \bar{X})(Y - \bar{Y})}{\sqrt{\Sigma(X - \bar{X})^2 \Sigma(Y - \bar{Y})^2}}$$

Expressed in this manner, the numerator of r provides a measure of the extent to which X and Y vary together—known as *covariation.* Because the range of values for the covariation will vary from one distribution to another, a means of standardization allowing for meaningful comparisons from one distribution to another is required. This is accomplished in the formula by dividing the numerator by the denominator, a value that would be achieved if all observations fell perfectly on a straight line (i.e., a perfect correlation). The ratio between these two terms is the simple correlation coefficient, and this measure will range in value from -1.0 to $+1.0$ for all distributions. A *positive correlation coefficient* indicates that as one variable increases (or decreases) in value, so does the other. A *negative correlation coefficient* indicates a decline in the values of one variable as the values of the other increase. A *zero correlation* implies the absence of a linear relationship between the two variables.

Because the definitional formula given previously is somewhat tedious to apply to an actual set of data, the computational formula which may be used to calculate r is expressed as follows:

$$r = \frac{N\Sigma XY - (\Sigma X)(\Sigma Y)}{\sqrt{[N\Sigma X^2 - (\Sigma X)^2][N\Sigma Y^2 - (\Sigma Y)^2]}}$$

For the data on state percentage of voting turnout and educational status, the r value calculated according to the preceding formula is .57.

The simple correlation (r), like ϕ and τ_b, has no intrinsic meaning of its own. It is simply a measure of strength. By squaring r, we obtain the coefficient of determination (r^2), which, as discussed previously, is a measure of the variance that is explained. We have already shown that the variance explained in this example is 33 percent (rounded), and the square of r (.57) does equal 0.33 (rounded).

Prior to considering some substantive examples of correlation and regression analysis, one final word of caution is in order. Correlations based on rates or averages and data collected at the aggregate level (such as that used in the example of state-level voting turnout) are sometimes known as *ecological correlations,* and as such, they must be used with extreme caution. Obviously, states do not vote or attend classes; people do. Information collected at the aggregate level is not necessarily indicative of behavior at the individual level (i.e., voter) and should not be so interpreted. We consider this important point more carefully at the end of this chapter.

Some Examples of Regression and Correlation Analysis

Norman R. Luttbeg makes good use of the scatterplot, regression, and correlation analysis in his examination of the relationship between each state's population percentage living in metropolitan areas and each state's murder rates and abortion rates in the American states.[15] Luttbeg's analysis is shown in Figure 9.3.

Figure 9.3 indicates positive relationships between the percentage of a state's population living in metropolitan areas for measures of both murder rates and abortion rates. A visual inspection of the scatterplots presented in Figure 9.3 also shows that the relationship between the percentage living in metropolitan areas and the abortion rates is stronger than the relationship between the percentage living in metropolitan areas and murder rates. This distinction is confirmed by the correlation coefficients (.34 between percentage living in metropolitan areas and murder rates versus .68 between percentage living in metropolitan areas and abortion rates). The proportion of a state's population living in metropolitan areas, Luttbeg concludes, is related to "many problems faced by states, such as murder and high abortion rates."[16]

Another interesting use of correlation analysis is provided by Alan Abramowitz, in his 1994 study examining the relationship between party identification (coded as a seven-point variable ranging from "Strong Democrat" to "Strong Republican") and a number of policy attitudes among white respondents to the 1988 National Election Study.[17] Abramowitz's results are shown in Table 9.15, where correlations for various subgroups (such as age, region, and education) are examined.

Noting stronger correlations between partisanship and many of these issues for younger voters, Abramowitz interprets these results to suggest that, "younger whites were affected more than older whites by a variety of issues that began to divide the parties during the 1960s, not just by racial issues."[18]

Another instructive application of the simple correlation coefficient is provided in William Taggart and Russell Winn's study of the factors associated with imprison-

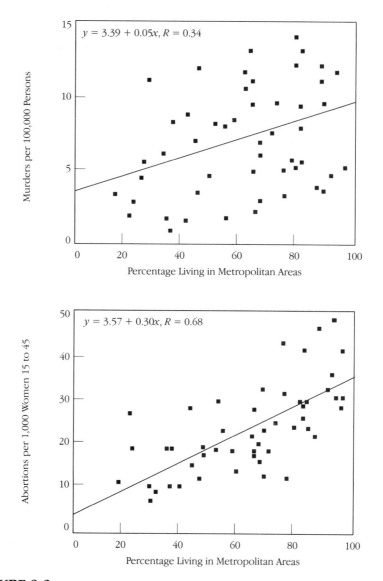

FIGURE 9.3

Murder and Abortion Rates versus Percentage Living in Metropolitan Areas

Source: Norman R. Luttbeg, *Comparing the States and Communities* (New York: HarperCollins Publishers, 1992), 24.

ment rates in the American states.[19] Their results, showing the correlations between incarceration rates and a number of state-level variables, are shown in Table 9.16.

Interpreting these data, Taggart and Winn note, "The variables displaying the strongest relationships are associated with crime, social characteristics, ideology and

TABLE 9.15

Partisan Polarization on Issues among Whites, by Demographic Characteristics in 1988

	Social Welfare Issues	Racial Issues	Defense Issues	Lifestyle Issues	Death Penalty	School Prayer
All whites (*n* = 1,103)	.36**	.17**	.24**	.08**	.19**	.02
Age						
17–44 (*n* = 638)	.34**	.23**	.32**	.16**	.21**	.11**
45 or older (*n* = 465)	.38**	.11**	.17**	.02	.16**	−.07
Region						
North (*n* = 791)	.39**	.20**	.28**	.09*	.19**	.03
South (*n* = 312)	.33**	.14**	.21**	.08	.21**	.07
Racial context						
Blacks < 15% (*n* = 730)	.36**	.18**	.29**	.09*	.20**	−.00
Blacks > 15% (*n* = 373)	.38**	.15**	.13**	.06	.16**	−.07
Education						
High school (*n* = 561)	.25**	.13**	.17**	.00	.11**	−.02
Some college (*n* = 269)	.41**	.19**	.28**	.15**	.15**	.02
Graduated college (*n* = 255)	.47**	.36**	.48**	.33**	.43**	.24**

* $p < .05$.

** $p < .01$.

NOTE: Coefficients are product–moment correlations between seven-point party identification scale and issue scales. Significance levels are based on one-tailed *t*-test.

SOURCE: Alan I. Abramowitz, "Issue Evolution Reconsidered: Racial Attitudes and Partisanship in the U.S. Electorate," *American Journal of Political Science* 38 (February, 1994), 13. Data source:

culture, alternatives to corrections, and the two demographic measures addressing change [change in population density and percent change in population]."[20]

SUMMARY

Some of the most commonly used statistics designed to measure the strength of a relationship between two variables have been examined in this chapter. In the next chapter, we examine some techniques for measuring the strength of a relationship existing among several variables, but before we do so, a few additional issues related to correlational analysis should be considered.

TABLE 9.16

Eight Hypotheses Concerning State Incarceration Rates in 1984: Pearson's Zero-Order Correlation Coefficients ($n = 48$)

Hypothesis/Variables	Correlation with Incarceration Rate
Hypothesis 1: Crime in 1980	
1. Violent crimes per 100,000 population	.69**
2. Property crimes per 100,000 population	.42**
Hypothesis 2: Economics in 1980	
1. Median family income	.05
2. Percentage of individuals below poverty level	.29*
Hypothesis 3: Social characteristics in 1980	
1. Percent of males between 20 and 29 years of age	.09
2. Percent nonwhite males	.58**
3. Percent nonwhite males between 20 and 29 years	.66**
Hypothesis 4: Demographics in 1980 and between 1970 and 1980	
1. Population	.19
2. Population density	−.07
3. Change in population density	.36*
4. Percent change in population	.31*
Hypothesis 5: Ideology and culture	
1. Percent vote for McGovern in 1972	−.41**
2. Conservatism in the early 1980s	.30*
3. Political culture circa 1970	.65**
Hypothesis 6: Sentencing and parole reforms as of 1983	
1. Adoption of determinate sentencing (0 = no; 1 = yes)	−.16
2. Mandatory sentencing index	.43**
3. Adoption of systemwide parole (0 = no; 1 = yes)	.18
4. Early release credit provision index	−.03
Hypothesis 7: Alternatives to corrections in 1984	
1. Probationers per 100,000 population	.38**
2. Designed capacity of community-based facilities	.41**
3. Ratio of community-based capacity to prison capacity	.02
Hypothesis 8: Institutional conditions	
1. Percent prison capacity in 1984	.08
2. Corrections organizational strength in 1977	.03
3. Designed capacity of prison facilities in 1984	.41**

*$p < .05$.
**$p < .01$.

SOURCE: William A. Taggart and Russel G. Winn, "Imprisonment in the American States," *Social Science Quarterly,* 74 (December, 1993), 742.

Try to Examine All the Data: Look for Outliers

A tremendous advantage of correlation analysis is its ability to summarize with a single number great amounts of data. Paradoxically, however, this summarization may become a disadvantage if we focus only on the correlation coefficient and overlook the actual data distribution. By ignoring the actual data, we run the risk of overlooking important deviations from the mainstream, and often, these deviations are just as interesting to the researcher and the broader academic community. In addition, cases that deviate from the major trends can effect the strength and nature of the relationship that otherwise would be reported.

When displaying the data in the form of a scatterplot, those values that deviate considerably from the regression line are known as **outliers.** In Figure 9.1, it can be seen that Hawaii had a relatively high value on education (approximately 80% had at least 12 years of education), but a relatively low voter turnout in the 1992 presidential election (about 42%). For this set of data, Hawaii would be considered an outlier, and its inclusion in this analysis weakens the degree of association between these two variables (with Hawaii deleted, the correlation between these two variables increases from 0.57 to 0.64).

Statisticians differ in their recommendations on how to deal with outliers. Some suggest that the analysis should be run with outliers excluded; others suggest that the analysis should be run both with outliers included *and* with outliers excluded, and *both* results should be reported.[21] At this point, students should at least be aware of the issues raised by outliers, as well as of the situations where the regression model does not work very well.

Beware of Ecological and Individualistic Fallacies

When examining the relationship between educational levels and voting turnout for the American states in the preceding analysis, it was mentioned that we must be cautious about drawing conclusions about individual behavior based on information collected at some aggregate level (such as the states). Here, we briefly describe the complex issues of ecological and individualistic fallacies in the interpretation of data.[22]

Ecological fallacy refers to the possibility of incorrectly reaching conclusions about the behavior of individuals based on data collected in the aggregate. For example, data collected at the county level showing wealthy counties to record higher proportions of Republican voters cannot necessarily be interpreted to mean that data collected from individuals in each county would show that wealthier individuals would always be more likely to vote Republican. Individuals composing a large unit of analysis (county, state, nation) do not necessarily reflect the behavior of the larger unit. To make inferences about individuals, the researcher needs to collect information at the individual level.

Conversely, an **individualistic fallacy** is made when inferences of group behavior are made on the basis of information collected from individuals. It should not be concluded from the finding that less wealthy individuals are less politically active that voting turnouts will be lower among counties with lower average income levels. If we wish to make a statement about voting behavior at the county level, we need to collect data at that level.

Of course, we may not always be in possession of precisely the data we need to analyze the relationship that interests us most. Often, for example, information on individuals is not available; we have to rely on data collected at the precinct, city, county, or state level. In such instances, researchers must be fully aware of the limitations of the available data and must be explicit about such limitations in reporting the results of the analysis.

Do Not Confuse Correlation with Causation

One of the most grievous errors that can be made in the application of correlation techniques is to assume that correlation is equivalent to causation. It is true that demonstrating correlation is an important first step toward establishing causation, but this is only the first step. Correlation does not necessarily imply causation. In the first place, correlation is an indication of *strength,* but not *direction,* of a relationship. A high correlation between two variables does not tell us which preceded the other. The time order of variables is not always obvious.

Equally important is the problem of spurious or confounding influences. Even when time sequence can be clearly established, it is still possible that the observed correlation between two variables may actually be the results of the influence of one or several other variables. That is, the apparent correlation between variables X_1 and X_2 may actually be the result of X_3's influence on both X_1 and X_2. If the influence of X_3 could be removed, it might be found that the observed correlation between X_1 and X_2 would vanish. This is the issue of control, to which we turn in the following chapter.

KEY TERMS

measures of association	scatterplot
phi coefficient	linear relationship
Cramer's V	coefficient of determination
contingency coefficient	simple correlation coefficient
proportionate reduction of error	unexplained variance
Lambda coefficient	explained variance
linear model	coefficient of nondetermination
regression equation	outliers
intercept	ecological fallacy
slope	individualistic fallacy
correlation coefficient	

EXERCISES

1. Reproduced again, is a table showing the relationship between party identification and opinions toward Bill Clinton's performance as president, as revealed in the 1994 American National Election Study:

Party Identification

Approval Rating	Republican	Independent	Democrat	Totals
Approval	106	239	462	807
Disapproval	412	245	125	782
Totals	518	484	587	1,589

NOTE: All responses other than those shown have been deleted.

    a. Using the chi-square value calculated in Exercise 1 for Chapter 8, calculate and present the Cramer's V and the contingency coefficient statistics for this table.

    b. Calculate also the lambda coefficient for this table.

    c. Based on these three measures of association, what can be said about the strength of relationship between partisanship and opinions of presidential performance, at least as revealed in the 1994 survey? Discuss also the differences in values represented by these three statistics, and tell what these differences tell us about the calculation and use of measures of association.

2. The following table presents, for a sample of ten states, the percentage of state population living in metropolitan areas (as of the 1990 census), and the rate of violent crime per 100,000 population.

State	Percentage of Population Living in Metropolitan Areas	Violent Crime Rate
Maine	36.1	132
Connecticut	95.7	540
Indiana	71.5	505
Iowa	43.2	303
Kansas	53.8	500
West Virginia	41.7	191
Kentucky	47.6	438
Louisiana	73.5	951
Wyoming	29.6	310
Nevada	84.4	677

SOURCE: *Statistical Abstract of the United States,* 1993.

    a. Construct a scattergram for the preceding set of data. On the basis of the scattergram alone, what can be said about the apparent relationship between percentage of population living in metropolitan areas and crime rate for those states.

    b. Compute the sample regression coefficient, the simple correlation coefficient, and the coefficient of determination for this set of data. What is the interpretation of each of these coefficients in relation to this set of data?

    c. What are the advantages and disadvantages of applying correlation and re-

gression analysis to data such as these? What do these coefficients tell us about this set of data, and what precautions should be taken in reporting the results?
3. From a publication such as the *Statistical Abstract of the United States,* or some other data source, select any measure other than crime rate for these same states, and calculate the correlation and regression coefficients between that variable and the percentage of population living in metropolitan areas. How does this relationship compare with that for crime rate, as revealed by these coefficients?
4. Examine recent issues of political science and policy-related journals, and locate articles using the following analyses:
   a. Cross-tabulation analysis—report the results.
   b. Correlation analysis—report the results.
   c. Simple regression analysis—report the results.
   d. Discuss the differing methodologies represented by these articles and the reasons why each was selected.

NOTES

1.   See James A. David, *Elementary Survey Analysis* (Englewood Cliffs, NJ: Prentice-Hall, 1971), 49.
2.   Charles L. Davis, "Religion and Partisan Loyalty: The Case of Catholic Workers in Mexico," *Western Political Quarterly* (March, 1992), 275–197.
3.   Ibid., 284.
4.   As presented in Linton C. Freeman, *Elementary Applied Statistics* (New York: John Wiley & Sons, 1965), 74.
5.   Renu Khator, "Recycling: A Policy Dilemma for American States?" *Policy Studies Journal* 21 (Summer, 1993), 210–223.
6.   Ibid., 218.
7.   See especially Leo A. Goodman and William H. Kruskal, "Measure of Association for Cross Classification," *Journal of American Statistical Association* 49 (1954), 732–764; M.G. Kendall, *Rank Correlation Methods* (London: Griffin, 1970); M. G. Kendall and A. Stuart, *The Advanced Theory of Statistics,* vol. 2 (New York: Hafner, 1973); and Robert H. Somers, "A New Asymmetric Measure of Association for Ordinal Variables," *American Sociological Review* 27 (1962), 799–811.
8.   For an elaboration, see Albert M. Liebetrau, *Measures of Association* (Newbury Park, CA: Sage Publications, 1983), 85– 88; and Herbert F. Weisberg, "Models of Statistical Relationship," *American Political Science Review* 68 (December, 1974), 1638–1655.
9.   This interpretation of gamma refers to the predictability of ordered pairs, not to individual cases.
10.   The argument presented here follows the distinction usually made between τ_b and τ_c. See Marija J. Norusis, *The SPSS Guide to Data Analysis,* 2nd ed. (Chicago: SPSS, 1991), 322–324; see also Nelson C. Dometrius, *Social Statistics Using SPSS* (New York: Harper-Collins, 1992), 311–315. However, Weisberg ("Models of Statistical Relationship") points out that the choice between τ_b and τ_c involves substantive as well as technical issues.
11.   Bryan D. Jones, Frank R. Baumgartner, and Jeffrey C. Talbert, "The Destruction of Issue Monopolies in Congress," *American Political Science Review* 87 (September, 1993), 657–671.
12.   Ibid., 664–665.

13. J. David Gopoian and Sissie Hadjiharalambous, "Late-Deciding Voters in Presidential Elections," *Political Behavior* 16 (1994), 55–78.
14. Somers, "A New Asymmetric Measure of Association for Ordinal Variables."
15. Norman R. Luttbeg, *Comparing the States and Communities* (New York: HarperCollins Publishers, 1992).
16. Ibid., 23.
17. Alan I. Abramowitz, "Issue Evolution Reconsidered: Racial Attitudes and Partisanship in the U.S. Electorate," *American Journal of Political Science* (February, 1994), 1–24.
18. Ibid., 12.
19. William Taggart and Russell Winn, "Imprisonment in the American States," *Social Science Quarterly* (December, 1993), 736–749.
20. Ibid., 743.
21. For a good discussion of this problem, see Franklin A. Graybill and Hariharan K. Kyer, *Regression Analysis* (Belmont, CA: Duxbury Press, 1994), 351–364.
22. For additional discussion of the very important topics of ecological and individualistic fallacies, see Louise H. Kidder, *Selltiz, Wrightsman and Cook's Research Methods in Social Relations,* 4th ed. (New York: Holt, Rinehart and Winston, 1980), 296–301.

CHAPTER 10

Sorting Out Relationships:
Analyzing Several Variables

Some years ago, political researchers examining the relationship between various state-level political variables (such as degree of two-party competition) and public policies adopted by those states (such as welfare expenditures) made some very interesting—and surprising—findings. Although much political theory suggested an independent effect of politics on public policy, these researchers found that when examined in the context of various *socioeconomic variables* (such as income, urbanization, and industrialization), the correlations between the political variables and the policy indicators were dramatically reduced.[1] One prominent scholar in this area was to conclude, "Most of the associations that occur between political variables and policy outcomes are really a product of the fact that economic development influences *both* political system characteristics *and* policy outcomes. When the effects of economic development are controlled, political factors turn out to have little influence on policy outcomes."[2]

When examining the relationship between two variables in the context of one or several additional variables, we may find the nature of the original *bivariate* (two-variable) relationship to be significantly altered. A relationship that at first appeared to be strong may be quite weak. Sometimes, we find the original relationship strengthened, and sometimes the original relationship is virtually unchanged.

It is also the case that political relationships are extremely complex, and it is unusual under any circumstance for one variable to be so strongly associated with another as to provide a complete and satisfactory explanation of that variable. To thoroughly understand a particular variable of interest, we often must examine that variable in reference to several independent variables.

Accounting for the influence of two, three, or more variables can improve our understanding of a dependent variable, and it can affect an original bivariate relationship in many ways. Because several variables are being examined at one time, the category of methods used in such analysis is termed **multivariate analysis.** We also return at this point to our earlier discussion of *control.*

STATISTICAL CONTROL

In Chapter 3, we talked about various research design options. It was noted there that when conducting nonexperimental research (such as survey research), researchers have much less control over the objects of study or over the effects of the independent variables than when conducting experimental research. Random assignment of subjects to treatment groups, as is possible when conducting experimental research, greatly helps to eliminate the confounding effects of various independent variables. Through random placement of subjects into various groups, the experimenter controls for extraneous factors, thus ensuring that control and treatment groups are, on average, similar in all respects and that they differ only in terms of their exposure to the independent variable or variables. Through careful pretesting, posttesting (immediately after the experimental treatment is administered), and follow-up testing procedures, researchers can reach reasonably firm conclusions about the isolated impact of the independent variable.

We noted also in Chapter 3 that experimental techniques sometimes can be used in political and policy research, but we also said that there are many situations when the procedure cannot be employed. When it is impossible to randomly assign subjects to various groups and to rigorously control the introduction of various treatment effects, some other means for control must be used. These other means involve techniques of *statistical control.*

Simply put, statistical controlling is an ex post facto method of manipulating the data so that respondents will be rendered equivalent on important variables, thereby eliminating the effects of confounding factors on the bivariate relationship being examined. Statistical control is less powerful than experimental control for a variety of reasons (although it does have a number of advantages, which are discussed at the conclusion of this chapter). One of the most important of its limitations is that to apply the technique effectively, all possible confounding factors (variables) need to be identified *prior* to conducting the study. If the information has not been collected, or cannot be obtained, appropriate control is impossible. Because no researcher can ever collect information on *every possible* variable, a great deal of time and thought must go into the data-collection effort. It is incumbent on the researcher to identify and collect information on all additional factors that might *reasonably* be expected to affect the original relationship.

The Confounding Influence of Third Variables: Spurious and Intervening Relationships

There are many obvious examples of relationships between two variables that, when examined in the context of a third variable, are found to be significantly altered. A high correlation might be found, for example, between grades in political science courses and grades in biology courses at a particular university. It almost certainly is the case, however, that achievement in one of these topics is not causally related to achievement in the other. More probably, some third variable, such as hours spent studying, explains grade variations in both subject areas. In such a situation, the relationship between grades in political science and grades in biology is said to be *spurious* (a term that is defined more completely subsequently); hours spent studying explains both variables. Another often-cited example of a spurious relationship is the one between the number of fire trucks responding to a fire and the extent of damage done. The more the trucks called, the greater the damage. Clearly, though, fire trucks are not the cause of fire damage. The size of the fire, itself, is responsible for both the number of fire trucks called and the size of the damage done. As one final example: A moderately strong relationship probably exists between political attitudes of siblings. People who are liberal on social issues probably tend to have brothers and sisters who are liberal also, and those who are conservative probably tend to have conservative brothers and sisters. Yet, such relationships might be found to be largely spurious after accounting for attitudes of parents and other commonly experienced environmental influences, such as education, peer associations, and so forth. These common experiences may be most directly related to the political attitudes of brothers and sisters.[3]

In contrast to these examples, many political situations are not so obvious. At the beginning of this chapter, we talked about the discovery, a few years ago, that the relationships between some political variables and some policy variables were largely reduced after controlling for various socioeconomic factors. The finding that political system characteristics seemed to have little independent effect on public policy not only was a surprise, but also was described as "very disturbing" to many political scientists.[4]

Researchers must make every reasonable effort to test and discard all possible confounding influences before concluding that a causal relationship apparently does exist. This effort is one of the most difficult phases of the research process. It is impossible, as mentioned previously, to actually examine *every* possible confounding influence. Literally, this would mean reexamining the original relationship, accounting for the possible influence of all other phenomena. Nevertheless, the researcher must examine and control for all third factors that might *reasonably* be expected to affect the original relationship. Theory helps to identify such variables, and so, too, do the results obtained by previous researchers.

Figure 10.1 illustrates the confounding roles that a third variable, "X_3," may play in the relationship between two variables, "X_1" and "X_2." As noted in Figure 10.1A in the case of a **spurious effect,** we are saying that Variable X_3 is the cause of the variation in both variables X_1 and X_2. Variables X_1 and X_2 may appear to be related, but this is only because of the effect of Variable X_3 on both. This is analogous to the aforementioned situation in which the hours spent studying (Variable X_3, in this case) was the actual cause of the variance in biology (Variable X_1) and in political science (Variable X_2) grades. A spurious relationship can be defind as one in which the original two variables have no causal relationship but are dependent on an alternative, third variable.

In the case of an **intervening effect** (Figure 10.1B), we are saying that Variable X_3 is an intervening or mediating factor, which helps explain in greater detail how the causal effect of Variable X_1 actually is transmitted to Variable X_2. As an example,

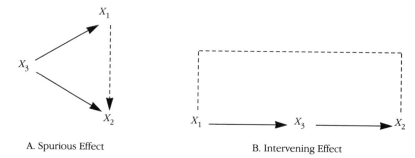

A. Spurious Effect   B. Intervening Effect

FIGURE 10.1

Confounding Roles Played by Third Variable

NOTE: Solid arrow denotes a nonzero correlation; broken arrow denotes relationship approaching zero after controlling for other variables.

Reader Note: Statistics, alone, cannot determine which of these two models correctly depicts the sequence of relationships among these three variables. In both cases, the researcher is predicting that the relationship between X_1 and X_2 will be substantially reduced when controlling for X_3. Determining which is the more appropriate model is a function of theory, past research, and common sense.

we may be examining the relationships between the political attitudes of grandparents (Variable X_1), parents (Variable X_3), and children (Variable X_2). The intervening model would suggest that the impact of grandparents' political attitudes on those of children is mediated by the attitudes of parents.

The important point to note about the preceding discussion is that whether testing for spurious or intervening effects, the predicted result of controlling for Variable X_3 is the same in each instance: The relationship between Variable X_1 and Variable X_2 will be substantially reduced. To determine whether a spurious or an intervening model most appropriately describes the relationship between the variables being examined, the researcher must rely on theory, past research, and—in many cases— good common sense. Statistical procedures cannot make these decisions.[5]

In the remainder of this chapter, three types of statistical controlling techniques are introduced. These are tabular control, partial correlation analysis, and the multivariate regression and logit techniques.

Controlling for a Third Variable with Tables

Cross-tabulation is a method of control useful when analyzing nominal or ordinal data.[6] Using cross-tabulation procedures, we reexamine the original relationship between the independent and dependent variables for each category of the control factor. The original correlation (represented by gamma, lambda, T_b, or whatever) is then compared with the correlation for each category of control, and any changes are said to result from the confounding influence of the third variable.

The best way to explain this technique of control is by example. Suppose we are

TABLE 10.1
Relationship between Party Identification and Public Attitudes toward Health-Care Reform

Support of Health-Care Reform		Party Identification: Republican	Democrat	Totals
	No	73	37	110
	Yes	67	123	190
Totals		140	160	300
		Gamma = .57 (rounded)		

Note: Hypothetical data.

interested in public attitudes toward health-care reform and the possible relationship between this and party identification. We might be testing the hypothesis that attitudes toward health-care reform are at least partially a function of a party affiliation: Democrats may be more supportive, Republicans less so. In order to test this hypothesis, assume further that through telephone interviewing, we have gathered information from 300 randomly selected voters in our city and that—for simplicity of illustration—their support for health-care reform is coded either as "no" or "yes." The relationship between party identification and support of health-care reform, as revealed in this survey, might appear as shown in Table 10.1.

The strength of the relationship between partisanship and support of health-care reform (as measured by the gamma coefficient) is found to be 0.57. Democrats are found to support reform in higher proportions than Republicans. There is, then, a moderately strong positive correlation between party identification and attitudes toward health-care reform existing among this sample. The question is whether this correlation will change when applying controls.

Assume further that in our survey, we asked respondents to indicate their level of income, and for ease of analysis, we have grouped everyone into just two income categories: "low" or "high." We may suspect that income, too, affects attitudes toward health-care reform. It may be that higher income respondents oppose health-care reform and that lower income respondents support such reform, regardless of party identification. In other words, perhaps it is level of income (or wealth) that is the more important factor in predicting attitudes toward reform of health care.

To test for this possibility, we may reexamine the original relationship between party identification and attitudes toward health care reform, *controlling for* levels of income (categorized simply as low or high). This technique actually divides the original table into two tables, one representing attitudes of low-income people and the other representing attitudes of high-income people. In this manner, the researcher can assess the impact of partisanship on health-care reform attitudes for each income group. When controlling in this manner, any number of possible results may be obtained. Table 10.2 illustrates one possibility.

TABLE 10.2

Relationship between Party Identification and Attitudes toward Health-Care Reform, Controlling for Income Levels (original relationship unchanged)

Support of Health-Care Reform	Income Level					
	Low			High		
	Republican	Democrat	Total	Republican	Democrat	Total
No	30	32	62	43	5	48
Yes	30	108	138	37	15	52
Total	60	140	200	80	20	100
	Gamma = .55 (rounded)			Gamma = 0.54 (rounded)		

NOTE: Hypothetical data.

It can be seen in Table 10.2 that regardless of level of income, Democrats are still more supportive, and Republicans less so, of health-care reform. In each control situation, the correlation coefficient (gamma) remains essentially unchanged from the original relationship (shown in Table 10.1).[7] We conclude in this instance that controlling for income levels has not affected the original relationship and that partisanship remains a factor of at least moderate importance in understanding attitudes toward health-care reform. Of course, other factors may also affect this relationship, and they too would have to be examined, but at least we can conclude that when controlling for income, the relationship between partisanship and attitudes toward health-care reform is *not spurious.*

Other results are possible when applying the technique of tabular control. Table 10.3 illustrates one of these. Here, it can be seen that the original correlation of 0.57 is eliminated when the control for level of income is applied. These results justify

TABLE 10.3

Relationship between Party Identification and Attitudes toward Health-Care Reform, Controlling for Income Levels (original relationship spurious)

Support of Health-Care Reform	Income Level					
	Low			High		
	Republican	Democrat	Total	Republican	Democrat	Total
No	9	21	30	64	16	80
Yes	51	119	170	16	4	20
Total	60	140	200	80	20	100
	Gamma = .0.00			Gamma = 0.00		

NOTE: Hypothetical data.

TABLE 10.4

Relationship between Party Identification and Attitudes toward Health-Care Reform, Controlling for Income Levels (original relationship altered)

Support of Health-Care Reform	Income Level					
	Low			**High**		
	Republican	**Democrat**	**Total**	**Republican**	**Democrat**	**Total**
No	33	27	60	40	10	50
Yes	27	113	140	40	10	50
Total	60	140	200	80	20	100
	Gamma = 0.67			Gamma = 0.00		

NOTE: Hypothetical data.

the conclusion that, when controlling for income, there is no relationship between partisanship and attitudes toward health-care reform. The original relationship (shown in Table 10.1) is said to be spurious. This finding, by the way, does not automatically lead to the conclusion that it is income that must be the cause of differing attitudes toward health-care reform. Before reaching such a conclusion, the relationship between income levels and attitudes toward health-care reform must be examined, *and* the results subjected to the same testing procedures as outlined previously.

Another possible result of tabular control is shown in Table 10.4, which illustrates an instance in which the association for one category of the control has been eliminated, but for the other has increased. How is this to be interpreted? Examining the data, it can be seen that for high-income respondents, partisanship is not a differentiating factor in terms of attitudes toward health-care reform (high-income Democrats and Republicans are evenly split in their attitudes). The correlation for this table is shown to be 0.00. For low-income respondents, however, partisanship is shown to be a very important factor. Low-income Democrats are far more likely to support health-care reform than low-income Republicans. The correlation of 0.67 indicates an even stronger relationship for this group than was originally noted (Table 10.1). It would be concluded, then, that party identification is *not* a factor helping to explain attitudes toward health-care reform for high-income people, but it is a very important factor explaining differences for low-income people.

One additional possible effect of cross-tabular control is illustrated in Table 10.5. Here, we see that the control has very dramatically altered the picture of the relationship between party identification and support for health-care reform as presented in Table 10.1. We see now that for low-income people, a much stronger correlation exists between party identification and health-care reform attitudes than was indicated in Table 10.1. Low-income Democrats are much more likely to support this measure than are low-income Republicans, and the correlation is shown to be 0.95.

TABLE 10.5

Relationship between Party Identification and Attitudes toward Health-Care Reform, Controlling for Income Levels (original relationship altered)

Support of Health-Care Reform	Income Level					
	Low			High		
	Republican	Democrat	Total	Republican	Democrat	Total
No	53	22	75	20	15	35
Yes	7	118	125	60	5	65
Total	60	140	200	80	20	100
	Gamma = 0.95			Gamma = −0.78		

NOTE: Hypothetical data.

For high-income respondents, the control shown in Table 10.5 has completely reversed the original relationship. Now, it can be seen that a strong relationship exists for high-income respondents, but this relationship is in a *negative* direction. In this instance, high-income Republicans are found to support health-care reform, high-income Democrats are in opposition. The correlation is shown to be −0.78. No doubt, the control in this instance would significantly alter the interpretation of the relationship between partisanship and attitudes toward health-care reform shown in Table 10.1.

It can be seen in these examples that controlling for the influence of a third factor can have any number of possible effects on an original relationship. The original relationship may be unchanged, or it may be altered in ways that substantially affect our interpretation of the results.

An interesting application of tabular control is provided by Barbara J. Burt-Way and Rita Mae Kelly, in their examination of the relationship between gender and political ambition of certain state and local elected officials.[8] One of their tables is presented in Table 10.6, in which they look at the relationship between level of political ambition and gender, controlling for type of elected official (local or state).

Table 10.6 shows that men have slightly more progressive ambitions than do women, and that the control for type of official (local or state) only slightly effects this relationship. The relationship between gender and ambition is somewhat stronger for state legislators than for officials from local jurisdictions. As Burt-Way and Kelly conclude, "It is evident that men have progressive ambition at a slightly higher rate than women."[9]

Another interesting use of tabular control is presented in David Hadwiger's examination of the relationship between voting turnout, election outcome, and citizen-sponsored ballot measures (referendums or initiatives) in a study of 276 California cities.[10] A portion of Hadwiger's results is shown in Table 10.7.

As Table 10.7 shows, inverse relationships are found between voter turnout and election outcome when controlling for type of citizen-sponsored measures. Refer-

TABLE 10.6
Levels of Political Ambition

	Local Officials		State Legislators	
Level of Political Ambition	**Men (n = 160) (%)**	**Women (n = 66) (%)**	**Men (n = 16) (%)**	**Women (n = 19) (%)**
Discrete	11.9	15.2	0.0	0.0
Static	46.8	56.1	56.3	68.4
Uncertain Progressive	6.9	7.6	31.2	21.1
Progressive	34.4	21.1	12.5	10.5
		Gamma = .230		Gamma = .301

NOTE: "Discrete" refers to those officeholders who stated they had definitely decided not to run for any office. "Static" refers to those who definitely planned to run for the same office, but who had no aspirations for higher office. "Uncertain Progressive" politicians were those who said they would consider higher office but had not decided whether to run. "Progressive" politicians were those stating they definitely will run for a higher office and have an office in mind.

SOURCE: Barbara J. Burt-Way and Rita Mae Kelly, "Gender and Sustaining Political Ambition: A Study of Arizona Elected Officials," *Western Political Quarterly* (March, 1992), 15.

endums are likely to *succeed* when turnout is high (over 45%); initiatives, on the other hand, are likely to *fail* in high-turnout elections. As Hadwiger concludes, these results "raise the interesting possibility that voters in high turnout elections are not more likely to vote against ballot measures, but rather are more likely to vote against the petitioners and for the status quo."[11]

Partial Correlation

Cross-tabulation control procedures are very useful, in that they allow us to examine the correlation between two variables for each level of the control variable. Thus,

TABLE 10.7
Turnout, Type of Measure, and Election Outcome

	Type of Citizen-Sponsored Ballot					
	Referendum: Turnout (%)			Initiative: Turnout (%)		
Outcome	**Low**	**Moderate**	**High**	**Low**	**Moderate**	**High**
Win	38.5 (5)	50.0 (2)	67.0 (2)	61.0 (11)	31.0 (5)	35.0 (7)
Lose	61.5 (8)	50.0 (2)	33.0 (1)	39.0 (7)	69.0 (11)	65.0 (13)

NOTE: Numbers in parentheses refer to the number of measures.

SOURCE: Adapted from David Hadwiger, "Money, Turnout, and Ballot Measure Success in California Cities," *Western Political Quarterly* (June, 1992), 542.

we are able to observe nuances in the relationships that would otherwise be undetected. In addition, cross-tabulation procedures may be used with any level of data, although it is most common to see the procedure used with nominal and ordinal data.

On the other hand, cross-tabulation procedures have two major disadvantages. First, cross-tabulation becomes very cumbersome when dealing with a control variable of several categories or especially when dealing with several control variables at the same time. In the aforementioned examples, we were always examining a single control variable having only two categories of control. Interpretation in such cases is relatively straightforward. Imagine, however, applying three or four control variables, each having several categories. A dozen or more tables might be generated, rendering the interpretation of such results quite complex and tedious.

More important, the application of cross-tabulation is limited by the size of the sample. Cross-tabulation divides the sample into smaller and smaller subsamples for each category of control. It does not take long, using this procedure, to exhaust all cases. Unless the number of cases is very large, it is difficult to apply more than two or three cross-tabulation controls at the same time.

A second method of control is the technique known as **partial correlation.** The partial-correlation technique is limited to interval-level data. However, it is not limited by sample size, and many controls can be applied even when the total number of observations is relatively small.

The partial-correlation technique extends the logic of simple regression analysis discussed in Chapter 9. There, we used knowledge of an independent variable (percentage of a state's population graduating from high school) to predict values of a dependent variable (voting turnout in the 1992 presidential election). We noted in Chapter 9 that the coefficient of determination (r^2) tells us the amount of variance reduction produced by the regression routine, and the r^2 for the analysis conducted in Chapter 9 was found to be 0.33.

Although education levels explained about one third of the variance in turnout rates, clearly, much variance remains unexplained. In Chapter 9, we called the amount of variance remaining in the dependent variable, after accounting for the independent variable, the "unexplained variance." Often, this value is termed the *residual* value. Residuals represent the deviations between the actual and the predicted values of the dependent variable. Residuals are helpful in understanding the concept of the partial correlation coefficient.

Assume that we are interested in the relationship between X_1 and X_2 but believe that a third factor, X_3, may also affect this relationship. It may be that we are testing a *spurious* model similar to that depicted in Figure 10.1A where we are suggesting that the association between X_1 and X_2 may really result from the fact that the two are related to X_3. The partial correlation routine tests for this by correlating the residuals of the regressions of X_1 on X_3 and X_2 on X_3. That is, two regression equations are generated: one predicting the values of X_1 based on X_3, the other predicting the values of X_2 based on X_3. The residual values that result represent the variation in both X_2 and X_1 that is unexplained by X_3. The correlation of these residuals, then, represents the correlation of X_2 and X_1, controlling for the effect of X_3

on each. The result is the partial correlation between X_1 and X_2, controlling for X_3.

A second way to think of the partial correlation coefficient is as an average of all the simple correlation coefficients between X_2 and X_1 that would result if the correlations were calculated for each value of X_3. For each value of X_3, a regression line could be plotted and a correlation coefficient calculated for the appropriate values of X_2 and X_1. The partial correlation coefficient is equivalent to the weighted average that would result from each of these separate simple correlations.[12]

Regardless of which interpretation is placed on the partial correlation coefficient, its computational formula may be presented as

$$rX_1 X_2 . X_3 = \frac{(rX_1 X_2) - (rX_1 X_3)(rX_2 X_3)}{\sqrt{1 - r^2 X_1 X_3}\ \sqrt{1 - r^2 X_2 X_3}}$$

Instead, the partial correlation may be defined more simply as

$$r_{12.3} = \frac{r_{12} - (r_{13})(r_{23})}{\sqrt{1 - r_{13}^2}\ \sqrt{1 - r_{23}^2}}$$

where X_1 and X_2 = dependent and independent variables
X_3 = control variable

In both of these formulas, the symbol to the right of the dot represents the control variable. Thus $r_{12.3}$ represents the partial correlation between X_1 and X_2, controlling for X_3.

An Illustration of Partial r

By way of illustration, consider the following hypothetical example. Assume that we are interested in the relationship between income and attitudes of racial tolerance. From a sample of 2,000 adults, we may have found a simple correlation of .40 between the two variables. Those with higher incomes were found to be more tolerant. However, we suspect that some other factor may be responsible for this apparent correlation. Having also collected information on education, the **correlation matrix** for the three variables might appear as follows:

	X_1 (racial tolerance)	X_2 (income)	X_3 (education)
X_1 (racial tolerance)	1.0		
X_2 (income)	0.40	1.0	
X_3 (education)	0.50	0.60	1.0

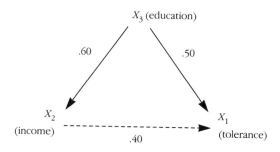

FIGURE 10.2
Proposed Three-Variable Model

We see that education is related to both variables, so, again, we may be dealing with a possible spurious situation. In this instance, the model we are testing might appear as shown in Figure 10.2.

Applying the formula, we see that the partial correlation between income and racial tolerance, controlling for education, is

$$r_{1\,2.3} = \frac{r_{12} - (r_{13})(r_{23})}{\sqrt{1 - r_{13}^2}\ \sqrt{1 - r_{23}^2}}$$

$$= \frac{0.4 - (0.5)(0.6)}{\sqrt{1 - 0.5^2}\ \sqrt{1 - 0.6^2}}$$

$$= 0.14$$

Here, the correlation between income and racial tolerance has been substantially reduced. In this hypothetical example, we would conclude that the relationship between income and racial tolerance is largely spurious. The important factor in each instance (at least until additional analysis indicates otherwise) is education. Those with higher education levels have higher incomes and are more racially tolerant.

One additional fact should be observed from this example of the calculation of the partial correlation coefficient. Examining the formula, it can be seen that the numerator is obtained by finding the value of the simple correlation coefficient between the independent and dependent variables (r_{12}) and then subtracting from that value the product of the simple correlation coefficients between the control variable and the independent variable (r_{23}) and the control variable and the dependent variable (r_{13}). From this calculation, it can be inferred that whenever the value of the product of the correlations between the control variable and the independent and dependent variables approximates the value of the correlation between the independent and the dependent variables, the partial correlation between the independent and the dependent variables will be reduced accordingly. If the two values are exactly the same, the partial correlation coefficient will be zero because $r_{12} - (r_{13}) (r_{23})$ would be equal to zero. In this example, had the simple correlation between income and tolerance been .30 (rather than .40), the partial correlation coefficient would have been 0.00. These relationships can assist in gaining a rough estimation of the magnitude of the partial correlation coefficient before actually calculating its value.

We have been discussing to this point the partial correlation between an independent variable and a dependent variable, controlling for one control variable. This value is also termed the *first-order partial correlation coefficient,* to indicate that only one variable is being controlled. Squaring the first-order partial correlation coefficient $(r^2_{12.3})$, we obtain a value analogous in interpretation to r^2. This value, known as the partial coefficient of determination, represents the variation in the dependent variable explained by the independent variable, when controlling for the third factor.

As was the case with cross-tabulation, it is possible, using partial correlation techniques, to control for more than one variable at a time. When controlling for the effects of two variables, the formula for the partial correlation coefficient is

$$r_{12.34} = \frac{r_{12.3} - (r_{14.3})(r_{24.3})}{\sqrt{1 - r^2_{14.3}} \ \sqrt{1 - r^2_{24.3}}}$$

By extension, it is possible to control for three, four, or more variables at the same time. It is important to remember, however, that no matter how many controls are attempted, the partial correlation routine will generate only one value. This differs from the cross-tabulation procedure, where a separate value is generated for each category of control.

Some Uses of Partial Correlation

An especially intriguing use of partial correlation analysis is provided by Arthur A. Goldsmith, in his examination of the factors related to democratization.[13] Taking as his units of analysis eighty-four "less developed countries" Goldsmith tests the hypothesis that change toward democracy will be associated with positive economic consequences. As he puts it, "since the Enlightenment, [this line of reasoning] has insisted that democracy has an economic edge over autocracy."[14] Goldsmith develops a measure of change toward democracy in these eight-four countries over the 1970s and 1980s, and he correlates this measure with various measures of economic health, controlling for per capita gross national product (GNP). His results are shown in Table 10.8.

Surprisingly, Goldsmith finds very little association between democratization and these economic variables, when controlling for GNP. (In addition, many of the rela-

TABLE 10.8

Partial Correlations with Freedom Change (controlled for per capita GNP)

Dependent Variable	Partial r	N	Interpretation
Country credit rating	.104	58	Increase in democracy is associated with rising credit risk (not predicted)
Political risk index	.232	26	Increase in democracy is associated with rising political risks for multinational corporations (not predicted)
General government consumption	−0.25	62	Increase in democracy is associated with rising public consumption (not predicted)
Domestic savings rate	.089	73	Increase in democracy is associated with falling savings rates (not predicted)
Export ratio	−.087	68	Increase in democracy is associated with rising exports (predicted)

Source: Arthur A. Goldsmith, "Political Freedom and the Business Climate: Outlook for Development in Newly Democratizing States," *Social Science Quarterly* 75 (March, 1994), 122.

tionships are in the wrong direction.) As he concludes, "On balance the statistical analysis fails to support the . . . opinion that establishing representative, constitutional government has advantages in fostering a favorable business climate. . . . Their greater openness and legitimacy do not appear, by themselves, to give democratizing regimes any important economic edge."[15]

Another interesting use of partial correlation analysis is provided by Alan I. Abramowitz.[16] Abramowitz's study on the relationship between party identification and a number of policy attitudes among white voters in the United States was reviewed in Chapter 9, where we looked there at the simple correlation coefficients he presented. In that same article, Abramowitz reexamined the correlations between party identification (which, it will be recalled, is a seven-point scale ranging from "Strong Democrat" to "Strong Republican") and each of these various policy attitudes, measured while *controlling for all other attitudes*. The results are shown in Table 10.9.

As shown in Table 10.9, racial attitudes have very little impact on party identification for these various groups of white voters. When controlling for the other factors, the correlation between "racial issues" and the party-identification variable is reduced to almost zero in every case. However, this reduction is not true for some other issue areas, such as social welfare. As Abramowitz concludes, "The data . . . show that attitudes toward racial issues were unrelated to party identification after controlling for attitudes toward other types of issues. . . . In contrast, attitudes toward traditional social welfare issues were strongly related to party identification after controlling for attitudes toward other types of issues."[17]

TABLE 10.9

Partial Correlations between Issues and Party Identification among Whites by Demographic Characteristics in 1988

	Social Welfare Issues	Racial Issues	Defense Issues	Lifestyle Issues	Death Penalty	School Prayer
All whites ($n = 1,103$)	.32**	.01	.16**	.01	.09**	−.05
Age						
17–44 ($n = 638$)	.27**	.04	.20**	.02	.09*	.00
45 or older ($n = 465$)	.35**	.03	.13**	−.00	.09*	−.08*
Region						
North ($n = 791$)	.34**	.04	.19**	−.00	.07*	−.05
South ($n = 312$)	.29**	−.05	.14**	−.01	.13**	.02
Racial context						
Blacks < 15% ($n = 730$)	.30**	−.01	.22**	.01	.11**	−.08*
Blacks > 15% ($n = 373$)	.34**	.03	.05	−.04	.07	.01
Education						
High school ($n = 561$)	.22**	.03	.14**	−.02	.06	−.05
Some college ($n = 269$)	.35**	.04	.14*	.03	.00	−.04
Graduated college ($n = 255$)	.30**	.02	.24**	.04	.23**	.02

* $p < .05$.

** $p < .01$.

Note: Coefficients are partial correlations between seven-point party identification scale and each issue scale controlling for all other issues. Significance levels are based on one-tailed t-test.

Source: Alan I. Abramowitz, "Issue Evolution Reconsidered: Racial Attitudes and Partisanship in the U.S. Electorate," *American Journal of Political Science* 38 (February, 1994), 14. Data source: American National Election Study, 1988.

MULTIVARIATE ANALYSIS

Up to this point, we have been discussing primarily the isolated impact of a single independent variable on a dependent variable. Control techniques (either cross-tabulation or partial correlation analysis) are useful to help clarify this relationship.

In addition, researchers are often interested in assessing the *relative* and *combined* impacts of a number of independent variables on a dependent variable. We would like to know the relative and combined impacts of all those variables related to voting turnout, or legislators' voting patterns, or per-capita spending on welfare among the states, and so forth. The classification of techniques useful for such exploration is *multivariate analysis,* which, as used here, includes multiple regression, multiple correlation, and logit techniques.

Multiple Regression

The general regression equation for multivariate analysis can be presented as an extension of the simple regression equation. In the case of two independent variables (X_1 and X_2), the multiple regression equation can be presented as

$$Y_p = a + b_1 X_1 + b_2 X_2$$

where Y_p = predicted values of Y
$\quad\quad a$ = Y intercept value
$\quad\quad b_1 X_1$ = partial regression of Y and X_1, holding X_2 constant
$\quad\quad b_2 X_2$ = partial regression of Y and X_2, holding X_1 constant

The *b* values generated by the multiple-regression routine are known as *partial slopes* because they represent the amount of change in the dependent variable associated with each independent variable, holding all other independent variables constant. The calculation of each constant is relatively straightforward:

$$a = \bar{Y} - (b_1 \bar{X}_1 + b_2 \bar{X}_2)$$

$$b_1 = \left(\frac{SY}{SX_1} \right) \frac{rYX_1 - rYX_2 \, rX_1 X_2}{1 - r^2 X_1 X_2}$$

$$b_2 = \left(\frac{SY}{SX_2} \right) \frac{rYX_2 - rYX_1 \, rX_1 X_2}{1 - r^2 X_1 X_2}$$

As shown, the regression estimates can all be calculated if we know the mean scores, standard deviations (represented by the symbol "S" in above formulas) and simple correlation coefficients for all the variables.

The partial slope of each independent variable generated through this routine is interpreted as the amount of expected change in the dependent variable (Y) associated with a one-unit change in the independent variable, holding constant (controlling for) all other independent variables. The regression equation represents our best estimate of the values of the dependent variable for any combination of values of the independent variables.

The partial slopes also allow us to compare the importance of the independent variables. If two subsamples of a population are being examined (such as men and women), the relative magnitudes of the partial slopes generated by separate regression equations for each subpopulation indicate the relative strength of each independent variable. The higher the value in the partial slope, the more important is that variable in explaining the dependent variable for the particular subpopulation.

If we wish to compare the relative impact of the various independent variables with each other, however, the partial slopes are of little use. This is because the variables in the equation may have been measured according to different scale values. One variable may be measured in terms of dollars, another in years of education, and still another in terms of grade point averages. With such disparate values, it makes little sense to compare the impact of a unit change of one variable with the impact of a unit change of another.

Therefore, if we wish to assess the relative importance of each predictive variable in a single regression equation, we make use of a statistic known as the **beta weight.** The beta weight (symbolized as β) is simply the slope that would be obtained if all variables were standardized; it measures change in the dependent variable in terms of standard deviation units for each of the independent variables, controlling for all others. The beta weight is thus known as the **standardized partial regression coefficient,** and its major advantage lies in allowing comparison of the *relative* impact of change in the independent variables on change in the dependent variable.

The beta weight for each independent variable is calculated by multiplying the partial slope by the ratio of the standard deviation of the independent variable to that of the dependent variable. In the case of two independent variables, X_1 and X_2, the beta coefficients β_1 and β_2 would be calculated as

$$\beta_1 = \left(\frac{SX_1}{SY} \right) b_1$$

$$\beta_2 = \left(\frac{SX_2}{SY} \right) b_2$$

The Multiple Correlation Coefficient

As was the case when considering the simple correlation coefficient, the **coefficient of multiple determination** (R^2) represents the proportion of the variance in the dependent variable explained by all the independent variables. R^2 is typically defined as the sum of the remaining variance in the dependent variable, which is explained by each independent variable after accounting for the influence of every other independent variable. In the case of two independent variables, the first variable (X_1) explains all the variance it can in the dependent variable, and the second variable (X_2) then explains all the remaining variance in Y that it can explain. The amount of variance in the dependent variable explained by X_1 is, as we have seen before, r^2yx_1.

The amount of remaining variance explained by X_2 will be expressed as the product of the variance in Y explained by X_2, controlling for X_1, multiplied by the proportion of variance in Y left unexplained by X_1.

In the case of two independent variables, these relationships can be expressed as

$$R^2_{y.x_1x_2} = r^2_{yx_1} + (r^2_{yx_2.x_1})(1 - r^2_{yx_1})$$

$$\begin{pmatrix} \text{total variance} \\ \text{in } Y \text{ explained} \\ \text{by } X_1 \text{ and } X_2 \end{pmatrix} = \begin{pmatrix} \text{proportion of} \\ \text{variance in } Y \\ \text{explained by} \\ X_1 \end{pmatrix} + \begin{pmatrix} \text{proportion of} \\ \text{variance in } Y \\ \text{explained by } X_2, \\ \text{in addition to} \\ \text{that explained} \\ \text{by } X_1 \end{pmatrix} \begin{pmatrix} \text{amount of} \\ \text{variance left} \\ \text{unexplained} \\ \text{by } X_1 \end{pmatrix}$$

It should be noted that the symbol for R^2 has only one character to the left of the dot. This is to signify that, in this case, the variable Y is the dependent variable and X_1 and X_2 are the independent variables. A more general symbol for R^2 is $R^2_{1.234...i}$, where variable 1 is the dependent variable and all those to the right are considered to be independent variables. R^2, as mentioned previously, is known as the coefficient of multiple determination. It ranges in value from 0.00 to $+1.00$. The multiple correlation coefficient (symbolized as R) is the positive square root of R^2. As was the case with r, R is a measure of how well actual values of Y fit with those predicted by the (in this case, multiple) regression equation.

Some Uses of Multiple Regression and Correlation

An interesting use of multiple regression and correlation is provided by Arthur H. Miller, Vicki L. Hesli, and William M. Reisinger, in their examination of those variables related to attitudes toward political reforms of a democratic nature in the former USSR.[18] Using survey data collected in Russia, Ukraine, and Lithuania in 1990–1992, the authors developed regression equations for data collected both in 1991 and in 1992, as presented in Table 10.10.

It can be seen that age, education, and gender are significantly related to proreform attitudes for both years (1991 and 1992), and that age clearly is the most important (beta of $-.276$ in 1991 and $-.259$ in 1992). As the authors conclude, "The propensity of younger people to be relatively more supportive of political change is apparent in both 1991 and 1992."[19] The total amount of variance in the reform measure is shown by the R^2 to be .15 in 1991 and .11 in 1992.[20]

Another interesting use of multiple regression and correlation is provided by Malcolm D. Holmes and his co-authors, who looked at these variables related to the severity of sentencing of felony defendants in El Paso, Texas.[21] Their results are shown in Table 10.11.

TABLE 10.10

Regression Equation Predicting Support for Political Reform

Independent Variables	1991		1992	
	b	**Beta**	**b**	**Beta**
Life satisfaction[a]	−.298**	−.070	.161*	.043
	(.029)		(.030)	
Age	−.058**	−.276	−.053**	−.259
	(.001)		(.002)	
Education	.279**	.160	.180**	.106
	(.013)		(.014)	
Gender[b]	.415**	.061	.446*	.069
	(.047)		(.051)	
Rural residence	−.755**	−.096	.021	.003
	(.056)		(.061)	
Income	.000	.011	.000	.071
	(.000)		(.000)	
Ethnicity				
Ukrainian	.124	.016	.195	.027
	(.055)		(.058)	
Lithuanian	2.74**	.112	.619*	.037
	(.168)		(.180)	
Constant	11.41		9.57	
Adjusted R^2	.15		.11	
Number of cases	2,188		1,936	

*$p < .01$.

**$p < .001$.

[a] Satisfied = high.

[b] Male = high.

NOTE: The proreform index ranges from 1 to 17, with high values indicating greater support for rapid reform. Standard errors are in parentheses.

SOURCE: Arthur H. Miller, Vickie L. Hesli, and William M. Reisinger, "Reassessing Mass Support for Political and Economic Change in the Former USSR," *American Political Science Review* 88 (June, 1994), 407. Data source: University of Iowa's Post-Soviet Citizen Surveys.

From these results, it can be seen that the severity of the conviction charge, the number of prior felony convictions, and the use of a firearm all are positively related to severity of sentence. Looking at ethnicity of judges, the authors concluded that "clearly Hispanic judges sentence Anglo and Hispanic defendants similarly, and Anglo judges give Hispanic defendants sentences the same as those awarded by Hispanic judges."[22] The multiple R^2 for this set of data (.52) shows that these variables account for slightly more than half of the variation in sentencing severity for this group of defendants.

TABLE 10.11

Unstandardized Coefficients, Standard Errors, and Standardized Coefficients for Regression of Sentence Severity on Legal, Resource, and Status Variables

Independent Variables	Unstandardized Coefficients	Standard Errors	Standardized Coefficients (beta weights)
Conviction charge severeity	1.67***	0.45	.17
Number of conviction charges	0.11	0.90	.01
Number of prior felony convictions	4.03***	0.38	.54
Degree of physical injury to victim	1.40	0.83	.08
Use of a firearm	5.24	2.06	.12
Pretrial release	−3.06***	0.91	−.18
Private attorney	−0.01	0.94	.00
Age of defendant	0.12**	0.04	.13
Female defendant	−0.60	1.55	−.02
Anglo judge–Anglo defendant[a]	—	—	—
Anglo judge–Hispanic defendant	3.98**	1.28	.23
Hispanic judge–Anglo defendant	4.15*	2.01	.11
Hispanic judge–Hispanic defendant	5.15***	1.42	.26
Constant	−7.14		
$R^2 = .52$			

* $p < .05$.

** $p < .01$.

*** $p < .001$.

[a] Category excluded from this set of dummy variables, which serves as the baseline for interpreting coefficients for included categories.

SOURCE: Malcolm D. Holmes, Harmon M. Hosch, Howard C. Daudistel, Dolores A. Perez, and Joseph B. Graves, "Judges' Ethnicity and Minority Sentencing: Evidence Concerning Hispanics," *Social Science Quarterly* 74 (September, 1993), 501.

Logistic Regression

Regression analysis has much theoretical and descriptive appeal. It has recently been described by one observer as "the most utilized tool of statistical inference by political scientists."[23] On the other hand, it also has been called "one of the most abused statistical techniques in the social sciences."[24] The model as described in this book thus far (called the "ordinary least squares linear regression model"—or OLS for short) makes a host of assumptions about the data, and these assumptions must be met if the technique is to be used appropriately.[25] While arguably some of these assumptions may be violated without much harm, others are critical, and when they are not met, this lack may lead to erroneous and misleading results.[26]

One of the most important of these assumptions is that the dependent variable is a continuous, interval measure. However, many of the variables that political and policy analysts are interested in explaining are dichotomous or multicategory nonordered measures. Examples are party identification (measured as Democrat, Republican, Independent), attitudes toward term limitations for members of Congress (measured as "favor" or "oppose"), and opinions about the type of recycling option that some community should adopt (e.g., "curbside pick-up," "several neighborhood drop-off points," or "a single central-city collection center"). All of these are qualitative measures, and the application of the OLS regression model can lead to mistaken and even absurd conclusions.

A simple example will illustrate one of the problems of using OLS linear regression techniques with dichotomous dependent variables. In its 1992 American National Election Study, the ICPSR asked respondents for whom they voted for president. Of the total sample, 1,357 said they voted either for George Bush or Bill Clinton. That survey also asked respondents to place themselves on a 7-point liberal or conservative scale (ranging from "extremely liberal" to "extremely conservative") and also placed respondents on a 7-point strength of partisanship variable, ranging from "Strong Democrat" to "Strong Republican." Taking the voting decision as the dependent variable and coding a vote for Bush as "0" and a vote for Clinton as "1" and coding the two independent variables on scales of from 1 to 7, the resulting OLS regression equation becomes:

$$Y_p = 1.4 - .07(X_1) - .15(X_2)$$

$$\text{where} \quad Y_p = \text{predicted vote}$$
$$(0 = \text{Bush})$$
$$(1 = \text{Clinton})$$
$$X_1 = \text{ideology, a scale ranging from}$$
$$1 = \text{extremely liberal to}$$
$$7 = \text{extremely conservative}$$
$$X_2 = \text{Strength of party identification,}$$
$$\text{a scale ranging from}$$
$$1 = \text{Strong Democrat to}$$
$$7 = \text{Strong Republican}$$

Solving this equation for the extreme values of the independent variables demonstrates the nonsensical predictions that can result. As an example, the predicted vote score for an individual who is "extremely liberal" (coded as 1) and a "Strong Democrat" (coded as 1) would be 1.18. Likewise, an individual who is "extremely conservative" (coded as 7) and a "Strong Republican" (coded as 7) would have a predicted vote score of −0.14. However, both of these predicted scores (1.18 and −0.14) fall outside the range of possible scores on this value (which ranged from "0" for a Bush vote to "1" for a Clinton vote). Obviously, it is impossible for anyone's score to be below 0.0 or above 1.0 on this voting choice measure, yet this is what would be predicted for these individuals, based on the OLS linear regression model generated for this set of data.

Models other than that assumed by linear regression, then, are appropriate under particular circumstances. Logistic regression is an often-used technique designed to test for nonlinear models.[27] *Logit* (logistic regression) models yield coefficients, called "maximum likelihood estimates" (MLEs), that look like regression coefficients. MLEs, however, are not as simply interpreted as regression coefficients. In logit analysis, the dependent variable is measured as the natural log of the ratio of the probability that the dependent variable is 1.0 to the probability of it being .00 (a measure known as the *log odds*). A positive MLE score for any variable means that this variable increases the log odds of an event occurring; a negative value of MLE means that the variable decreases the log odds of occurrence.

Consider again the example presented previously, where regression analysis was used to predict the expected vote for Clinton or Bush in the 1992 presidential election, based on the independent variables, strength of party identification, and degree of liberalism/conservatism. The corresponding logistic regression equation for these same variables is shown here:[28]

$$L_p = 7.2 - .97(X_1) - .71(X_2)$$

where X_1 = Ideology (as defined previously)
X_2 = Strength of party identification (as defined previously)

Because the signs of both coefficients are negative, the results can be interpreted as showing that being conservative and being strongly Republican both decrease the log odds of voting for Clinton.

One of the attractive features of logit analysis is that it permits the analyst to estimate probabilities of occurrence. Solving the logit equation developed here for those who are extremely liberal (coded as "1"), and who consider themselves strong Democrats (coded as "1") yields the following result:

$$L_p = 7.2 - .97(1) - .71(1)$$
$$= 5.52$$

Translating this number back to the probability of voting for Clinton (which was coded as "1") is accomplished by the following formula:

$$P_{y = 1} = \frac{e^{5.52}}{1 + e^{5.52}}$$

where e = a value known as Euler's constant, always set at 2.71828

$$P_{y = 1} = \frac{103.9437}{1 + 103.9437}$$

$$= .9905 \text{ (rounded)}$$

Interpreted, this means that those persons who are extremely liberal and consider themselves strong Democrats have a 99 percent chance of voting for Clinton. Similarly, those who are extremely conservative (coded as 7) and consider themselves strong Republicans would be shown to have less than a 1 percent chance of voting for Clinton. In this manner, logit analysis permits the estimation of the probability of an event occurring for any combination of predictor variables.

A number of measures of how well the logit equation fits the data have been developed. One of these is to compare the predicted values to actual values and then to calculate the *proportion of cases correctly predicted.*[29] The equation presented previously correctly predicts 88.38 percent of voter choice, as revealed in the 1992 American National Election Survey.

Most computer programs also will calculate a statistic known as "pseudo-R^2." One commonly used pseudo-R^2 is represented by the following formula:[30]

$$\text{pseudo-}R^2 = c/(N + c)$$

where c = the Chi-Square value of the equation
N = number of cases

Pseudo-R^2 ranges between 0 and 1.0, approaching 1.0 as the quality of the model improves.

Logistic regression analysis of dichotomies, as discussed previously, is a special case of multicategory nominal dependent variables. The model can be extended to the case of dependent variables with multiple categories (*polytomous* dependent variables). In such a case, the logistic coefficients that result are interpreted as the effect of each independent variable on categories of the dependent variable, relative to one category selected as the default, or reference, category.

Some Uses of Logit Analysis

Two recently published studies well illustrate the use of logit analysis. In the first, Todd Donovan and Joseph R. Snipp examined public support for the initiative to limit the number of terms that California legislators may serve (known in California as "Proposition 140").[31] Donovan and Snipp tested several hypotheses about the relationship between various group memberships and support for this proposition. Specifically, they proposed that support for term limitations would have more support "among members of groups least represented by the status-quo legislature."[32] Their logistic regression results (based on telephone polls of California voters) are shown in Table 10.12.

As shown in Table 10.12, three models influencing voter support for term limitation actually were tested. The overall fit of each model is statistically significant (as revealed by the chi-square values). They find, as assumed, that younger voters and women were more likely to indicate support for term limitations. However, as they say, "the underrepresentation hypothesis is not supported by the [negative] coefficient for Hispanic voters."[33] Their results also show partisan contacts to be signifi-

TABLE 10.12

Factors Influencing Support for California's Term Limitation Proposition 140 Maximum Likelihood Estimates (MLE)

Variable	Model 1	Model 2	Model 3
Intercept	.640*	.541	.780*
	(.499)	(.508)	(.513)
Age	−.018***	−.018***	−.019***
	(.007)	(.007)	(.007)
Female	.346*	.356*	.390*
	(.236)	(.237)	(.241)
Black	−.123	−.001	−.185
	(.675)	(.689)	(.681)
Hispanic	−.316	−.306	−.338
	(.377)	(.377)	(.381)
Republican	.504**	.646***	.397*
	(.243)	(.272)	(.252)
Conservative		−.225	
		(.331)	
Age × strength of party attachment		.007	
		(.007)	
Media information			−.149
			(.141)
Contacted by Democrats			−1.154*
			(.760)
Contacted by Republicans			.871**
			(.488)
N	324	324	324
Model chi-square (improvement)	12.7**	14.2**	19.5**
Pseudo R^2	.562	.561	.558

* $p < .10$ (one-tail).

** $p < .05$ (one-tail).

*** $p < .01$ (one-tail).

NOTE: Estimated by logistic regression with data from the Oct. 30, 1990, Field Poll. Dependent variable = 1 if respondent intended to vote in favor of Prop. 140, 0 if otherwise. Values in parentheses are standard errors of the MLE. Model 1 chi-square based of 5 d.f., Model 2 on 7 d.f., Model 3 on 9 d.f. Pseudo R^2 is constructed with the Aldrich and Nelson (1984, 55–57) formula.

SOURCE: Todd Donovan and Joseph R. Snipp, "Support for Legislative Term Limitations in California: Group Representation, Partisanship, and Campaign Information," *Journal of Politics* 56 (May, 1994), 498.

cantly related to attitudes toward term limitations. They say, "voters who have been contacted by the Democratic party are less likely to support [term limitations], while voters contacted by the Republicans are more likely [to do so]."[34]

The second example reviewed here is a study by Donald R. Songer, Sue Davis,

TABLE 10.13
Logit Coefficients for the Likelihood of a Liberal Vote on Obscenity Cases,
1981–1990

Independent Variables	MLE	SE
Intercept	−4.672	
Region	1.240	0.52**
Appointing president	1.118	0.26***
Bookstore	3.892	0.96***
Individual	−1.885	0.56***
Film	−1.408	0.49**
Prior	1.592	0.58***
Adult	3.958	1.10***
Magazine	−1.503	0.51**
Judge gender	−0.709	0.85

*Significant at .05.

**Significant at .01.

***Significant at .001.

NOTE: Percentage categorized correctly = 86.2% (false positive = 20%; false negative = 11.6%).
Reduction in error = 53.2%. $-2 \times LLR$ = 144.92. Model chi square = 109.93, df = 9, $p < .0001$.
Number of cases = 210, mean of dependent variable = .295.

SOURCE: Donald R. Songer, Sue Davis, and Susan Haire, "A Reappraisal of Diversification in the
Federal Courts: Gender Effects in the Courts of Appeals," *Journal of Politics* 56 (May, 1994), 433.

and Susan Haire, in which they examined effects on decisions by federal appellate
judges.[35] In general, Songer, Davis, and Haire hypothesize that the decisions of
women judges "will be more liberal than their male counterparts."[36] They looked
at decisions of all regular judges of the United States Courts of Appeals from 1981
to 1990 in the areas of search and seizure, employment discrimination, and obscenity cases. Table 10.13 shows their logistic results for obscenity cases.

First, it can be seen that the model does a very good job of predicting the votes
of judges. Slightly over 86 percent of the 210 decisions are correctly predicted. Gender of the judge, however, is shown to *not* be an important variable. As the authors
conclude, "the gender of the judge appears to have no effect on the likelihood of a
liberal vote when other factors are taken into account. The coefficient for gender
[−0.709] is small and statistically insignificant."[37]

SUMMARY

A variety of methods of statistical control have been discussed in this chapter. These
methods are often used in nonexperimental research situations (such as survey research). The point has been stressed here (as it was also in Chapter 3) that the true
experiment is superior in ascertaining the direction of causation.

Nonetheless, survey research has advantages of its own, and it is appropriate to point out these advantages in this concluding section. Perhaps the greatest advantage of survey research is its facilitation of the selection of a representative sample to be studied. Whatever results may be obtained from an experimental study of drug-education programs in a local school system or of decision making by a particular city council may apply only to that school system and that city council. These results are not necessarily generalizable to any other school system or any other city council. Only at the greatest expense and trouble could even one experimental and one control group randomly selected from some large population (such as all high school students or all city council members) be assembled in one location for the purpose of participating in a true experimental research situation. However, at a reasonable cost, we can interview a random sample of the population (high school students, city council members, or even the American electorate), and we can then generalize from the results of that sample to the entire population. So, survey research facilitates the selection of a representative sample and enhances our ability to generalize from that sample to a whole population.

The second advantage flowing from this is expense. Surveys may be less costly than a true experiment would be. This is especially true if interviews are solicited by phone or by mail.

Finally, as pointed out by Simon and Burstein, in survey research "you can get closer to the 'real' . . . variables than with a laboratory experiment."[38] By this, it is meant that survey research, unlike laboratory research, does not construct an artificial situation—people are not asked to play roles. In survey research, we deal with people as they are—poor, rich; employed, unemployed; Democrat, Republican; politically active, politically inactive; and so forth. Taking people as they really are provides insights that are impossible in a simulated laboratory situation.

Although methods of statistical control are inferior to those used in the true experimental situation when it comes to assessing the extent and direction of causation, these methods have many advantages of their own. Using these techniques, researchers can, at a reasonable cost, reach reasonable inferences of causality, and through proper sampling techniques, they can generalize these conclusions to the larger population. Besides, many problems and situations that we wish to study simply are not amenable to experimental manipulation. As one student of social science research has put it, "the most important social scientific . . . research problems do not lend themselves to experimentation, although many of them do lend themselves to [methods of statistical control]."[39]

KEY TERMS

multivariate analysis
spurious effect
intervening effect
cross-tabulation
partial correlation

correlation matrix
beta weights
standardized partial repression coefficient
coefficient of multiple determination

EXERCISES

1. A researcher is interested in the relationship between the public's attitude to- ward marijuana use and age. From a sample of 245 people interviewed in a par- ticular community, the following results were obtained (all data are hypothetical):

Attitudes toward Marijuana Use	Age		
	35 or Less	Over 35	Totals
More tolerant	80	50	130
Less tolerant	40	75	115
Totals	120	125	245

a. Examining the *cell entries* in this table, what would the researcher conclude about the relationship between age and attitudes toward marijuana use for this sample?

b. Using the formulas presented in Chapter 9, calculate the gamma coefficient for this table. How does this coefficient assist in measuring the relationship between age and attitudes toward marijuana use?

   Additionally, the researcher included in the survey questions pertaining to education (for simplicity, dividing the sample into those attending and those not attending college). After reexamining the original relationship, controlling for the education variable, the results shown in Table 10.14 were obtained.

TABLE 10.14
Public Attitudes toward Marijuana Use, by Age and by Education

Attitudes toward Marijuana Use	Not Attending College			Attending College		
	35 or Less	Over 35	Totals	35 or Less	Over 35	Totals
More tolerant	3	7	10	77	43	120
Less tolerant	22	58	80	18	17	35
Totals	25	65	90	95	60	155

c. How is the original relationship between attitudes toward marijuana use and age affected by the control for education, as revealed by the cell entries in the preceding table?

d. Calculate the gamma coefficients for each control table. How do these com- pare with the original coefficient calculated previously, and what does this comparison reveal about the controlled relationship?

e. Summarize the relationships among age, education, and attitudes toward marijuana use, as revealed by these tables. What is the likely explanation for these findings?

2. Based on a survey conducted in a particular community, a researcher has found that the following matrix shows that simple correlation coefficients exist among these variables: income, education, and attitudes toward stricter antipollution legislation. (All data are hypothetical.)

	Income	**Education**	**Attitudes toward Pollution Legislation**
Income	1.0	—	—
Education	.58	1.0	—
Attitudes toward pollution legislation	.25	.45	1.0

a. Based *only* on the matrix of simple correlation coefficients, what conclusions might be reached regarding the nature of relationships among these variables?
b. Calculate the *partial correlation coefficient* between income and attitudes toward pollution legislation, using the formula presented in this chapter.
c. Compare the partial correlation coefficient with the original simple correlation coefficient (shown previously), and discuss how the control may alter your conclusion about these relationships.
d. Discuss the general importance of controlling for variables in political and policy research, and describe how such techniques may improve our understanding of relationships.

3. In a 1993 article, Todd Donovan used multiple regression analysis to examine for several California cities the relationship between a number of community variables and the extent to which those cities developed policies of economic development (measured as the number of economic-development policies adopted by cities). Donovan's results are shown in Table 10.15.
a. Based on the information presented in this table, what can be said about the relationships between this set of variables and the adoption of economic-development policies, at least by this set of cities?
b. Which of these variables can be said to be *most important* in explaining adoption of economic-development policies, which are *least important,* and which coefficients demonstrate these distinctions? Which variables appear to be *statistically significant* in their association with economic-development policy adoption, and which statistic shows this?
c. How much of the *total variance* in policy adoption is accounted for by these variables? Which statistic shows this?
d. Donovan concludes from his analysis that, "cities that are larger [adopt] more policies to promote development . . . older communities also adopt more policies . . . cities housing higher proportions of commuters [adopt] more policies [and] cities with higher levels of homeownership display a sig-

TABLE 10.15

Relationship of Community Variables to Economic Development Policies

Independent Variables	Dependent Variable: Number of Economic Development Policies Adopted		
	Regression Coefficient	Standardized Coefficient	T-Value
Degree of community controversy*	−1.410	−.197	2.24
Proportion of residents white-collar professionals	0.040	.036	0.38
City unemployment levels	0.345	.123	0.97
Median family income	−4.6E-04	−.498	3.49
Population change (1980–89)	−0.012	−.040	0.46
Influence of private neighborhood groups*	2.052	.113	1.31
Mayor's office in charge of economic development activities	−2.811	−.206	2.49
Influence of private business groups*	−0.967	−.063	0.71
Size (logged population)	0.540	.074	0.67
Area	0.122	.264	2.12
Age (year of incorporation)	0.055	.279	2.43
Proportion homeowners	0.131	.313	2.67
Per capita tax revenue	−0.014	−.077	0.77
Proportion commuters	0.075	.215	2.00
Constant	119.53		
F value = 5.05 R^2 = .439 n = 114			

* These variables were measured by means of mailed questionnaire to officials of the various cities. Most other variables were obtained from the U.S. census, or from the California Department of Finance.

Source: Todd Donovan, "Community Controversy and the Adoption of Economic Development Policies," *Social Science Quarterly* 74 (June, 1993), 386–402.

nificant association with higher levels of [economic development] policy adoption." Identify the statistics in Table 10.15 supporting these conclusions. Are there any additional conclusions that could be reached concerning these relationships? What would these be?

4. Howard Frant[40] uses logit analysis of American cities greater than 50,000 in population, to examine the relationship between a number of community variables (including whether the cities use the city manager form of government) and the communities' commitment to use of civil-service procedures in their employment and personnel procedures. Two indicators of civil-service commitment are examined: whether the local civil-service commission has substantive powers, and whether civil service commission, or some other agency, hears personnel appeals. His results are shown in Table 10.16.

TABLE 10.16

Logit Coefficient Estimates for Measures of Civil Service

Independent Variables	Dependent Variables			
	Substantive Powers?		Appeals?	
Intercept	−3.948*	(−2.41)	−1.358	(−0.83)
City manager?	−0.874*	(−2.24)	−1.064*	(−2.49)
Number of municipal employees	0.645*	(3.05)	0.373	(1.97)
Per-capita income	0.000094	(1.08)	0.0001	(1.03)
Percent of population with more than high school education	−0.0206	(−1.20)	−0.0233	(−1.19)
Suburb?	0.826	(1.83)	−0.421	(−0.85)
City age	0.020	(1.44)	0.0078	(0.50)
Northeast	−1.613*	(−2.16)	−3.88*	(−4.12)
North central	−0.580	(−1.19)	−1.621*	(−2.90)
South	−0.600	(−1.40)	−0.921	(−1.97)
Pseudo-R^2 =	.19		.26	
Number of cases	222		202	

*Significant at .05 level or better (two-tailed test).

NOTE: Numbers in parenthesis are t-values. Note also the use of three dummy variables as measures of regionalism.

SOURCE: Howard Frant, "Rules and Governance in the Public Sector: The Case of Civil Service," *American Journal of Political Science* 37 (November, 1993), 990–1007.

    a. Based on this analysis, what could be concluded about the relationship between these community characteristic variables and the extent of civil service powers and appeals in American cities? How are these determinations made?

    b. Which of these variables are statistically significantly related to the dependent variables, and which are not? How are these determinations made?

    c. Overall, how well does this model fit the data? That is, how much do these variables assist in understanding variations in the use of civil-service procedures among American cities?

    d. Frant concludes that, "in manager cities the probability of a civil service personnel system is lower [than in other cities]," and that, "aside from some of the regional [variables], none of the variables intended to capture cultural differences has a statistically significant effect." Identify those statistics in this analysis that support these conclusions.

5. Applications to political and policy research literature

    a. Review any issues of recent political science and policy-related journals, and identify at least three articles using ordinary least squares multiple regression techniques and at least three articles using logit analysis.

    b. Discuss the reasons why the researchers selected these techniques.

c. Discuss the conclusions that can appropriately be drawn from each mode of analysis. What are the advantages and disadvantages of each technique, as indicated by your review?

NOTES

1. See Richard E. Dawson and James Robinson, "Inter-Party Competition, Economic Variables, and Welfare Policies in the American States," *Journal of Politics* 25 (May, 1963), 265–289.

2. Thomas R. Dye, *Understanding Public Policy* (Englewood Cliffs, NJ: Prentice-Hall, 1981), 328; emphasis added. See also, Thomas R. Dye, *Politics, Economics, and the Public* (Chicago: Rand McNally, 1966).

3. Greenberg, in an early study of socialization, found political similarities among siblings to be largely "confined to partisanship and related attitudes, such as feelings of distress or pleasure over the outcome of an election campaign. Aside from party preference, the influence of the family seems to be primarily indirect and to influence attitudes toward authority, rules, and compliance." See Edward S. Greenberg, *Political Socialization* (New York: Atherton Press, 1970), 71.

4. Thomas Dye, *Understand Public Policy Book*, 329. Over the past several decades, the relationships among politics, policy, and socioeconomic variables have been examined many times, and political scientists today have a much more complete view of how and under what circumstances political variables influence policy outcomes. Dye, in this book, does a good job of summarizing much of this research; see especially pages 325–337.

5. Actually, in some instances, statistical procedures can be used to identify models that appear to best fit the data, and they can be of some assistance in clarifying the relationships within a set of variables. For a discussion, see Hayward R. Alker, *Mathematics and Politics* (New York: Macmillan Publishing, 1968).

6. A number of coefficients have been developed for use with nominal and ordinal data, which are similar in interpretation to the partial correlation coefficient used with interval-level data (discussed subsequently). Included are the partial gamma, the partial tau-b, and the partial Somers's *d*. Most of these are based on weighted-average coefficients for categories of data. These partial coefficients are sometimes used in political and policy research. For an introduction, the student is advised to consult James A. Davis, "A Partial Coefficient for Goodman and Kruskal's Gamma," *Journal of the American Statistical Association* 62 (March, 1967), 189–193; and Robert H. Somers, "A Partitioning of Ordinal Information in a Three-Way Cross-Classification," *Multivariate Behavior Research* 5 (April, 1970), 217–239.

7. Correlation coefficients produced when applying the technique of tabular control are sometimes called "conditional correlation coefficients" because they refer to associations under certain conditions—in this case income. See David Knoke and George W. Bohrnstedt, *Statistics for Social Data Analysis,* 3rd ed. (Itasca, IL: F. E. Peacock Press, 1994), 244.

8. Barbara J. Burt-Way and Rita Mae Kelly, "Gender and Sustaining Political Ambition: A Study of Arizona Elected Officials," *Western Political Quarterly* (March, 1992), 11–25.

9. Ibid., 15.

10. David Hadwiger, "Money, Turnout, and Ballot Measure Success in California Cities," *Western Political Quarterly* (June, 1992), 539–547.

11. Ibid., 543.
12. See Hubert M. Blalock, *Social Statistics* (New York: McGraw-Hill Book Company, 1979), 455–477, for an excellent brief discussion of the partial correlation coefficient.
13. Arthur A. Goldsmith, "Political Freedom and the Business Climate: Outlook for Development in Newly Democratizing States," *Social Science Quarterly* (March, 1994), 115–124.
14. Ibid.
15. Ibid., 122–123.
16. Alan I. Abramowitz, "Issue Evolution Reconsidered: Racial Attitudes and Partisanship in the U.S. Electorate," *American Journal of Political Science* 38 (February, 1994), 1–24.
17. Ibid., 14.
18. Arthur H. Miller, Vickie L. Hesli, and William M. Reisinger, "Reassessing Mass Support for Political and Economic Change in the Former USSR," *American Political Science Review* 88 (June, 1994), 399–411.
19. Ibid., 407.
20. The authors report a statistic labeled, "adjusted R^2." The unadjusted R^2 value almost always increases with the inclusion in a regression equation of additional independent variables, regardless of how important those variables actually are. The adjusted R^2 statistic is designed to compensate for the number of independent variables. See Blalock, *Social Statistics,* 486–487.
21. Malcolm D. Holmes, Harmon M. Hosch, Howard C. Daudistel, Dolores A. Perez, and Joseph B. Graves, "Judges' Ethnicity and Minority Sentencing: Evidence Concerning Hispanics," *Social Science Quarterly* 74 (September, 1993), 496–506.
22. Ibid., 501. The reader should note that "ethnicity of judges" in this case was measured as a set of what are called "dummy variables." In such situations, *all but one* of the categories of a nominal variable are treated as separate variables, and all cases are assigned scores of "1" or "0," depending on their presence or absence in each category. The newly created variables are inserted into the regression equation and treated as interval variables. The group that is excluded (in this instance, Anglo judges' sentencing of Anglo defendants) serves as a reference group against which comparisons can be made. For a further discussion of the use of dummy variables in regression analysis, see Larry D. Schroeder, David L. Sjoquist, and Paula E. Stephan, *Understanding Regression Analysis* (Newbury Park, CA: Sage Publications, 1986), 56–58.
23. George A. Krause, "Is Regression Analysis Really Leading Political Science down a Blind Alley," *PS: Political Science and Politics* 27 (June, 1994), 187–190.
24. John H. Aldrich and Forrest D. Nelson, *Linear Probability, Logit, and Probit Models* (Newbury Park, CA: Sage Publications, 1989), 9.
25. For a listing and discussion of these assumptions, see Michael S. Lewis-Beck, *Applied Regression* (Newbury Park, CA: Sage Publications, 1980), 26–46.
26. For an interesting and instructive exchange of views on the use of regression analysis in political research, see Krause, "Is Regression Analysis Really Leading Political Science down a Blind Alley," and James P. McGregor, "Procrustes and the Regression Model: On the Misuse of the Regression Model," *PS: Political Science and Politics* 26 (December, 1993), 801–804.
27. Next to logit, probably the most commonly used nonlinear regression routine is the probit model. *Probit* estimates values of the coefficient of the dependent variable by use of the normal distribution, or z scores. In a binary situation (where the dependent variable takes on only two values), the results of probit and of logit typically are very similar, and the choice is largely a matter of individual preference. Because logit applies

to *polytomous* (multiple category) dependent variables, it has been highlighted in this discussion.

28. Note. Both the OLS regression equation presented previously and the logistic equation presented here were generated using the statistical package, SPSS/PC+.

29. For problems with this measure, see Aldrich and Nelson, *Linear Probability, Logit, and Probit Models,* 57.

30. As proposed by Aldrich and Nelson, *Linear Probability, Logit, and Probit Models,* 57.

31. Todd Donovan and Joseph R. Snipp, "Support for Legislative Term Limitations in California: Group Representation, Partisanship, and Campaign Information," *Journal of Politics* 56 (May, 1994), 492–501.

32. Ibid., 493.

33. Ibid., 498.

34. Ibid., 499.

35. Donald R. Songer, Sue Davis, and Susan Haire, "A Reappraisal of Diversification in the Federal Courts: Gender Effects in the Courts of Appeals," *Journal of Politics* 56 (May, 1994), 425–439.

36. Ibid., 429.

37. Ibid., 432.

38. Julian L. Simon and Paul Burstein, *Basic Research Methods in Social Science,* 3rd ed. (New York: Random House, 1985), 166.

39. Fred N. Kerlinger, *Foundations of Behavioral Research,* 2nd ed. (New York: Holt, Rinehart and Winston, 1973), 392.

40. Howard Frant, *Rules and Governance in the Public Sector: The Case of Civil Service,* American Journal of Political Science 37 (November, 1993), 990–1007.

11

Preparing the Report:
Writing and Rewriting

After the topic has been selected, hypotheses have been developed, information has been collected, and data have been analyzed, it is time to prepare the research report. It is tempting, when reaching this stage, to think that the hard work is over and that writing the final report will bring the project quickly and easily to conclusion. This thinking is mistaken. Writing is hard work. Aaron Wildavsky, one of political sciences's most respected and prolific scholars (and also former president of the American Political Science Association), found that writing, "is not only a mental but a physical process." "Oftentimes," he said, "you get stuck in the course of writing. You sit at your desk and nothing happens."[1]

Writing is not easy—even for professionals—and the report preparation phase of the research process is as important as any other to the successful completion of the project. All that most readers are going to know about your research will be contained in the final written report. A sloppy presentation can give the impression (sometimes correctly, sometimes incorrectly) that the research is sloppy. Not even the most brilliantly designed and carefully executed study will be very favorably received unless that study is presented effectively.

Unfortunately, it is not possible to provide a specific set of instructions that will guarantee success in writing the final report. In this sense, the final stage of the research process is similar to the beginning, selecting a topic: Both are highly individualized, and both largely reflect the personality and specialized interests and skills of the researcher. Nonetheless, as in the topic-selection stage, some guidelines can be offered to assist in the writing process.

WRITING HANDBOOKS AND STYLE MANUALS

As a beginning for writing, students should pick up and review one or more of the several writing handbooks and style manuals dealing with the writing process and with the style, format, and presentation for research papers. **Writing handbooks** are reference tools. They give rules for grammar, punctuation, spelling, sentence and paragraph structure, and they include guidelines on usage and on writing terminology. Handbooks present a review of the entire writing process, with suggestions on structure, organization, and revisions. **Style manuals** provide detail for the presentation of references, footnotes, and bibliographic information. Additionally, a number of other guides and books about writing are available, which offer suggestions on a variety of writing tasks. Among the most widely circulated of these handbooks, manuals, and guides are the following.

Writing Handbooks

William Strunk, Jr., and E.B. White, *The Elements of Style,* 3rd ed. (New York: Macmillan, 1979) [available now in electronic format, for use with PC and Apple Macintosh computers].

Laurie Kirszner and Stephen Mandell, *The Holt Handbook,* 4th ed. (Fort Worth, TX: Harcourt Brace, 1995).

H. Ramsey Fowler and Jane E. Aaron, *The Little, Brown Handbook,* 5th ed. (New York: HarperCollins, 1992).

Jim Corder and John Ruszkiewicz, *Handbook of Current English,* 8th ed. (Glenview, IL: Scott, Foresman, 1989).

Style Manuals

The Chicago Manual of Style, 14th ed. (Chicago: University of Chicago Press, 1993).

MLA Handbook for Writers of Research Papers, 3rd ed. (New York: Modern Language Association, 1988).

Publication Manual of the American Psychological Association, 4th ed. (Washington, DC: American Psychological Association, 1994).

Kate L. Turabian, *A Manual for Writers of Term Papers, Theses, and Dissertations,* 5th ed. (Chicago: University of Chicago Press, 1987).

Other Books about Writing

Michael Ivers, *The Random House Guide to Good Writing* (New York: Random House, 1993).

Joseph M. Williams, *Style: Toward Clarity and Grace* (Chicago: University of Chicago Press, 1990).

Phyllis Cash, *How to Develop and Write a Research Paper,* 2nd ed. (Englewood Cliffs, NJ: Prentice-Hall, 1988).

James D. Lester, *Writing Research Papers: A Complete Guide,* 7th ed. (Glenview, IL: Scott, Foresman, 1993).

Roberta H. Markman, Peter T. Markman, and Marie L. Waddell, *Ten Steps in Writing the Research Paper,* 4th ed. (Hauppauge, NY: Barron's Educational Series, 1989).

Donald J. D. Mulkerne and Donald J. D. Mulkerne, Jr., *The Perfect Term Paper,* 4th ed. (New York: Doubleday, 1988).

Donald Murray, *The Craft of Revision,* 2nd ed. (Fort Worth: Harcourt Brace, 1995).

These texts will provide invaluable guidance in the important areas of proper footnoting; bibliographic preparation; the handling of quoted material; the proper preparation of tables, charts, captions, and figures; punctuation, and so forth. Following are some additional guidelines for the structure, style, and length of your report.

STRUCTURE OF THE RESEARCH REPORT

An examination of any issue of any scholarly journal will reveal that research reports vary greatly in structure. It is not possible, or even desirable, to expect all reports to conform to a rigid format. There are, nevertheless, a few features common to most research reports. The following may be considered a checklist by which students may evaluate their report or the work of others.

1. The Title. The **report title** should be concise, clear, and specific; it should direct the reader immediately and without ambiguity to the focus of this research paper. Titles such as "Race Differences in Abortion Attitudes"; "Ethnicity, Gender, and Police–Community Attitudes"; "Capital Punishment Decisions in State Supreme Courts"; and "Trends in Work Force Sex Segregation, 1960–1990" all accomplish these goals.[2]

2. The Abstract. Often, an **abstract** will be included on the title page or as the first page of a report. The abstract is a brief statement summarizing the focus, methodology, and findings of the report. A typical abstract will be no longer than 150 words. Following is the abstract included with Richard Nadeau, Richard Niemi, and Timothy Amato's study, "Expectations and Preferences in British General Elections":

> We address two questions: How do people form their expectations about the likely winner of the next general election? and What are the links between expectations and votes? Using data collected by the Gallup organization in Great Britain, we find that the expectations formation process (1) has a significant inertia component but also a rapid adjustment to current information; (2) reflects voters' ability to translate economic expectations into political forecasts; and (3) is "time-bounded," possessing special characteristics immediately before and after a general election. The analysis also confirms the existence of a small bandwagon effect, whereby expectations that one party will win inflate that party's vote. The ability of voters to make reasonable forecasts without being unduly influenced by their own preferences suggests that under normal circumstances voters are expressing real preferences and not simply following the crowd.[3]

3. The Introduction. Depending on the length and complexity of the research being reported, the **introduction** to the research paper may be accomplished by

a single sentence, or a single paragraph, or several related ones. Regardless, the introduction should accomplish two goals: It must clearly state the theme or purpose of this particular research project; and it must make the reader understand why the topic is important and how the results might be used. The introduction is frequently the most difficult—and most important—section of the paper, in part because this section sets the tone for the entire report. Without promising more than can possibly be delivered, the writer must use the introduction to demonstrate the importance of this research effort and to sufficiently stimulate the reader's interest to press on with the report.

Consider the introductory *sentence* of Anna Madamba and Gordon De Jong's article, "Determinants of White-Collar Employment: Puerto Rican Women in Metropolitan New York":

> If we wish to understand reasons for the severely disadvantaged status of some minority and majority population groups in America's cities, it is necessary to explain both who obtains jobs and who obtains good jobs.[4]

This sentence nicely tells the reader *what* the focus of this article is going to be and *why* it is important. All introductions should accomplish these two objectives.

4. Statement of Hypotheses. Frequently, the **hypotheses** (research questions) being pursued will be formally presented at the end of the introductory section. Here, the independent, dependent, and control variables should be clearly identified; the direction and nature of expected relationships should be discussed; and all variables and concepts should be introduced.

As an example, Michael W. Giles and Keanan Hertz end the introductory section of their article, "Racial Threat and Partisan Identification," with the following paragraph:

> The present study reexamines the relationship between black political threat and the decline in white support for the Democratic party. Adopting the power approach, we hypothesize that as blacks constitute a larger component of a given political context, defection of white voters from the Democratic party will increase. Moreover, we hypothesize that this relationship will be conditioned by white social class and will vary temporarily with the salience of race in the political arena.[5]

5. Review of the Literature. The statement of hypotheses typically is followed by a section describing for the reader the **relevant research** that exists on this particular problem. The literature review should explain to the reader the theoretical context of the problem being examined: Where does this particular research project fit in the general knowledge area being studied? For class projects, especially, it is not expected or necessary to review every possible book, article, and manuscript that might relate to the topic. The concern is more than those key sources that relate most directly to the research project being pursued.

6. Research Design and Methods. The next section of the report discusses and justifies the study's **research design and methodology.** The type of data collected and the method of data collection should be detailed. If the research involves

sampling, the researcher must describe the population sampled, the techniques of sampling, the rate of completed surveys or interviews, and any biases that may have resulted. If questionnaires are used, the researcher should discuss the type of questionnaire and the procedures for coding the information. If other sources of information are used, the researcher should indicate who collected the data, by what techniques, and under what circumstances. Here, the researcher should also indicate the methods adopted for testing the hypotheses. If this is to be an experimental research design, the researcher should indicate how the control and experimental samples were selected, how testing was conducted, and how representative are the samples of the total population. If a nonexperimental research design is selected, the researcher should indicate which statistics were used to test the hypotheses and why they were selected.

7. Presentation of Findings. The body of the report is reserved for the **presentation of analysis and results**. This is the heart of the report; in the opinion of the reader, the project will stand or fall largely on the effectiveness of this section. Special care must be taken to ensure that the results of the analysis are presented as clearly and unambiguously as possible. This means that the report should be presented in a manner most convenient for the reader. Tables, charts, and figures should be presented in the body of the text near the point of discussion, not at the end. Critical points should be presented in the text itself, not relegated to footnotes. All quotes should be properly cited, and the sources of all data and information should be clearly presented. From the data presented, the reader should be able to evaluate the appropriateness of the statistics calculated and discussed.

At this stage, the writer should ask, "Have I made my case as convincingly as possible? Are the data presented in a manner that facilitates the reader's understanding of what I am saying? Have I made it possible for the reader to evaluate the conclusions I have made?" The celebrated writer Kurt Vonnegut once observed, "Readers . . . have a tough job to do, and they need all the help they can get [from writers]."[6]

8. Summary and Conclusions. The report should contain a brief **summary and conclusions** section. Here the researcher summarizes the major points of the paper; discusses, once again, the implications for the hypotheses (and theory) being tested; and points to the direction for needed future research. Concluding their study of capital punishment decisions by state supreme courts, Melinda Hall and Paul Brace stated

> Our [study] of death penalty decision making presents a striking challenge to the notion that political considerations have been removed from the process of assigning the death penalty. . . . Stated broadly, legal rules, no matter how detailed, seemingly do not remove discretion from the process of judicial decision making. Moreover, this discretion, inherent in the system, is exercised predictably according to the judges' preferences and other political calculations. . . . More basically, irrespective of the constraints of the law, judicial decisions intrinsically are political in nature.[7]

Also, the conclusion typically includes a statement or two about the *limitations* of the study. Those interested in the topic will benefit not only from your findings, but also from the *problems* encountered in conducting your research. All political and policy research has limitations. By candidly discussing the problems faced and how and why they were handled as they were, the researcher not only provides the reader with additional criteria for evaluating this particular research, but also—just as important—he or she provides valuable guidelines and directions to those contemplating future work in the field. In this sense, interested readers learn not only from your findings but also from the problems you faced along the way.

WRITING STYLE

Any manual of writing style will advise writers to stress stylistic *virtues* (such as writing with clarity, precision, care, conciseness, and honesty), and to avoid stylistic *vices* (such as using the passive voice, jargon, and vague and sexist language). Yet, it is much more difficult to define just what these terms mean and more difficult still to instruct someone in the art of effective writing style. Even William Strunk and E. B. White (whose little book, *The Elements of Style*[8] is a classic in the field) admit that, "There is no satisfactory explanation of style, no infallible guide to good writing, no assurance that a person who thinks clearly will be able to write clearly, no key that unlocks the door, no inflexible rules by which the young writer may shape his course."[9]

With all these obstacles confronting the writer, one might think it impossible to develop or improve good writing style. It is true, however, that the writing style of almost any author can be improved. As a start, students should read Strunk and White's *The Elements of Style*. It is a little book (85 pages), but almost everyone will find there numerous helpful suggestions. At the conclusion of the book, Strunk and White list 21 suggestions that would help improve anyone's writing style.

One of the suggestions identified by Strunk and White should be particularly stressed: Revise, and rewrite. It is almost never the case that the first draft of a manuscript is the best final product. Almost any written work, regardless of how brief or informal, can be improved by rewriting. Aaron Wildavsky, the political scientist whose observations on writing introduced this chapter, stated that, "I know of no better way of improving writing than continuous revision."[10] Likewise, noted economist John Kenneth Galbraith commented,[11]

> To write adequately one must know, above all, how bad are one's first drafts. They are bad because the need to combine composition with thought, both in their own way taxing, leads initially to a questionable, even execrable result. With each revision the task eases, the product improves. Eventually there can be clarity and perhaps even grace.

A good suggestion, especially for beginning writers, is that after completing the first draft, set aside the paper and move on to other projects or simply relax for a while. Come back to the manuscript in a day or two, refreshed and prepared to assume seriously the role of self-critic. At this stage, as a writer, you must step back from the details and complexities of the research itself, and for every sentence and every paragraph and every section, ask yourself once again: "Have I made the points I want to make as clearly and precisely as possible?" On reexamination, even the most experienced writer invariably will discover areas of confusion and ambiguity that can be improved by revision. The secret to successful writing is rewriting.

REPORT LENGTH

Probably the question most asked by students assigned a research project is, "How long should the final report be?" It is impossible to provide an answer that will satisfy all research situations. Doctoral dissertations often are 300 pages or longer, and master's theses frequently run in excess of 100 pages. At the other extreme, more narrowly focused topics may be handled nicely in a dozen pages or less. Most journals in political science prefer manuscripts of around 30 to 40 double-spaced pages, and many include a section entitled "research notes," where preliminary research articles of about a half-dozen pages or so are published. Student research reports can range from 10 to 50 pages but probably average around 20 to 25 pages in length.

Manuscript length can vary widely; perhaps the best that can be said is that the paper should achieve its purpose as briefly and as parsimoniously as possible. The purpose of the *research report,* unlike the *literature review,* is not to detail exhaustively every book, article, and manuscript that might possibly relate to the area or to review *all* arguments that have been advanced on one side of the issue or the other. Some of this level of detail, of course, is necessary and desirable, but the primary purpose of the research paper is to convey to the reader the results of this particular analysis and to do so as expeditiously as possible. The test of success is whether the reader is convinced that the argument has been made as forcefully and as effectively as possible and whether the skeptical or curious reader can replicate from the data presented the author's own results. If this goal has been accomplished, the paper is long enough. If not, the paper should be strengthened (but not necessarily lengthened) in these critical areas.

SUMMARY

This text began with the themes that (1) political and policy research can be an enjoyable, pleasurable experience; and (2) for greatest satisfaction, research should be carried out in a systematic, orderly process. By amply referencing published research of practicing political and policy scientists, it is hoped that the first of these themes has been well illustrated. The focus of this text has been on the second theme: the conduct of systematic political research. We have explored each of the major stages of research—from topic selection, to hypothesis formation, to research design, to literature review, to data collection, to data analysis, to report writing—and we have reviewed those techniques and methods most helpful at each stage.

When conducting your own research, or serving as part of a research team, you will find that research is a deeply rewarding and tremendously exciting process. There is, as Wildavsky put it, "elation at discovery."[12] There is another, even more important lesson to learn about scientific research. Even with the best of research guides, with the most advanced of computers, with the most sophisticated statistical programs, and with the highest quality of data, research success is not guaranteed. All these tools help maximize the likelihood of research success, but the ingredient missing from the list is the human intellect. No technique can guarantee scientific breakthroughs; no computer can guarantee a successful research effort. Above all else, it is the human imagination that remains the key to creative research. This key, as it turns out, is the truly exciting aspect of political research: blending the imagination with available technology to produce the highest quality research product—which is speculative, experimental, and innovative—research that, in a word, is *imaginative.*

In conducting research, it is hoped that the student will benefit from the correct use of the methods and tools discussed in this text. It is even more strongly hoped that the student will recognize and never lose sight of the difference between the *techniques* of research and the *creativity* of research. Creativity is a product of the human imagination—not the computer, not the technique, not the method. It is creativity in scientific research that is to be cherished and pursued above all. This is the final, and most important, lesson of this book: The imagination, uninhibited and unrestrained, stands without challenge as the greatest of all research tools.

KEY TERMS

writing handbooks
style manuals
report title
abstract
introduction

hypothesis
relevant research
research design and methodology
presentation of analysis and results
summary and conclusions

EXERCISES

1. Select a recent issue of a political science or policy-related journal in an area of particular interest to you. Examine each empirically oriented article in that issue, and for each of these articles, report the following:
   a. The introductory sentence or paragraph indicating the focus of the study and why it is important
   b. The hypotheses being tested
   c. The design of the research, including the type of data examined and the method of data collection
   d. The methods used to test the hypotheses
   e. The study's conclusions
2. Critically analyze each study reviewed in the preceding item. Include in your analysis a discussion of the following:
   a. Was the author's introduction stated clearly and precisely? How could the introduction be improved?

b. Were the author's hypotheses stated so that the independent and dependent variables were easily identified? Could they have been stated more clearly? If so, how?

c. Do you find the research design to have been adequate for the problem addressed? If not, how might it have been improved? What alternative sources of data, or means of data collection, might you suggest?

d. Were the techniques of analysis appropriate for the hypotheses tested and data employed? Why or why not?

e. Were the conclusions reached appropriate, based on the analysis presented. Why or why not?

f. What *one* major weakness do you find in *each* study? What suggestions would you offer to future researchers to overcome this weakness?

NOTES

1. Aaron Wildavsky, *Craftways: On the Organization of Scholarly Work* (New Brunswick: Transaction Publishers, 1989), 4–5.

2. All of these are titles of articles appearing in the March 1994 issue of *Social Science Quarterly.*

3. Richard Nadeau, Richard G. Niemi, and Timothy Amato, "Expectations and Preferences in British General Elections," *American Political Science Review* 88 (June, 1994), 371–383.

4. Anna B. Madamba and Gordon F. De Jong, "Determinants of White-Collar Employment: Puerto Rican Woman in Metropolitan New York," *Social Science Quarterly* 75 (March, 1994) 53.

5. Michael W. Giles and Kaenan Hertz, "Racial Threat and Partisan Identification," *American Political Science Review* 88 (June, 1994), 318.

6. Kurt Vonnegut, "How to Write with Style," *Newsweek on Campus* (April, 1987), 54–55, cited in Thomas E. Cronin, *The Write Stuff* (Englewood Cliffs, NJ: Prentice-Hall, 1990), 1.

7. Melinda Gann Hall and Paul Brace, "The Vicissitudes of Death by Decree: Forces Influencing Capital Punishment Decision Making in State Supreme Courts," *Social Science Quarterly* 75 (March, 1994), 148.

8. William Strunk, Jr., and E. B. White, *The Elements of Style,* 3rd ed. (New York: Macmillan Publishing, 1979).

9. Ibid., 66.

10. Wildavsky, *Craftways,* 36.

11. John Kenneth Galbraith, *A Life in Our Times: Memoirs* (Boston: Houghton Mifflin, 1981), 535.

12. Wildavsky, *Craftways,* 34.

Listing of Major Political Science and Policy Journals

Students may find the following information useful as a way to identify those political science and policy journals most likely to contain articles and research on topics of particular interest.

Information contained herein is taken largely—but not exclusively—from Fenton Martin and Robert Goehlert, *Political Science Journal Information* (Washington, DC: American Political Science Association, 1990), a publication that lists and describes the major political science journals. Grouping of journals by subject area is mine, not that of the original authors. Many journals, it should be noted, may be grouped in more than one category; in such cases, I have tried to place journals in those groups that seem to be of primary focus. It should be noted also that no attempt is made here to list the many specialized policy journals such as those in education, environment, criminal justice, health care, welfare, and so forth.

ALL AREAS OF POLITICS AND PUBLIC AFFAIRS

American Political Science Review. All areas of political science, including articles on American politics, international relations, political theory, comparative politics, and political methodology.

British Journal of Political Science. All fields of political science, including political philosophy and political sociology.

International Political Science Review/Revue Internationale de Science Politique. Studies on central and currently controversial themes in political science and on those areas of inquiry in the discipline where new concepts and methodologies are developing.

Journal of Political Science. All areas of political science.

The Journal of Politics. All areas of political science, with a primary focus on American politics and government.

Political Science Quarterly. All areas of government, politics, public affairs.

Political Studies. All areas of political science, with special attention to British domestic or foreign policy.

Politics & Society. Political and social criticism of contemporary society, with a philosophical and commentary approach.

Polity. All areas of political science, including political theory, comparative politics and American government.

Western Political Quarterly. All areas of political science, including American politics and government, international politics, political theory, and public policy.

AMERICAN POLITICS IN GENERAL: CONGRESS AND THE PRESIDENCY

American Journal of Political Science. U.S. government and politics mainly, but including some articles on international and comparative politics; strong interest in research methodology.

American Politics Quarterly. All areas of American government, including urban, state, and national politics; focus on political parties, public opinion, political theory, legislative behavior, administrative organization, and intergovernmental relations.

Congress and the Presidency. The presidency, Congress, the interactions between them, and national policy making in the framework of political science and history.

Presidential Studies Quarterly. Any study directly or indirectly related to the U.S. presidency.

COMPARATIVE POLITICS

Canadian Journal of Political Science. Focus on Canadian politics, with some articles dealing with international affairs or political thought.

Comparative Political Studies. Any area of comparative politics and comparative political economy, with articles based on theoretical and empirical research, especially quantitative analysis.

Comparative Politics. Comparative analysis of political institutions and behavior, with an interdisciplinary approach.

Comparative Strategy: An International Journal. Principles and practices of politics in the contemporary world; application of theoretical perspectives, empirical investigations, and historical analyses to strategic problems.

European Journal of Political Research. European comparative studies, relying heavily on quantitative analysis.

Government and Opposition: A Quarterly Journal of Comparative Politics. Comparative studies of political development; most articles deal with political situations in specific nations.

Journal of Developing Areas. Economics, political science, public administration, international relations, sociology, business, geography, history, anthropology, demography—with focus on Third World or less-developed regions of developed countries.

Journal of Development Studies. Economic and social development of Third World countries.

Legislative Studies Quarterly. All aspects of parliaments and legislatures, their relations to other political institutions, their functions in the political system, and the activities of their members, both within these institutions and outside them.

Parliamentary Affairs: A Journal of Comparative Government. All aspects of government and politics directly or indirectly connected with a parliament and with parliamentary systems throughout the world.

West European Politics. Current issues relating to Western Europe.

ELECTORAL STUDIES, PUBLIC OPINION

Electoral Studies. Elections in democratic countries anywhere in the world, electoral systems, and theories of electoral behavior.

Public Opinion Quarterly. Public opinion polls, communication, research methods, attitudes.

FEDERALISM/STATE AND LOCAL

Journal of Urban Affairs. Urban research and policy analysis.

Publius: The Journal of Federalism. Issues dealing with federalism, intergovernmental relations, and state and local government in the United States and other federal polities.

Urban Studies. Economic and social contributions to the field of urban and regional planning.

INTERDISCIPLINARY

The Social Science Journal. All social science disciplines represented; articles may be discipline-specific or may have interdisciplinary foci.

Social Science Quarterly. Any topic appealing to readers in more than one social-science discipline.

Social Science Research. All social-science areas; deals quantitatively with substantive issues.

INTERNATIONAL AFFAIRS/ INTERNATIONAL RELATIONS

Alternatives: A Journal of World Policy. International relations, technology, lifestyles, economic development, human rights, new international economic order, militarism, and international security.

Foreign Affairs. International affairs, energy, history, economics, political affairs (domestic and international) as they touch on the world scene.

Foreign Policy. International relations, economics, political science, history/political science.

International Interactions. International relations and policy-oriented research with a solid theoretical basis.

International Organization. All fields of international relations, international organization, political economy, and comparative foreign policy.

International Security. All aspects of international security affairs.

International Studies Quarterly. Broad research within the field of international studies, particularly of an interdisciplinary nature.

Journal of Conflict Resolution. Interdisciplinary, focusing on peace and war within and between nations.

Journal of Peace Research. Areas and themes relevant to the scientific understanding of conflict and the conditions for peace, defined not only as absence of war, but also including social justice.

Orbis: A Journal of World Affairs. International affairs, especially U.S. foreign policy.

War & Society. Military history, broadly defined.

World Development. International development studies, particularly with an interdisciplinary focus.

World Policy Journal. In-depth analysis of issues affecting U.S. foreign and domestic policy; coverage includes security issues, regional developments, and environmental issues.

World Politics. International relations, comparative politics, political theory, foreign policy, and national development, as well as history, geography, economics, military affairs, and sociology.

LAW AND POLITICS

The Journal of Law and Politics. Law of the political process, federalism, separation of powers, political science, public-policy analysis, multidisciplinary approaches to politicolegal problems.

Law & Society Review. The cultural, economic, political, psychological, and social aspects of law and legal systems.

PERSPECTIVES ON POLITICAL SCIENCE: MATHEMATICAL MODELING, TEACHING, RESEARCH

Mathematical Social Science. Analysis of human ecosystems, analysis of quality of life, analysis of structures and adaptive systems, automata theory, cluster analysis, decision theory, game theory, kinship systems, mathematical social sciences.

Perspectives on Political Science. State of the profession, application of social science concepts to the study of politics.

Talking Politics. Topics broadly related to teaching of political science in high schools and colleges.

POLITICAL BEHAVIOR: COMMUNICATION, PSYCHOLOGY, SOCIALIZATION

Political Behavior. Political psychology and political sociology broadly. Political socialization and recruitment; citizen and elite behavior; behavioral aspects of institutions.

Political Communication and Persuasion. Emphasis on mass media, propaganda, psychological warfare, political persuasion, and the peacekeeping roles of political communicators.

Political Psychology. Theoretical and research articles dealing with the relationships of psychological and political processes.

POLITICAL THOUGHT: POLITICAL HISTORY, POLITICAL PHILOSOPHY

History of Political Thought. Political theory, history of political ideas, and philosophy. Roughly half the articles deal with classic names of political science such as Plato, Rousseau, and Thomas More.

Journal of Theoretical Politics. Theory, social science theory, and especially political theory.

Philosophy & Public Affairs. Philosophy and political science.

Philosophy of the Social Sciences. Philosophy of the social sciences.

Political Theory. History of political thought, modern theory, American political thought, conceptual analysis, political theory and political science.

The Review of Politics. International orientation, with a diversified focus on American, European, and international politics, political theory, and analysis of institutions.

Socialism and Democracy. Theory and practice of socialism; socialism and democracy.

PUBLIC POLICY/PUBLIC ADMINISTRATION

Administration and Society. Public and human service organizations, their administrative processes, and their effect on society.

Evaluation Review. Form for researchers, planners, and policy makers engaged in development, implementation, utilization, and evaluation of public programs and policy.

Governance: An International Journal of Policy and Administration. Governmental organizations, administration and personnel, policy processes and issues, emphasis on comparative research with theoretical significance.

Journal of Policy Analysis and Management. Focus on the interrelationship between political science and management science; articles frequently explore the connection between politics and the implementation of social policy.

Journal of Policy Modeling. Economics, sociology, political science, management, business, international relations.

Journal of Public Policy. Articles that relate social science concepts to the practice, institutions, and problems of government.

Policy and Politics. British and comparative public policy.

Policy Review. All aspects of American public policy—both foreign and domestic policy—and public controversy.

Policy Sciences. Research and review articles, with emphasis on public policy; approach is interdisciplinary, drawing on management and political science theory.

Policy Studies Journal. Applications of political and social sciences to important policy problems in areas such as defense, poverty, labor, education, environment, energy, housing, unemployment, and health.

Policy Studies Review. Applications of political and social sciences to important policy problems.

Public Administration Review. All areas of public administration.

WOMEN'S STUDIES

Women & Politics: A Quarterly Journal of Research and Policy Studies. Articles that assist in the behavior, performance, and problems of women who participate in either mass or elite politics.

APPENDIX **B** Areas under the Normal Curve

Fractional parts of the total area (10,000) under the normal curve, corresponding to distances between the mean and ordinates, which are z standard deviation units from the mean.

z	00	01	02	03	04	05	06	07	08	09
0.0	0000	0040	0080	0120	0159	0199	0239	0279	0319	0359
0.1	0398	0438	0478	0517	0557	0596	0636	0675	0714	0753
0.2	0793	0832	0871	0910	0948	0987	0126	0164	1103	1141
0.3	1179	1217	1255	1293	1331	1368	1406	1443	1480	1517
0.4	1554	1591	1628	1664	1700	1736	1772	1808	1844	1879
0.5	1915	1950	1985	2019	2054	2088	2123	2157	2190	2224
0.6	2257	2291	2324	2357	2389	2422	2454	2486	2518	2549
0.7	2580	2612	2642	2673	2704	2734	2764	2794	2823	2852
0.8	2881	2910	2939	2967	2995	3023	3051	3078	3106	3133
0.9	3159	3186	3212	3238	3264	3289	3315	3340	3365	3389
1.0	3413	3438	3461	3485	3508	3531	3554	3577	3599	3621
1.1	3643	3665	3686	3718	3729	3749	3770	3790	3810	3830
1.2	3849	3869	3888	3907	3925	3944	3962	3980	3997	4015
1.3	4032	4049	4066	4083	4099	4115	4131	4147	4162	4177
1.4	4192	4207	4222	4236	4251	4265	4279	4292	4306	4319
1.5	4332	4345	4357	4370	4382	4394	4406	4418	4430	4441
1.6	4452	4463	4474	4485	4495	4505	4515	4525	4535	4545
1.7	4554	4564	4573	4582	4591	4599	4608	4616	4625	4633
1.8	4641	4649	4656	4664	4671	4678	4686	4693	4699	4706
1.9	4713	4719	4726	4732	4738	4744	4750	4758	4762	4767
2.0	4773	4778	4783	4788	4793	4798	4803	4808	4812	4817
2.1	4821	4826	4830	4834	4838	4842	4846	4850	4854	4857
2.2	4861	4865	4868	4871	4875	4878	4881	4884	4887	4890
2.3	4893	4896	4898	4901	4904	4906	4909	4911	4913	4916
2.4	4918	4920	4922	4925	4927	4929	4931	4932	4934	4936
2.5	4938	4940	4941	4943	4945	4946	4948	4949	4951	4952
2.6	4953	4955	4956	4957	4959	4960	4961	4962	4963	4964
2.7	4965	4966	4967	4968	4969	4970	4971	4972	4973	4974
2.8	4974	4975	4976	4977	4977	4978	4979	4980	4980	4981
2.9	4981	4982	4983	4984	4984	4984	4985	4985	4986	4986
3.0	4986.5	4987	4987	4988	4988	4988	4989	4989	4989	4990
3.1	4990.0	4991	4991	4991	4992	4992	4992	4992	4993	4993
3.2	4933.129									
3.3	4995.166									
3.4	4996.631									
3.5	4997.674									
3.6	4998.409									
3.7	4998.922									
3.8	4999.277									
3.9	4999.519									
4.0	4999.683									
4.5	4999.966									
5.0	4999.997133									

Source: Harold O. Rugg, *Statistical Methods Applied to Education,* Boston: Houghton Mifflin Company, 1917, Appendix table III, pp. 389–390. Reprinted with the kind permission of the publisher.

APPENDIX C Distribution of χ^2

							Probability							
df	.99	.98	.95	.90	.80	.70	.50	.30	.20	.10	.05	.02	.01	.001
1	.0³157	.0³628	.00393	.0158	.0642	.148	.455	1.074	1.642	2.706	3.841	5.412	6.635	10.827
2	.0201	.0404	.103	.211	.446	.713	1.386	2.408	3.219	4.605	5.991	7.824	9.210	13.815
3	.115	.185	.352	.584	1.005	1.424	2.366	3.665	4.642	6.251	7.815	9.837	11.341	16.268
4	.297	.429	.711	1.064	1.649	2.195	3.357	4.878	5.989	7.779	9.488	11.668	13.277	18.465
5	.554	.752	1.145	1.610	2.343	3.000	4.351	6.064	7.289	9.236	11.070	13.388	15.086	20.617
6	.872	1.134	1.635	2.204	3.070	3.828	5.348	7.231	8.558	10.645	12.592	15.033	16.812	22.457
7	1.239	1.564	2.167	2.833	3.822	4.671	6.346	8.383	9.803	12.017	14.067	16.622	18.475	24.322
8	1.646	2.032	2.733	3.490	4.594	5.527	7.344	9.524	11.030	13.362	15.507	18.168	20.090	26.125
9	2.088	2.532	3.325	4.168	5.380	6.393	8.343	10.656	12.242	14.684	16.919	19.679	21.666	27.877
10	2.558	3.059	3.940	4.865	6.179	7.267	9.342	11.781	13.442	15.987	18.307	21.161	23.209	29.588
11	3.053	3.609	4.575	5.578	6.989	8.148	10.341	12.899	14.631	17.275	19.675	22.618	24.725	31.264
12	3.571	4.178	5.226	6.304	7.807	9.034	11.340	14.011	15.812	18.549	21.026	24.054	26.217	32.909
13	4.107	4.765	5.892	7.042	8.634	9.926	12.340	15.119	16.985	19.812	22.362	25.472	27.688	34.528
14	4.660	5.368	6.571	7.790	9.467	10.821	13.339	16.222	18.151	21.064	23.685	26.873	29.141	36.123
15	5.229	5.985	7.261	8.547	10.307	11.721	14.339	17.322	19.311	22.307	24.996	28.259	30.578	37.697

df														
16	5.812	6.614	7.962	9.312	11.152	12.624	15.338	18.418	20.465	23.542	26.296	29.633	32.000	39.252
17	6.408	7.255	8.672	10.085	12.002	13.531	16.338	19.511	21.615	24.769	27.587	30.995	33.409	40.790
18	7.015	7.906	9.390	10.865	12.857	14.440	17.338	20.601	22.760	25.989	28.869	32.346	34.805	42.312
19	7.633	8.567	10.117	11.651	13.716	15.352	18.338	21.689	23.900	27.204	30.144	33.687	36.191	43.820
20	8.260	9.237	10.851	12.443	14.578	16.266	19.337	22.775	25.038	28.412	31.410	35.020	37.566	45.315
21	8.897	9.915	11.591	13.240	15.445	17.182	20.337	23.858	26.171	29.615	32.671	36.343	38.932	46.797
22	9.542	10.600	12.338	14.041	16.314	18.101	21.337	24.939	27.301	30.813	33.924	37.659	40.289	48.268
23	10.196	11.293	13.091	14.848	17.187	19.021	22.337	26.018	28.429	32.007	35.172	38.968	41.638	49.728
24	10.856	11.992	13.848	15.659	18.062	19.943	23.337	27.096	29.553	33.196	36.415	40.270	42.980	51.179
25	11.524	12.697	14.611	16.473	18.940	20.867	24.337	28.172	30.675	34.382	37.652	41.566	44.314	52.620
26	12.198	13.409	15.379	17.292	19.820	21.792	25.336	29.246	31.795	35.563	38.885	42.856	45.642	54.052
27	12.879	14.125	16.151	18.114	20.703	22.719	26.336	30.319	32.912	36.741	40.113	44.140	46.963	55.476
28	13.565	14.847	16.928	18.939	21.588	23.647	27.336	31.391	34.027	37.916	41.337	45.419	48.278	56.893
29	14.256	15.574	17.708	19.768	22.475	24.577	28.336	32.461	35.139	39.087	42.557	46.693	49.588	58.302
30	14.953	16.306	18.493	20.599	23.364	25.508	29.336	33.530	36.250	40.256	43.773	47.962	50.892	59.703

For larger values of df, the expression $\sqrt{2\chi^2} - \sqrt{2df - 1}$ may be used as a normal deviate with unit variance, remembering that the probability for χ^2 corresponds to that of a single tail of the normal curve.

SOURCE: Reprinted from R. A. Fisher and F. Yates, *Statistical Tables for Biological, Agricultural and Medical Research*, 6th ed. (London: Longman, 1974), Table IV. Used by permission of the authors and Longman Group Ltd.

APPENDIX D   Distribution of *t* Values

	Level of Significance for One-Tailed Test					
df	.10	.05	.025	.01	.005	.0005
	Level of Significance for Two-Tailed Test					
	.20	.10	.05	.02	.01	.001
1	3.078	6.314	12.706	31.821	63.657	636.619
2	1.886	2.920	4.303	6.965	9.925	31.598
3	1.638	2.353	3.182	4.541	5.841	12.941
4	1.533	2.132	2.776	3.747	4.604	8.610
5	1.476	2.015	2.571	3.365	4.032	6.859
6	1.440	1.943	2.447	3.143	3.707	5.959
7	1.415	1.895	2.365	2.998	3.499	5.405
8	1.397	1.860	2.306	2.896	3.355	5.041
9	1.383	1.833	2.262	2.821	3.250	4.781
10	1.372	1.812	2.228	2.764	3.169	4.587
11	1.363	1.796	2.201	2.718	3.106	4.437
12	1.356	1.782	2.179	2.681	3.055	4.318
13	1.350	1.771	2.160	2.650	3.012	4.221
14	1.345	1.761	2.145	2.624	2.977	4.140
15	1.341	1.753	2.131	2.602	2.947	4.073
16	1.337	1.746	2.120	2.583	2.921	4.015
17	1.333	1.740	2.110	2.567	2.898	3.965
18	1.330	1.734	2.101	2.552	2.878	3.922
19	1.328	1.729	2.093	2.539	2.861	3.883
20	1.325	1.725	2.086	2.528	2.845	3.850
21	1.323	1.721	2.080	2.518	2.831	3.819
22	1.321	1.717	2.074	2.508	2.819	3.792
23	1.319	1.714	2.069	2.500	2.807	3.767
24	1.318	1.711	2.064	2.492	2.797	3.745
25	1.316	1.708	2.060	2.485	2.787	3.725
26	1.315	1.706	2.056	2.479	2.779	3.707
27	1.314	1.703	2.052	2.473	2.771	3.690
28	1.313	1.701	2.048	2.467	2.763	3.674
29	1.311	1.699	2.045	2.462	2.756	3.659
30	1.310	1.697	2.042	2.457	2.750	3.646
40	1.303	1.684	2.021	2.423	2.704	3.551
60	1.296	1.671	2.000	2.390	2.660	3.460
120	1.289	1.658	1.980	2.358	2.617	3.373
∞	1.282	1.645	1.960	2.326	2.576	3.291

Source: Abridged from R. A. Fisher and F. Yates, *Statistical Tables for Biological, Agricultural and Medical Research,* 6th ed. (London: Longman, 1974), tab. III. Used by permission of the authors and Longman Group Ltd.

APPENDIX E Distribution of *F* Values

p = .05

$n_2 \backslash n_1$	1	2	3	4	5	6	8	12	24	∞
1	161.4	199.5	215.7	224.6	230.2	234.0	238.9	243.9	249.0	254.3
2	18.51	19.00	19.16	19.25	19.30	19.33	19.37	19.41	19.45	19.50
3	10.13	9.55	9.28	9.12	9.01	8.94	8.84	8.74	8.64	8.53
4	7.71	6.94	6.59	6.39	6.26	6.16	6.04	5.91	5.77	5.63
5	6.61	5.79	5.41	5.19	5.05	4.95	4.82	4.68	4.53	4.36
6	5.99	5.14	4.76	4.53	4.39	4.28	4.15	4.00	3.84	3.67
7	5.59	4.74	4.35	4.12	3.97	3.87	3.73	3.57	3.41	3.23
8	5.32	4.46	4.07	3.84	3.69	3.58	3.44	3.28	3.12	2.93
9	5.12	4.26	3.86	3.63	3.48	3.37	3.23	3.07	2.90	2.71
10	4.96	4.10	3.71	3.48	3.33	3.22	3.07	2.91	2.74	2.54
11	4.84	3.98	3.59	3.36	3.20	3.09	2.95	2.79	2.61	2.40
12	4.75	3.88	3.49	3.26	3.11	3.00	2.85	2.69	2.50	2.30
13	4.67	3.80	3.41	3.18	3.02	2.92	2.77	2.60	2.42	2.21
14	4.60	3.74	3.34	3.11	2.96	2.85	2.70	2.53	2.35	2.13
15	4.54	3.68	3.29	3.06	2.90	2.79	2.64	2.48	2.29	2.07
16	4.49	3.63	3.24	3.01	2.85	2.74	2.59	2.42	2.24	2.01
17	4.45	3.59	3.20	2.96	2.81	2.70	2.55	2.38	2.19	1.96
18	4.41	3.55	3.16	2.93	2.77	2.66	2.51	2.34	2.15	1.92
19	4.38	3.52	3.13	2.90	2.74	2.63	2.48	2.31	2.11	1.88
20	4.35	3.49	3.10	2.87	2.71	2.60	2.45	2.28	2.08	1.84
21	4.32	3.47	3.07	2.84	2.68	2.57	2.42	2.25	2.05	1.81
22	4.30	3.44	3.05	2.82	2.66	2.55	2.40	2.23	2.03	1.78
23	4.28	3.42	3.03	2.80	2.64	2.53	2.38	2.20	2.00	1.76
24	4.26	3.40	3.01	2.78	2.62	2.51	2.36	2.18	1.98	1.73
25	4.24	3.38	2.99	2.76	2.60	2.49	2.34	2.16	1.96	1.71
26	4.22	3.37	2.98	2.74	2.59	2.47	2.32	2.15	1.95	1.69
27	4.21	3.35	2.96	2.73	2.57	2.46	2.30	2.13	1.93	1.67
28	4.20	3.34	2.95	2.71	2.56	2.44	2.29	2.12	1.91	1.65
29	4.18	3.33	2.93	2.70	2.54	2.43	2.28	2.10	1.90	1.64
30	4.17	3.32	2.92	2.69	2.53	2.42	2.27	2.09	1.89	1.62
40	4.08	3.23	2.84	2.61	2.45	2.34	2.18	2.00	1.79	1.51
60	4.00	3.15	2.76	2.52	2.37	2.25	2.10	1.92	1.70	1.39
120	3.92	3.07	2.68	2.45	2.29	2.17	2.02	1.83	1.61	1.25
∞	3.84	2.99	2.60	2.37	2.21	2.09	1.94	1.75	1.52	1.00

(table continues)

299

Appendix E (continued)

p = .01

$n_2 \backslash n_1$	1	2	3	4	5	6	8	12	24	∞
1	4052	4999	5403	5625	5764	5859	5981	6106	6234	6366
2	98.49	99.01	99.17	99.25	99.30	99.33	99.36	99.42	99.46	99.50
3	34.12	30.81	29.46	28.71	28.24	27.91	27.49	27.05	26.60	26.12
4	21.20	18.00	16.69	15.98	15.52	15.21	14.80	14.37	13.93	13.46
5	16.26	13.27	12.06	11.39	10.97	10.67	10.27	9.89	9.47	9.02
6	13.74	10.92	9.78	9.15	8.75	8.47	8.10	7.72	7.31	6.88
7	12.25	9.55	8.45	7.85	7.46	7.19	6.84	6.47	6.07	5.65
8	11.26	8.65	7.59	7.01	6.63	6.37	6.03	5.67	5.28	4.86
9	10.56	8.02	6.99	6.42	6.06	5.80	5.47	5.11	4.73	4.31
10	10.04	7.56	6.55	5.99	5.64	5.39	5.06	4.71	4.33	3.91
11	9.65	7.20	6.22	5.67	5.32	5.07	4.74	4.40	4.02	3.60
12	9.33	6.93	5.95	5.41	5.06	4.82	4.50	4.16	3.78	3.36
13	9.07	6.70	5.74	5.20	4.86	4.62	4.30	3.96	3.59	3.16
14	8.86	6.51	5.56	5.03	4.69	4.46	4.14	3.80	3.43	3.00
15	8.68	6.36	5.42	4.89	4.56	4.32	4.00	3.67	3.29	2.87
16	8.53	6.23	5.29	4.77	4.44	4.20	3.89	3.55	3.18	2.75
17	8.40	6.11	5.18	4.67	4.34	4.10	3.79	3.45	3.08	2.65
18	8.28	6.01	5.09	4.58	4.25	4.01	3.71	3.37	3.00	2.57
19	8.18	5.93	5.01	4.50	4.17	3.94	3.63	3.30	2.92	2.49
20	8.10	5.85	4.94	4.43	4.10	3.87	3.56	3.23	2.86	2.42
21	8.02	5.78	4.87	4.37	4.04	3.81	3.51	3.17	2.80	2.36
22	7.94	5.72	4.82	4.31	3.99	3.76	3.45	3.12	2.75	2.31
23	7.88	5.66	4.76	4.26	3.94	3.71	3.41	3.07	2.70	2.26
24	7.82	5.61	4.72	4.22	3.90	3.67	3.36	3.03	2.66	2.21
25	7.77	5.57	4.68	4.18	3.86	3.63	3.32	2.99	2.62	2.17
26	7.72	5.53	4.64	4.14	3.82	3.59	3.29	2.96	2.58	2.13
27	7.68	5.49	4.60	4.11	3.78	3.56	3.26	2.93	2.55	2.10
28	7.64	5.45	4.57	4.07	3.75	3.53	3.23	2.90	2.52	2.06
29	7.60	5.42	4.54	4.04	3.73	3.50	3.20	2.87	2.49	2.03
30	7.56	5.39	4.51	4.02	3.70	3.47	3.17	2.84	2.47	2.01
40	7.31	5.18	4.31	3.83	3.51	3.29	2.99	2.66	2.29	1.80
60	7.08	4.98	4.13	3.65	3.34	3.12	2.82	2.50	2.12	1.60
120	6.85	4.79	3.95	3.48	3.17	2.96	2.66	2.34	1.95	1.38
∞	6.64	4.60	3.78	3.32	3.02	2.80	2.51	2.18	1.79	1.00

$$p = .001$$

n_2\\n_1	1	2	3	4	5	6	8	12	24	∞
1	405284	500000	540379	562500	576405	585937	598144	610667	623497	636619
2	998.5	999.0	999.2	999.2	999.3	999.3	999.4	999.4	999.5	999.5
3	167.5	148.5	141.1	137.1	134.6	132.8`	130.6	128.3	125.9	123.5
4	74.14	61.25	56.18	53.44	51.71	50.53	49.00	47.41	45.77	44.05
5	47.04	36.61	33.20	31.09	29.75	28.84	27.64	26.42	25.14	23.78
6	35.51	27.00	23.70	21.90	20.81	20.03	19.03	17.99	16.89	15.75
7	29.22	21.69	18.77	17.19	16.21	15.52	14.63	13.71	12.73	11.69
8	25.42	18.49	15.83	14.39	13.49	12.86	12.04	11.19	10.30	9.34
9	22.86	16.39	13.90	12.56	11.71	11.13	10.37	9.57	8.72	7.81
10	21.04	14.91	12.55	11.28	10.48	9.92	9.20	8.45	7.64	6.76
11	19.69	13.81	11.56	10.35	9.58	9.05	8.35	7.63	6.85	6.00
12	18.64	12.97	10.80	9.63	8.89	8.38	7.71	7.00	6.25	5.42
13	17.81	12.31	10.21	9.07	8.35	7.86	7.21	6.52	5.78	4.97
14	17.14	11.78	9.73	8.62	7.92	7.43	6.80	6.13	5.41	4.60
15	16.59	11.34	9.34	8.25	7.57	7.09	6.47	5.81	5.10	4.31
16	16.12	10.97	9.00	7.94	7.27	6.81	6.19	5.55	4.85	4.06
17	15.72	10.66	8.73	7.68	7.02	6.56	5.96	5.32	4.63	3.85
18	15.38	10.39	8.49	7.46	6.81	6.35	5.76	5.13	4.45	3.67
19	15.08	10.16	8.28	7.26	6.61	6.18	5.59	4.97	4.29	3.52
20	14.82	9.95	8.10	7.10	6.46	6.02	5.44	4.82	4.15	3.38
21	14.59	9.77	7.94	6.95	6.32	5.88	5.31	4.70	4.03	3.26
22	14.38	9.61	7.80	6.81	6.19	5.76	5.19	4.58	3.92	3.15
23	14.19	9.47	7.67	6.69	6.08	5.65`	5.09	4.48	3.82	3.05
24	14.03	9.34	7.55	6.59	5.98	5.55	4.99	4.39	3.74	2.97
25	13.88	9.22	7.45	6.49	5.88	5.46	4.91	4.31	3.66	2.89
26	13.74	9.12	7.36	6.41	5.80	5.38	4.83	4.24	3.59	2.82
27	13.61	9.02	7.27	6.33	5.73	5.31	4.76	4.17	3.52	2.75
28	13.50	8.93	7.19	6.25	5.66	5.24	4.69	4.11	3.46	2.70
29	13.39	8.85	7.12	6.19	5.59	5.18	4.64	4.05	3.41	2.64
30	13.29	8.77	7.05	6.12	5.53	5.12	4.58	4.00	3.36	2.59
40	12.61	8.25	6.60	5.70	5.13	4.73	4.21	3.64	3.01	2.23
60	11.97	7.76	6.17	5.31	4.76	4.37	3.87	3.31	2.69	1.90
120	11.38	7.31	5.79	4.95	4.42	4.04	3.55	3.02	2.40	1.56
∞	10.83	6.91	5.42	4.62	4.10	3.74	3.27	2.74	2.13	1.00

SOURCE: Abridged from R. A. Fisher and F. Yates, *Statistical Tables for Biological, Agricultural and Medical Research,* 6th ed. (London: Longman, 1974), tab. III. Used by permission of the authors and Longman Group Ltd.

Glossary

abstract A brief (usually 150 words or less) summary of the information contained within an article, a book, or another information source; generally descriptive, but evaluative information may also be available; for reports of research, the abstract summarizes the hypotheses, the methodology, and the findings of a given investigation.

alternative–form method A means of assessing reliability by administering two versions of the same test to the same group of individuals on more than one occasion, then comparing their results on each occasion.

analysis of variance *F*–test A statistical technique that allows for comparisons of differences among multiple samples or categories, based on the assumption that each observed value of the dependent variable can be thought of as a sum of these three terms: the mean score for all observations, the deviation of the observed value's group mean from the overall mean, and the deviation of each observed value from its observed group mean (see Appendix E).

anonymity A means of ensuring confidentiality, by concealing the identity of research participants from the investigator, as well as from other persons.

applied research Empirical investigation that focuses on questions intended to lead to immediate or direct assistance in addressing practical concerns.

bar graph A graphic presentation of data, in which each vertical (or horizontal) bar represents a given category of a variable, and the height (or length) of each bar indicates the value for that variable; for a graph of frequencies, the height of each bar indicates the frequency of responses for the given category of variable.

basic research Empirical investigation in which fundamental questions are probed, regardless of whether the findings may offer immediate or direct assistance in addressing practical concerns.

beta weight A statistic that indicates the slope that would be obtained if all variables were standardized; it measures change in the dependent variable in terms of standard–deviation units for each of the independent variables, controlling for all others; it allows for comparison of the *relative* degree to which changes in the independent variables effect changes in the dependent variable.

between–groups sum of squares   A value obtained when calculating an F–ratio for groups being compared, which is derived by subtracting the overall mean from the mean of each group, squaring each difference, multiplying the squared value by the number of observations in a given group, and then summing the results.

case–study design   A research design whereby an investigator gathers many data about a particular individual or set of individuals, often making use of interview data, observational data, and case–history data supplied by the individuals under investigation.

census   A method of gathering information about all individuals within a given population.

chi–square test   A test of statistical significance (χ^2), used for determining the extent to which observed values in a contingency table deviate from the values that would have been expected if the two variables had no relationship to one another (i.e., for determining whether the two variables are independent of each other in the population), such as when cross–tabulating nominal or ordinal variables.

closed–ended question   Question to which a respondent is expected to give only a limited response, such as a forced–choice response.

cluster sampling technique   A means of selecting population samples by choosing individuals at random within particular clusters of communities, rather than by choosing participants at random from the population as a whole.

codebook   An explicit listing of how each datum should be recorded for each respondent, providing a distinctive number for each possible acceptable response to each question in a survey.

codesheet   A sheet of paper with columns and rows used for recording data regarding individual respondents.

coding   The process whereby a researcher assigns numbers to all possible acceptable responses to all items in a survey.

coefficient of determination   The proportionate amount of variance in the dependent variable that is explained by the independent variable, expressed as a reduction–of–variance ratio, symbolized as r^2.

coefficient of multiple determination   The proportion of the variance in the dependent variable, which is explained by all of the independent variables; represented as R^2, this coefficient is typically defined as the sum of the remaining variance in the dependent variable explained by each independent variable, after the influence of every other independent variable has been accounted for.

coefficient of nondetermination   A measure of the proportionate amount of variance in the dependent variable, which is not explained by the independent variable.

coefficient of reproducibility   The ratio of error responses to the total number of possible responses for a given scale.

coefficient of scalability   An indication of how well a scaling routine actually improves the ratio of error responses to the total number of possible responses for a given scale.

coefficient of variation   A measure of dispersion used for comparing the dispersion of two or more groups around the mean of each group; calculated as CV =

$s \div \bar{X}$, where CV = coefficient of variation, s = standard deviation, and $\bar{X}$ = mean.

column marginals   The sums of each column in a table of nominal or ordinal data.

composite measure   A combination of responses to two or more items, or a combination of scores.

concept   An idea that represents and organizes a set of characteristics or phenomena.

concept operationalization   The translation of abstract concepts into a form that can be objectively defined, observed, and measured.

confidentiality   An ethical principle of research, whereby an investigator (a) safeguards the privacy of each individual who provides information to the investigator, and (b) conceals the identity of each information provider.

construct validity   The extent to which the underlying theoretical framework of a scale is supported by the responses to individual items on the scale, such that the particular relationships of responses predicted by the theory are actually confirmed (e.g., if the theory predicts that liberal attitudes toward civil rights correspond with liberal attitudes toward religious freedom, individuals who respond strongly to one also respond strongly to the other).

content validity   The extent to which a scale assesses all aspects of a given hypothetical construct being assessed.

contingency coefficient   A measure of association, based on chi–square, most appropriate for comparing contingency tables of the same size.

control group   Research participants who are *not* exposed to an experimental treatment, thereby serving as controls for extraneous influences on the outcomes of the treatment.

control variable   A variable that an experimenter is controlling while manipulating the independent variable and observing its effects on the dependent variable.

convenient sampling technique   A method of selecting individuals from a population of interest, in which the representativeness of the sample is given less emphasis than is the convenience of obtaining information from those individuals.

correlation matrix   A *matrix* (tabular display of information in rows and columns) indicating the *correlation* (degree of association) between each variable such that all possible correlations between pairs of variables are represented in the matrix.

Cramer's *V*   A measure of association, which is a modification of the phi coefficient, applicable to any size of contingency table.

criterion validity   The extent to which performance on a given scale accurately predicts performance on another measure of the hypothetical construct being assessed.

cross–sectional research   An investigation involving the study of a representative sample of individuals from a population, in which the researcher cannot directly manipulate which individuals will be exposed to a particular independent variable, but in which the investigator attempts to evaluate the strength and direction of statistical relationship between an independent variable and one or more dependent (outcome) variables.

cross–tabulation   A method for analyzing the degree of association between nominal or ordinal data.

cumulative percentile   The percentage of respondents who score at levels equal to or less than a given value.

decile range   The range for the middle 80 percent of the data in a given distribution (not considering either the highest 10% or the lowest 10% of the data).

degrees of freedom   The number of values in a given distribution, which are free to vary, after particular constraints are imposed.

dependent variable   A characteristic or an event that a researcher is trying to explain, understand, or predict, based on manipulation of an independent variable.

dictionary   A book comprising an alphabetical listing of terms, along with their meanings; may be specific to the terms used in a particular field of interest.

directional hypothesis   A research hypothesis that predicts the direction of the relationship between the independent and the dependent variables.

discriminative power   The degree to which a given item can aid in highlighting the differences among individuals regarding an attribute of interest.

disproportionate sampling technique   A method for ensuring that individuals from a particular category within a population are disproportionately overrepresented in a given sample; usually used when a proportionate sample would be so small that the data would be difficult to interpret; statistical weightings may be used to compensate for oversampling.

ecological fallacy   An incorrect inference that the behavior shown by individuals will necessarily be the same as the behavior shown by groups to which those individuals belong.

empirical research   Investigation in which a researcher attempts accurately to describe (measure, label, categorize, and compare) the observable characteristics of events, to observe the relationships among events, and perhaps eventually to predict how a particular event may influence one or more other events.

encyclopedia   A comprehensive source of information regarding a particular subject or regarding a broad range of subjects, usually organized as an alphabetical series of articles on each relevant topic.

evaluation research   Empirical investigation that assesses and judges the effectiveness of particular policies or the outcomes of particular agencies or programs of political action.

experimental or treatment group   Research participants who are exposed to an experimental treatment.

experimental research design   A format for investigation in which an experimenter obtains an experimental and a control group, exposes the experimental group to the treatment variable, and measures the effects.

explained variance   The amount of variance in the dependent variable that is explained by the dependent variable; the ratio of explained variance to total variance provides the measure for the coefficient of determination.

external validity   An indication that an observed relationship between a given independent variable and a given dependent variable applies not only to the sample of individuals under investigation, but also to the population of individuals from which the sample was drawn.

factor analysis   A statistical technique for identifying a relatively small number of underlying factors within a large body of data; these factors can be used for identifying key relationships among sets of interrelated variables.

factor loading   The degree to which each item on a given scale is related to each underlying factor.

factorial design   A format for research in which an investigator uses the statistical technique of factor analysis to identify a relatively small number of underlying factors that can account for relationships within sets of many interrelated variables.

follow–up surveys   A means of collecting information from participants, either in writing or through an interview, in which the information is gathered some time after the conclusion of an initial phase of information gathering.

follow–up test   A test given some time after the conclusion of an experiment, the results of which are used by an investigator to assess long–term influences of the independent variable on the dependent variable.

frequency distribution   A tabulation of data, listing the response of each individual for each category or interval being tabulated.

frequency polygon   A histogram in which the midpoints of the top of each bar are connected, forming a solid line.

gamma   A symmetrical (nondirectional) test for assessing the strength of relationship between ordinal-level variables.

gopher   A menu–based computer tool designed to facilitate searches for information in an on–line database, proceeding from more general to more specific topics available on the Internet.

Guttman technique   A method of designing scales, which is intended to ensure that all of the items selected to be used on a given scale actually measure the same attribute.

histogram   A bar graph of interval data, in which the width of each bar is proportional to the size of each interval, and the height of each bar is proportional to the frequency of responses for each interval, so that the area of each bar (width × height) aptly represents the frequencies for each interval.

hypertext   A format for documents, which allows persons who view a given document to select particular key words within the document, thereby gaining access to related documents.

hypothesis   Explicit statement of belief regarding the expected relationship between two or more concepts or variables.

independent variable   A characteristic or an event that a researcher is manipulating, in order to understand, explain, or predict its influence on a dependent variable.

index   An alphabetized listing of topics and their associated locations within a book or within a body of research material (e.g., an on– line database).

individualistic fallacy   An incorrect inference that the collective behavior of a group of individuals will necessarily be the same as the individual actions shown by members of the group.

intercept   A constant value to be calculated for a given regression equation, which may be plotted as the distance from the origin of coordinate axes to a given point where a regression line crosses the referent axis.

internal consistency A measure of correlation among scale items, used for determining whether the items all measure the same hypothetical construct.

internal validity An indication that a given independent variable appears accurately to predict observed changes in a given dependent variable.

Internet An on–line system offering both access to various databases and electronic–mail (E–mail) service to persons in virtually all research settings, as well as to persons who subscribe through private providers.

interquartile range The range for the middle 50% of the data in a given distribution (not considering either the highest 25% or the lowest 25% of the data).

interrupted time–series design A format for research whereby an investigator attempts to assess the influence of an independent variable by taking measures of the dependent variable at various intervals prior to the introduction of the independent variable and then taking further measures of the dependent variable at multiple intervals following the introduction of the independent variable; the investigator then analyzes the data obtained, to see whether a pattern of change may be observed.

interval variable A variable for which numeric labels indicate not only a rank ordering among assigned values, but also precise, constant intervals between numbers.

intervening effect The influence of a third variable that helps to explain how the independent variable leads to variation of the dependent variable.

interview Broadly, a method of asking questions and recording people's responses to those questions; more narrowly, a research method whereby a researcher conducts a survey either in person or via telephone.

introduction A brief statement of the purpose of a report, informing the reader of why the particular topic is important and of interest to the reader.

judgment sampling A method of selecting individuals from a population of interest, in which a researcher attempts to obtain a representative sample by choosing individuals who, in the researcher's opinion, appear to represent the population.

lambda coefficient A proportionate reduction of error statistic based on the notion that values of the dependent variable can be predicted, given the values of the independent variable.

Likert scaling technique A means of measuring responses to items in terms of a continuum reflecting intensity of agreement or disagreement with a particular statement; responses are then combined to create an index regarding each individual's overall responses on the attribute of interest.

line diagram A graph in which individual points are connected by a continuous line; often used for showing changes over time.

linear model A straight-line relationship between two interval variables which can be defined by the regression equation $Y = a + bX$, where X is a given value of the independent variable, Y is the corresponding predicted value of the dependent variable, and a and b are constants.

listserver Computer center for distributing information about a given topic, offering both electronic mail (E–mail) services and relevant files to users of the Internet who subscribe to the given computer center.

mean   The arithmetic average, calculated as $\bar{X} = \Sigma X \div N$, where $\bar{X}$ is the mean, ΣX is the sum of all values, and N is the total number of values in the distribution; used mainly for determining a central tendency within interval data.

mean deviation   A measure of dispersion, calculated by (a) finding the absolute value of the difference between each observation and the mean $|X - \bar{X}|$; i.e., ignoring positive [+] vs. negative [–] signs, which otherwise would result in a sum of zero), (b) summing the absolute values ($\Sigma |X - \bar{X}|$) of these deviations from the mean, and (c) dividing this sum by the total number of observations ($\Sigma |X - \bar{X}| \div N$).

mean squares   A value obtained when calculating an F–ratio for groups being compared, which is derived by obtaining the within– groups sum of squares and then dividing this number by the within– group degrees of freedom (simply sum the number of cases, and subtract 1, for each group).

mean squares between groups   A value obtained when calculating an F–ratio for groups being compared, which is derived by obtaining the between–groups sum of squares, and then dividing this number by the between–groups degrees of freedom (the sum of the number of groups, minus 1).

measure of association   Assesses the strength of a relationship between one or more independent variables and one or more dependent variables; such a measure also facilitates the comparison of relationship strength across various relationships.

measure of central tendency   A numeric calculation indicating typical, representative information about a set of data, such as the mean, the median, and the mode; facilitates comparison of characteristics.

measure of dispersion   A numeric calculation indicating the variability within a set of data, such as the range, the variance, and the standard deviation; facilitates comparison of characteristics within and across data sets.

median absolute deviation   A calculation of dispersion based on finding the median (middle value) of the absolute values (ignoring positive [+] or negative [–] signs) of all of the deviations from the median value for the distribution.

median   The middle value in a distribution, which evenly divides a distribution into two groups of equal size; used mainly for determining a central tendency within ordinal data.

mode   The value for which there is the greatest frequency of response within a given distribution; used mainly for determining central tendency within nominal data.

multivariate analysis   An examination of several independent variables at one time.

nominal variable   A variable for which numeric labels are used to identify category membership, not quantitative variations across individuals (e.g., in designating 0 as male and 1 as female).

nondirectional hypothesis   A research hypothesis that predicts a relationship between the independent and the dependent variables but that does not state the direction of that relationship.

nonprobability sampling method   Any method of selecting a sample for which the probability of being selected is unknown or not equal.

normal curve   A symmetrical distribution that is unimodal and that has equivalent values for the mean, the median, and the mode; additionally, in a normal distribution, about 68% of all values can be expected to fall within an area one standard deviation above or below the mean, more than 95% of all values will fall within two standard deviations above or below the mean, and more than 99% of values will fall within three standard deviations above or below of the mean.

normative analysis   An examination of issues in which an individual considers data within the context of personal values, beliefs, and preferences, with a view to shaping policy.

null hypothesis   An assertion that there is *no* relationship between the independent variable and the dependent variable.

observational techniques   Methods for obtaining data, in which researchers directly observe the actions of individual participants, usually in the participants' natural settings, rather than in a laboratory.

on–line database system   Computer–based body of data organized in a manner that allows for various means of gaining access to information (e.g., through indexes); often, such systems provide access to multiple databases simultaneously.

on–line library catalog system   A comprehensive means of electronically storing, organizing, and updating information regarding the contents of a library, which may be accessible to researchers using a computer terminal; often structured in ways that are very similar to those of the traditional card–catalog system, although frequently, computerized systems offer greater flexibility than traditional card–based library catalogs.

one group pretest–posttest design   A format for research in which an experimental group serves as its own control group; specifically, the individuals in the group are given a *pretest* (a test given prior to exposure to an experimental treatment), are exposed to an experimental treatment, and then are given a *posttest* (a test given after their exposure to the experimental treatment); although the changes observed at the posttest may be due to exposure to the experimental treatment, the experimenter cannot rule out the possibility that other variables may have influenced the outcome at posttest (including the taking of the pretest).

one–tailed test   A means of assessing the statistical significance of a directional hypothesis.

open–ended question   Question to which a respondent is invited to give any response that the respondent deems appropriate, without limitations imposed by the interviewer.

operational   Capable of being defined in terms of observable measurements.

ordinal variable   A variable for which numeric labels indicate a rank ordering among assigned values, but for which the particular numbering system and intervals between numbers is arbitrarily determined (e.g., in indicating degree of conservatism on a scale from 0 to 10).

outliers   Values that deviate from the predominant trends, which can influence the observed strength of the relationship between the independent and the dependent variable; as plotted on a graph, outliers deviate considerably from the regression line.

panel–study design   A format for research in which the investigator cannot determine who will or will not be exposed to an independent variable, but in which the researcher is able to collect data at various time intervals and to measure whether a statistical relationship exists between an independent variable and a dependent variable, as they may change over time.

partial correlation   A method of controlling for confounding influences of a third variable which considers the amount of variance remaining in the dependent variable after accounting for the variance explained by the independent variable.

phi coefficient   A measure of association for nominal data when both the independent and dependent variables are *dichotomous* (i.e., each has only two values); calculated by obtaining the chi– square value, dividing that value by the sample size (n), and then finding the square root of that quotient.

pictograms   A stylized pie chart, in which each item in the chart is represented by an icon for the particular item.

pie chart   A graph for representing part:whole categorical relationships, in which a circle represents a whole amount, which is divided into proportional segments (pie–shaped wedges), such that the size of each categorical wedge is equivalent to the proportion of that part to the whole being represented by the circle.

political documents   A heading within a menu–based tool for the Internet; comprises various subheadings containing resources on political and policy–related issues.

posttest   A test given *after* exposure to an independent variable, such as an experimental treatment.

presentation of analysis and results   A description of what the researcher found, based on the researcher's analysis of the findings, in light of the hypotheses, presented so that the researcher's analysis is aptly supported, yet so that others may critically evaluate the findings and infer alternative explanations, as appropriate.

pretest   A test given *before* exposure to an independent variable, such as an experimental treatment.

probability sampling techniques   Any method of selecting a sample which is drawn so that each element of the population has a known and typically equal chance of being selected.

qualitative variable   A variable that may represent differences or changes among attributes (e.g., religion or gender), rather than in degrees of magnitude.

quantitative variable   A variable that may represent increases or decreases in magnitude (e.g., more conservative than, lower income than).

questionnaire   A list of questions prepared by a researcher and given to participants, in order to solicit their responses; usually, the list is presented in writing, and respondents are expected to answer in writing.

quota sampling   A method of selecting individuals from a population of interest, in which the researcher attempts to obtain a representative sample by choosing individuals who have particular characteristics (e.g., ethnicity, gender, region of the country, socioeconomic status), based on their proportionate representation in the population.

range   An indication of variation, often used for ordinal data, calculated by subtracting the lowest value from the highest value in a given distribution.

ratio variable   A variable for which numeric labels indicate a rank ordering among assigned values, precise and constant intervals between numbers, and having a natural zero point.

regression equation   An expression of the relationship between an independent variable and a dependent variable, whereby the predicted value of the dependent variable Y is $a + bX$, where X is a given value of the independent variable, and a and b are constants to be calculated.

relevant research   A portion of a report, which offers an overview of studies that relate to the topic of the report, indicating how the investigation being reported may be integrated into the body of research in the field.

reliability   The extent to which the same individual exhibits the same scores on repeated administration of a given measure.

report title   A concise, clear, and specific label for a research paper, which directly informs the reader of the focal topic of the paper.

research design   A plan for conducting an investigation, whereby a researcher maps out a method for conducting research.

research hypothesis   An assertion that a relationship exists between an independent variable and a dependent variable.

response bias   The tendency for respondents to be influenced by the context in which information is gathered (e.g., the kinds of questions asked, the way in which the questions are asked, or the setting in which the questions are posed), thereby yielding somewhat distorted answers.

row marginals   The sums of each row in a table of data.

sample   A representative group of individuals about whom information is gathered, in order to acquire information about the population from which the sample is obtained.

sampling error   The degree to which the values for a given sample differ from the values that would be obtained from the population of interest.

scaling   A means for measuring phenomena that are believed to exist but that cannot be assessed directly (e.g., racial prejudice or political activism), in which two or more measures are combined to form a single score that is assigned to each individual respondent.

scatterplot   A graphic representation depicting the relationship between the independent variable (X) and the dependent variable (Y), as plotted on coordinate axes, with the points representing the intersecting X and Y observations for each case.

simple correlation coefficient   A statistic indicating the strength of the relationship between variables, expressed as r, obtained by finding the square root of r^2 (the coefficient of determination).

simple random sample   A representative group of individuals, who are selected by a method that ensures that each member of the population of interest has an equal likelihood of being selected for study.

skewed   A characteristic of a distribution, in which the mean, the median, and the mode have different values; for example, in a *negatively skewed distribution,* the mean value is below the median score, and in a *positively skewed distribution,* the mean value is above the median score.

slope   A constant value to be calculated for a regression equation, which reveals the extent of change in the dependent variable associated with a one-unit change in the independent variable.

Somers' *d*   A statistic which allows for testing of asymmetric relationships between ordinal independent and the dependent variables.

split–half method   A means of assessing reliability by dividing a scale into two subscales that are believed to measure the same hypothetical construct and then administering both halves of the test to a group of individuals, then comparing their results on each half of the test.

spurious effect   A relationship between an independent and a dependent variable shown to vanish when considering the effects of a third variable.

standard deviation   A widely used measure of dispersion for interval data, calculated by obtaining the square root of the variance.

statistical significance   The degree to which the observed relationship between the independent and the dependent variable is predicted by the research hypothesis and is *not* a result of random fluctuations in the data.

stratified sampling technique   A method for obtaining a representative sample for a population in which individuals from two or more categories are chosen in proportion to their representation in the population.

structured interview routine   A method of conducting an interview, in which a researcher asks a predetermined, uniform list of questions that are identical for each respondent.

structured observational techniques   A set of observational methods whereby a researcher chooses participants, designs a situation in which participants are observed, provides guidelines for the interaction, and perhaps even intervenes during the observation.

style manual   Guidebook providing detailed information regarding the requirements for the written format of materials for a particular discipline, including information on how to handle references, footnotes, bibliographical material, tables, and so on.

summary and conclusions   A brief recapitulation of the key points in a report, describing how the findings did or did not support the hypotheses, and pointing the way to new investigations leading from the study described in the report.

survey techniques   A set of research methods in which researchers collect information from participants, either in writing (e.g., a questionnaire) or through an interview (e.g., via telephone or face–to–face); relies on the interviewer's ability to elicit candid self–reports and on the interviewee's ability to respond accurately and honestly about the information of interest.

systematic political research   Investigation of political science and policy issues, in which the researcher carefully follows a well–planned series of steps.

***t*–test**   Statistical method for comparing the magnitude of difference between means for two samples or groupings.

tau–*b* A symmetrical (nondirectional) test for assessing the strength of relationship between ordinal independent and dependent variables.

tau–*c* A symmetrical (nondirectional) test for assessing the strength of relationship between ordinal independent and dependent variables used for tables of unequal number of rows and columns.

testing (or instrument) reactivity A phenomenon whereby the act of taking a test or completing a survey actually influences the response obtained.

test–retest method A means of assessing reliability by administering the identical test to the same group of individuals on more than one occasion, then comparing their results on each occasion.

two–tailed test A means of assessing the statistical significance of a nondirectional hypothesis.

Type I error A mistake arising when a researcher incorrectly infers that a relationship that is observed in a given sample also exists in the population of interest.

Type II error A mistake arising when a researcher incorrectly infers that because no relationship is observed in a given sample, no relationship exists in the population of interest.

unexplained variance The amount of variance that is not explained by the relationship between the independent and the dependent variables.

univariate analysis An examination of information in which only one variable is studied at any one time, such as in describing distributions of data.

unstructured interview format A method of conducting an interview, in which a researcher may obtain a wide range of information on a particular topic, without following a predetermined list of questions.

unstructured observational techniques A set of observational methods whereby a researcher observes individuals in their natural settings, engaged in whatever actions they may choose for themselves, without any prompting from the researcher.

validity The extent to which a given assessment instrument actually measures what is designed to measure.

variable Something that varies or a placeholder for information that may be designated as having any of two or more values.

variance Also known as the mean-squared deviation, this measurement of dispersion is calculated as follows: variance $= \Sigma (X - \bar{X})^2 \div N$, where $X =$ each observation; $\bar{X} =$ mean of all observations; $\Sigma (X - \bar{X})^2 =$ the sum of the difference between each observation and the mean, squared; and $N =$ total number of observations.

variation ratio An indication of variation within nominal data; calculated as $1 -$ [(total number of cases in the modal category) $\div$ (total number of cases)].

web A means for retrieving information from the Internet, which is available in various forms (e.g., text, charts, graphs, pictures, and sound), and which may be viewed temporarily, sent to an E–mail (electronic mail) address for subsequent retrieval, or printed as "hard copy".

within–groups sum of squares A value obtained when calculating an *F*–ratio for groups being compared, which is derived by multiplying the square of the standard deviation of each group by one less than the number of cases in the group, and then summing the results.

writing handbook   Resource that provides information on the writing process, such as how to organize, structure, revise, and edit written material; includes information on grammar, punctuation, spelling, and the structure of sentences and paragraphs, as well as guidelines on usage.

***z* score**   A standard score, which tells in units of standard deviation how far a particular score lies above or below the mean.

Acknowledgments   *(continued from p. ii)*

Figure 3.2: "Illustration of Interrupted Times-Series Design: Views about Environmental Protection Regardless of Cost" from Robert Cameron Mitchell, "Public Opinion and the Green Lobby: Poised for the 1990s?" in Norman J. Vig and Michael E. Kraft, eds., *Environmental Policy in the 1990s*, page 86. Copyright © 1990 by Congressional Quarterly, Inc. Reprinted with the permission of Congressional Quarterly Press.

Box 3.2: "Pitfalls of Time-Series Analysis" adapted from Donald T. Campbell and H. L. Ross, "The Connecticut Crackdown on Speeding: Time-Series Data in Quasi-Experimental Analysis," *Law & Society Review* 3, no. 1: 33–53. Reprinted with the permission of Law & Society Review Association.

Box 4.1: "Participant Observation" from Carol M. Swain, *Black Faces, Black Interests*, pp. 227–229. Copyright © 1993 by the President and Fellows of Harvard College. Reprinted with the permission of Harvard University Press.

Table 4.1: "Techniques for Increasing Percentage of Mailed Questionnaire Returns" adapted from Delbert C. Miller, *Handbook of Research Design and Social Measurement*, fifth edition, pp. 144–155. Copyright © 1991 by Sage Publications, Inc. Reprinted with the permission of the publisher.

Box 4.2: "Even Experts Make Mistakes" from Michael R. Kagay, "Poll on Doubt of Holocaust is Corrected, *"New York Times* (July 8, 1994). Copyright © 1994 by The New York Times Company. Reprinted with the permission of the *New York Times.*

Page 75: Recommendations for conducting personal interviews from Lewis Anthony Dexter, *Elite and Specialized Interviewing* (Evanston, IL: Northwestern University Press, 1970). Reprinted with the permission of the publisher.

Table 4.2: "Choosing among the Mailed Questionnaire, Face-to-Face Interviewing, or Telephone Survey" adapted from Delbert C. Miller, *Handbook of Research Design and Social Measurement*, fifth edition, page 168, and James H. Frey, *Survey Research by Telephone*, page 76. Copyright © 1989, 1991 by Sage Publications, Inc. Reprinted with the permission of the publisher.

Table 4.3: "Sample–Size Requirements for Varying Degrees of Error Tolerance and Confidence Levels" adapted and extended from Charles H. Backstrom and Gerald D. Hursh, *Survey Research* (Evanston, IL: Northwestern University Press, 1963), page 33. Reprinted with the permission of the publisher.

Box 5.3: "Using Existing Data: The Relationship between Presidential Character and Exercise of Executive Clemency" from P. S. Ruckman, Jr., "Presidential Character and Executive Clemency: A Reexamination," *Social Science Quarterly* 76 (March 1995): 213–221. Copyright © 1995 by University of Texas Press. Reprinted with the permission of the author and publisher.

Page 123: Index of citizen activity from Sidney Verba, Kay Lehman Schlozman, Henry Brady, and Norman H. Nie, "Citizen Activity: Who Participates? What Do They Say?," *American Political Science Review* 87 (June 1993): 303–318. Copyright © 1993 by The American Political Science Association. Reprinted with the permission of the publisher.

Pages 125 and 126: Short quote and "Scale of Attitudes toward Hiring Minorities" from Frank J. Thompson and Bonnie Brown, "Commitment to the Disadvantaged among Urban Administrators: The Case of Minority Hiring," *Urban Affairs Quarterly* 33 (March 1978): 355–378. Copyright © 1978 by Sage Publications, Inc. Reprinted with the permission of the publisher.

Figure 6.4: "Scale of Attitudes toward Capital Punishment" from J. Balogh and M. A. Mueller," A Scaling Technique for Measuring Social Attitudes toward Capital Punishment," *Sociology and Social Research* 45 (1960): 24–26. Reprinted by permission.

Table 6.1: "Scale of Adolescent Substance Use" from Judy A. Andrews, Hyman Hops, Dennis Ary, Edward Lichtenstein, and Elizabeth Tildseley, "The Construction, Validation, and Use of a Guttman Scale of Adolescent Substance Use: An Investigation of Family Relationships," *Journal of Drug Issues* 21 (Summer 1991): 557–572. Copyright © 1991 by Journal of Drug Issues, Inc. Reprinted with the permission of the publisher.

Table 6.2: "Profeminism Scale" from Lee Ann Banaszak and Eric Plutzer, "Contextual Determinants of Feminist Attitudes: National and Subnational Influences in Western Europe," *American Political Science Review* 87 (March 1993): 147–157. Copyright © 1993 by The American Political Science Association. Reprinted with the permission of Lee Ann Banaszak and the publisher.

Box 7.1: "Deciding Authorship: Use of Descriptive Statistics" from Frederick Mosteller and David L. Wallace, *Inference and Disputed Authorship: The Federalist* (Reading, Mass.: Addison–Wesley, 1964). Reprinted with the permission of Springer-Verlag, New York.

Figure 7.2: "Illustration of a Frequency Polygon" from William G. Jacoby, "The Structure of Ideological Thinking in the American Electorate," *American Journal of Political Science* 39 (May 1995): 325. Reprinted with the permission of The University of Wisconsin Press.

Figure 7.4: "Illustration of a Pictogram" from "Unemployment: A Burden on Youth," *New York Times* August 12, 1993). Copyright © 1993 by The New York Times Company. Reprinted with the permission of the *New York Times.*

Figure 7.5: "Pictogram Showing Price of Oil Increase," *Time* (April 9, 1979): 57. Copyright © 1979 The Time, Inc. Magazine Company. Reprinted with the permission of *Time.*

Figure 7.6: "Voter Participation in Presidential Elections, 1880–1992" from Milton C. Cummings, Jr. and David Wise, *Democracy under Pressure*, seventh edition, page 309. Copyright © 1993 by Harcourt Brace & Company. Reprinted with the permission of the publisher. Figures from 1880 through 1916 from Robert E. Lane, *Political Life* (New York: The Free Press, 1965), page 20. Copyright © 1959 by The Free Press. Reprinted with the permission of the publisher.

Figure 7.7: "Trends in Class Bias, Using Various Measures of Socioeconomic Status" from Jan E. Leighley and Jonathan Nagler, "Socioeconomic Bias in Turnout 1964–1988: The Voters Remain the Same, "*American Political Science Review* 86 (September 1992): 730. Copyright © 1992 by The American Political Science Association. Reprinted with the permission of the authors and publisher.

Figure 7.9: "Illustration of Graphic Distortion" from Donald R Byrkit, *Statistics Today: A Comprehensive Introduction* (Menlo Park, CA: Benjamin/Cummings Publishing Company, 1987, page 25. Copyright © 1987 by The Benjamin/Cummings Publishing Company, Inc. Reprinted with the permission of the author.

Table 7.5: "Mean Comparisons: Differences between White and Black Childbearing Women and Differences between All White and Black Respondences by Survey Year" from John Lynxwiler and David Gay, "Reconsidering Race Differences in Abortion Attitudes," *Social Science Quarterly* 75, no. 1 (March 1994): 67–84. Copyright © 1994 by University of Texas Press. Reprinted with the permission of the author and publisher.

Table 7.6: "Annual Compensation of Governors, Grouped by Region" from *The Book of the States, 1992–1993*. Copyright © 1992–93 by The Council of State Governments. Reprinted with the permission of the publisher.

Table 8.3: "Form of Local Government by Population Group" from John J. Harrigan, *Politics and Policy in States and Communities,* fifth edition, page 169. Copyright © 1994 by HarperCollins College Publishers, Inc. Reprinted with the permission of the publisher.

Table 8.5: "Community Opinion of Saturn by County, June 1990 and June 1991 (percentages)" from David Folz et al., "Saturn Comes to Tennessee: Citizen Perceptions of Project Impacts," *Social Science Quarterly* (December 1993): 797. Copyright © 1993 by University of Texas Press. Reprinted with the permission of the publisher.

Box 8.1: "Importance of the Chi-Square Test" excerpted from Ian Hacking, "Trial By Number," *Science* (November 1984): 69–70. Reprinted by permission.

Table 8.8: "*t*–Tests of Environmental Concerns between Richer and Poorer Nations" from Steven R. Brechin and Willett Kempton, "Global Environmentalism: A Challenge to the Postmaterialism Thesis?," *Society Science Quarterly* (Fall 1994): 253. Copyright © 1994 by University of Texas Press. Reprinted with the permission of the publisher.

Table 8.11: "Support for Presidential Civil Rights Proposals" from James D. King and James W. Riddlesperger, Jr., "Presidential Leadership of Congressional Civil Rights Voting," *Policy Studies Journal* 21, no. 3 (1993): 548. Copyright © 1993 by Policy Studies Organization. Reprinted with the permission of the publisher.

Table 8.12: "Analysis of Variance for Voting Technologies (*n* = 265)" from Peter A. Shocket, Neil R. Heighberger, and Clyde Brown, "The Effect of Voting Technology on Voting Behavior in a Simulated Multi–Candidate City Council Election," *Western Political Quarterly* (June 1992): 531. Copyright © 1992 by the University of Utah. Reprinted with the permission of the authors and *Political Research Quarterly* (formerly *The Western Political Quarterly*).

Table 9.1: "Suggested Verbal Interpretations of Correlation Coefficients" adapted from James A. Davis, *Elementary Survey Analysis* (Englewood Cliffs, New Jersey: Prentice-Hall, 1971), page 49. Copyright © 1971 by Prentice–Hall, Inc. Reprinted with the permission of the publishers.

Box 9.1: "Correlation as a Diagnostic Tool" excerpted from Lawrence K. Altman, "A Bald Spot on Top May Predict Heart Risk," *New York Times* (February 24, 1993). Copyright © 1993 by The New York Times Company. Reprinted with the permission of the *New York Times*.

Table 9.3: "Religiosity and Partisan Loyalty: 1986 *New York Times* Survey" from Charles L. Davis, "Religion and Partisan Loyalty: The Case of Catholic Workers in Mexico," *The Western Political Quarterly* (March 1992): 285. Copyright © 1992 by the University of Utah. Reprinted with the permission of the author and *Political Research Quarterly* (formerly *The Western Political Quarterly*).

Table 9.8: "Contingency Table Analysis for States' Recycling Efforts" from Renu Khator, "Recycling: A Policy Dilemma for American States?," *Policy Studies Journal* 21 (Summer 1993): 217. Copyright © 1993 by the Policy Studies Organization. Reprinted with the permission of the publisher.

Table 9:10: "The Correspondence between Tone and Venue in Congressional Hearings on Pesticides and Civilian Nuclear Power" from Bryan D. Jones, Frank R. Baumgartner, and Jeffrey C. Talbert, "The Destruction of Issue Monopolies in Congress," *American Political Science Review* 87 (September 1993): 663. Copyright © 1993 by The American Political Science Association. Reprinted with the permission of Bryan Jones and the publisher.

Table 9.11: "Political Characteristics of Voters by Time of Decision: Kandall's Tau–*b* Coefficients for the Relationships between Political Characteristics of Voters and Time of Decision (early, middle, late)" from J. David Gopoian and Sissie Hadjiharalambous, "Late Deciding Voters in Presidential Elections, *Political Behavior* 16 (1994): 64–65. Reprinted with the permission of Plenum Publishing Corporation.

Figure 9.3: "Murder and Abortion Rates versus Percentage Living in Metropolitan Areas" from Norman R. Luttbeg, *Comparing the States and Communities,* page 24. Copyright © 1992 by Norman R. Luttbeg. Reprinted with the permission of HarperCollins College Publishers, Inc.

Table 9.15: "Partisan Polarization on Issues among Whites, by Demographic Characteristics in 1988" Alan I. Abramowitz, "Issue Evolution Reconsidered: Racial Attitudes and Partisanship in the U.S. Electorate," *American Journal of Political Science* 38 (February 1994): 13. Reprinted with the permission of The University of Wisconsin Press.

Table 9.16: "Eight Hypotheses Concerning State Incarceration Rates in 1984: Pearson's Zero–Order Correlation Coefficients (*n* = 48)" from William A. Taggart and Russell G. Winn, "Imprisonment in the American States," *Social Science Quarterly* 74 (December 1993): 742. Copyright © 1993 by University of Texas Press. Reprinted with the permission of the publisher.

Table 10.6: "Levels of Political Ambition" from Barbara J. Burt-Way and Rita Mae Kelly," Gender and Sustaining Political Ambition: A Study of Arizona Elected Officials," *The Western Political Quarterly* (March 1992): 15. Copyright © 1992 by the University of Utah. Reprinted with the permission of the authors and *Political Research Quarterly* (formerly *The Western Political Quarterly*).

Table 10.7: "Turnout, Type of Measure, and Election Outcome" from David Hadwiger, "Money, Turnout, and Ballot Measure Success in California Cities," *The Western Political Quarterly* (June 1992): 542. Copyright © 1992 by the University of Utah. Reprinted with the permission of the author and *Political Research Quarterly* (formerly *The Western Political Quarterly*).

Table 10.8: "Partial Correlations with Freedom Change (controlled for per capita GNP)" from Arthur A. Goldsmith, "Political Freedom and the Business Climate: Outlook for Development in Newly Democratizing States," *Social Science Quarterly* 75 (March 1994): 122. Copyright © 1992 by University of Texas Press. Reprinted with the permission of the publisher.

Table 10.9: "Partial Correlations between Issues and Party Identification among Whites by Demographic Characteristics in 1988" from Alan L. Abramowitz, "Issue Evolution Reconsidered: Racial Attitudes and Partisanship in the U.S. Electorate," *American Journal of Political Science* 38 (February 1994): 14. Reprinted with the permission of The University of Wisconsin Press.

Table 10.10: "Regression Equation Predicting Support for Political Reform" from Arthur H. Miller, Vickie L. Hesli, and William M. Reisinger, "Reassessing Mass Support for Political and Economic Change in the Former USSR," *American Political Science Review* 88 (June 1994): 407. Copyright © 1994 by The American Political Science Association. Reprinted with the permission of Arthur H. Miller and the publisher.

Table 10.11: "Unstandardized Coefficients, Standard Errors, and Standardized Coefficients for Regression of Sentence Severity on Legal, Resource, and Status Variables" from Malcolm D. Holmes, Harmon M. Hosch, Howard C. Daudistel, Dolores A. Perez, and Joseph B. Graves, "Judges' Ethnicity and Minority Sentencing: Evidence Concerning Hispanics," *Social Science Quarterly* 74 (September 1993): 501. Copyright © 1994 by University of Texas Press. Reprinted with the permission of the publisher.

Table 10.12: "Factors Influencing Support for California's Term Limitation Proposition 140 Maximum Likelihood Estimates (MLE)" from Todd Donovan and Joseph R. Snipp, "Support for Legislative Term Limitations in California: Group Representation, Partisanship, and Campaign Information," *Journal of Politics* 56 (May 1994): 498. Copyright © 1994 by University of Texas Press. Reprinted with the permission of the publisher.

Table 10.13: "Logit Coefficients for the Likelihood of a Liberal Vote on Obscenity Cases, 1981–1990" from Donald R. Songer, Sue Davis, and Susan Haire, "A Reappraisal of Diversification in the Federal Courts: Gender Effects in the Court of Appeals," *Journal of Politics* 56 (May 1994): 433. Copyright © 1994 by University of Texas Press. Reprinted with the permission of the publisher.

Table 10.15: "Relationship of Community Variables to Economic Development Policies" from Todd Donovan, "Community Controversy and the Adoption of Economic Development Policies," *Social Science Quarterly* 74, no. 2 (June 1993): 386–402. Copyright © 1993 by University of Texas Press. Reprinted with the permission of the author and publisher.

Table 10.16: "Logit Coefficient Estimates for Measures of Civil Service" from Howard Frant, "Rules and Governance in the Public Sector: The Case of Civil Service," *American Journal of Political Science* 37 (November 1993): 900–1007. Reprinted with the permission of The University of Wisconsin Press.

Page 279: "Expectations and Preferences in British General Elections" from Richard Nadeau, Richard G. Niemi, and Timothy Amato, *American Political Science Review* 88 (June 1994): 371–383. Copyright © 1994 by The American Political Science Association. Reprinted with the permission of the publishers.

Page 280: "Racial Threat and Partisan Identification" from Micheal W. Giles and Kaenan Hertz, *American Political Science Review* 88 (June 1994): 318. Copyright © 1994 by The American Political Science Association. Reprinted with the permission of the authors and the publisher.

Page 281: Excerpt from "The Vicissitudes of Death by Decree: Forces Influencing Capital Punishment Decision Making in State Supreme Courts" by Melinda Gann Hall and Paul Brace, *Social Science Quarterly* 75 (March 1994): 148. Copyright © 1994 by University of Texas Press. Reprinted with the permission of the publisher.

Appendix B: "Areas under the Normal Curve" from Harold O. Rugg, *Statistical Methods Applied to Education* (Boston: Houghton Mifflin Company, 1917), Appendix table III, pp. 389–390. Reprinted with the permission of the publisher.

Appendix C: "Distribution of χ^2 abridged from Ronald A. Fisher and Frank Yates, *Statistical Tables for Biological, Agricultural, and Medical Research,* sixth edition, Table IV. Reprinted with the permission of Longman Group, Limited on behalf of the Literary Executor of the late Sir Ronald A. Fisher, F.R.S. and Dr. Frank Yates, F.R.S.

Appendix D: "Distribution of *t* Values" abridged from Ronald A. Fisher and Frank Yates, *Statistical Tables for Biological, Agricultural, and Medical Research,* sixth edition, Table III. Reprinted with the permission of Longman Group, Limited on behalf of the Literary Executor of the late Sir Ronald A. Fisher, F.R.S. and Dr. Frank Yates, F.R.S.

Appendix E: "Distribution of *F* Values" abridged from Ronald A. Fisher and Frank Yates, *Statistical Tables for Biological, Agricultural, and Medical Research,* sixth edition, Table V. Reprinted with the permission of Longman Group, Limited on behalf of the Literary Executor of the late Sir Ronald A. Fisher, F.R.S. and Dr. Frank Yates, F.R.S.

Author Index

Subject Index